THOMAS LANGLEY

THOMAS LANGLEY
AND THE
BISHOPRIC OF DURHAM
1406–1437

by

R. L. STOREY

*An Assistant Keeper of
the Public Records*

Published for the Church Historical Society

LONDON
S.P.C.K
1961

First published in 1961
by S.P.C.K.
Holy Trinity Church, Marylebone Road, London N.W.1
Printed in Great Britain by
William Clowes and Sons, Limited
London and Beccles

CONTENTS

PREFACE

THIS is the third book about a medieval bishop of Durham to be published within the last five years, but each deals with a distinct phase in the history of the Bishopric: Mr G. V. Scammell's *Hugh du Puiset, Bishop of Durham* (Cambridge, 1956) concerns the period of final territorial expansion, while Dr C. M. Fraser in her *History of Antony Bek* writes of the great age of legal definition, when the Bishop won recognition of established privileges but was refused further aggrandisement. It is not until the time of Thomas Langley that the organization of the palatine government can be traced in ample detail, for if his pontificate lacks the illumination given by chroniclers to earlier periods, it has left us his episcopal register and many records of his chancery and exchequer.

I have incurred many debts of gratitude in the preparation of this book, the chief to Dr J. Conway Davies, at whose suggestion and under whose guidance I first began to study Langley's career. I have received much kindness and assistance in the various repositories and libraries where I have worked, particularly from my friends and colleagues in the Public Record Office and the Prior's Kitchen at Durham. Of those who have given encouragement and valued criticism I wish especially to thank Mr K. B. McFarlane and Professor H. S. Offler. I am most grateful to the Church Historical Society for undertaking the publication, and to Dr Rose Graham and Dr R. F. Hunnisett for reading the proofs. Through all the stages of this book's preparation I have made many calls on my wife's expert assistance, and I am aware that without her support the work would not have reached this stage. For errors and disputable conclusions I take sole responsibility.

R. L. STOREY

Bishop's Stortford
1 November 1960

ABBREVIATIONS

CCR.	*Calendar of Close Rolls.*
CFR.	*Calendar of Fine Rolls.*
CPL.	*Calendar of Papal Letters.*
CPR.	*Calendar of Patent Rolls.*
CPS.	Exchequer: Treasury of Receipt: Council and Privy Seal (The number of the file only follows).
DCD.	Dean and Chapter of Durham.
DKR.	*Reports of the Deputy Keepers of the Public Records.*
GD.	Records of the Justices Itinerant: Gaol Delivery Rolls.
PPC.	*Proceedings and Ordinances of the Privy Council of England*, ed. N. H. Nicolas (Record Commission, 1834–7).
Reg.	DCD. Register of Bishop Langley.
Reg.	*The Register of Thomas Langley*, ed. R. L. Storey (Surtees Society, 1955–).
Reg. IPM.	(Public Record Office) Palatinate of Durham: Chancery Records: Cursitor's Records: Abstracts of Inquisitions *post mortem*, Register II.
RG.	DCD. Receiver-General's Records.
Rot.	(Public Record Office) Palatinate of Durham: Chancery, *etc.*: Rolls of Bishop Langley.
Rot. Parl.	*Rotuli Parliamentorum* (1783).
Rot. Scot.	*Rotuli Scotiæ*, ed. D. Macpherson and others (Record Commission, 1814–9).
Scr. Tres.	*Historiæ Dunelmensis Scriptores Tres*, ed. J. Raine (Surtees Society, 1838).
SS.	Surtees Society.
VCH.	*Victoria County History.*

Note: Manuscript sources in the Public Record Office are cited without any prefix.

I

THE BISHOP'S SECULAR CAREER

THOMAS LANGLEY,[1] Bishop of Durham, was one of the most prominent figures in English public life in the early fifteenth century, and in his long tenure of the see of St Cuthbert achieved many reforms in the governments of both the diocese and the county palatine committed to his rule; yet despite his obvious importance, very little can be discovered of him as a man except by inference, for only rarely did he attract the notice of the small number of chroniclers writing in his lifetime. In more recent times, only one individual study has been made of his life, but the writer's interest was confined to Langley's activities as diocesan and he based his account almost entirely on the Bishop's register.[2] With this valuable exception, Langley has received attention only because a notice of his life had to be given in some series, as one in the line of Bishops of Durham [3] or Chancellors of England,[4] as a supposed graduate of Cambridge [5] or even as a worthy of the parish of Eccles in Lancashire.[6] None of these studies is exhaustive or entirely accurate, and the total number of sources consulted by all these writers is less than half the material that has proved profitable; very few records concerning

[1] The surname is spelt "Longley" at least as often as "Langley" in contemporary records, but the latter is preferred: it is the present form of his place of origin and has been traditional in Durham from before the date of his death.

[2] A. Hamilton Thompson, "Thomas Langley, Bishop of Durham 1406–1437", *Durham University Journal*, *1945*, pp. 1–16.

[3] *Scriptores Tres* (Chambre), pp. 146–7; W. Hutchinson, *The History and Antiquities of the County Palatine of Durham* (Newcastle-upon-Tyne, 1785–94), Vol. I, pp. 325–35; R. Surtees, *The History and Antiquities of the County Palatine of Durham* (Durham, 1816–40), Vol. I, pp. lv–lvii; *VCH. Durham*, Vol. II, pp. 22–4, 161.

[4] Lord Campbell, *Lives of the Lord Chancellors* (1846), Vol. I, pp. 315 & 336; E. Foss, *The Judges of England* (1848–51), Vol. IV, pp. 338–40.

[5] J. & J. A. Venn, *Alumni Cantabrigienses*, Part I (Cambridge, 1922–7), Vol. III, p. 45.

[6] E. Baines, *History of the County Palatine and Duchy of Lancaster* (1836), Vol. III, pp. 152–5. See also *Dictionary of National Biography* and J. H. Wylie, *History of England under Henry the Fourth* (1884–98), Vol. II, pp. 344, 483–5.

the first forty years of Langley's life have been discovered, but for the remaining thirty-five the quantity is very great indeed.

I LANCASHIRE BACKGROUND

The few references to Thomas Langley in fourteenth-century records offer only a bare outline of the first forty years of his life. He was born soon after 1360, for in 1433 he described himself as a septuagenarian.[1] His later benefactions to the parish of Middleton, five miles north of Manchester, indicate his birth-place. In the north-west corner of the parish is Langley, from which a family of some standing in Lancashire had taken its name. In 1394, one Roger de Longley died seised of the manors of Accrington and Prestwich as well as other lands in the same district.[2] He was presumably the head of the family to which Thomas belonged, but was not his father: his name was William.[3] The manor of Middleton was held by the Bartons, but the vill of Langley belonged to a branch of the family of Langley until 1466, when it is said to have been sold to James Radcliffe of Radcliffe.[4] The mullet on Thomas Langley's arms of *paly argent et vert* indicates that he belonged to a junior branch of the family. His origin, therefore, if humble was not obscure; although it was not sufficiently privileged to make his career easy, neither was it an obstacle to any promotion his natural ability might earn.

The nature of Thomas Langley's education is unknown. There is a tradition that he went to Cambridge,[5] but proof of this cannot be found. If he did ever attend a university, it is certain that he did not take a degree: not a single instance of his being styled "Master" has been seen. The obvious career for the talented younger son of a "gentle" family was as a clerk; he could expect the patronage of influential friends to assist his advancement in the Church. Langley's career began in the service of the family of Radcliffe of Radcliffe, a few miles from his home. On

[1] *Reg.* no. 1041.
[2] *DKR. 39*, p. 541.
[3] *CPR. 1413–1416*, p. 206.
[4] F. Gastrell, *Notitia Cestriensis* (Chetham Society, 1845–50), Vol. II, Part 1, p. 99, n. 2.
[5] The earliest authority appears to be Wharton (*Anglia Sacra* (1691), Part I, p. 775), who is followed by the historians of Durham. No contemporary warrant is given in Venn, *Alumni Cantabrigienses*. Godwin gives no details of Langley's education (*A Catalogue of the Bishops of England* (1601), p. 528).

4 August 1385, he was instituted Rector of the church of Radcliffe, on the presentation of James Radcliffe. Langley was described as a clerk, showing that he was then in minor orders. He held the church for five months only,[1] but never broke his connection with the Radcliffes. When he became Bishop of Durham, two members of the family were attached to his household: George was a member of his diocesan council and received a number of Durham benefices; and John, to whom the Bishop granted a dispensation for his illegitimacy, was treasurer of the episcopal household.[2] Langley was empowered by the Pope to grant a number of dispensations for marriage in the prohibited degrees, and two members of the Radcliffe family were given such dispensations. Langley collated William Radcliffe to a prebend at Auckland.[3]

The Radcliffes were one of the greatest families in Lancashire. It was a short step from their service to that of the Duke. Thomas, the younger brother of Langley's first patron, was one of Gaunt's esquires; he was twice knight of the shire and held various offices and commissions in the county. He and Langley were among the feoffees in Gaunt's manor of Barnoldswick.[4] It is most likely that it was Thomas Radcliffe who first introduced Langley to the Duke. When this happened is not known; in 1407, it was said that Langley had served Gaunt and Henry IV from the days of his youth.[5] Langley's resignation of the church of Radcliffe at the end of 1385 may have been made because of his change of employment. He soon won Gaunt's confidence: in 1394, he was sent to speak to Richard II, then in Wales, regarding certain of the Duke's affairs.[6] As the relations between Gaunt and the King were then amicable,[7] Langley would have been favourably received. In the following year, on 23 July, his estate as a prebendary of the royal free chapel of St Martin-le-Grand was ratified,[8] and on 12 February 1396 he was given the rectory of

[1] Lambeth: Register of Archbishop Courtenay, ff. 350 & 353v.
[2] *Reg. Langley*, no. 478; and see below, p. 75.
[3] *Reg.* nos. 220 & 272.
[4] J. S. Roskell, *Knights of the Shire for the County Palatine of Lancaster* (Chetham Society, 1937), pp. 72–4.
[5] *ab annis teneris* (Hutchinson, *History of Durham*, I, p. 332).
[6] Duchy of Lancaster: Accounts (Various), bundle 32, no. 21; partly printed in J. Armitage-Smith, *John of Gaunt* (Westminster, 1904), p. 448.
[7] Ibid. 341, 354–6; W. Stubbs, *The Constitutional History of England* (Oxford, 1890–6), Vol. II, p. 511.
[8] *CPR. 1391–1396*, p. 609.

St Alphege, London, a benefice in the gift of the Dean of that chapel.   It is a fair inference that the King was responsible for Langley's presentation: he wished to please the Duke and reward his trusted clerk.   On 15 February 1397, Langley exchanged the church of St Alphege for a canonry in St Asaph Cathedral with the prebend of Meifod.[1]   A month later, on 17 March, he was ordained priest in Coventry Cathedral, with this prebend as his title.[2]   Gaunt presented him to the church of Castleford, in the honour of Pontefract, and he was admitted on 26 September 1398; on the same day, he was granted the Archbishop's licence for non-residence for three years.[3]   A further indication of Langley's standing is that Gaunt appointed him one of the executors of his will.[4]

Langley's early connection with the Duchy and county of Lancaster had great significance for his later career.   Firstly, of course, it accounts for his later rise, his selection for high office by Henry IV.   His loyalty to the House of Lancaster, so marked throughout his life, arose from the same cause.   He remained on terms of friendship with other servants of the Duchy who became royal ministers at the same time.   Of more particular significance was the political nature of the environment in which he had spent the first forty years of his life.   The liberties of the Duke of Lancaster were most extensive: he was authorized by royal charters to have his own chancery in the county, where he could issue writs under his seal; he had also his own exchequer exercising in the county the jurisdiction enjoyed elsewhere by the royal exchequer, and could appoint his justices to hold crown and all other pleas; he enjoyed, in fact, all the liberties and *jura regalia* pertaining to a county palatine.[5]   It was under this form of administration that Langley had lived, and his important position in the Duke's service would have enabled him to become experienced in its machinery.   When he became Bishop of Durham, he became lord of a franchise with almost identical privileges.

    [1] G. Hennessy, *Novum Repertorium Ecclesiasticum Parochiale Londinense* (1898), p. 86.
    [2] Lichfield: Act Books, no. 6, fo. 156.
    [3] York: Register of Archbishop Scrope, fo. 17.
    [4] *Wills of Kings*, ed. J. Nichols (1780), p. 163; *Testamenta Eboracensia* (SS. 1836, 1855, & 1864), Vol. I, p. 234.
    [5] Armitage-Smith, pp. 207–8; R. Somerville, *History of the Duchy of Lancaster*, Vol. I (1953), pp. 56–66, 115–28.

His earlier experience made it easy for him to enter into the position of a count palatine; being already acquainted with the organization necessary for the government of a private regality, he would have been able, from the very beginning of his pontificate, to provide for the smooth operation of the administrative machinery of Durham. He would, moreover, have been fully aware of the extent of his rights and jealous for their preservation and for their full recognition.

There is no doubt that Bishop Langley appreciated this resemblance, for when he chose men to assist him in the administration of Durham, he frequently selected fellow-Lancastrians. A noticeable number of the men collated to benefices in his gift were described as clerks of the diocese of Coventry and Lichfield, the diocese in which Lancashire lay. Three successive receivers-general of Durham, John Newton, Nicholas Hulme, and Richard Buckley, and two treasurers of the Bishop's household, Hulme and John Radcliffe, were all natives of this diocese.[1] William Mablethorp, who acted as one of the Bishop's auditors, held a similar position in the Duchy. John Thoralby, a clerk first in the Duchy chancery and later in that of the King, was one of Langley's most trusted councillors.[2] Thomas Holden, a member of Langley's household before he became Bishop, was appointed steward of Durham.[3] Two members of the family of Strangways held important offices: Robert was chief forester of Weardale,[4] and James, later chief justice of the county of Lancaster, was also one of the Bishop's justices.[5] Langley was not merely favouring old friends and associates by bestowing offices and benefices upon them, but securing the services of men he knew and could trust, men, like himself, experienced in palatine administration. Other Lancastrians were employed in the Bishop's diocesan government, the most notable being Thomas Lyes, first as registrar and later as vicar-general, and Thomas Hebden, the spiritual chancellor.[6]

Another connection with the Duchy was preserved by Langley's duties in the execution of John of Gaunt's will. As the most junior of the executors, and as one of the two clerks in the body of distinguished persons appointed, a great amount of the routine business would have devolved upon Langley, particularly in the

[1] Below, pp. 74–5, 78–9. [2] Below, p. 101.
[3] Below, pp. 93, 102. [4] Rot. A. m. 5.
[5] Below, p. 63. [6] Reg. I, pp. xv & xviii–xix.

first months after Gaunt's death but to a lesser extent throughout the following years.   It was not until 1403 that the executors were able to attend to the Duke's desires for the foundation of chantries; in this year royal licences were obtained for the establishment of chantries in St Paul's, London, and in the collegiate church of St Mary at Leicester.[1]   Langley's interest in these foundations is reflected in entries in his episcopal register; these concern the appropriation of the church of Preston, Lancashire, to St Mary's,[2] and presentations of chaplains to the chantries by himself and other executors.   The last presentation recorded was made by Langley alone, on 1 February 1436;[3] he had outlived all his co-executors.

The endowment of chantries was a common practice in Langley's day.   It had become almost a tradition for men who rose to greatness in both Church and State to erect these founda-tions at the places of their birth, for reasons mainly pious, no doubt, but also as memorials to their fame in their native parishes. Just as Chichele at Higham Ferrers, Kemp at Wye, and Skirlaw at Swine, so Langley endowed a religious foundation at his birthplace.   The church at Middleton was in a ruinous con-dition before he had it entirely rebuilt.   On 22 August 1412, the Bishop of Coventry and Lichfield granted Langley a licence to consecrate the new church, the high altar and two additional altars, one of these being dedicated to the Virgin Mary and St Cuthbert.[4]   After his death, his executors erected a chantry at this altar,[5] for one priest to celebrate masses for the souls of the Kings of England, Langley, and his ancestors.   As in his Galilee foundation at Durham—where, incidentally, his parents were commemorated[6] —the incumbent had also "to teach one grammer skole fre for pore children".[7]   Nothing remains of Langley's church at Middleton to-day, except the tower,[8] but the school survived the Reformation; it was re-founded, with an additional endowment, in the reign of Elizabeth I.[9]

[1] *CPR. 1401–1405*, pp. 210 & 214.   [2] *Reg.* no. 29.
[3] Ibid. 547 & 1187.   [4] *Reg.* no. 276.
[5] *CPR. 1436–1441*, p. 399; *DKR. 34*, p. 170.
[6] *CPR. 1413–1416*, pp. 206–7.
[7] *Lancashire Chantries* (Chetham Society, 1862), pp. 119–21; A. F. Leach, *English Schools at the Reformation* (Westminster, 1896), Part II, p. 116.
[8] *VCH. Lancaster*, Vol. V, p. 153.
[9] Ibid. II, pp. 575–7.

Another instance of Langley's later activities in Lancashire was his participation in the foundation of the collegiate church of Manchester. The founder was Thomas, Lord de la Warre; he and Langley were old friends. When Langley visited Swineshead, near Boston, on 24 October 1408,[1] he had presumably gone there to see De la Warre, who was Rector of Swineshead.[2] De la Warre usually appointed Langley or some of the Bishop's clerks as his proctors in Parliament.[3] He enfeoffed Langley and other trustees in lands which they subsequently granted to the college. The royal licence for the foundation was granted on 22 May 1421.[4] In the following August, despite the fact that he must have been fully occupied by his duties as Chancellor of England, Langley went through Lancashire on his way to Durham, and spent three or four days in Manchester, obviously attending to business relating to the college. The Bishop of Coventry and Lichfield, in licensing the erection of the college, authorized Bishop Langley and Thomas de la Warre to make its statutes. The foundation was of a warden, eight priests to be fellows of the college, and a number of other ministers and servants; the first warden was installed in 1428.[5] When the Pope confirmed the local Bishop's licence, he gave Langley authority to make new statutes and amend or abolish those already existing if he saw fit.[6] Langley's experience of collegiate churches in his diocese of Durham would have been most valuable when he framed the statutes for Manchester, and it is clear that they were designed to prevent the common abuse of non-residence. The warden's salary had to be sufficient to support his dignity, but the stipends of the fellows were such as to make it necessary for them to stay in residence: each priest had £4 a year, but an allowance of 16d. a week was added for commons. That these small stipends were due to policy and not necessity is shown by the fact that after all deductions had been made from the endowment of £260 p.a., a surplus of some £56 was left for charity, repairs, and other requirements. The regulations were apparently successful in preventing non-

---

[1] For Langley's itinerary, see Appendix A.
[2] *Complete Peerage*, ed. V. Gibbs (1910–59), Vol. IV, pp. 150–1.
[3] Parliamentary Proxies, files 45, no. 2212; 46, no. 2294; 48, no. 2385; 52, nos. 20, 22, 24, 26–7.
[4] *CPR. 1416–1422*, p. 366.
[5] Gastrell, *Notitia Cestriensis*, Vol. II, Pt. I, p. 59.
[6] *CPL*. VII, p. 475.

residence, for in 1545 it was reported that the warden, fellows, and other ministers were all resident "at this daye", keeping hospitality together according to their statutes.[1] Through his participation in this foundation, Langley retained an interest in Lancashire until the end of his life, and in his will he bequeathed some of his books to the college.[2]

2 THE KING'S CLERK, 1399–1407

When John of Gaunt died on 3 February 1399, his son and heir, Henry of Derby, was in exile, and his estates were seized by Richard II; yet within little more than six months the House of Lancaster was saved from ruin and Henry was King. The plots and rebellions of the first years of his reign show that the revolution was far from popular, but one group of men certainly had cause to rejoice: the servants of the Duchy, rescued from the threat to their livelihood, could expect much of their future. "The Lancastrians looked well after their own." [3] To no one of these Duchy servants was the triumph of Henry of Derby to bring greater success than to Thomas Langley. He had not joined the Duke in exile, but had stayed to perform his duties as Gaunt's executor. Richard had confirmed his possession of the church of Castleford and canonry of St Asaph's on 3 April, and one of the nobles accompanying Richard to Ireland had appointed him an attorney in England.[4] It may safely be presumed, however, that when Henry returned to England in the summer of that year, Langley did not hesitate to join him: the confidence and favour that the new King was to bestow from the first days of his reign indicated that Langley's loyalty to the House of Lancaster had outweighed all considerations of personal safety in the months of crisis, and that Henry was glad to accept the services of his father's trusted clerk.

With the accession of Henry IV, Langley became "the King's clerk"; this title was applied to him on 11 October, a fortnight after the reign began, when he had resigned his church of Castleford.[5] Only one record has been found to establish the nature of

---

[1] *Lancashire Chantries*, pp. 7–10.   [2] *Scr. Tres*, Appendix, p. ccxlv.
[3] E. F. Jacob, in Introduction to *The Register of Henry Chichele* (Canterbury and York Society, 1937–47), Vol. I, p. xxv.
[4] *CPR. 1396–1399*, pp. 380, 502, & 519.
[5] *CPR. 1399–1401*, p. 178.

his employment during the next two years: on 22 December 1399, the Keeper of the Great Wardrobe was ordered to issue livery to Thomas Langley, *nostre secretaire*, for the coming feast of Christmas.[1] As no other clerk is known to have held this office until 1402,[2] it seems most probable that Langley retained it until his promotion in 1401. His work would have required constant attendance upon the King, for as Secretary he was the keeper of the royal signet, the smallest and most personal of the King's seals. The place of the signet in the royal administration in this period is not a little obscure; it lacked the prestige of the Great Seal, and also of the Privy Seal, yet it had the valuable function of causing the keepers of these two instruments to issue their more authoritative letters, and it was often used to attest the King's less formal missives to other officers and subjects.

The personal standing of the Secretary is best revealed by his record of ecclesiastical preferment. Langley's first Crown presentation was to the archdeaconry of Norfolk, on 29 October 1399. In 1401, he was granted prebends in York Minster [3] and in the royal free chapel of Bridgnorth. On 1 July, the King gave him the deanery of York.[4] The Archbishop confirmed his appointment on 20 January 1402 and he was installed by proxy five days later, but Langley was unable to make his title effective as the Pope claimed the deanery and bestowed it upon a cardinal. The King refused to allow this provision, and at length a bargain was made: the Cardinal was given the archdeaconry of Exeter and Langley was provided to the deanery, in which he was again installed in 1403.[5] In the meanwhile, he had occupied a second prebend at York and others at Lincoln, Salisbury, and Wells. He was truly described as *benebeneficiatus*.[6] This prosperity marked the King's appreciation of his Secretary's work, and promised greater favour in the future: the deanery of York was the major English benefice below episcopal rank, and

---

1 Exchequer K.R.: Accounts, Various, box 649 (unsorted).

2 J. Otway-Ruthven, *The King's Secretary and the Signet Office in the XV Century* (Cambridge, 1939), p. 152.

3 J. le Neve, *Fasti Ecclesiae Anglicanae*, ed. T. D. Hardy (Oxford, 1854), Vol. II, p. 484, & Vol. III, p. 205.

4 *CPR. 1399–1401*, pp. 470 & 506.

5 *Foedera, Conventiones, Literae* (etc.), ed. T. Rymer (1704–35), Vol. VIII, p. 291; *CPR. 1401–1405*, p. 212; *CPL.* V, p. 537; Le Neve, III, p. 124.

6 Exchequer K.R.: Ecclesiastical Documents, bundle 8, no. 24; *CPR. 1401–1405*, pp. 61 & 89; *CPL.* V, p. 537; Le Neve, II, p. 152, & III, p. 209.

most of those who had recently held it had been advanced to
bishoprics.

The duties of the royal Secretary could be very exacting when
his master was as beset with enemies as Henry IV, and as vigorous
in going to meet them.   The first threat to the new King was a
plot by friends of Richard II to attack Henry and his family when
they were staying at Windsor after Christmas.   The King was
forewarned, however, and was able to overcome the conspirators.
Langley would have shared in the alarm and was given a memento
in the form of a magnificent bed forfeited by one of the rebels.[1]
In the following summer, after the failure to restore the long truce
made by Richard II in 1396, Henry attempted to force an end to
the open hostility shown by Scotland since his accession.   He
ordered a military concentration at York in June, and after further
fruitless diplomatic exchanges with the Scottish King advanced by
way of Durham and Newcastle to the gates of Edinburgh.   As in
the past, the Scots refused to join battle and forced the English
army to withdraw by ensuring that it was unable to find supplies
in their country; the English invasion lasted a mere fortnight.[2]
Langley was with the King throughout the campaign: while the
Keeper of the Privy Seal remained at Newcastle, the Secretary is
known to have gone as far as Leith, where he wrote a warrant on
12 August.[3]   While it is not inconceivable that he had attended
Gaunt in the Marches fifteen years earlier,[4] Langley's participation
in the expedition of 1400 is his first established introduction to the
Border country and its problems, and also led to his earliest
recorded visits to the city of Durham.

The following twelve months saw two further campaigns by the
King, both in Wales against the rebels led by Owen Glyndwr: the
first took place shortly after the Scottish expedition, the next in
October 1401.   Although on this second occasion he advanced as
far as Caernarvon, he was no more successful than in the previous
year, and bad weather and short supplies forced him to withdraw.
Henry returned to London, and went on to Hertford Castle.[5]

---

[1] CCR. 1399–1402, p. 321.

[2] Wylie, Henry the Fourth, Vol. I, pp. 126–40.

[3] CPR. 1399–1401, pp. 351–70; cf. Chancery: Warrants for the Great Seal,
file 603.

[4] R. L. Storey, "The Wardens of the Marches of England towards Scotland,
1377–1489", English Historical Review, 1957, pp. 595–8.

[5] Wylie, op. cit. I, pp. 242–6.

Here on 3 November he appointed Langley Keeper of the Privy Seal[1] in succession to Richard Clifford. Clifford had been consecrated as Bishop of Worcester four weeks earlier[2] and had presumably waited until the King had returned from Wales before surrendering the office. Every Keeper of the Privy Seal could expect promotion to a bishopric, but it was a convention that he should resign once he had been consecrated; the Privy Seal was considered to be beneath the episcopal dignity. Thus no particular political importance need be attached to Clifford's replacement by Langley; this was the only government change at that time. Yet there was some significance in Langley's appointment. Previously, Henry had selected for the offices of Chancellor, Treasurer, and Keeper of the Privy Seal men who had served under Richard II without being too closely associated with the more unpopular acts of the late King. Henry's policy had been to seek support by conciliatory measures, and he found it expedient to choose ministers for their practical experience of administration rather than for their political leanings.[3] Langley, on the other hand, was obviously a Lancastrian partisan; his appointment suggests that Henry was feeling more free to consult his personal preferences in the choice of ministers.

Langley's first fourteen months in office passed quietly; he was not often absent from Westminster, and then only to visit royal residences in its neighbourhood.[4] He was thus left comparatively free to acquire a thorough knowledge of the operations of his new office. This department held a key position in the royal administration and was the third great office of state, ranking after Chancery and the Exchequer. There were very few aspects of government in which the Privy Seal had no part, for its warrants made their way into all offices and to the King's ministers throughout his realm, abroad in Guienne as well as at home in England and Wales. Most of the letters sent out from Chancery under the Great Seal, all payments other than regular fees and pensions made by the Exchequer, and all issues of money, arms, livery, and other articles from the various royal wardrobes and other accounting offices were authorized by warrants under the Privy Seal.

---

[1] Exchequer of Receipt: Warrants for Issues, box 17, no. 345.
[2] W. Stubbs, *Registrum Sacrum Anglicanum* (Oxford, 1897), p. 84.
[3] Stubbs, *Constitutional History*, III, pp. 15 & 34.
[4] Chancery Warrants, files 611–18.

The seal was widely known and had full authority, and the King's subjects respected its directions to perform services of all kinds. The Privy Seal was extensively used in diplomacy, when the King wished to correspond with foreign princes on less formal terms than the traditional practice of Chancery permitted in its letters. The development and growth of the Privy Seal Office in the course of the fourteenth century had made it a target of critical interest in the reign of Richard II.   Attempts were made by his political adversaries to make it amenable to their control; while the King, hampered in the exercise of his prerogative, tried to circumvent this restraint by the wide use of his signet.   It has been observed that these circumstances caused the Privy Seal to go "out of court".[1]   This was not the case when Langley was Keeper, however, for the King made far greater use of the Privy Seal than of the signet, and was generally able to direct it by word of mouth.   The Privy Seal Office itself was established in the capital, and like other Keepers, Langley rented the London inn of a bishop,[2] but he had his own room in at least one royal manor,[3] and after his first year as Keeper again became one of the King's most constant companions.   He thus enjoyed a position of great influence, not only by virtue of the widespread activity of the Privy Seal, but also because he was one of Henry's closest advisers.   The Keeper was an *ex officio* member of the King's Council, the executive body which, whether in attendance on the King or meeting in his absence, transacted the routine business of government.

The year 1402 had seen warfare on two fronts: while the King had made a third profitless expedition into Wales, an invasion by the Scots was decisively defeated at Humbledon Hill by the Wardens of the Marches, the Earl of Northumberland and his son Henry Percy.   The King decided to go north to assist the Percies in the summer of 1403, but when he reached Burton-on-Trent on 17 July, he learnt that Henry Percy was in open rebellion, and wrote to order the Council to join him.[4]   Langley for

---

[1] T. F. Tout, *Chapters in the Administrative History of Medieval England* (Manchester, 1920–33), Vol. V, pp. 50–4, 205–11.

[2] H. C. Maxwell-Lyte, *Historical Notes on the Use of the Great Seal* (1926), p. 198.

[3] An instrument was made *in quadam camera domini Thome Longley* in Eltham manor on 27 December 1401 (Reg. Scrope, fo. 5v).

[4] *PPC*. I, pp. 207–8.

one obeyed this command promptly, and had joined the King at Shrewsbury by 21 July.[1] The two armies were then ready for battle, but in an attempt to prevent bloodshed, the King sent the Abbot of Shrewsbury and Langley [2] to Henry Percy, to offer him peace and a pardon. Percy was apparently impressed by the King's envoys, and sent his uncle, the Earl of Worcester, to explain the causes of the rising. The Earl was a hostile emissary, however, who is reported to have accused the King of unjustly seizing the crown, and he returned to his nephew with an unfavourable report. The armies then joined battle, Henry Percy was killed and his forces completely routed.[3]

The King now redirected his forces to the north of England. The Earl of Westmorland had deterred the Earl of Northumberland from joining his son, but the King wanted to enforce his submission. In addition, there was still a threat of invasion from Scotland. Langley wrote to the Exchequer from Lichfield on 25 July that the King had learnt that a Scottish attack was imminent, and required arms to be bought and sent to Pontefract in all possible haste.[4] Henry reached York on 8 August, when Langley took the opportunity to be personally installed in his deanery, and officiated in the Minster when the Archbishop celebrated mass for the King.[5] The main object of the King's visit to York was to receive the surrender of the Earl of Northumberland, on 11 August; a few days later, at Pontefract, he arranged for the custody of the Earl's castles by royal officers.[6] Langley now returned to Westminster, but he rejoined Henry at Worcester on 3 September and accompanied him on another brief excursion into Wales. The King was so short of funds when he reached Carmarthen that Langley advanced the modest sum of ten marks to help to pay the garrison.[7]

The defeat of the Percies was the King's most notable achievement in 1403; he had survived a serious threat to his crown, but

---

[1] Chancery Warrants, file 620.

[2] *Clericus de privato sigillo* (*Thomae Walsingham Historia Anglicana* (Rolls Series, 1863–4), Vol. II, p. 257).

[3] Ibid. II, pp. 257–8; M. V. Clarke & V. H. Galbraith, "The Deposition of Richard II", *Bulletin of John Rylands Library, 1930*, p. 179.

[4] Warrants for Issues, 18/599.

[5] Le Neve, III, p. 124; *The Fabric Rolls of York Minster* (SS. 1858), pp. 193–5.

[6] Walsingham, II, p. 259; *Foedera*, VIII, p. 330.

[7] Chancery Warrants, files 620–1; Warrants for Issues, 18/604.

this negative success had been followed by another expensive campaign in Wales. He had now completely emptied his treasury and was therefore obliged to call Parliament. When it met on 14 January 1404, the administration was strongly criticized and the King's financial weakness made him unable to resist a demand to name the members of his Council. The intention of this move was not to make Henry accept councillors nominated by the opposition, but rather to impress on the existing Council a sense of responsibility to Parliament, particularly in financial matters.[1] It was very active in the succeeding months, holding frequent sessions at Westminster from the end of April until the second week of June.[2] For the latter part of this period it acted in the absence of the King, who had departed for the north to compel the Earl of Northumberland to fulfil his promise to admit royal custodians to his castles. Langley stayed in London until 20 June before following the King, presumably in the company of the Chancellor and others of the Council.[3] The Earl had been called to Pontefract, and on 9 July made an agreement with the King and Council to surrender his Border castles in return for lands of equal value.[4] At Pontefract, plans were also made for the defence of the Marches towards Scotland, and a truce was concluded with Scottish representatives.[5] Henry then retired to his Duchy estates in the north Midlands. Langley went back to London, but for a few days only. He rejoined the King, accompanying him as he travelled from manor to manor.[6] Henry's object was doubtless to economize by living on his estates, but he was able to dispense with the Council while he did so: the petitions granted in the summer of 1404 were examined by the King alone. The Keeper of the Privy Seal was the only member of the Council in regular attendance.[7]

Langley had now been Keeper for nearly three years, and the time was due for him to receive the customary reward for such service, a bishopric. Robert Braybrook, Bishop of London, had

<hr />

1 *Rot. Parl.* III, p. 530; J. F. Baldwin, *The King's Council in England during the Middle Ages* (Oxford, 1913), pp. 153–5.

2 CPS. 12.

3 Chancery Warrants, file 623.

4 Walsingham, II, p. 263; *Foedera*, VIII, pp. 364–5.

5 *Rot. Scot.* II, pp. 167 & 169; *CPR. 1401–1405*, p. 408.

6 Wylie, op cit. IV, p. 292; Chancery Warrants, file 623.

7 CPS. 13.

died on 27 August. The royal licence for an election was issued on 10 September, and the Chapter, no doubt inspired by some expression of the King's wishes, chose Langley for their Bishop on 10 October.[1] The King informed the Pope that he wished Langley to be provided to London, and the Archbishop of Canterbury, who had already written to the Pope on behalf of Robert Hallam, Chancellor of Oxford University, now wrote again to Rome to commend Langley, "his dear friend", whose virtues as well as his long service to John of Gaunt and King Henry made him a worthy candidate.[2] The Pope, Innocent VII, ignored Langley's nomination and canonical election, and on 10 December provided Roger Walden, the former Archbishop of Canterbury.[3] Langley's natural disappointment would have been palliated to some extent by his promotion to the highest position in the royal administration. The Chancellor, Henry Beaufort, had been translated from the see of Lincoln to that of Winchester, and he resigned the Great Seal some two weeks before he received the temporalities of his new diocese,[4] which he presumably wished to be free to visit. Langley was appointed to succeed him on 2 March.[5]

As Chancellor, Langley had high and numerous responsibilities. He was firstly the King's chief minister, and as such held a permanent and influential position in the Council. He had to ensure that the administrative machinery of Chancery functioned efficiently. Chancery was still the principal organ of government, although its adaptability to new demands was restricted by the traditions and the routine developed over three centuries. Letters under the Great Seal were the most solemn expression of the King's commands, and of his assent to numerous activities on the part of his subjects. By the issue of writs, the Chancellor held an important place in the operations of the courts of common law,

---

[1] *CPR. 1401–1405*, p. 422; F. Godwin, *De Praesulibus Angliae Commentarius*, ed. W. Richardson (Cambridge, 1743), p. 186.

[2] *Royal Letters, Henry IV* (Rolls Series, 1860), pp. 415–16. The writer's name is not known, but it is not conceivable that anyone other than the Archbishop would have ventured to propose a candidate for a bishopric to the Pope. The Chancellor, Beaufort, might have done so, but would have been more likely to recommend Langley or some other "King's clerk".

[3] *CPL*. VI, p. 6. See below, p. 18, for the conclusion of this episode.

[4] *CPR. 1405–1408*, p. 1.

[5] R. L. Storey, "English Officers of State, 1399–1485", *Bulletin of the Institute of Historical Research, 1958*, p. 85.

and he was himself able to exercise jurisdictions in both common law and equity.   As was appropriate to the dignity of his office, Langley lived in considerable state.   He continued to occupy the London inn of the Bishop of Coventry and Lichfield until after his promotion to the see of Durham.[1]   Apart from the clerks of Chancery, his household included laymen of gentle birth.[2]   On one occasion at least, the King was his guest: on 6 February 1406, Henry thanked him for his hospitality.[3]

Attendance of the King's Council accounted for a considerable proportion of Langley's time.   In the month following his appointment, while the King was absent from London, the Council met almost daily at Westminster, with only the Chancellor, Treasurer, and Keeper of the Privy Seal regular in their attendance.[4]   On 1 April, the Great Council assembled at St Albans,[5] and Langley lodged there until its dismissal on 6 April. Instead of returning to the capital immediately, he went on into Norfolk to make a visitation of his archdeaconry.   He stopped at Baldock on 7 April, at Babraham on the following day, and at Shouldham, near King's Lynn, on the 11th; thence he crossed Norfolk to Corton, a few miles south of Great Yarmouth, a journey that took him a whole week, and spent another four days on the road to Thetford, where he arrived on 22 April.   He then returned to London.[6]   This visitation, for such it clearly was, was a remarkable event: a visitation by an archdeacon in person was not a common occurrence in the later Middle Ages, and by an archdeacon who was also Chancellor of England probably unknown.   An archdeaconry was then regarded as a sinecure, the duties to be performed by an official, while the income went to support a favoured royal or episcopal minister.   Langley's contemporaries who were, like himself, both archdeacons and high government officials, obtained papal licences to hold visitations by deputy.   Langley had never obtained an indult to visit by deputy.   When he was Keeper of the Privy Seal, he was too much occupied by secular affairs to hold a visitation, but his

---

1 *Reg.* no. 12.
2 *Ancient Deeds*, Vol. III, no. C.3317.
3 Chancery Warrants, 1360/36.
4 CPS. 19; Wylie, op. cit. IV, p. 293.
5 Walsingham, II, p. 268.
6 *CCR. 1402–1405*, pp. 442, 490, 500, 505 & 508; *CFR. 1399–1405*, p. 266; *CPR. 1401–1405*, p. 461.

interest in his archdeaconry is revealed by his obtaining, on 29 December 1402, the King's licence to certify direct to Chancery all persons excommunicated in the archdeaconry.[1] Also, unlike some archdeacons, Langley appears to have been on amicable terms with his Bishop, Henry Despenser of Norwich: he carried out some business for him at court, and acted as one of his attornies in Parliament.[2]

The last, and most serious, rising against Henry IV took place in the summer of 1405. The real leaders were the Earl of Northumberland, the Earl Marshal, and Lord Bardolf, but Archbishop Scrope of York put himself forward as its figurehead and published a manifesto against Henry's administration. The King received news of the revolt when he was at Hereford, on 22 May, where he issued orders for the assembly of the shire levies of the midland counties.[3] He hastened to the scene of the revolt, and wrote to the Council from Derby on 28 May to inform it of the rebellion, asking his councillors to join him at Pontefract with such forces as they could raise.[4] Before Henry reached Yorkshire, the main part of the rising had been suppressed by the politic treachery of the Earl of Westmorland, who, by feigning to parley, had captured the Archbishop and Earl Marshal. Northumberland and Bardolf, too late to help their fellow-conspirators, retired further north.

The Council, meanwhile, had been prompt to obey Henry's summons. Although it had met at Westminster on 30 May, Langley, at least, reached Nottingham the next day, where the King was waiting. On 6 June, Langley was at Bishopthorpe, the Archbishop's manor, where Henry had set up his head-quarters,[5] and was thus close at hand on 8 June when Archbishop Scrope was hastily given a form of trial and executed immediately afterwards, despite the Archbishop of Canterbury's intercession. According to one account of Scrope's death, the King was reluctant to have him executed, but the royal councillors insisted on this extreme measure.[6] As Henry's first councillor, Langley

---

[1] CPR. 1401–1405, p. 187.
[2] Anglo-Norman Letters and Petitions, ed. M. D. Legge (Anglo-Norman Text Society, 1941), p. 109; Parliamentary Proxies, file 42, no. 2090.
[3] CPR. 1405–1408, p. 66.
[4] PPC. I, pp. 264–5.
[5] CPS. 21 & 22; CFR. 1399–1405, p. 272; CPR. 1405–1408, p. 21.
[6] Incerti Scriptoris Chronicon Angliae, ed. J. A. Giles (1848), p. 45.

must be suspected of complicity, but a second account indicates that it was the secular members of the Council, certain knights, who pressed for the capital sentence.[1] These accounts are mere excuses for the King, however; he had to explain his action to Archbishop Arundel, and ecclesiastics generally, and put the blame on his advisers. His position had been gravely endangered by Scrope's treason, and he was well acquainted with the dictum *necessitas non habet legem*.[2] His mind had been made up over a week before the dramatic scene at Bishopthorpe. On 1 June, he had granted that John Tilton should have the pension that "he who is next created archbishop of York" would be obliged to pay a royal clerk.[3] Scrope was not the first prelate or priest to suffer death by Henry's command.[4]

The archbishopric of York was thus vacant. On 17 June, the King's licence was given for an election. Langley, the Dean, was his nominee. He was elected, and on 8 August Henry gave his assent and asked the Pope to give his confirmation.[5] Master John Catrick had already been sent to the Roman *Curia*, doubtless to explain the reasons for Scrope's execution. He took with him letters designed to win Henry the favour of the Cardinals of Naples and Florence, the King having granted, on 18 June, that they might obtain provision to English benefices to a total annual value of £200.[6] Another concession was the admission of Roger Walden to the bishopric of London. The see had been vacant for several months while, presumably, the King pressed Langley's claims. With Langley's election to York, the question of his promotion to London could be set aside and Walden was given licence, on 24 June, to enter into possession.[7] The King's surrender on this point failed to placate the Pope. Innocent refused to countenance Langley's election to York: he naturally regarded the execution of Scrope as an affront to the Church, and the nomination of the King's Chancellor as his successor as an additional insult. Nor had it been particularly creditable for

---

[1] *Eulogium Historiarum sive Temporis* (Rolls Series, 1858–63), Vol. III, p. 407.
[2] Lyte, *Great Seal*, p. 130.
[3] Warrants for the Privy Seal, file 3, no. 138; Chancery Warrants, 626/4359.
[4] Wylic, I, pp. 275–8, 428.
[5] *Foedera*, VIII, p. 407; *CPR. 1405–1408*, pp. 21 & 48.
[6] Warrants for Issues, 20/286; Warrants for the Privy Seal, 3/147 & 149; Chancery Warrants, 626/4391.
[7] *CPR. 1405–1408*, p. 22.

Langley to have accepted promotion in the circumstances, although it is possible that the delay of six weeks between the issue of the licence for the election and the King's confirmation was due to Langley's reluctance to fill Scrope's place. The Pope excommunicated all who had taken part in the execution and provided Robert Hallam to the vacant see. The King forbade both the publication of the sentence and the provision of the Pope's candidate. Relations with Rome remained in a strained condition for some time, the archbishopric lay vacant until after Langley's promotion to Durham,[1] and it was left to Innocent's successor, Gregory XII, to offer absolution to those who had been guilty of Scrope's death. He commissioned Langley and the Bishop of Lincoln as his mandataries for this purpose on 12 April 1408.[2]

With the death of Scrope, the most serious part of the rebellion had been crushed, but Northumberland and Bardolf were still at large. While the King went further north to reduce the Earl's castles and forced him to take sanctuary in Scotland, the Council returned to Westminster to hold sessions there throughout July. It then rejoined the King at Pontefract, whence they all departed on 14 August and travelled by way of Leicester and Worcester to Hereford. In September, Henry made another incursion into Wales, and in his absence, Langley went to Coventry,[3] probably to raise a loan; both he and Henry were once more at Worcester on 29 September,[4] and the year's military operations were concluded. For the second time in three years, an unsuccessful rebellion, followed by a campaign against the elusive rebels of Wales, had reduced the King to bankruptcy and obliged him to seek relief by calling Parliament.

When Langley, as Chancellor, formally opened Parliament on 1 March 1406, his address was conciliatory in tone: he placed particular emphasis on the King's desire for counsel and for the well-being of his subjects. The Commons were not moved to make an early grant of subsidies, and with the approach of Easter, Parliament was prorogued for three weeks on 3 April.[5]

[1] A. Hamilton Thompson, *The English Clergy and their Organisation in the Later Middle Ages* (Oxford, 1947), pp. 18–19.
[2] *CPL*. VI, p. 98.
[3] CPS. 22; *CCR. 1402–1405*, pp. 525–9; *CPR. 1405–1408*, pp. 35–58.
[4] *CCR. 1402–1405*, p. 525.
[5] *Rot. Parl.* III, pp. 567 & 569.

Langley again spent the vacation visiting his archdeaconry of Norfolk; on 12 April, he was at Corton, and travelled slowly westwards through Norwich to King's Lynn, where he arrived on 18 April. As he went, he issued some writs touching local matters of a legal nature, and took a recognizance at West Dereham on 20 April.[1] Then he returned to Westminster for the second parliamentary session, which was no more profitable than the first so far as the King was concerned. Although he made concessions, including the nomination of his Council, no subsidies were granted and a further prorogation was necessary.[2]

During the summer, Langley at last attained the episcopal dignity. He was provided to the see of Durham by a bull of 14 May, and was consecrated in St Paul's, London, on 8 August by Archbishop Arundel, who was assisted by Bishops Beaufort of Winchester and Clifford of London, at Langley's request. Being unable to visit his diocese immediately, the new Bishop appointed vicars-general on 10 August.[3] The King would have been most reluctant to change his Chancellor at that time: Chancery was always closely associated with Parliament, and Langley had presumably become well acquainted with the leading elements in the "Long Parliament" of 1406 and understood their attitude to the government. As a further session was due, Henry would have wished to retain the minister who was best informed on this subject. Moreover, if Langley were to resign the Great Seal then, whatever his motive, his replacement might have appeared as a sign of weakness on the King's part: it would have appeared that he had dismissed the chief minister of his much criticized administration. Langley therefore remained in office for a further six months, until a month after the close of Parliament. Its third session lasted for more than two months. It again asked the King to name his councillors, drew up some thirty articles for the reform of the government which the King was constrained to accept, and at length granted subsidies. Langley was then able, on 22 December, to inform the Commons that they were dismissed.[4]

The main burden of Parliament's complaints had been directed against the inefficiency of the administration and, in particular,

---

[1] *CCR. 1405–1409*, pp. 123–6; *CPR. 1405–1408*, p. 186.
[2] *Rot. Parl.* III, pp. 571 & 579.
[3] *Reg.* nos. 1, 10 & 12; and below, p. 166.
[4] *Rot. Parl.* III, pp. 568, 579, 585–9, 603; *PPC.* I, p. 295.

against the government's failure to defend the country against attacks by its enemies. This criticism might have been the reason for Langley's resignation of the Great Seal on 30 January 1407.[1] This was Stubbs' view.[2] As the first minister of the administration, Langley might have been held responsible for the criticisms made against it. This explanation of his resignation cannot be accepted; incompetence would have been the last charge made against Langley. Apart from the record of his government, both spiritual and temporal, in Durham, the mere fact that so exacting a master as Henry V employed him as Chancellor for five years is sufficient warrant to exonerate him from the accusation of inefficiency; it is no exaggeration to say that Langley was one of the ablest administrators of his day. In any case, the parliamentary criticism of 1406 was less than just: the chief cause of the Crown's weakness was the inadequacy of its financial resources.

A further reason for rejecting any suggestion that Langley had suffered in reputation is the fact that on the same day as he resigned the Great Seal he was appointed a member of the King's Council, with an annual salary of two hundred marks.[3] Later in the year, on 5 May, the King granted a charter confirming the franchises of the Bishopric of Durham, and gave as one of the causes moving him the special affection he had for Langley.[4] The reasons for Langley's resignation are most likely to be connected with his promotion to the episcopate. There was still at that time some prejudice against a bishop holding secular office [5] and Langley may have shared this feeling at that particular moment. He did not visit Durham until a further six months had passed, but he may well have wished to have more freedom from royal business in order to attend to the problems of his secular and diocesan administrations. He had held office under the King for more than seven years, in a time of great stress, of rebellions and troublesome Parliaments; he must have felt the need for some rest from the rigours of office. He could not have resigned the Great Seal before Parliament had been dismissed, and he took the

[1] *Foedera*, VIII, p. 464; *CCR. 1405–1409*, p. 250.

[2] *Constitutional History*, III, p. 61.

[3] Warrants for Issues, 23/264.

[4] Hutchinson, *History of Durham*, I, p. 332; *Calendar of Charter Rolls*, Vol. V, p. 432.

[5] *The St Albans' Chronicle, 1406–1420*, ed. V. H. Galbraith (Oxford, 1927), p. 10.

earliest opportunity to do so; for Archbishop Arundel would not relieve him without considerable persuasion.[1]   Langley's surrender of the Great Seal marked the end of a chapter in his life; he was no longer merely "the King's clerk", owing his position in the state to the office the King conferred upon him.   He now stood as a public figure in his own right, for as Bishop of Durham he was both a high ecclesiastic and a powerful secular magnate. His position, as well as the experience he had acquired of the details of government, his record of loyal service in times of crisis and the fact that he was still in the prime of life, ensured his future prominence as a statesman of the first rank.

3   COUNCILLOR AND DIPLOMAT, 1407–1417

In the ten years that followed his resignation of the Great Seal, Bishop Langley held no office of state, although it might be said that he remained a "cabinet minister", even that he was at times "secretary of state for foreign affairs".   His prominence as a diplomat in the negotiations between England and France in the few years preceding the renewal of the Hundred Years War is the most apparent though not the only reason for regarding this period of his career as one of particular interest.   He also had an important rôle in the English participation in the Conciliar Movement, and his association with this activity as well as Anglo-French diplomacy is highly significant.   At the same time, his position as member of a royal Council subject to partisan influences deserves attention.   Throughout these years Langley was making himself familiar with the administrations of his diocese and county palatine, and taking the part traditionally required of a Bishop of Durham in the troubled affairs of the Marches towards Scotland; these local interests made it necessary for him to pass several months of each year in the north of England.[2]

Langley had been appointed to the King's Council on 30 January 1407,[3] and remained in the capital to attend its sessions until the end of the Trinity term.   He spent the summer in his diocese, being enthroned at Durham on 4 September.   On 24 October, when the seventh Parliament of the reign was opened

---

[1] *The St Albans' Chronicle, 1406–1420*, p. 10.
[2] See Appendix A, pp. 226–32 below.
[3] Warrants for Issues, 23/264.

at Gloucester, Langley was the first-named of the triers of petitions from Gascony; [1] this appointment presaged his new responsibilities in the diplomatic field. The state of relations between England and France had been practically one of open warfare since the accession of Henry IV, whom the government of Charles VI regarded as a usurper; it no longer adhered to the treaty for a truce of twenty-eight years concluded with his son-in-law, Richard II, in 1396. Although sporadic civil war in France weakened its government, it had committed many hostile acts: Gascony was invaded and partly conquered, an alliance was made with Owen Glyndwr, and in the Channel there were frequent clashes between French and English ships. There was an improvement in relations from the summer of 1407, when an English delegation visited France. The French then proposed to send an embassy, which was granted letters of safe-conduct on 27 September. When it arrived at Gloucester early in December, Langley was appointed to lead the English representatives, who were empowered to treat for a perpetual peace and marriage alliance, or for local or general truces. In the event, it was agreed, on 7 December, that there should be a truce in Guienne from 15 January to 15 April 1408, so that it should be possible for further negotiations to be conducted in a more friendly atmosphere. [2]

The result of this conference was meagre in comparison with the terms of the English commission, although the area covered by the terms of the truce was larger than any since 1399. The real significance of the agreement, however, was that it was the prelude to a notable increase in diplomatic exchanges. That the discussions were not confined to national differences is suggested by a phrase in the preamble to the English commission: the negotiations were undertaken in the belief that an understanding with France was an essential prerequisite for English participation in the international movement to reunite the Church. [3] The Great Schism had then existed for close on thirty years, since 1378, when the College of Cardinals had abandoned Urban VI and elected another Pope, Clement VII. Since that year western

---

[1] *Rot. Parl.* III, pp. 608–9.
[2] *Foedera*, VIII, pp. 484–5, 499, 504–9.
[3] "Au fin que mieulx puissons entendre a l'apaisement du Schisme qi est en l'Esglise" (Ibid. VIII, p. 504).

Europe had two rival obediences, which its own political divisions fostered and perpetuated: Clement's court at Avignon was supported by France and the Spanish kingdoms; while England and Germany became the principal allies of the Urbanist Popes. France took the lead in devising measures to end this disgraceful situation, but England was lukewarm and her distrust of the French was a further obstacle. By the close of 1407, it was recognized in France that the intransigent attitude of the rival Popes had made "the way of cession", namely that both should resign, an impossible policy, and that the only course offering a solution was conciliar action. Her ambassadors at Gloucester would inevitably discuss this great problem with Langley and his colleagues, and strive to allay English suspicion that France's attitude was merely one of national self-interest. Langley would have listened to the French diplomats with particular attention, for as Bishop of Durham he experienced one of the most pernicious consequences of the Schism: since England had supported the party of Urban VI, Scotland had inevitably followed France into the Avignonese camp, and the Durham cell of Coldingham and other English churches in the diocese of St Andrews thus became subject to the rival obedience. In 1390, the Urbanist Pope granted Bishop Skirlaw of Durham full powers of episcopal jurisdiction in Berwick-upon-Tweed and all other parts of the diocese of St Andrews already ruled by the English King or that he might conquer in the future; this jurisdiction was inherited by Langley when he succeeded Skirlaw.[1] The Bishop of Durham therefore had a particular interest in any activity to end the Schism, as he also had in the condition of Anglo-French relations: a treaty of peace or truce with France could probably be extended to embrace her Scottish ally, as it had been ten years earlier, and thus give relief to the Bishop's estates and subjects in Northumberland. The King employed Langley in his dealings with France because he trusted in his discretion and ability, but the Bishop himself was most directly anxious for reasons both secular and ecclesiastical to bring this diplomacy to a successful conclusion.[2]

When the French embassy had departed from Gloucester, Langley returned to his diocese for Christmas, and made his way back to London early in January 1408. In the following month, the Earl of Northumberland made his last desperate gesture of

[1] Below, pp. 145–6.   [2] See also p. 35, note 2.

rebellion: he left Scotland with his henchman Bardolf to enlist an army on his estates in North Yorkshire, and met defeat and death at Bramham Moor on 19 February. The King came to Yorkshire to restore order, with Langley in attendance, and while Henry was lodged in the Bishop's manor of Wheel Hall, near York,[1] Langley stayed at Howden, not far distant. French diplomats came to the King after he had moved on to Pontefract, and on 15 April they agreed to an extension of the truce until 30 September.[2] As one of the English representatives was Richard Holme, the Bishop's spiritual chancellor, who was with him at Howden on the day of the treaty,[3] Langley would have been kept closely informed of these discussions and may even have had some direct conversation with the Frenchmen; it is unlikely that he wasted the opportunity to obtain news of recent French activity to end the Schism. He would have learnt that the clergy of France had threatened to withdraw their obedience from the Avignonese Pope if reunion had not been accomplished by 24 May, a threat they were to fulfil. A matter of more immediate concern to the Bishop, however, was the pacification of Yorkshire; he remained in the county throughout May, spending its latter part at North-allerton, in the centre of the disaffected area. He then made an extensive tour of his estates, going to Norham Castle, on the Border, and then back to Durham to conduct a visitation of the county. His preoccupation in this task must account for his inability to attend Convocation at York on 20 August: it had been summoned to consider the reunion of the Church, and in par-ticular an invitation by a number of cardinals to attend a General Council to be held at Pisa.[4]

Langley was once more in London by mid-October, and would have been present when Cardinal Ugoccione came to urge England's adherence to the conciliar movement. The Cardinal's intervention was decisive: Henry was now determined that England should be represented at Pisa. There was a second session of that summer's Convocation at York in December, and this time Langley did attend and was appointed to lead the delegation of the northern province to the General Council.[5] His selection was inevitable, even if the King had not required

---

[1] Wylie, *Henry IV*, IV, p. 297.   [2] *Foedera*, VIII, pp. 513–19.
[3] *Reg.* no. 65.   [4] *Reg.* nos. 91 & 95.
[5] York: Register of Archbishop Bowet, Vol. I, fo. 291v.

his nomination, for his political standing made him a more influential representative than either Archbishop Bowet or Bishop Strickland of Carlisle, while other reasons, already mentioned, made him a particularly suitable choice. His appointment by Convocation, however, occasioned a complication in the course of the King's negotiations with France. It had been agreed at a recent meeting of representatives of both countries that Henry should send an embassy led by an archbishop or bishop to Paris to meet a French commission on 3 February 1409, and he hoped to conclude a treaty of peace and possibly also a marriage alliance. In November 1408, he decided that Langley should lead this embassy, but its departure was delayed, presumably on account of the King's grave illness in January, and an envoy was sent to France to explain why the ambassadors had not been despatched.[1] The King's incapacity accounts for his delay in deciding whether Langley should go to Paris or to Pisa, and it was not until 20 March that he determined that the Bishop should attend the General Council.[2]

Langley departed from London at the end of March and arrived in Pisa on 7 May. He was thus two weeks later than Robert Hallam, Bishop of Salisbury, who led the English delegation and acted as its chief spokesman in the Council's debates.[3] There is only one notice of Langley's activities: he celebrated mass before the Council on 13 June.[4] His influence must have been considerable, however, for he held powers of attorney from fourteen bishops and one hundred and three abbots and priors.[5] After the two rival Popes had been declared deposed, Alexander V was elected, on 26 June. On 7 July, he granted Langley the power to collate to a number of benefices in his own gift. This grant cannot have been sought by Langley, for it had no value to him and he did not even trouble to have it recorded in his register. He was granted five other faculties on 18 July,[6] which he had presumably requested of the Pope to replace the useless grant of the 7th. It would thus appear that if the earlier grant

---

1 Warrants for Issues, 24/236 & 298; *Foedera*, VIII, p. 571.
2 Chancery Warrants, 1362/44.
3 *Sacrorum Conciliorum Collectio*, ed. J. D. Mansi (Florence & Venice, 1759–98), Vols. XXVI, cols. 1139 & 1140, and XXVII, col. 348.
4 Vatican Library: Thome Trotati Manuale Concilii Pisan. fo. 64v.
5 Mansi, op. cit. XXVII, cols. 348–50.
6 *CPL.* VI, pp. 151–2, 154–5; *Reg.* nos. 139, 213–21.

were made on Alexander's own motion, it was in recognition of Langley's work in the Council, possibly even in promoting the Pope's election.

The last session of the Council of Pisa was held on 7 August. Langley returned to England in leisurely fashion; it is likely that he did not arrive in London many days before 17 October, when Henry recognized Alexander as Pope. The Bishop went on to his diocese at the end of November, and remained there until he was obliged to return to take his place in the Parliament that met at Westminster on 27 January 1410. In his absence, two ministerial changes—of the Chancellor and Treasurer—had marked the success of a political group led by Henry, Prince of Wales, and the Bishop of Winchester, whose brother Thomas Beaufort was the new Chancellor. This success was ratified in Parliament on 2 May, when the King named the Prince, the Bishops of Winchester, Durham, and Bath and Wells, the Earls of Arundel and Westmorland, and Lord Burnell as his councillors. This Council, small in comparison with its predecessors and composed solely of peers, was presumably nominated by the Prince; Langley and Bubwith, the Bishop of Bath, the only career administrators, would have been retained to widen its basis. On 9 May Prince Henry told Parliament that Langley and the Earl of Westmorland would not be able to attend the Council regularly, on account of their responsibilities on the Scottish border, and Bishop Chichele of St David's and the Earl of Warwick were therefore also appointed councillors.[1] Langley did attend the Council in the following month of June, and again in October. At the end of November, he accompanied it to Leicester, where the King was staying,[2] and then went on to his diocese. In March 1411, he came to London to attend a meeting of the Great Council,[3] but spent the next five months in the north, partly in continuing his interrupted visitation of the archdeaconry of Durham.

The record of Langley's attendance of the King's Council since his appointment in May 1410 shows him to have been one of its least regular members, and throughout the period of Prince Henry's ascendancy he did not receive his salary as a councillor.[4]

[1] *Rot. Parl.* III, pp. 632 & 634.
[2] *PPC.* I, pp. 331–40; and II, pp. 4–5; *CCR. 1405–1408*, pp. 133–5, 175, 182 & 188; Wylie, *Henry IV*, IV, p. 300.
[3] *PPC.* II, pp. 6–7.
[4] Exchequer of Receipt: Issue Rolls, 605–9.

His recognized responsibilities in the north do not account for his infrequent attendance, for there were no Scottish attacks in the summer of 1411, and although he was appointed to treat with Scottish representatives on 23 May, he appears to have taken no part in these negotiations.[1]   The true explanation would seem to be that he was at best lukewarm in his support of the Prince's party. Langley has been described as "an adherent of the Beaufort party",[2] and there is some justification for this opinion. His association with Henry Beaufort was of long standing, dating from the early years when he was a clerk in the household of Beaufort's father, John of Gaunt; he had chosen Beaufort to assist in his consecration as Bishop of Durham,[3] and in 1407 had been associated with him in a licence to grant certain lands to John Beaufort, Earl of Somerset.[4]   Langley's first loyalty, however, was always given to the King, and Henry IV distrusted his half-brother Bishop Beaufort, even suspecting him of encouraging Prince Henry to supplant him on the throne; despite their close kinship, he would not appoint Beaufort an executor of his will. Langley never forfeited the King's confidence: when Henry appeared to be dying in January 1409, Langley was one of the small group of ministers and old Duchy servants who stayed around him,[5] and he was appointed an executor of Henry's last will in 1413.   When they were together at Leicester in November 1410, the King must have voiced his misgivings to Langley, who from that time ceased to take his place in the Council.

While Langley was in his diocese in the summer of 1411, news came to England that Pope John XXIII had elected him and Bishop Hallam of Salisbury to the cardinalate on 6 June.   He had created a total of fourteen cardinals on that day, chosen from the most eminent churchmen of several countries, including Pierre d'Ailly, Filastre, and Zabarella.[6]   The Pope's motive in making so catholic a selection was undoubtedly a desire to gain the diplomatic support of the European powers against both his Italian enemies and the two rival Popes, for despite the Council

[1] Below, p. 148.   [2] C. L. Kingsford, *Henry V* (1923) p. 63, note.
[3] *Reg.* nos. 10 & 11.   [4] *CPR. 1405–1408*, p. 342.
[5] *Testamenta Vetusta*, ed. N. H. Nicolas (1826), Vol. I, pp. 17–18; *CCR. 1405–1409*, p. 498.
[6] Ciaconi, *Vitae et Res Gestae Pontificum Romanorum et S.R.E. Cardinalium* (1677), Vol. III, col. 803; F. Cristofori, *Storia dei Cardinali di Santa Romana Chiesa* (Rome, 1888), p. 268.

of Pisa, the Urbanist and Avignonese parties continued to maintain their own popes. The King received the news of these elections with mixed feelings: he fully appreciated the honour to his country, but placed too much value on the counsel of the two Bishops to wish them to leave England to take up continual residence in Rome. He thus wrote to the Pope to excuse Hallam and Langley from accepting their cardinalates, and as this letter was written before an official notice of the elections had been received from Rome,[1] it would appear that Langley could not have been consulted before it was despatched. While it is undeniable that England could ill-afford to lose these two distinguished churchmen, the King was probably also unwilling to commit himself to too cordial a support of a Pope whose reputation and policies were to occasion his deposition four years later.

The outbreak of civil war in France in 1411 led to a new turn in English diplomatic policy; both factions turned to England for assistance, and Prince Henry and the Council made an alliance with the Duke of Burgundy. Bishop Chichele acted as leader of the English representatives in the preceding negotiations, in which Langley took no part. The King had no liking for the Burgundian connection and broke it after resuming full control of the government. In the Parliament of November 1411, he thanked his councillors for their services and dismissed them. A new Council was named, although the only appointment of which a record remains was that of Archbishop Bowet of York.[2] Archbishop Arundel again became Chancellor and a new Treasurer was also appointed. Langley was a member of the re-formed Council, and came to attend it regularly, taking his salary.[3] He had obviously anticipated spending a larger proportion of his time in royal service than he had done in the previous eighteen months when, on 1 September, before leaving his diocese to attend Parliament, he appointed a vicar-general for the reason that he expected to be absent continually because of the business committed to him by the King.[4] In February 1412, when a Burgundian embassy came to London, Langley was appointed to lead the English commission[5] and since discussions with

1 British Museum: Harley MS. 431, fo. 1.
2 *Rot. Parl.* III, p. 649; Warrants for Issues, 28/217.
3 Issue Rolls, 609, m. 11, and 610, mm. 11 & 13.
4 *Reg.* no. 226.
5 *Foedera*, VIII, p. 721; Warrants for Issues, 28/222.

representatives of the rival French group were taking place at the same time, his instructions must have been to avoid committing the King and to secure from the Burgundians promises of concessions that would cause the Armagnac faction to increase its offers for English support. In the event, the Armagnacs promised to restore Aquitaine and Henry entered into an active military alliance.

After a brief visit to his diocese in the Easter vacation, Langley resumed his attendance of the Council. He appears to have assisted Prince Henry in an attempted reconciliation with his father, for when the Prince came to London for this purpose on 30 June, he lodged with the Bishop before visiting the King.[1] He was not immediately successful, but was reconciled before the King's death. Langley remained in attendance on Henry IV until the very end of the reign; his absences from the capital in the summer of 1412 and in the following winter were comparatively short, and he was in London when Henry died on 20 March 1413. The supervisors of Henry's last will, which does not survive, were the Prince and Archbishop Arundel; and Archbishop Bowet, Bishop Langley, and three other Lancastrians were its executors. Their task was onerous: Henry had died so heavily in debt that the executors were at first reluctant to undertake the administration. It was granted in Parliament in 1413 that they should be given the sum of 25,000 marks in composition for the goods that Henry V had inherited in order to settle the late King's obligations, but the greater part of this sum had not been paid ten years later. The executors of Henry IV received their final acquittance from the Archbishop of Canterbury in 1429.[2]

The steady loyalty Langley had given to Henry IV might well have prejudiced his standing with the new King, but in fact Henry V gave no indication of any animosity against the Bishop and soon came to hold the same high regard that his father had shown for Langley's capabilities as counsellor, diplomat, and administrator. Langley was a member of the Privy Council from the beginning of the reign and a trier of petitions in Henry V's first Parliament.[3] From the end of the year he can

---

[1] *A Chronicle of London*, ed. N. H. Nicolas (1827), p. 94.

[2] *Rot. Parl.* IV, pp. 206–8, 280–2, 323–4; *Foedera*, IX, pp. 9–10; *CPR. 1413–1416*, p. 54, and *1422–1429*, pp. 64, 188–9; *Reg. Chichele*, II, pp. 421–31.

[3] Chancery: Charter Rolls, nos. 180–2; *PPC.* II, pp. 131–5; *Rot. Parl.* IV, pp. 3–4.

be seen to emerge as the King's chief adviser on foreign policy, a position he was to retain for more than three years. When ambassadors of the French King came to London in December, Langley, who was their host, headed the commissioners who on 24 January 1414 concluded a treaty for a general truce to last until 31 January 1415.[1] Henry had not attempted an early resumption of the Burgundian alliance he had favoured in his father's lifetime, but continued to treat with both French parties with the object of perpetuating their division and forcing competing offers of concessions from them. In the negotiations held in the Bishop of Durham's inn, the prospects of peace and the marriage of the King to Princess Katherine, daughter of Charles VI, had been favourably discussed. On 31 May, Henry appointed Bishops Langley of Durham and Courtenay of Norwich, the Earl of Salisbury and others, as his ambassadors to treat with the French King.[2] They departed from London on 10 July and arrived in Paris on 8 August; the citizens were very impressed with the size of the embassy, estimated at five hundred strong, and the magnificence of its entertainment by the Duke of Berri. King Charles and his Council were absent from the capital, however, and had not appointed any representatives to treat with the English commissioners, who therefore departed after stating Henry's terms for peace. They returned to London on 3 October.[3]

As a consequence of the embassy's failure, Parliament, which met on 19 November, made grants for war, but the Great Council asked that hostilities should not be begun before it was certain that negotiations would produce no result.[4] Henry had already decided to send another embassy, and on 3 November the Exchequer made payments to Langley, Courtenay, and other ambassadors about to depart for France; they received their formal commission on 5 December.[5] The embassy set out from

[1] J. H. Wylie & W. T. Waugh, *The Reign of Henry the Fifth* (Cambridge, 1914-29), Vol. I, p. 156; *Foedera*, IX, pp. 88-9, 91-101.
[2] Ibid. IX, pp. 102-4, 131-3.
[3] Exchequer L.T.R.: Foreign Accounts, no. 47, rot. C.; Accounts, Various, 321/20 & 26, and 620/20; N. de Baye, *Journal* (Soc. de l'Hist. de France, 1885, 1888), Vol. II, p. 190; *Chronique du Religieux de Saint Denys* (Coll. des Docs. Inédits, 1829-52), Vol. V, p. 376; J. Juvenal des Ursins, *Histoire de Charles VI*, ed. D. Godefroy (Paris, 1653), p. 281; *Foedera*, IX, pp. 131-3.
[4] *Rot. Parl.* IV, pp. 34-5; *PPC*. II, pp. 150-1.
[5] Issue Roll 619, m. 4; *Foedera*, IX, pp. 183-8.

London on 14 December, and, after being delayed by high seas at Southampton which caused it to turn back and cross from Dover, arrived in Paris before 24 January 1415, when the existing truce was prorogued until 1 May.[1] The English ambassadors again made a sensation with their splendour and company of six hundred horsemen; they were lavishly entertained by Charles VI, who held tournaments and banquets in their honour.[2] The course of the negotiations cannot have been equally cordial, for the English embassy began with a claim for the cession of the French crown to King Henry, and followed its rejection with demands for enormous concessions of territory and money. These terms were gradually reduced as the French made counter-offers, but as the last and most generous of these was less than the embassy was empowered to accept,[3] it returned to London where Bishops Courtenay and Langley were greeted with popular derision "because they had achieved nought".[4] Although the French had promised to send an embassy, the King clearly expected to gain nothing from it and made his final arrangements for a military expedition to France. Amongst the measures decided at meetings of the Great Council in April, which Langley attended, were the appointments of the Duke of Bedford as Lieutenant of the Realm, and of the Archbishop of Canterbury, the Bishops of Winchester and Durham, the Earl of Westmorland and five other lords to the Council, with whose advice Bedford was to govern while the King was abroad.[5]

The promised French embassy did not arrive until June, when Henry and his court were at Winchester and Bishops Courtenay and Langley met it outside the city on the last day of the month.[6] The French offered even larger concessions than at Paris, but they were insufficient for Henry, and the discussions, which were conducted in an atmosphere of mutual distrust, finally broke down on 6 July. After the embassy's departure, Henry went on

---

[1] Foreign Accounts, no. 48, rot. B. (dorse); *Foedera*, IX, pp. 197–200.

[2] *Chron. St Denys*, V, p. 408; J. Juvenal, pp. 285–6; J. de Waurin, *Recueil des Chroniques* (Rolls Series, 1864–91), Vol. II, p. 164; J. le Fèvre, *Chronique* (Soc. de l'Hist. de France, 1876, 1881), pp. 211–12.

[3] *Foedera*, IX, pp. 208–15.

[4] Adam of Usk, *Chronicle 1377–1419*, ed. E. Maunde Thompson (1904), p. 125. But see Appendix A, p. 231, for the date of Langley's return.

[5] *PPC.* II, pp. 153–8.

[6] *Le Procès de Maître Jean Fusoris* (Memo. de Soc. de l'Hist. de Paris, 1901), p. 157.

to Southampton and ordered the musters of his army to be taken.[1] He made dispositions in case he died on the campaign, and on 22 July granted a great part of his Duchy of Lancaster possessions to a group of feoffees for the purpose of executing his will, which was sealed on 24 July. Langley, who was one of the feoffees and was also appointed an executor of the will, was bequeathed a missal and a breviary.[2] After the royal army had sailed for France, he hastened from Southampton to Durham. This was his second visit to the Bishopric that year, and both on this occasion and in May the cause of his journey was the threat of invasion from Scotland.[3] He remained in his diocese until the end of September, when he came to London to attend Parliament and the Council.

The King returned to England in November, and spent the following year promoting a number of alliances that were to isolate France from outside support. The Emperor Sigismund visited the country with the object of mediating between England and France, but was eventually persuaded to become Henry's ally. Langley was in London during most of Sigismund's visit, and accompanied the Emperor and King to Calais in September 1416.[4] He remained there for nearly a month, while Henry received the fealty of the Duke of Burgundy and arranged a short truce with France. Langley was at Westminster to attend Parliament, and after his appointment on 8 December to a commission to negotiate with Scottish representatives for the release of their King,[5] made his way to the north of England in some haste. He had other royal business there, for Henry hoped to employ the Duke of Bourbon and the Sieur de Gaucourt, who had been captured in 1415, as his emissaries to Charles VI, and Langley was his principal agent in discussions with these and other French magnates imprisoned in Pontefract Castle. He visited Pontefract with three English peers in January 1417 to discuss the preparation of written obligations to ensure that Bourbon and Gaucourt would return to England after performing their mission, and a report of this meeting was sent to the King.

---

[1] *Foedera*, IX, p. 287.
[2] *CPR. 1413–1416*, pp. 356–7; *Foedera*, IX, pp. 289–93.
[3] Below, p. 149.
[4] C. L. Kingsford, "An English Historical Collection of the Fifteenth Century", *English Historical Review, 1914*, p. 510.
[5] Below, p. 150.

Henry sent further instructions to Langley, who obtained bonds from two of the prisoners on 18 January.[1] He also "remembred the said Duc of Burbon that he write to yow [the King] with his awen hand how he contynuth his wille and entent in the matire secret".[2] The nature of this matter is revealed by a letter Henry wrote to his representative with the German Emperor on 25 January: the prisoners had been asked, presumably by Langley, if they would recognize Henry as King of France; at first they refused to do this, but later agreed that Bourbon should go to France to advise Charles to surrender Normandy and the lands ceded to Edward III by the Treaty of Brétigny; if Charles rejected this advice, Bourbon would recognize Henry as King of France. The project was being kept a close secret in order to safeguard Bourbon, and Henry, who wrote this letter with his own hand, said that none knew of it "save [the Bishop of] Derham and I".[3]

These discussions with the French prisoners were the last Anglo-French negotiations in which Langley took part: the series of conferences that ended with the Treaty of Troyes were conducted, on the English side, by members of the Council with the King in Normandy. He had been the King's chief diplomatic adviser in two periods, from the time of the Gloucester Parliament in 1407 until his departure for the Council of Pisa in 1409, and again from the beginning of 1412 for the five years following; it is not possible to add to the bare record of his appointments to commissions in the first period, but his position in the second can be illuminated further. In the two great embassies Henry V sent to Paris, Bishop Courtenay acted as spokesman, as his noble birth and university training so well fitted him to do, but that Langley was the most influential member of the embassies cannot be doubted: in the first, he alone was referred to in the commission as "our councillor".[4] The two Bishops transacted other business for the King when they were in Paris in 1414, Henry who had it in mind to found a convent of the Celestine Order in England having charged his ambassadors to make enquiries about the Order in France. They visited the Celestine house in Paris and while

1 *Foedera*, IX, pp. 423-7.
2 Ancient Correspondence, Vol. LVII, no. 79.
3 *Foedera*, IX, pp. 427-30.
4 Ibid. IX, p. 132.

Courtenay talked with the Prior in his garden and tasted his fruit, Langley examined the constitutions of the house, comparing them with the Rule of St Benedict.[1]   This incident brilliantly illumines the rôles of the two Bishops, of Norwich as the courtier and Durham the professional expert, perhaps rougher of tongue than his noble colleague but sharp in the interpretation of diplomatic formulae.   Langley was also entrusted with the preparation of the King's foreign correspondence: it was reported at a meeting of the Council held soon after the return of the second embassy that he had made drafts of letters to be sent to King Charles, his Secretary, and the Duke of Berri.[2]   His latest commission, the secret discussions with the French prisoners, offers the most conclusive proof of the extent to which Henry relied on his gifts of persuasion and discretion.

Langley told the King his immediate plans when he wrote from Pontefract on 18 January 1417: "This same Monday at nyght, with Goddes grace, I shal mete my lord of Westmerland at York, and there abide al Tyseday to solicite the chevance that ye have commanded us.   And from thennes atte first I go to Duremward, with youre gracious leve, to sumwhat ordcyn for my litell and symple governance." [3]   He was once more in London from the end of March, where the Council was making plans for the King's second expedition to France; on 2 May, he went to Mortlake to seek Henry's consent to some of its arrangements.[4]   He attended the Great Council at Reading,[5] and then accompanied the King to Southampton, where the fleet and army were assembling. Amongst Henry's final dispositions before he embarked were the appointments of Langley as Chancellor on 23 July and of the Duke of Bedford as Lieutenant of the Realm two days later.[6]   As the King intended to wage a methodical campaign of conquest, and anticipated a long absence from England, it was essential that he should leave the administration in the hands of an experienced minister in whose loyalty and competence he had the

---

[1] *Fusoris*, p. 220.

[2] *PPC.* II, pp. 153–4.   In the letter to King Charles, Langley blamed Anglo-French enmity as a principal cause of the perpetuation of the schism in the Church (*Chron. St Denys*, V, 506–10).

[3] Ancient Correspondence, Vol. LVII, no. 79.

[4] *PPC.* II, pp. 231–2.

[5] Usk, p. 130.

[6] *CCR. 1413–1419*, p. 435; *CPR. 1416–1422*, pp. 112–13; *Foedera*, IX, pp. 472 & 475.

most complete confidence. The sequel will show how much Henry V depended on Bishop Langley for the well-being of the government of England.

4 CHANCELLOR OF ENGLAND, 1417–1424

There is no record surviving of any ordinance for the government of England in 1417 similar to that of 1415, when before his departure overseas the King appointed both a Lieutenant and a Council to advise him.[1]   It is most likely, however, that Henry named the councillors who were to assist Bedford in 1417, since a phrase in the Lieutenant's commission leaves no doubt of the Council's importance: Bedford was empowered to summon and hold Parliaments and Great Councils, grant licences for elections by capitular bodies and assent to the election of minor prelates, receive fealties of feudal tenants and grant them livery, in all of which activities as well as in other matters touching his governance he was to act with the advice and assent of the King's Council "and not otherwise".[2]   This was not the only restriction on the Lieutenant's authority: despite his absence and military and diplomatic commitments in France, Henry V kept a firm grasp on the reins of government in England, and because he did so the standing of his Lieutenant was less potent in fact than in theory, while the position of the Chancellor was correspondingly enhanced.

The King's ability to direct the operations of the administration in England depended to a considerable degree upon the speed with which he could communicate with it.   The existence of an efficient messenger service is testified by the Chancery records, which show that letters sealed by the King in different parts of Normandy were generally delivered at Westminster ten days later and two instances have been traced where the interval was only eight days.[3]   It was therefore only in times of particular emergency that the Council was obliged to take action on its own initiative; for the most part, it was able to refer to the King.   In the same way as when the King was in England, the Council sent him lists of articles on various subjects, in which it made sugges-

---

[1] *PPC.* II, p. 157.
[2] *CPR. 1416–1422*, pp. 112–13; *Foedera*, IX, pp. 475–6.
[3] Chancery Warrants, 1364/44 and 1365/5; *CPR. 1416–1422*, pp. 132 & 414.

tions of action to be taken. There exist two such lists that were sent to Henry, one concerning the government of Calais, the other the administration of North Wales; against the various articles, some of them dealing with matters of no great moment, the King gave his directions or signified his assent to the Council's proposals.[1] Surviving records of the King's correspondence with his ministers as well as notices of letters sent by him to other subjects [2] also attest to the attention he paid to English affairs. Henry continued to exercise all the prerogatives appertaining to his English crown and remained the sole fount of royal patronage; presentations to benefices and secular appointments, grants of corrodies and wardships, were all kept at his disposal, and subjects had to send him their petitions for pardons, licences, and redress.

When the King took such a close interest in English affairs, it is obvious that his Lieutenant hardly enjoyed viceregal status. His chief responsibility was the defence of the realm, for in the King's absence he was commander-in-chief of all military forces already in existence or that might be formed when need arose. He was also required to preserve law and order in the country: Henry wrote to his Lieutenant in 1420 to "se that justices of pees, shereves, eschetours, coroners, and suche officers as shul be maad be suche persones as ben able and worthy therto, and that ben no troublers in thaire contrees".[3] By virtue of his commission, the Lieutenant took the place of the King in Parliament, but although its petitions were addressed to him he was unable to answer them, and had to forward them to the King.[4] The records of Chancery reveal that his power to cause letters to be issued under the Great Seal was also very limited. The King's injunction that the Lieutenant should rule only with the Council was closely observed: private petitions made to him were referred to it,[5] nor was he even permitted to enjoy the privilege of ordering such minor conveniences as appointing commissioners to take food for his household or men for his ship: they were appointed by warrants of the Council.[6] When Bedford wrote to Langley for a

---

[1] *PPC.* II, pp. 318–19, 363–7.
[2] Issue Rolls 643, m. 23, and 646, mm. 3 & 12.
[3] Chancery Warrants, 1543/19.
[4] *Rot. Parl.* IV, p. 128.
[5] CPS. 32 & 35; *PPC.* II, p. 296.
[6] *CPR. 1416–1422*, pp. 254, 327, 397–8.

licence to permit him to export grain, his warrant was submitted to the Council, which gave its assent with the proviso that the Duke should answer for the payment of customs.[1]   On the other hand, the Lieutenant's influence in the Council must have been considerable since, as the King's deputy, he would have presided over those meetings he attended.   The small number of Council lists that are available, however, suggest that the Lieutenant was as often absent as not: his military duties occasionally required him to travel about the country, while the councillors continued to meet at Westminster.[2]

As Chancellor, Langley was the leading member of this Council, and he would have taken the Lieutenant's place as its president when he was unable to attend.   The other official members were the Keeper of the Privy Seal, until 1418, when he went to France, and the Treasurer's deputy.   A small number of prelates and secular peers sometimes sat in the Council: between the time of the King's departure and his return three and a half years later, out of a total of fifteen recorded sessions, the Archbishop of Canterbury is known to have attended five times, the Bishop of Winchester and Sir John Pelham twice, and the Duke of Exeter, the Bishop of Bath and Wells, and the Earl of Westmorland once. For the most part, however, the number in attendance was very small, with the Chancellor and Under-Treasurer as the only regular members: [3] on three known occasions, letters of Privy Seal were made "by the order of the Lieutenant and with the consent of the Chancellor"; [4] at other times, similar letters were made "by the advice of the Council" when Langley alone was present.[5]   While the small number of lay peers remaining in England tended to be engaged on the defence of the seas and of the northern Marches, an increasing proportion of the bishops was called upon to join the King, an exodus that not only weakened the Council but inevitably also had adverse effects on the country's ecclesiastical polity.   This latter circumstance is illustrated by the grant to Langley by the vicar-general of the diocese of London of commissions to celebrate ordinations and

---

1 Chancery Warrants, 1543/14.
2 E.g. Chancery Warrants, 1537/3 & 7; 1543/14.
3 CPS. 33; Chancery Warrants, 1542/3 & 13; Early Chancery Proceedings, 5/60; *PPC.* II, pp. 218, 239 & 261.
4 CPS. 32 & 33.
5 CPS. 33 & 34.

consecrate the Abbot of Colchester, in December 1418.[1] Langley
therefore carried an unduly heavy burden for more than three
years, and that Henry realized this and provided a remedy by
increasing the strength of the Council is shown by records of an
improved attendance both during and after his visit to England
in 1421. From this time onwards, Archbishop Chichele, the
Bishops of Bath and Wells, Winchester and Worcester, and the
Keeper of the Privy Seal were regular members of the Council.[2]

The work of Henry V's Council in England, particularly in the
years 1418–1420, must be regarded largely as the personal
achievement of Bishop Langley. Since the King continued to
direct his government, the Council's activities were mostly of a
routine, executive nature, but the volume of this business was
very great indeed. In addition to the normal work of the
Council about the law and administration of England, it had also
to arrange for the supply of money, military stores, and reinforcements to the King, organize fleets "to keep the seas", and occasionally to take some part in negotiations with foreign powers.
Langley's long experience as an administrator would have
enabled him to cope with the numerous matters laid before the
Council; even when the Lieutenant was able to be present, he
would have had to rely on the Chancellor's knowledge of the
mechanism of government, and the absence from the country of
other potential councillors made this dependence complete. The
King's correspondence with his Lieutenant and Chancellor makes
it clear that he placed the responsibility for the English administration on these two officers in equal measure; he rarely addressed
his letters to the Council. In their turn, Langley and the
Lieutenant sent Henry their separate reports on the condition of
the country.[3] It is apparent that the King regarded them as
restraints on each other: the Lieutenant was expected to ensure
that Langley performed his duties, while the Chancellor had to
see to it that the Lieutenant did not abuse his position.

Henry's correspondence with his Lieutenant usually included
orders that he should act with the Chancellor and others of the
Council in preparing the particular measures required. This

[1] *Reg.* II, nos. 512–14.
[2] CPS. 34 & 36; Chancery Warrants, 1543/34 & 49B; *PPC.* II, pp. 286, 288,
289, 293, 300, 303 & 315.
[3] *Collection Générale des Documents Français qui se trouvent en Angleterre*, ed.
J. Delpit (Paris, 1847), p. 229.

injunction appears in letters to Bedford concerning breaches of the truce with Brittany and negotiations with Flanders.[1]   Bedford was directed to restore the temporalities of Salisbury to John Chandler, but the Chancellor was sent a similar warrant.[2]   On 17 March 1418, Henry told Bedford to join Langley in discussing repairs to the property of the bishopric of St David's with Benedict Nicholl, who had recently been provided to that see.[3]   Langley appears to have executed this commission: on 2 May, Nicholl made bonds in Chancery not to sue his predecessor's executors for repairs, and Langley reported this arrangement to the King on 4 May.[4]   Other instances could be cited of Henry writing to both Lieutenant and Chancellor on the same matter.[5]   The King's letters to Langley likewise required him to consult with the Lieutenant, as when he informed the Chancellor in February 1419 that the King of Castille was planning to attack the south coast and ordered him to prepare defensive measures with the advice of Bedford "and of other suche as semeth to youre discrecion".[6] Henry committed other business of a military nature to Langley: he had to arrange for the Duke of Exeter to join the King, organize the transport of the Prior of Kilmainham and his soldiers to France, and make indentures with the Constable of Fronsac in Guienne and with the Warden of the West March.[7] Henry wrote twice in 1419 to ask Langley to make sure that the Duke of Orleans was being securely guarded.[8]   In 1418, Langley sent the King reports on negotiations being conducted with Flemish and Genoese representatives, and Henry wrote back to approve of the arrangements made: "alle this we committe to yow and to the remenant of oure counseil to be wroght after youre discrecions and comun advis".[9]

Apart from correspondence of this varied nature, which arose from Langley's position as first councillor, Henry also wrote to him on business that concerned him as Chancellor.   Most of the

[1] *PPC*. II, pp. 243–4, 250.
[2] Chancery Warrants, 1543/9 and 1364/9; Lyte, *Great Seal*, p. 191.
[3] Ibid. 175.
[4] *CCR. 1413–1419*, p. 502; Chancery Warrants, 1364/53.
[5] Ibid. 1364/61 and 1365/26.
[6] Ancient Correspondence, XLIII, no. 162.
[7] *Excerpta Historica*, ed. S. Bentley (1831), pp. 388–9; Chancery Warrants, 667/931 and 1366/13; and see below, p. 152.
[8] Chancery Warrants, 1365/12; *Foedera*, IX, p. 801.
[9] *PPC*. II, pp. 255–7.

King's warrants for letters under the Great Seal were simply orders for grants to be made in the form directed, but in a small number Henry required Langley to exercise his discretion, as when he felt Robert FitzHugh's title to a prebend of Dublin to be in doubt, and again when the King was uneasy about the continued possession of the hospital of St Anthony by the Dean of St Martin-le-Grand; in both these cases, Langley was asked to find a lawful solution on certain lines.[1] The delegation to the Chancellor of questions touching the royal conscience was not new, and was a principal cause of the growth of Chancery's judicial activities, but Henry V's absence and major preoccupations in France led to a marked acceleration in this development. Petitions claiming redress that could not be sought in a court of common law were still submitted to the King, but he had little time to consider them, and therefore referred them to the Chancellor. In a letter of 22 May 1421, he told Langley that he could not hear a suit because of his hasty departure from England: he had ordered the parties to appear before the Chancellor, who was to hear the dispute.[2] One letter sent by Henry from France enclosed a petition to which "we have take but litel heed",[3] a second charged Langley to call the parties to a dispute and "doo unto hem both right and equite, and in especial that ye see that the porer partye suffre no wrong".[4] Again and again the Chancellor was directed to enquire into the truth of complaints and ordain a remedy "by your good avys", as right and reason required.[5]

The delegation by the King of petitions he was unable to consider was only one of the reasons for the extraordinary increase in the Chancellor's judicial work between 1417 and 1421. Before departing for Normandy in 1417, the King had made an ordinance in Council that suspended the taking of all assizes, with the object of protecting the rights of his soldiers.[6] In consequence, with the removal of the traditional common law remedy, plaintiffs approached the Chancellor for redress in alleged cases of *novel disseisin*: more than two hundred of such bills survive, a figure

---

[1] Chancery Warrants, 1365/6 & 23.
[2] Ancient Correspondence, XLIII, no. 159.
[3] Chancery Warrants, 1365/32.
[4] *Proceedings in Chancery* (Record Commission, 1827–32), Vol. I, p. xvi.
[5] Chancery Warrants, 667/905, 1364/66 & 71 and 1365/9.
[6] *Rot. Parl.* IV, p. 147.

that exceeds the total of petitions for equitable remedies presented to chancellors before 1413. Nor was this the sum of litigation brought to Langley, for another two hundred bills asked him to find remedies for a wide variety of grievances, of which breach of covenant and corruption of the normal forms of justice by "maintenance" constitute the greater part.[1] The fact that Henry was referring petitions to Langley probably became common knowledge, and suitors hoped to avoid delay by making immediate resort to the Chancellor. This is not the place to examine the procedure followed by the Chancellor in attending to petitions, but evidence is available in the Chancery rolls and suggests that a good number of suitors were successful in their applications for redress. The great volume of bills sent into Chancery, a current that began in 1417 and continued to increase throughout the following century and beyond, reveals a popular esteem for its equitable jurisdiction that was established when Thomas Langley was Chancellor to Henry V.

Another important aspect of the Chancellor's work was his position as the government's spokesman in Parliament; it was a task calling for considerable qualities of diplomacy in these years, because the King had received large subsidies before 1417 yet continued to need money to finance his wars. Langley's address to Parliament on 16 November 1417 on the text "Be valiant and show yourselves men, and you shall obtain glory" [2] must have been unusually stirring, for it won the rare distinction of finding itself quoted, with poetic licence, in the rhyming chronicle of Thomas Elmham;[3] the Commons responded with a grant of two tenths and two fifteenths.[4] Later that year, Langley went into the Convocation of Canterbury and persuaded the clergy to grant the King a subsidy.[5] The next time Langley addressed Parliament, on 16 October 1419, he obviously thought the Commons would be reluctant to grant more taxes, for the text he chose was "Let us not be weary in well-doing." [6] Complaints were made about the export of money, but a grant of subsidies was eventually conceded.[7] These duties in Parliament were infrequent, however, and for the most part Langley's work in the

---

1 Early Chancery Proceedings, bundles 4 & 5.
2 1 Macc. 2.64.
3 *Memorials of Henry the Fifth* (Rolls Series, 1858), p. 155.
4 *Rot. Parl.* IV, pp. 106–7.   5 *Reg. Chichele*, III, pp. 39–40.
6 Gal. 6.9.   7 *Rot. Parl.* IV, pp. 116–18.

capital was divided between the Council and Chancery; sometimes he conducted official business at his manor of Old Ford, as in July 1420, when there was an outbreak of the plague in London.[1] He made four journeys to Southampton with other members of the Council: in April 1418, when it went to take the musters of the Duke of Exeter and other contingents sailing for Normandy;[2] in August of the following year, to organize the port's defence against an expected attack by Spanish ships;[3] in April 1420, to review the Duke of Bedford's retinue and the Earl of Devon's naval force;[4] and once more two years later, to arrange for the passage of the Queen and Bedford to France.[5]

It was inevitable that the pressure of government business should prevent the Bishop from paying many visits to Durham. He was in his diocese in August and September of 1418. The threat of invasion may account for his journey, but at the same time he had a survey made of his estates in the county palatine and found some recreation by hunting in his park at Wolsingham.[6] It was two years before his next visit, when Langley travelled in the company of the Duke of Gloucester, the Lieutenant, as far as York,[7] and then went on and spent some four weeks in the Bishopric. The King's return to England in February 1421 enabled the Chancellor to celebrate Easter in his cathedral city, but he had to depart in haste when Henry sent for him.[8] He joined the King at the episcopal manor of Howden, where a Scottish embassy had come to discuss the release of their King;[9] they returned to London at the end of April. Six weeks later, Langley was at Dover to see Henry sail to France for the third and last time.

The Chancellor was in Westminster during July 1421, and then made another journey to the north of England. He first went to Manchester, where his business was the erection of the collegiate church, the licence for which had been granted on 22 May.[10]

---

1 CPS. 33; CCR. 1419–1422, p. 77.
2 CPR. 1416–1422, p. 201.
3 Ancient Correspondence, XLIII, no. 162; CPR. 1416–1422, pp. 270, 323–4.
4 Ibid. 319.
5 Ibid. 426–8, 441 & 443.
6 DCD. Bursar 1418–1419, m. 4d.; and see below, pp. 152 & 70.
7 Chancery Warrants, 1537/4; CPR. 1416–1422, pp. 298 & 312.
8 Reg. fo. 275.
9 CPR. 1416–1422, p. 335; Rot. Scot. II, pp. 228–9.
10 CPR. 366.

After four days in Manchester, he crossed the Pennines to Durham by way of Skipton-in-Craven. This visit by Langley to the north merits a detailed account as an illustration of how the Chancellor spent a "vacation"; he continued to transact Chancery business all the time, legal as well as secretarial, and had the Great Seal and presumably a number of Chancery clerks with him. As he travelled, he issued royal letters in connection with the elections of priors,[1] commissions of the peace for Cumberland and Westmorland [2] and original writs; [3] ordered elections of coroners in Cambridge and Yorkshire and appointed officers in the port of Newcastle-upon-Tyne.[4] On 2 September, he went to Gateshead to take security from Henry Percy that he would not injure William Mitford, who had sent the Chancellor a petition alleging that Percy had expelled him from certain lands.[5] At Bishop Auckland, three days later, Marmaduke Lumley and Richard Neville entered into bonds to observe the settlement of a dispute; [6] Langley had doubtless mediated to produce this agreement. He remained in his diocese until 19 September, and was in York on the following day. Convocation met there on 22 September, summoned for the purpose of granting the King a subsidy. Langley felt that his personal intervention was necessary to persuade the clergy to make this grant; they were becoming increasingly reluctant to grant taxes, and this time they complained that excessive rains and floods had added to their burdens. They were induced, however, to grant the King a tenth.[7] Langley then returned to London, and remained fully engaged upon the *negocia regis et regni* until the following summer.

Bishop Langley was on his way back to the capital after passing the summer vacation of 1422 in his diocese when he met a messenger bringing him the news that Henry V had died at Vincennes on 31 August.[8] The King was now the infant Henry of Windsor, and a group of his father's councillors, led by Bishop Beaufort, was anxious to gain control of the government and

---

[1] *CPR.* 393 & 395.
[2] Ibid. 451 & 461.
[3] Exchequer L.T.R.: Originalia Roll, 186, m. 63.
[4] *CCR. 1419–1422*, p. 250; *CPR.* 394.
[5] *CCR.* 226; Early Chancery Proceedings, 4/159.
[6] *CCR.* 208.
[7] Below, pp. 211–12.
[8] The messenger who passed through Biggleswade on 10 September was almost certainly going to Langley (*Rot. Parl.* IV, p. 194).

prevent the Duke of Gloucester from exercising the authority of regent. This contention must have begun immediately after the death of Henry V had been reported in England, and the councillors appear to have won the first round before 28 September, when Langley surrendered the Great Seal to Henry VI at Windsor,[1] a fiction which indicated that Gloucester had been debarred from the regency. No new Chancellor or other ministers were appointed until Parliament had met to approve the form of government in the royal minority. A week after it had assembled, on 16 November, it was announced that in view of the known wisdom of Henry V, who had chosen men of tried ability to be his ministers, his Chancellor, Treasurer, and Keeper of the Privy Seal should be restored to their offices.[2] Parliament also appointed four additional supervisors of Henry V's will, of whom Langley was one.[3] That he took this duty in earnest is shown by the record of his having the will in his possession for some time, until he surrendered it in 1426.[4] He had other business committed to him by the late King, as one of the feoffees of the Lancastrian estates and also as a trustee of the lands designated by Henry for the nunnery of Syon; the endowment of this new foundation was not completed until 1431.[5]

Langley's position as Chancellor cannot now have carried all the responsibilities he had borne under Henry V, but he was sufficiently occupied by official business to have to stay in London over Christmas. He was able to go to Durham for Easter 1423, and again in the summer, although this longer vacation had to be interrupted in September by a visit to York to confer with a Scottish embassy.[6] He delivered his last parliamentary sermon at Westminster on 20 October, a simple homily on the text "Fear God, honour the King." It was a restive Parliament, more ready to ask questions and make proposals about the Council than to grant supplies; it did not do this until 28 February 1424,[7] thus delaying the departure of the Chancellor for Durham, where he

---

[1] *CCR. 1422–1429*, p. 46; *Foedera*, X, p. 253.
[2] *Rot. Parl.* IV, p. 171; *CPR. 1422–1429*, p. 109; *Foedera*, X, p. 259.
[3] *Rot. Parl.* IV, pp. 172–3.
[4] *PPC.* III, p. 190.
[5] *Rot. Parl.* IV, pp. 243–7; *CPR. 1416–1422*, pp. 34–5, and *1422–1429*, pp. 205–7; *Ancient Deeds*, Vol. II, nos. B. 3819, 3871 & 3874.
[6] Below, pp. 153–4.
[7] *Rot. Parl.* IV, pp. 197, 200 & 201.

was to take part in negotiations with James I of Scotland. Langley remained in his diocese for a month after the conclusion of the Treaty of Durham,[1] and resumed his attendance of the Council at Westminster on 28 May. After the close of the sessions of the Trinity term, on 16 July, he resigned the Great Seal at Hertford Castle,[2] a fitting place for his final surrender of office, for it was here that Henry IV had appointed him Keeper of the Privy Seal more than twenty-two years before. No political motive need be sought for his resignation: he had been Chancellor for seven years, in a period of great stress, and as he was now more than sixty years of age he must have felt unable to continue in office.

5 LAST YEARS AS A ROYAL COUNCILLOR, 1424–1435

Langley's surrender of the Great Seal in 1424 did not mark the end of his career in royal service.   Although there is no record of his immediate appointment to the Council, as there was in January 1407, he remained a member and was present at its sessions in the Michaelmas term.   It would appear that he fell ill after his return from Westminster, for he remained at Bishop Auckland, probably from Christmas, until 19 April 1425; an ordination service in the chapel of the manor on 3 March had to be taken by the suffragan, and when the Rector of Stanhope came to resign his church the Bishop received him in the parlour instead of the chapel.[3]   Langley was able to travel to London at the end of April, where he went to attend Parliament.   He was a trier of petitions,[4] and remained in the capital until July, presumably until Parliament was dismissed on the 14th; he also attended some sessions of the Council.   He was once more in his diocese in August, and it is unlikely that he had any intention of returning to London that year.   On 20 November, however, he went to Raby Castle to receive Richard Neville's oath as an executor of the first Earl of Westmorland [5] and he was in London a fortnight later.   Despite the approach of Christmas, which he preferred to spend in his diocese, and his apparent desire to withdraw from

---

1 Below, pp. 154–5.
2 *CCR. 1422–1429*, p. 154; *Foedera*, X, pp. 340–1.
3 *Reg.* nos. 629 & 630.
4 *Rot. Parl.* IV, p. 261.
5 Reg. fo. 297v.

political affairs in the capital, Langley felt obliged to make this journey at that time and his motive can readily be ascertained.

The Duke of Gloucester had returned to England in April after the failure of his attempt to conquer his wife's estates in the Low Countries, and from this time his relations with Bishop Beaufort "passed from the stage of political rivalry to that of personal competition".[1] This animosity threatened to occasion violence on 29 October, when some of Beaufort's servants tried to force a way into the city of London, which was loyal to Duke Humphrey, and the mediation of Archbishop Chichele and the Prince of Portugal was required to prevent an ugly fraças. Langley would have learnt of this incident, and also that the Duke of Bedford had been urged to return from France, when he was at Raby; Richard Neville was Beaufort's nephew and may have persuaded Langley to intercede in the dispute. As in 1410,[2] it is easy to suspect Langley of being a supporter of Henry Beaufort, for to the ties of long association was now added the link provided by Langley's connection with the Nevilles,[3] yet on the occasions when Beaufort was criticized in the Council, or when his partisans openly opposed Gloucester, Langley did not emerge as one of his adherents.[4] Langley continued to regard himself as primarily the King's servant, and it therefore became his duty to work for the conciliation of the two princes; that he was the partisan of neither Gloucester nor Beaufort is attested by the depictions of both contestants in the St Cuthbert window he gave to York Minster.[5]

Langley's part in the attempts to reconcile Beaufort and Gloucester cannot be established, but in addition to his position in the Council and the respect his reputation must have commanded, he had a further opportunity to extend his influence: when the Duke of Bedford arrived in London on 10 January 1426, he was lodged in Langley's inn.[6] Parliament met at Leicester on 18 February, with Langley as a trier of petitions. On 7 March, Beaufort and Gloucester agreed to submit their differences to the

---

[1] K. H. Vickers, *Humphrey, Duke of Gloucester* (1907), p. 164.
[2] Above, p. 28.
[3] Below, pp. 105–8.
[4] Below, pp. 49–50.
[5] J. T. Fowler, "On the St. Cuthbert Window in York Minster", *Yorkshire Archaeological Journal, 1877*, pp. 258–64; F. Harrison, *The Painted Glass of York* (1927), p. 219.
[6] *The Brut* (Early English Text Society, 1906 & 1908), p. 433.

arbitration of a commission of nine councillors, of whom Langley
was one; its work was concluded five days later, when the Duke
and Bishop were formally reconciled.   Parliament was prorogued
for Easter on 20 March [1] and Langley observed the feast at
Bishop Auckland.   He returned to Leicester after the recess and
attended the Council there regularly.   His position as a councillor had been ratified by a formal appointment in Parliament,
and he was entitled to an annual salary of two hundred marks,
but on 1 June he asked the Council to excuse him from further
attendance: as long as he lived, he said, he would continue to
serve the King, but now he was old and long years of royal
service had both impaired his health and caused him to neglect
his diocese, and the safety of his soul would be imperilled if he
did not devote his last years to his church.[2]   That this application was refused is shown by records of Langley's continued
attendance of the Council at Westminster in July, at Reading in
November, and again at the capital in December.   There is less
evidence of his movements in 1427, but he was present at the
Council on 6 March and fairly regularly from May to July.

The fifth Parliament of the reign was opened at Westminster
on 13 October and for once Langley's name does not appear in
the lists of triers of petitions.   Although he was in London during
the parliamentary session, he appears to have absented himself
from the Council; he was in the capital because it was his duty
as a peer to attend Parliament, and because he wished to transact
some business concerning the will of Henry IV.[3]   On 21 January
1428, he excused himself from attendance of Parliament's second
session on the grounds of ill-health.[4]   He made only one visit to
London in this year, to be present on 1 June when the Council
made arrangements for the education of the young King, a
subject in which Langley showed particular interest.[5]   He continued to attend the Council until 11 July, and then returned to
the north.   He was therefore not present when Cardinal Beaufort
returned to London from his pilgrimage, and Gloucester and the
Council made a formal protest in the King's name against the
legatine commission given to him by Martin V, although he was

[1] *Rot. Parl.* IV, pp. 295–9, 301.
[2] *PPC.* III, pp. 197–8, 266.
[3] *Rot. Parl.* IV, pp. 316, 323–4.
[4] *Reg.* no. 701.
[5] *PPC.* III, pp. 296–300; and see below, p. 51.

permitted to make preparations for the crusade he was to lead against the Hussites in Bohemia. Beaufort came north in January 1429 to meet the King of Scots, and it would appear that Langley received him in his manor of Crayke about 16 January, when the Bishop issued commissions for the proclamation of the crusade in the diocese of Durham.[1] Langley was at Westminster to attend the Great Council, where on 17 April he concurred with the other magnates in deciding that Cardinal Beaufort should not take his customary part as Bishop of Winchester in the coming feast of the Garter. Langley was again present on 3 May, when it was agreed that his friend Richard Neville should assume the title of Earl of Salisbury.[2] The presence of Langley's signature on a Privy Council warrant of 10 May [3] is the only indication that he attended the smaller body during this visit to the capital.

A commission to negotiate with Scottish representatives caused Langley to be at his Border fortress of Norham on 13 July.[4] He was in his diocese until 8 September, and then went south. He probably intended to be present when Parliament was opened on 22 September, but on reaching Howden on the 12th wrote that sickness prevented his attendance.[5] His indisposition was of short duration, for he was with the Council on 10 October. On 6 November, he performed the office traditional to the Bishops of Durham, for the second time, when Henry VI was crowned at Westminster.[6] Langley's visits to the capital now became even less frequent. His employment in negotiations with the Scots was almost the sum of his services to the King in 1430, and that his single appearance at the Council, on 6 November, was connected with this activity is shown by his appointment to another commission in the following week.[7] On 2 January 1431 he again alleged bodily infirmity when appointing his proctors for Parliament,[8] although he was well enough to make the journey from Bishop Auckland to Howden that same week. He did attend the Great Council in November, when the Duke of Gloucester made another attack on his uncle the Cardinal; the magnates rejected a motion to deprive Beaufort of the see of Winchester, but agreed to the issue of a writ of *præmunire*. Bishop Lumley of Carlisle was

---

1 Below, p. 157.
2 *PPC*. III, pp. 322–6.
3 Chancery Warrants, 1545/8.
4 Below, p. 157.
5 *Reg.* no. 823.
6 *Historical Collection of a Citizen of London* (Camden Society, 1876), p. 168.
7 *PPC*. IV, p. 70; and see below, p. 158.
8 *Reg.* no. 897.

alone in urging the postponement of all action until Beaufort had returned to England, but he was joined by Archbishop Kemp and four secular peers in opposing a proposal to increase Gloucester's salary.   Langley gave no such indication of allegiance to the Cardinal.   He attended meetings of the Privy Council on 29 and 30 November,[1] and was once more at Bishop Auckland in time for Christmas.

It is probable that Langley now hoped to remain free to devote himself entirely to the affairs of his diocese and county palatine, for it would appear that he withdrew Thomas Lyes' commission as his vicar-general.   On 12 April 1432, however, he reappointed Lyes because he was obliged to attend Parliament.[2]   He was in London when Parliament was opened on 12 May and was appointed a trier of petitions; one matter discussed in Parliament that interested him was the will of Henry V.[3]   As his commission to the vicar-general also stated, however, the Bishop had to attend to business of his own and concerning his church.   This vague formula may be accepted as an allusion to the growing tension between Langley and a number of his tenants; he would have wished to seek legal advice and make sure of influential support lest it might be required.   The development of this conflict into an outright attack on the Bishop's franchise twelve months later caused Langley to resume his place in the King's Council; earlier it had seemed that he was anxious to relinquish it, now he turned it to his advantage.   He was on the road for London within a fortnight of the invasion of his liberty by a royal commission on 1 April 1433,[4] after observing Easter in his diocese. The resumption of his duties in the Council is indicated by his association with its other members in guaranteeing repayment of a loan to the King by Cardinal Beaufort, on 24 May,[5] and by his presence in the "Starred Chamber" on 20 June when a legal cause was heard.[6]   He continued to attend after Parliament was opened on 8 July, where he was again appointed to try petitions.[7] Langley was therefore in a very favourable position for the promotion of his own petition and his long record of royal service was another factor that weighed for him when it was considered.

[1] *PPC.* IV, pp. 100–8.
[2] *Reg.* no. 983.
[3] *Rot. Parl.* IV, pp. 388 & 399.
[4] Below, pp. 119–20, 127–8.
[5] *PPC.* IV, pp. 162–3.
[6] Baldwin, *King's Council*, pp. 525–9.
[7] *Rot. Parl.* IV, p. 419.

The Bishop's petition had been granted before Parliament was prorogued for the summer,[1] but he felt it necessary to return to the capital for the second session. At its close, on 21 December, he was finally excused from further membership of the Council on account of his age.[2] He remained in London after Parliament's dismissal because he was expecting further proceedings concerning his palatinate.[3] He did attend the Council on 1 February 1434, but he must have been called in because of his special knowledge of Anglo-Scottish relations, which were discussed then.[4] Langley returned to Durham later that month, but was once again at Westminster early in November, when he attended the Council and signed bills laid before it.[5] He then accompanied the councillors to Cirencester, where they discussed Henry VI's precocious conduct, and advised him to respect the decisions of his councillors.[6] That Langley should have made this long journey indicates the extent of his concern for the King's education, and he probably felt it to be as much a duty to the memory of Henry V as to his son to take this interest. He was still somewhat occupied with the administration of the late King's estate and had the will of 1417 in his possession. He attended the Parliament that met at Westminster on 10 October 1435, and on 8 November surrendered this will in its presence.[7] He was still admitted to a place in the Privy Council, signing bills there on 26 October and 8 November.[8] Langley did not wait until the dismissal of Parliament on 23 December; by then he had nearly completed his last journey from the capital.

[1] Below, pp. 128–9.
[3] Below, p. 129.
[5] CPS. 55.
[7] Rot. Parl. IV, p. 488.
[8] CPS. 56; British Museum: Campbell Charters, VIII, 2.

[2] Rot. Parl. IV, p. 446.
[4] PPC. IV, p. 446.
[6] PPC. IV, pp. 287–9.

II

THE COUNTY PALATINE OF DURHAM

THE secular franchise of the Bishops of Durham was the greatest liberty in size of territory as well as extent of jurisdiction in the medieval realm of England. Its core was the county of Durham and wapentake of Sadberge, now an integral part of the modern county but for centuries, by reason of its late acquisition by the bishops, a distinct unit. Here, and in the outlying lands in Northumberland, the "shires" of Norham, Island, and Bedlington, the Bishop exercised an authority equal in its scope to that of the King elsewhere in the realm; until the nineteenth century, when the last remaining privileges of the Bishop were taken from him, these lands were known as "The Bishopric". In addition to this territory, the Bishop of Durham was also the lord of considerable estates in Yorkshire—Allertonshire, Howdenshire, and the manor of Crayke—although only in the last-named did he enjoy a franchise as wide as that of the County Palatine.[1] The King's writs were excluded from the Bishopric; it was the Bishop's writ alone that "ran" there, and when the episcopal see was vacant and the temporalities taken into the King's hands, a special *sede vacante* seal was brought from the royal Exchequer for use in the palatine chancery.[2] The common law of England was observed in Durham, but it was administered by the Bishop's justices. It was possible to appeal from the Bishop's court to King's Bench by means of a writ of error, but instances of such an appeal were few and only one has been noticed in the time of Langley's rule.[3] Again, if a subject of the Bishop holding lands by royal letters patent or in possession of royal letters of protection was involved in a suit touching his land, he could claim aid of the King and the proceedings would have to be suspended.[4]

---

[1] *Placita de Quo Warranto* (Record Commission, 1818), pp. 187–8.
[2] *Ancient Kalendars and Inventories of the Treasury of H.M. Exchequer* (Record Commission, 1836), Vol. II, p. 73.
[3] Below, p. 133.   [4] Below, p. 66.

The "acid test" of palatine privilege lay in the question of the disposal of lands of traitors against the Crown. It had been established in 1327 that the Bishop of Durham could take all forfeitures in his liberty, and even this decision was based upon a precedent of 1267.[1] The Statute of Treasons of 1351 had made no provision for the exemption of forfeitures due to the lords of liberties.[2] When Ralph Lumley rebelled against Henry IV in 1400, his lands were seized by the King as forfeited to him and royal commissioners made a survey of all of Lumley's lands, including those in Durham; the King granted most of them to the Earl of Somerset. In 1405, Lumley's son John petitioned the King for livery, which was granted to him.[3] The King also claimed the lands in Durham forfeited by Henry Percy, and appointed a commission to enquire into treasons committed in the Bishop's liberty.[4] Bishop Skirlaw apparently made no protest against these proceedings. Langley was less pusillanimous; he obtained from Henry IV and Henry V confirmations of the liberties of his palatinate, including that of taking forfeitures.[5] When the judgement against the Earl of Cambridge, Henry Lord Scrope, and Thomas Grey for their treason was confirmed by Parliament in 1415, a proviso was made for those claiming forfeitures in their liberties.[6] Langley consequently seized the lands in his franchise that had been held by Grey and made a grant of the custody of Scrope's lands in Durham.[7]

Some infringements of the liberties of Durham did occur when Langley was Bishop. The advowsons of churches were among the temporalities of the Bishopric. Although the Crown had no right to present to any church in Durham when the see was occupied, it did so on a few occasions. On 5 March 1409, the King presented John Legburn to the church of Sedgefield.[8] Langley did not

---

[1] *CPR. 1266–1272*, p. 63, & *1330–1334*, p. 360; and see G. T. Lapsley, *The County Palatine of Durham* (1900), pp. 41–5.

[2] *Statutes of the Realm* (Record Commission, 1810–28), Vol. I, p. 320.

[3] *Rot. Parl.* III, p. 459; Chancery Misc. Inquisitions, file 274; *CPR. 1399–1401*, pp. 173, 219 & 281, *1401–1405*, pp. 19 & 425, & *1405–1408*, p. 7; CPS. 19; *CCR. 1402–1405*, p. 439.

[4] *CPR. 1401–1405*, pp. 406–7, 426.

[5] *Cal. Charter Rolls*, V, pp. 432, 454–5.

[6] *Rot. Parl.* IV, p. 67.

[7] Durham: Auditors' Records: Sheriffs' Accounts, no. 3, m. 1; Rot. B. m. 12d.; and see below, pp. 251–2 (c. 9).

[8] *CPR. 1408–1413*, p. 54.

reject the nomination,[1] presumably because Legburn was an old friend.[2] Even so, the presentation was undesirable in principle, and four days after it had been made, Langley, who was then in London, obtained an exemplification of the judgement of Edward I by which Antony Bek was restored his regalian privileges in Durham.[3] This was a case of *quid pro quo*: Langley had accepted the King's nominee, but in return had secured a recognition of his liberties from Henry IV. A breach of privilege dating from the time of his predecessor was remedied in 1410, when Langley complained that the Exchequer had appointed a commission to make enquiries about the sums raised by the Mayor and townsmen of Hartlepool by virtue of a grant of murage to them by the King in 1400. As a result of this protest the prejudicial commission was revoked[4] and in the future Langley exercised the sole right to grant murage to the towns of his palatinate[5] without any interference by the Crown. From 1410 until 1416, the Bishop prosecuted a suit in Parliament, Chancery, and King's Bench for the recovery from the Mayor and citizens of Newcastle-upon-Tyne of the southern third part of the bridge crossing the River Tyne between that town and Gateshead. This portion of the bridge had been lost to the Bishopric since 1383, when the men of Newcastle removed the "Cuthbertstones" marking the boundary; they later erected a tower on the Bishop's portion. A jury drawn from Cumberland and Westmorland eventually found for the Bishop, who took seisin of his third of the bridge on 28 January 1417.[6] Langley met his most severe test as ruler of the Bishopric in 1433, when his vigilant jealousy for its liberties aroused him to take immediate counter-action.[7]

Statutes enacted in Parliament were obeyed in Durham, although the county did not send knights to represent it. On the other hand, ordinances made by the King in Council were not

---

[1] Legburn's admission was not registered, but he held the church until 1424 (*Reg.* no. 614).

[2] He was another of Gaunt's executors and entertained Langley at his house in Westminster in 1412 (*Reg.* no. 217).

[3] *Foedera*, VIII, pp. 572–5.

[4] *CPR. 1399–1401*, p. 355, & *1408–1413*, p. 264.

[5] Rot. A. m. 2, B. mm. 16d. & 20d.

[6] King's Bench: *Coram Rege* Roll, Michaelmas 2 Henry V, mm. 13–15; *Scr. Tres.* Appendix, p. ccvii.

[7] Below, pp. 119–29.

considered binding in the palatinate; thus Henry V's ordinance
suspending assizes [1] was not observed, as the record of an assize
of *novel disseisin* taken at Durham in 1420 testifies.[2] Durham did
not pay lay subsidies granted by Parliament. This was the rule
up to 1435, when a graduated tax on all lands, including those in
the Bishopric, was granted to the King.[3] The Bishop was ordered
on 29 January 1436 to arrange for the assessment and collection
of this tax in his liberty, and he appointed a commission for
this purpose on 6 March. On 29 May, however, the Crown
appointed a second commission;[4] no doubt there had been
opposition to the subsidy in Durham that had caused delay in
its collection. Eventually, instead of paying the subsidy, the
tenants of the Bishopric paid the King a fine of £100 which he
was pleased to accept, saying that it exceeded the sum the subsidy
would have yielded.[5] The principle of immunity from parliamentary taxation was thus upheld. In 1433, Parliament had
sought that commissions should be appointed in every county to
take from every man of substance an oath not to "maintain"
robbers and other lawless men.[6] The Crown appointed these
commissions on 1 May 1434 and made lists of the men of each
county who were to take the oath; in view of the Bishop of
Durham's franchise, he was told merely to attend to the administration of the oath to such inhabitants of the Bishopric as he saw
fit.[7] In somewhat tardy compliance, Langley gave orders on
12 August that five knights, fifty-one esquires and eighteen other
men, including the Mayors of Hartlepool and Stockton and some
forest officials, should come before him in Durham Cathedral on
23 September to take the oath; in his return, he did not report
that any of these men had failed to comply with his summons.[8]
This incident illustrates that, while the Bishop of Durham was
expected to obey parliamentary enactments, it was left to him to
put them into effect. The franchise of Durham was respected,
but at the same time it was understood that the Bishopric was
part of the realm of England and subject to its laws.

---

[1] Above, p. 41.   [2] DCD. Cartulary IV, ff. 135v.–6v.
[3] *Rot. Parl.* IV, p. 486.   [4] *CFR. 1430–1437*, p. 262; Rot. C. m. 10.
[5] Exchequer of Receipt: Receipt Rolls, no. 749, m. 13; *CPR. 1436–1441*,
p. 43.
[6] *Rot. Parl.* IV, pp. 421–2.
[7] *CPR. 1429–1436*, pp. 370–413; Rot. C. m. 8.
[8] *Reg.* no. 1122.

The Bishop of Durham had two states: he was both temporal ruler of the county palatine and ordinary of the diocese—the secular lord of his tenants but also their father-in-God. The Prior of Durham was the foremost subject of the diocese, but he was also, by virtue of his large territorial possessions, one of the chief barons of the county. The Bishop had to act in his two capacities when a prior was elected: as secular lord, his licence for an election had firstly to be obtained, and his assent to the Chapter's choice had also to be given under the great seal of his temporal chancery; while as ordinary, the Bishop was required to make a formal examination of the election proceedings, confirm the appointment, and order the induction of the new prior.[1] That it was still possible for there to be some confusion between the Bishop's two states as late as the fifteenth century is shown by the proceedings of the Chapter of Durham in 1416. The Bishop was abroad when Prior Hemmingburgh died. The monks met to consider how to sue a licence to elect his successor, and found that the great canonist, "the Archdeacon", had stated that a licence could be obtained from a bishop's vicar-general. Some doubt was expressed, so that it was decided to communicate with the Bishop directly.[2] It would, in fact, have been an error to have sought a licence from the vicar-general. The words of "the Archdeacon" had been wrongly interpreted, for he referred not to a vicar *in spiritualibus*, but to the vicegerent a temporal ruler would appoint to rule over his domains during his absence.[3] Langley had not appointed a vicegerent; his vicar-general had authority in spiritual matters only.

The two-fold aspect of the Bishop's power was also exemplified in the employment of the spiritual weapon of excommunication. According to English practice, an ordinary could call upon the Crown for its aid against a person who had remained in a state of excommunication for a period exceeding forty days. The King then directed a sheriff to seize the person named and hold him until he had made his peace with the Church. The same practice was observed in Durham, where the Bishop, as ordinary, directed his temporal chancellor to order the sheriff to arrest

---

[1] Below, pp. 199–200.
[2] DCD. 2.6.Pontificalia 9; Cartulary III, ff. 298v.–299.
[3] "Archidiaconus" (Guido de Bayso), *Rosarium super Decreto* (Venice, 1495), Dist. LXIII, c. 16.

excommunicated subjects of the county palatine. The position of the spiritual courts in Durham was thus particularly strong: action could be taken speedily. In one case, ten days after the sheriff had been ordered to arrest an excommunicated woman, it was reported that she had submitted; the Bishop was then asked to release her from his prison.[1] The Bishop's regality gave him an advantage over other prelates, including his metropolitan, the Archbishop of York. They had to apply to him when invoking the aid of the secular arm in Durham.[2] While the Bishop's temporal power was valuable to his spiritual authority, the positions could be reversed: the spiritual arm could be employed to support the secular administration. The Bishop could excommunicate his subjects for offences against his temporalities. The county palatine was the patrimony of St Cuthbert; attacks upon the Bishop's property were therefore acts of sacrilege. Langley made considerable use of his power to excommunicate persons who perpetrated offences against his temporal possessions or who in other ways violated the peace of the county. Monitions were issued against unknown miscreants who escaped the notice of his secular government.[3] Durham lay in the Bishop's peace, not in that of the King; as lord palatine or as ordinary, it was his responsibility to preserve order in the county.

I LAW AND ADMINISTRATION

When Bishop Langley opened his suit in defence of the privileges of the see of Durham in Parliament in 1433, he gave a short account of the constitution of his franchise: between Tyne and Tees, he said, and in the lordship of Norham and manor of Bedlington, he and all his predecessors had the "liberty" of a county palatine, with their own chancery, exchequer, and court where all pleas and assizes were taken, their own justices, sheriffs, coroners, escheators, and other ministers such as the kings of England had been wont to employ whenever need arose or for the execution of parliamentary statutes; the bishops of Durham issued their own original and judicial writs, held a county court, possessed their private mint, and were accustomed to grant their peace to subjects who submitted after being outlawed. This description of the Bishop's franchise was based almost word for

[1] DCD. Reg. III, fo. 80. [2] *Reg. Langley*, no. 349. [3] Below, pp. 114–16.

5

word on the statement of claims made by Antony Bek to Edward I's justices in 1293, which had been admitted by Edward I and his Council in Parliament; Henry IV had confirmed this judgement in 1409. Even if the form of government in Durham was not as ancient as Langley seemed to believe, there was no doubt that it had existed for nearly two centuries.[1] There had been administrative reforms since Bek's time, and Langley himself made some contributions to the efficiency of his secular government, but its general pattern had been established many years before his accession.

Durham city was the capital of the Bishop's lay franchise as well as of his diocese. In the cliff-bound promontory held in the loop of the River Wear stood the Cathedral and Convent of Durham and, guarding its open end, the Bishop's castle; between lay the Palace Green, with the hall where the justices sat, the mint and houses used as offices by the palatine chancery and exchequer and as residences by various ministers. North of the castle was the walled town, which could be entered by crossing either Framwellgate Bridge or Elvet Bridge; in Saddler Street stood the Bishop's gaol and in the Bailey the town-houses of his tenants-in-chief.[2] The territory administered from this capital was equally small and compact. The most distant part of the Bishopric, Norhamshire and Islandshire, was to some extent independent of the government in Durham city, and had its own centre in Norham Castle. The wapentake of Sadberge was also to a lesser degree, and more in name than in fact, a separate lordship; like Norham, it had its own justices, sheriff, and escheator, but in Sadberge these offices were held by the same men who exercised them in the county of Durham. Neither territory had its own chancery, however, and both were subject to the chancery in Durham.

The pattern of government in the Bishopric reproduced on a smaller scale many of the features of the royal administration of England. This was inevitable with regard to the enforcement of law and order because of the observance of the common law of the realm and statutory legislation in the palatinate. The development of a secretarial organization similar to that of the King was the natural consequence of the continuous promotions of royal clerks to the episcopal see: Langley was the fifth suc-

[1] *Rot. Parl.* IV, p. 427; *Foedera*, VIII, pp. 572–5.
[2] *VCH. Durham*, III, pp. 23–5.

cessive bishop who had been Keeper of the Privy Seal, and from even earlier times, since the episcopate of William II's minister Ranulph Flambard, the Bishopric had been ruled by men thoroughly acquainted with the practices of the royal government and who applied its methods to their temporal administration. Richard de Bury (1333–45) was responsible for the organization of the Durham chancery in the later Middle Ages; he had separated it from the diocesan secretariat, which became a household department.[1]   The great seal of the Bishopric, showing the Bishop enthroned on the obverse and as a mounted secular baron on the reverse,[2] and the rolls recording the majority of the commissions and letters that passed under it, were housed in the secular chancery in Durham.   William Chancellor, a layman, held the office of palatine chancellor throughout Langley's pontificate together with the office of constable of Durham Castle, to which he had been appointed by the King in 1406, during the vacancy of the see.[3]   There was also an office of clerk of chancery and keeper of its rolls which was granted to William Raket for life in 1437.[4]

Before Langley's accession, the chancery kept only one series of rolls, and he immediately introduced the practice of keeping two sets, one for letters patent—commissions, major appointments, grants, licences, and pardons—and a second for letters close, which included appointments of minor officials but was principally employed to record writs of *diem clausit extremum* and livery in respect of feudal tenants, and for the enrolment of recognizances to the Bishop and various written agreements made between his subjects.[5]   Although the chancery reverted to the tradition of keeping only one roll after nine years of the new method,[6] it returned to this practice in 1430 [7] and continued to observe it under Langley's successors.   The rolls give notes of the warrants for the issue of letters under the great seal, the most common of which are *per breve de privato sigillo* and *per ipsum episcopum*.   The number of surviving privy seal warrants is very small, but they indicate that the clerks of the Durham chancery were careless in

---

1 *Reg. Langley*, I, p. xiii.
2 Reproduced in Plate V, illustrating C. H. Hunter Blair, "Medieval Seals of the Bishops of Durham", *Archæologia, 1922*, pp. 1–24.
3 *CPR. 1405–1408*, p. 175.   4 Rot. C. m. 13.
5 Rot. A., & B. mm. 1–7.   6 Rot. B. mm. 7–20, & E.
7 Rot. C. & D.

the way they recorded warrants. A warrant under the Bishop's privy seal, dated 1 July 1431, ordered the issue to Robert Eure of a licence to fortify his house at Bradley. The licence was issued on 20 January 1432, and the enrolment shows no warrant.[1] No warrant is given for the issue of the licence for the election of a prior of Durham in 1416, although a copy of the warrant, a privy seal, was entered in the episcopal register.[2] The copy of a licence for the acquisition of lands is noted *per ipsum episcopum* when the warrant was one of privy seal.[3] No signet warrant survives, although there are a few direct references to this seal in notices of warrants, such as *per billam de signeto, per litteram domini de signeto*.[4] Presumably *per ipsum episcopum* usually indicated the signet just as *per ipsum regem* indicated the King's signet in the usage of his chancery. On the other hand, the use of this formula cannot be regarded as a clear reference to the Bishop's signet in every case in view of the notice just given of this term being used when the privy seal was intended. *Per ipsum episcopum* did not always mean that a written warrant had been received in the chancery: for instance, on 21 September 1407 the custody of some lands was granted on the Bishop's authority, as announced by the steward.[5] No doubt many other letters under the great seal were ordered in this way and many were issued when the Bishop was so close at hand that he could have given verbal instructions for their preparation.

The Bishop's council was able to authorize letters under the great seal [6] and many matters were inevitably left to the chancellor's own discretion. The feudal aspects of the Bishop's government—the seizure of land after the death of a tenant, the inquisition *post mortem*, and livery to the heir—lay, for the most part, in the chancellor's sphere; no warrants were necessary and none were mentioned. Outside this field, however, the noting of absence or warrants cannot be regarded as evidence of the limits of the chancellor's authority: as has been shown before, there was much laxity in the recording of warrants. In all probability few of the letters enrolled, except those concerning the descent of landed property, were issued without the Bishop's personal order. Judicial writs were, however, issued without the Bishop being

---

[1] Durham: Chancery Records: Warrants and Grants, file 1, d; Rot. C. m. 5.
[2] *Reg.* nos. 420 & 421.   [3] Rot. B. m. 17; Durham Warrants, 1, a.
[4] Rot. C. m. 6.   [5] Rot. A. m. 9.   [6] Below, p. 103.

consulted, as was the practice in the royal Chancery. Letters of exemplification did not require warrants and, again in imitation of royal practice, were not enrolled in the Bishop's chancery.[1] The resemblance in diplomatic between royal and palatine letters under the great and privy seals is very close, although the Durham chancery did not follow that of the King in giving its letters the dates of their warrants.[2]

Closely associated with chancery in its superintendence of the Bishop's feudal rights in the Palatinate were the escheators of Durham (and Sadberge) and Norham, who were directed by writs of *diem clausit extremum* to hold inquisitions *post mortem* into the lands of tenants-in-chief, which they seized for the Bishop, to whom they accounted for the issues, until they received further writs to give livery to the heirs. Other inquisitions were taken *ex officio*, when the escheator investigated cases of alienation, seizing lands that were found to have been alienated without the Bishop's licence.[3] The escheator was also sheriff, and a further divergence from royal practice, indeed from statutory obligation, was that the offices were held for the duration of the episcopal pleasure. Langley appointed only four sheriffs and escheators in Durham and Sadberge, Percival Lindley in 1406, Sir William Claxton in 1416, Robert Eure in 1420, and Sir William Bowes in 1436.[4] The last appointment was undoubtedly connected with the imminence of war on the Border,[5] because Bowes had had a long, distinguished, and extremely profitable career in the wars in France.[6] The sheriff was the principal agent for the enforcement of the Bishop's peace and the operations of his courts of law: he executed original and judicial writs and arrested and guarded suspected criminals[7] as well as obdurate excommunicates.[8] William Claxton's zeal in this respect outran the desires of the Bishop who wrote, under his signet, to bid the sheriff refrain from casting the Mayor of Hartlepool into prison.[9] Numerous other writs and commissions were directed to the sheriffs, ranging from directions to distrain for debts due to the Bishop to orders to assist the King's Admiral.[10] Most of the letters on the close rolls

1 DCD. 3.3. Pontificalia 4 & 5.   2 Lyte, *Great Seal*, p. 247.
3 Reg. IPM. fo. 196; and see below, p. 123.
4 Rot. A. m. 1, B. mm. 8 & 19, & C. m. 11.   5 Below, pp. 160-1.
6 *The Itinerary of John Leland*, ed. L. T. Smith (1906-10), Vol. II, p. 9.
7 Rot. D. m. 15.   8 DCD. Reg. III, ff. 80, 98v. & 99.
9 DCD. Locellus 25, no. 56.   10 Rot. D. mm. 7 & 16.

were directed to these officers in one or other of their capacities,
and it is therefore hardly remarkable that an under-sheriff was
regularly employed for the somewhat meagre annual fee of
6s. 8d.,[1] a sum doubtless augmented by gifts from litigants.

The Bishop's coroners were financial officers of some importance [2] but also had their part in the administration of the
law.   Writs directed against the sheriff were sent to them for
execution,[3] as was customary in the realm, and when John Horne
was accidentally drowned at Shincliffe ford, Robert Jackson, the
coroner of Easington ward, took the view of the body, but for
performing this duty the Prior of Durham gave him 8s., including
the fee of 16d. due to the sheriff's clerk.   The coroner of Chester
ward also received a fee of half a mark from the Prior for viewing
the body of John Naylor, who "died through misfortune".[4]   If
these payments were irregular so too were other features of the office
of coroner in Durham.   Elsewhere in England this officer was
elected in the county court,[5] but the Bishop appointed four of his
five coroners, the coroners' fiscal responsibilities, another unique
feature, making their selection a matter of some concern to him.
While the coroners of the four wards of the county—Chester,
Darlington, Easington, and Stockton—were appointed by letters
under the great seal of the Bishopric, the office of coroner in the
wapentake of Sadberge was hereditary; its performance was one
of the services attached to a tenement comprising three messuages,
a croft, and an hundred acres of land.[6]

The judicial system of Durham was notably more simple than
that of the realm, for where the King had his courts of King's
Bench and Common Pleas at Westminster, and peripatetic
justices of assize and gaol delivery, the Bishop appointed a single
commission to attend to all kinds of legal actions.   The personnel
of the Durham judiciary was a mixture of palatine ministers and
professional lawyers: the steward of Durham was the first-named
in the Bishop's commissions; Robert Wycliffe, a clerk who had
been palatine chancellor to Bishop Skirlaw,[7] was a member until
1427, when William Chancellor took his place; and Sir William

1 DCD. Cartulary, IV, fo. 93v.
2 Below, pp. 69–70.   3 Rot. B. m. 20d.
4 DCD. Bursar, 1418–1419, m. 3d. & 1428–1429, m. 3d.
5 I have had the benefit of consulting the proofs of Dr R. F. Hunnisett's *The
Medieval Coroner* (Cambridge, 1961).
6 Reg. IPM. fo. 190v.   7 *DKR. 33*, p. 84.

Eure was a justice for some years. These justices were unpaid, but fees of £10 and £6 3s. 4d. a year were paid to the chief and second justices, who were the expert members of the commission: Richard Norton, Bishop Langley's chief justice from 1406, was also, from 1413, Chief Justice of Common Pleas until his death in 1420, and his successor in Durham, James Strangways, who had previously been second justice,[1] was successively a justice of Common Pleas, second justice in the county palatine of Lancaster, and eventually, in 1436, chief justice there.[2] The Bishop also had a serjeant-at-law, known as his attorney-general after 1424, receiving an annual retainer of 40s., and a clerk to the justices, who was paid £4 a year.[3] This clerk was occasionally required to sit as a justice when one of the regular members of the commission was not available.[4] The justices were appointed for both the county of Durham and wapentake of Sadberge, although in 1415 John Killingall was appointed to take assizes in Sadberge only and to act as a justice of gaol delivery in partnership with James Strangways.[5] Langley later came to appreciate the political importance of the commission of the peace,[6] but saw no need to appoint his first commission before 1410, and his second until twelve years later. Thereafter he made appointments more frequently and gradually brought the size of the commission from ten members in 1410 to sixteen in 1436. In addition to the justices of assize and the sheriff, some ministers, like the receiver-general, and a number of local magnates, including the first Earl of Westmorland, received the commission.[7] There was a separate commission of the peace for Sadberge,[8] which also had its own gaol.[9] The lordship of Norham and Island likewise had its own commissions of the peace, and of assize and gaol delivery, which were both composed of the sheriff of Norhamshire and two or three of the Bishop's tenants there, usually without any expert members, unlike Durham. In 1431, however, the steward, chancellor, and two professional palatine judges were included in

---

1 Rot. A. m. 1, & E. 7, 8 & 17.
2 Foss, *Judges*, IV, pp. 207–8, 361; Somerville, *Duchy of Lancaster*, p. 451.
3 RG. 188714, 189809, 189782, 189810, 190184 & 188686.
4 Rot. B. mm. 17 & 18d., E, mm. 8, 12 & 16, & C. mm. 7 & 11.
5 Rot. A. m. 11.
6 Below, p. 132.
7 Rot. A. m. 7, E. mm. 8, 12 & 16, & C. mm. 7 & 11.
8 Rot. B. m. 12.   9 Reg. IPM. fo. 167.

the commission of assize for Norham.[1]   A commission of *oyer et terminer* was appointed in Durham in 1412 to investigate allegations by the Earl of Westmorland that unknown miscreants had broken into his parks at Raby and Brancepeth and stolen his game.[2]

Sessions of the Bishop's justices of assize were held at least three times a year and may have been held five times.   Several references to sessions in September have been found, and to others in December, January, February, March, April, and July, but no complete list for any one year can be reconstructed; two notices indicate that in 1421 the next session after 3 January was 27 March, and that in 1428 the next after 25 February was 23 September.[3]   One day appears to have been regarded as sufficient for the transaction of business, for 28 September 1422 was appointed for assizes at Durham and the following day for assizes at Sadberge; the sessions were then adjourned to 20 and 21 December because the pestilence was rife in Durham.[4]   An adjournment from 24 September to 4 January following was made necessary by a fresh outbreak in 1416.[5]   There is another cause for supposing that the Bishop's justices were not too oppressed with business: the record of fines imposed by the justices in the year 1420–1 shows that less than 8s. was received from twenty-six offenders, and a total of 15s. 7d. in 1422–3.[6] The profits of justice also included the fines paid in chancery for original writs, which cost between twenty and forty pence;[7] the annual receipts in chancery from the issue of letters of all kinds were sometimes only £2.[8] Bishop Langley would not have agreed that *justitia est magnum emolumentum*.

A certain amount of litigation took place in the Bishop's chancery.   An increase in the number of surviving records of pleas heard there, and the appointment of an attorney for the Bishop in his chancery in 1425,[9] suggest a development in its judicial activities, particularly after the survey and other measures taken to reform the administration in 1418.   Langley had good

---

[1] J. Raine, *North Durham* (1852), p. 46.   [2] Rot. A. m. 9d.

[3] DCD. Cartulary IV, ff. 93v., 112v. & 193; Reg. III, ff. 79v., 93, 174v. & 175; Locelli 5, no. 40, & 21, no. 25.

[4] Rot. E. m. 8d.   [5] Rot. B. m. 10.

[6] DCD. Granator's roll for 1341, dorse.   (I am indebted to Dr C. M. Fraser for this reference.)

[7] Rot. B. m. 1.   [8] Below, p. 72.   [9] Rot. E. m. 12.

cause to appreciate the potentialities of his chancery as a court of law. The suit of John Binchester against the Bishop, heard in chancery on 27 April 1424, gives the pattern of such proceedings. An inquisition taken before Ralph Eure and John Newton, two of the commissioners who surveyed the Bishop's estates,[1] on 30 August 1418, had found that Donald Hesilrig had granted certain lands in East Rainton to Prior Hemmingburgh without the Bishop's licence; the lands were therefore seized by the Bishop. Binchester claimed that Hesilrig had granted him all his (Hesilrig's) lands in East Rainton, and that he (Binchester) had held the lands until he was expelled by reason of the inquisition. This he was ready to verify, and he sought that the Bishop's hand might be removed. John Aslakby, the Bishop's attorney, followed and said that he was ready to prove that Prior Hemmingburgh had acquired the lands in question. It was then decided by the court that the matter should be sent before the justices of assize, to be tried by a jury. The sheriff was therefore instructed to call twenty-four men of East Rainton to appear before the justices in Durham on 19 December. On that day the chancellor gave the record of the plea to the justices, but as some of the jurors failed to appear the case was adjourned to 12 April 1425. The jury then swore that Hesilrig had given the land to Binchester, to whom it was therefore restored.[2]

The other cases are very similar. Lands held by John Heron, a tenant of the Bishop, were entered after his death by Richard Lestrang and others by virtue of a deed made to them by Heron. The lands were seized by the Bishop, for whom it was alleged that the deed was without value,[3] presumably because the Bishop had not given his licence for the transaction. An inquisition taken after the death of the Earl of Westmorland led to the seizure of some of his lands as it had been found that they had been held of the Bishop. The Abbot of Blanchland claimed that the lands were his by right of his church.[4] William Rome, a chantry chaplain in Durham city, claimed that certain lands seized by the Bishop had been granted to him personally; while it was contended against him that the lands had been granted to the chantry in mortmain, without the Bishop's licence.[5] Again,

---

[1] Below, p. 70.
[2] Rot. E. m. 11; DCD. Cartulary IV, ff. 112d. & 193.
[3] Rot. E. m. 13.   [4] Rot. E. m. 15.   [5] Rot. E. m. 15.

three men were called into chancery to give reason why they should not forfeit a bond made to the Bishop, with the condition that it should be held void while they kept the peace. It was shown against them that one of their number had made a disturbance at Sadberge and attacked a man. In reply, it was said that the injuries were inflicted in self-defence.[1]   In all these cases the issue was not settled in the chancery, but was sent for determination by a jury. Each dispute was narrowed to a simple question of fact which could be verified or not by jurors.

A somewhat more complicated case, of which fuller details than usual are extant, merits some attention. Sir William Blakiston, a tenant of the Bishop, died about 1 June 1418.[2] On 18 August, the inquisition *post mortem* was held at Auckland and the Bishop's escheator seized the lands.[3] The heir, Nicholas Blakiston, although a minor, was granted custody of the lands at an annual rent of forty marks, on 26 September.[4] Subsequently, Thomas Langton complained that he had held some lands at Blakeston, by the feoffment of William Hutton, which same lands had now been seized and granted to the custody of Nicholas. On Langton's petition, a commission was appointed to hold an inquisition into his claims.[5] The inquisition, held on 20 April 1419, found that Langton had indeed been disseissed from his lawful tenements. He therefore sought that the Bishop's letters patent granting custody to Nicholas Blakiston should be revoked. The latter was therefore summoned, by the sheriff, to appear in chancery on 2 January 1420 to give cause, if he could, why the letters patent should not be revoked. On that day Blakiston appeared, presumably by attorney as he was taking part in the King's campaign in France, and showed royal letters of protection to himself, to have force for one year from the day of issue, 6 December 1419.[6] Langton was unable to continue his suit until the royal letters of protection had expired and Blakiston was back in England. On 8 April 1422, Blakiston appeared in the Durham chancery, as summoned, and claimed that he need not answer without the Bishop's aid because of the letters patent granting the custody; the hearing was therefore adjourned until

---

1 Rot. D. m. 12.
2 Writ of *diem clausit extremum* on 4 June 1418 (Rot. B. m. 14d.).
3 DCD. Locellus 5, no. 11.   4 Rot. B. m. 18.   5 Rot. B. m. 17d.
6 *Catalogue des Rolles Gascons, Normans et François*, ed. T. Carte (1753), Vol. II, p. 239.

21 September, and then again until 21 December. In the interval Langton applied to the Bishop for licence to proceed, and on 2 December Langley sent to the chancellor his writ of privy seal, ordering him to proceed despite Blakiston's plea, but not to give judgement without first consulting the Bishop. This writ was read in chancery. Blakiston then said that the letters patent should stand because his father had died seized of the lands which Langton claimed. Langton denied this, and both parties said that they were prepared to have their case decided by a jury. The proceedings in chancery were then concluded, and the record was handed over to the justices of assize on 8 January 1423.[1]

These accounts of proceedings in chancery[2] all have one feature in common: in every case the Bishop was involved, either directly as a party or indirectly through his aid being called upon by a party citing his letters patent in defence. This litigation is therefore comparable with that of the "Latin" or common law side of the royal Chancery, and was the logical application to the regalian liberty of Durham of the principle *coram rege terminari debet placitum quod ipsum tangit*.[3] The Bishop could no more be impleaded in his courts than the King, and complaints of alleged injustice by the Bishop or his ministers could only be heard in his chancery. His licence had to be obtained before his letters patent could be challenged in chancery, or, indeed, before any suit against him could be tried in one of his courts. His claim to this prerogative was challenged in 1433.[4] There is no doubt that it was popularly resented, although it was clearly an attribute of his regalian liberties. The similarity with proceedings in the "Latin side" of the King's Chancery was more than one of principle: it extended to methods of procedure. The course of the pleadings to the eventual passing of the record to the justices was the same as that in the royal court.[5]

2 REVENUE AND FINANCIAL ORGANIZATION

A contemporary estimate of the wealth of Durham is given in the Lollard scheme said to have been mooted in the Parliament of 1410, when proposals were made for the application

---

[1] DCD. Locellus 5, no. 11.   [2] See also below, pp. 118, 123–4, 132–3.
[3] Bracton, quoted by L. Ehrlich, *Proceedings against the Crown (1216–1377)* (Oxford Studies in Social and Legal History, 1921), p. 23.
[4] Below, pp. 123–6.   [5] Ehrlich, op. cit. pp. 168–73.

of the revenues of bishops and religious houses to educational
and secular purposes: the Bishopric and Convent of Durham were
said to be worth 20,000 marks (£13,333 6s. 8d.) in annual revenue.
This was an excessive estimate, but that the Bishop and Convent
came second in the list and were equated in total value with the
combined revenues of the Archbishop of Canterbury, Christ
Church, St Augustine's, and three other houses, as with the
yearly value of the see of Lincoln and the Convents of Ramsey
and Peterborough,[1] is a good indication of popular opinion about
Durham's prosperity.   It is impossible to assess medieval incomes
in modern terms, but the wealth of a particular person can be
realized by comparison with his contemporaries.   Five accounts
of Bishop Langley's receiver of Durham still survive, and they
show gross receipts of £2,942 in 1416–17, £3,586 in 1419–20,
£2,860 in 1424–5, £2,903 in 1428–9, and £2,568 in 1435–6.[2] The
annual average of these receipts is £2,970, but other sources not
included in these accounts probably gave the Bishop another
£1,000,[3] bringing the total to nearly £4,000.   In 1436, assess-
ments were made of the incomes of the laity for a special subsidy
to the King, and although it has been shown that the figures
returned must have been somewhat less than the real incomes
concerned,[4] they indicate that only two lay peers, the Duke of
York and the Earl of Warwick, had incomes exceeding £3,000.[5]
Comparison with the Bishop's spiritual peers must be based on
the returns given in the *Valor Ecclesiasticus* of 1535; here the annual
revenue of the Bishop of Durham is said to be £3,128.   The see
of Winchester was wealthier by £1,064 and Canterbury by £95,
but the next prelates in order of wealth, the Archbishop of York
and the Bishops of Bath and Wells, Exeter, and Lincoln, had
incomes falling into the £1,500–£2,000 group.[6]   It may therefore
be concluded that Bishop Langley was one of the five richest
landowners in England and probably inferior only to the Bishop
of Winchester in order of financial precedence.

[1] *St Albans Chronicle*, p. 53.

[2] RG. 189809, 189782, 189810, 190184 & 188686.

[3] Below, pp. 69 & 71.

[4] T. B. Pugh and C. D. Ross, "The English Baronage and the Income Tax
of 1436", *Bulletin of the Institute of Historical Research, 1953*, pp. 1–28.

[5] H. L. Gray, "Incomes from Land in England in 1436", *English Historical
Review, 1934*, p. 614.

[6] *Valor Ecclesiasticus* (Record Commission, 1810–34), Vols. I, pp. 7 & 123,
II, pp. 2 & 291, IV, p. 7, & V, pp. 1 & 300.

The largest part of the Bishop's revenue was formed by rents of two kinds, feudal dues and farms. The tenants-in-chief of the Bishopric held their lands by various kinds of services which usually included the payment of certain sums at the exchequer in Durham. The collection of these feudal rents was the responsibility of the coroners of the four wards and the wapentake of Sadberge: the account roll of a coroner describes him as being also "the collector of all the free farms and of the exchequer", and the receipts listed are the fixed sums paid by hereditary tenants who were usually people of some social standing.[1] There were also in each ward about ten collectors, whose duty it was to collect the rents and farms of demesne lands, some held in free tenure and others in bondage, from the tenants in various episcopal manors.[2] While the coroners were officers of some importance, recruited from the Bishop's tenants-in-chief and appointed by letters patent under the great seal of the Bishopric after taking an oath for the true performance of their duties,[3] the collectors were men of lower rank and were probably appointed by the Bishop's steward. In the annual audit, the sums received by the coroners and collectors were shown together in the accounts of each ward; for the year 1419–20, the total receipts at the exchequer were £735 from Darlington, £684 from Chester, £593 from Easington, £298 from Stockton, and £29 from the wapentake of Sadberge. The bailiffs of the four bailiwicks of Evenwood, Darlington, Middleham, and Stockton accounted separately, and in this year produced a total of £116.[4] The Bishop's lands in Norhamshire, whose receiver accounted at Durham, added little or nothing to his revenue because of the devastation in this territory; in 1406, a total of £1,477 was said to be owed by the tenants in Norhamshire.[5] The revenues received from the Yorkshire estates of Crayke, Allertonshire, and Howdenshire were not included in the account of the receiver of Durham, although their separate receivers rendered their accounts there. Statements made by these three officers in the middle of the century show that Allerton then produced £411, Howden £547, and Crayke £47.[6]

The revenues from the estates in County Durham steadily declined during Langley's pontificate, though this fall had,

---

[1] RG. 188879.   [2] RG. 188620.   [3] Rot. B. m. 19d.
[4] RG. 189782.   [5] RG. 190005.
[6] RG. 189881, 190237 & 189882.

indeed, begun before his accession. In 1385–6, Bishop Fordham had received £2,572 from the four wards and Sadberge,[1] but Langley had £2,445 from these sources in 1416–17 [2] and the total fell gradually until in the last year for which his accounts are available, 1435–6, it was £2,127.[3] This decline in revenue was general in all the wards, Sadberge, and the four bailiwicks, and although only five rolls of the receiver of Durham in Langley's pontificate are available, the gradual pattern of this fall in revenue, which continued after his death,[4] precludes the possibility that in the years for which the rolls are missing the lost income was all recovered as arrears. Attempts certainly were made to obtain for the Bishop all the rents due to him. The coroners were kept under rigorous pressure: for instance, John Birtley, who was appointed coroner of the ward of Chester in 1410, made a bond to the Bishop for £300 on 27 January 1416, with the condition that he would produce all the arrears of rents for the time he was coroner at Michaelmas following. Two years later, further bonds were made by other persons that they would bring Birtley to the Bishop's gaol if he did not find £80 owing in his accounts within a month.[5] On 26 February 1437, the coroners of the four wards came into chancery and made bonds to the Bishop in respect of their debts to him, which totalled £168.[6] In 1418, Langley planned a comprehensive review of his financial resources. The steward, constable, receiver-general, and four other ministers made a complete survey of his estates, listing the feudal rents and farms due from his lands in the county of Durham, which were recorded as on 15 August of that year; [7] and at the same time, a register of returns of inquisitions *post mortem* and *ex officio* was made, the earliest of which dated from the second quarter of the previous century. Later inquisitions were recorded in this volume,[8] and Langley's successors continued the practice of making registers of this sort. In 1419, Langley appointed a receiver to levy and collect all rents due to him from the beginning of his pontificate until within a few days of the date of the survey.[9]

The most important of the other regular revenues of the

1 *Bishop Hatfield's Survey* (SS. 1856), pp. 260–5.
2 RG. 189809.   3 RG. 188686.
4 RG. 189811; see also *Valor Ecclesiasticus*, V, p. 299.
5 Rot. B. mm. 2, 7 & 13d.   6 Rot. D. m. 15d.
7 Rentals and Surveys, portfolio 21, no. 29.
8 Reg. IPM.   9 Rot. B. m. 18.

exchequer were the pensions paid to the Bishop from a number of churches and the profits of his forests and mines. A total of £91 13s. 4d. was paid each year by the Bishop of Carlisle and a number of religious houses in respect of fourteen appropriated churches in Northumberland; the sequestrator in this archdeaconry collected these rents and accounted for them in the palatine exchequer. The Bishop had some difficulty in receiving these rents, and occasionally sequestrated these churches when payments had fallen into arrears.[1] After the appropriation of the church of Staindrop by the college established there in 1412, a rent of 40s. was paid to the exchequer and the sequestrator of Durham was made responsible for its collection.[2] The sequestrators were also held to account for fines and charges for probate made in the course of their judicial activities,[3] but these sums, together with the profits of the consistory court, procurations, and other spiritual revenues, did not find their way into the temporal exchequer, although they must have passed into the Bishop's private coffers. Mines and forests yielded about £250 each year; nearly half this sum came from the farm of a group of coal-mines held by Ralph Eure, and the master forester accounted for nearly all the remainder. His account included the farm of a few mines,[4] but these were usually farmed directly.[5] The account of a surveyor of the Bishop's lead-mines in Weardale does not show any profit,[6] but lead sold by the Bishop between 1428 and 1431 produced £858; these receipts were not recorded on the contemporary roll of the receiver of Durham.[7] Coal was sold to some burgesses of Newcastle-upon-Tyne for £50 in 1424–5 and for £13 6s. 8d. in 1428–9.[8] The Bishop exploited his mines and gradually increased his revenue from this source; in 1435–6 he had £66 13s. 4d. from Gateshead and £53 6s. 8d. from Whickham, where a new mine had been sunk.[9] In 1430, a miner of Stanhope undertook to work a new shaft of a lead-mine, and in 1432, the Bishop made an indenture with a man who was going to smelt iron;[10] an iron forge had already been developed in 1408–9.[11]

[1] *Reg.* nos. 290 & 397.
[2] RG. 189782.
[3] DCD. Cartulary III, fo. 354.
[4] RG. 190030.
[5] RG. 189809.
[6] RG. 190012.
[7] RG. 190014, 190015 & 190184.
[8] RG. 189810 & 190184.
[9] RG. 188686.
[10] Rot. D. mm. 2d. & 3d.
[11] G. T. Lapsley, "The Account of a Fifteenth-Century Iron Master", *English Historical Review, 1899,* pp. 509–29.

The preservation of the Bishop's forests was a constant source of trouble, for poaching of the episcopal game was a popular misdemeanour. Suspected offenders were obliged to make bonds in chancery to desist from this unlawful sport,[1] but those who escaped detection, and other persons who destroyed the Bishop's trees, were threatened with a different order of penalty.[2]

The total of receipts at the palatine exchequer was completed by a number of miscellaneous payments, some of them profits of the Bishop's regality, though these did not include any taxation of the Bishop's subjects, for even if he had the right to impose taxes, which is improbable, it is certain that Langley never did so on his own account. The chancellor accounted for money paid for writs, charters, and respites of homage; in one year he received nearly £40, but his receipts in two other years were less than £2.[3] The sheriff and escheator brought in about £100 each year, made up of fines before the justices of assize and of the peace, for suit of court and offences against the Statute of Labourers, which rarely exceeded £10 in one year; receipts from lands taken "into the Bishop's hands" on the death of tenants and for other causes; waifs and strays, and wreck, for which he sometimes had nothing to show.[4] The sheriff and escheator of Norham and Islandshire produced smaller sums for similar receipts.[5] There was a mint at Durham, where Mulkin of Florence, the Bishop's coiner, worked under the supervision of Richard Buckley, the keeper of the mint, and paid into the exchequer 5d. for each pound troy of silver he coined; the largest sum he paid was 76s. 3d. in 1416–17.[6] In 1424–5, Peter Tilliol paid £16 13s. 4d. for a recognizance and Alan Mercer of Newcastle £15 in part payment of a recognizance for £28 13s. 4d.[7] The farm of the burgh of Gateshead and the Bishop's fishery and mills there yielded £26 5s. 0d. in 1416–17;[8] other burghs were leased to farmers, Darlington for six years at an annual rent of £66 13s. 4d., in 1421, and Durham, also for six years, at a rent of £62 13s. 4d., in 1434.[9] Nicholas Hulme and Richard Buckley were granted the custody of certain lands in the minority of the late tenant's heir and had to account for their receipts.[10] These

---

1 Rot. B. m. 11d., & D. mm. 1 & 2.
2 Below, pp. 115–16.
3 RG. 189809, 189810 & 188686.
4 RG. 189600–5.
5 Durham Sheriffs' Accounts, nos. 3 & 4.
6 RG. 189809.
7 RG. 189810.
8 RG. 189809.
9 Rot. D. m. 13, & E. m. 7d.
10 Rot. C. m. 7.

two clerks were ministers of the Bishop, and he obviously preferred to grant such custodies to men whom he could trust to
produce the stipulated rents: in 1416–17, the master forester and
two other officers paid the receiver £36 13s. 4d in respect of lands
of minors in their custody.[1] The wardship of Isabella Heron
was sold for £51 13s. 4d.[2] A number of small rents—for Le
Bisshopemedow at Durham and a messuage in Gateshead,[3] for
instance—were paid direct into the exchequer. The sale of certain
episcopal property was sometimes recorded there, of a boat to the
clerk of the King's works at Berwick-upon-Tweed, and coal and
wool to burgesses of Newcastle.[4]

It must be emphasized that the revenues described above were
those paid into the exchequer at Durham, that is, to the Bishop's
receiver of Durham. Throughout Langley's pontificate this
position was held by William Chancellor in addition to the offices
of chancellor of the palatinate and constable of Durham Castle,
where the Bishop's treasure was stored.[5] The receiver, like the
other officials who handled the Bishop's money, made an annual
account at Michaelmas which showed the totals paid to him by
the coroners and collectors in the wards, the bailiffs of the four
bailiwicks, the forester and the sheriff, and others as already
described, but the receipts he recorded were of the actual sums
of money delivered to him by these officers. These sums were
not the gross receipts, because in the accounts of all these ministers
allowances were made for expenses and other issues: the sheriff,
for instance, took a fee of £10, paid £1 to the clerk of the crown,
and spent a few pence on the purchase of parchment and ink.[6]
The receiver's practice of listing only deliveries of cash did simplify
his own account, but it makes it inadequate as a statement of the
Bishop's revenue. In the five surviving account rolls of William
Chancellor it is shown that he received nothing from the bailiff of
Stockton because the revenues of this manor were all applied to
building work there.[7] This form of accounting is very different
from that observed at the royal Exchequer: the year's revenue
at Stockton would there have been recorded as received and then
assigned to the clerk of the works, and entries of this transaction

---

[1] RG. 189809.
[2] RG. 190184.
[3] RG. 189809.
[4] RG. 189810 & 190184.
[5] DKR. 32, p. 305.
[6] RG. 189602.
[7] RG. 189809, 189782, 189810, 190184 & 188686.

6

made on both the receipt and issue rolls; it was not material that the actual cash had never been delivered. Another shortcoming in the accounts of Langley's receiver, the omission of receipts from the Bishop's estates in Yorkshire,[1] also detracts from their value.

The account rolls of the receiver of Durham were therefore neither statements of all the Bishop's gross revenue nor full records of his expenditure. It would be strange if no complete account, giving all these particulars, had been kept, and accident, which has destroyed the greater part of all the account rolls of Langley's time, may be responsible for the present absence of this "key" account. The accounts of the receiver of Durham cannot be accepted as the central record of the Bishop's financial organization, not only because of their demonstrable deficiencies but also because the receiver was not the chief financial officer of the Bishopric. The Bishop also had a receiver-general,[2] the precise nature of whose responsibilities cannot be determined in the absence of his accounts; that these were made is testified by the record of a payment to an auditor for his expenses in coming to Durham in March 1420 to hear the receiver-general render his account.[3] A more complete picture of Bishop Langley's income and expenditure could have been drawn had at least one of these accounts survived.

The introduction to Durham of the title of receiver-general was another of Langley's innovations and its first notice belongs to the year of account 1416–17, when the office was held by John Newton.[4] Newton was the treasurer of the Bishop's household in the period 1406–9,[5] and was described as the Bishop's treasurer in 1413–14.[6] Nicholas Hulme became treasurer of the household by December 1419 at the latest[7] and succeeded Newton as receiver-general in 1421.[8] On 1 December 1422, Richard Buckley was appointed receiver-general and, unlike his two predecessors, received letters patent of appointment under the great seal, which stated merely that the Bishop gave the office to Buckley for the duration of his pleasure.[9] Buckley remained receiver-general until the end of Langley's pontificate, while the

1 Above, p. 69.
2 The distinction between these two officers has not always been noticed (e.g. Lapsley, *County Palatine*, pp. 92–3).
3 RG. 189782.   4 RG. 189809.   5 RG. 188714.
6 RG. 188926.   7 DCD. Additional Doc. 108.
8 RG. 190043.   9 Rot. E. m. 8.

position of treasurer of the household was held from 1424, if not earlier, by John Radcliffe.[1]　Langley's last two treasurers of the household were, as their title suggests, members of his *familia* who would have accompanied him wherever his business led him.[2] When Newton held this office, however, the case was somewhat different.　He was presumably an early associate of the Bishop, since he was, if not a Lancastrian, at least a native of the diocese of Coventry and Lichfield, and he was a witness to Langley's first episcopal act, the appointment of vicars-general made in London two days after his consecration.[3]　After this date, however, Newton only appeared as a witness to episcopal *acta* at places on the Bishop's estates in Durham and Yorkshire,[4] and when Langley went to the Council of Pisa in 1409 he appointed Newton and Alan Newark to fill vacancies in benefices in the Bishop's gift during his absence.　The second commissioner did not act, but Newton collated three benefices in the following summer and autumn, when the record of these transactions shows him to have been in Durham city.[5]　Newton's title before 1416 is misleading, but it can be explained by reference to the roll of Bishop Fordham's receiver of Durham for the year 1385–6, which shows that an officer known as the Bishop's treasurer received large amounts of money at the palatine exchequer and was able to explain why other sums were not forthcoming at the audit, while a second officer known as the clerk of the household was responsible for the care of the money delivered to that department.[6]　Like Fordham's treasurer, Newton and his successors as Langley's receivers-general were the resident managers of the Bishop's financial organization.　The issue of letters patent to Buckley in 1422 marked the completion of the process by which an office originating in the episcopal household became a recognized part of the government of the Bishopric.

The receiver-general collected the bulk of the revenues of the palatine exchequer in excess of the requirements of the administration in the county.　As treasurer of the household, Newton had received nearly all the arrears collected by the receiver of Durham in the period 1406–10 [7] and as receiver-general took £1,958 in 1416–17 and £1,873 two years later; and Richard

---

1 RG. 189810.　　　　2 Below, pp. 96–8.　　　　3 *Reg.* no. 12.
4 Ibid. 66, 158, 164, 189, 217 & 326.　　　　5 Ibid. 121–4.
6 *Hatfield's Survey*, pp. 268–75.　　　　7 RG. 188714.

Buckley received £1,119 in 1424–5, £917 in 1435–6, but only
£238 in 1428–9, when the largest sum went directly into the
household.[1] In addition to these receipts at the exchequer of
Durham, the receiver-general was paid the surpluses from the
Yorkshire estates,[2] nearly £1,000 a year,[3] and possibly money
from other sources, including the profits of the Bishop's spiritual
jurisdiction. The receiver-general was held to account for his
administration of these funds,[4] although for want of records it is
not known how he spent them. Allowances were made at the
annual audit for money paid by him to the official of Durham,
the clerk of the works, the stockman, and the bailiff of Gateshead,[5]
but the largest part of his funds would have been sent to the
household. In a letter to Newton, Langley wrote that he was
expecting to incur heavy expenses in the near future, and was
sending Nicholas Hulme, the treasurer of the household, to
explain their nature to Newton. The receiver-general was to
give Hulme the largest sum he could make available, and, an
interesting commentary on the times, either provide Hulme with
an escort "since the roads are now more perilous than they ever
have been, or by some other manner, the surest and most secret
you know". Langley further asked that Newton should inform
him by return when he could send more money, and how much,
"so that we can best arrange for our governance this year. And
since we do not wish that the contents of this letter should be
made known to any but our two selves, we have written this
letter by our own hand".[6] This unique document emphasizes
two important features of the receiver-general's work, the concentration in his hands of the Bishop's liquid resources and his
position as the most trusted of the palatine officials.

Other fragments of the Bishop's correspondence with John
Newton further underline the receiver-general's standing in the
government of the Bishopric. A second letter required Newton
to inform the Bishop "how much of our money you have in your
hands from your receipts from Durham, Allerton and Howden",
and then to go to the manor of Bishop Auckland to examine the
Bishop's beds, cloths, and fur coverings, making repairs where

---

1 RG. 189809, 189782, 189810, 188686 & 190184.
2 Below.   3 Above, p. 69.
4 RG. 189782.   5 RG. 189809, 190043 & 190307.
6 DCD. Additional Doc. 108 (French), and see below, p. 94.

necessary.[1] One letter referred to an indenture between the
Bishop and a mason who was engaged to erect part of a tower in
Norham Castle: Newton was to pay the mason what was owing
to him after he had learnt of the progress of the work from the
receiver of Norham.[2] Of yet greater interest, however, are the
articles sent by Langley in answer to numbers of enquiries and
proposals from Newton concerning a variety of administrative
measures. A letter sent with one set of articles acknowledged a
a letter from Newton reporting the escape of certain persons from
Durham Cathedral, possibly from sanctuary there, and also said
that Langley had directed to the vicar-general a commission for
an exchange of benefices [3] which Newton had apparently commended. The articles mostly referred to the accounts of William
Claxton as sheriff and the appointment of his successor,[4] but they
also included observations on arrangements for the mines in
Weardale and a note that if the coroner of Chester ward could
not be persuaded to stay in office for a further year another was
to be appointed in his place.[5] The second set of articles answered
articles from Newton and Richard Buckley, and were carried by
Richard Burton, clerk of the works, who, as the previous articles
had required, had gone to London to discuss arrangements with
the Bishop. In these articles, Langley expressed his satisfaction
with the agreement made with the coroner of Chester ward and
the suggestion that William Alwent should be coroner of Darlington ward; he had sent his warrant of privy seal to the chancellor
to make Alwent's commission. Other warrants to the chancellor
for various writs and commissions were also carried by Burton;
two of the writs had been drafted with the advice of John
Thoralby. Some matters were referred to other ministers: the
chancellor was to find a remedy in the question of the measure-
ment of keels (of coal) at Newcastle, and James Strangways, one
of the Bishop's justices of assize, was to attend to the case of
Henry Gateshead. The articles concluded with a note that
Richard Buckley was to see to the livery of cloth for robes to
Thomas Surtees and John Hutton, and with a list of names of
persons who were to be given hay from the stores at Auckland,
Middleham, and Stockton; some was to be retained for the

---

1 DCD. Additional Doc. 105 (*French*).   2 Ibid. 109.
3 This is *Reg.* no. 528.   4 Below, pp. 84–5.
5 DCD. Additional Docs. 102 & 103.

Bishop's use, but the Dean of Auckland was to have as much as he needed, the Prior of Durham, the suffragan, and Thomas Holden were to have a certain number of cartloads, and the remainder was to be distributed among the Bishop's poor tenants in those districts.[1]

The receiver-general thus appears to have taken an interest in every branch of the secular government of Durham, in the appointment of officials and the administration of justice no less than in the control of the Bishop's finances; the care of the Bishop's beds at Auckland, the livery of cloth and distribution of hay were domestic arrangements that had probably been the responsibility of the treasurer of the household in previous years, but the other business presumably once belonged to the province of the steward or chancellor. Occasional notices in Langley's letters to Newton also reveal the latter's interest in diocesan affairs: he had collated to benefices in 1409, was appointed custodian of the Priory of Durham during its vacancy in 1416, and sometimes received commissions to sequestrate benefices or arrange their exchange.[2] No less remarkable than the concentration of all this business in the hands of one official is the degree of attention given by the Bishop to every aspect of his government, as the lists of articles testify, and it was because of the tightness of the control exercised by Langley that Newton was permitted to possess such an extensive influence. The Bishop did not appoint a lieutenant to act during his long and uncertain absence abroad in 1409, but the fact that it was to Newton that he delegated his powers of ecclesiastical patronage, appurtenances of his temporal estate which the Bishop jealousy preserved,[3] indicates that he preferred Newton before the other officers of the administration of Durham as the repository of his confidence. The receiver-general was the agent of personal government by an absent ruler.

The ecclesiastical careers of the three successive receivers-general underline the value Langley put on their services. John Newton, Nicholas Hulme, and Richard Buckley were all natives of the diocese of Coventry and Lichfield; like the other clerical members of the temporal government of Durham, none was a graduate. Newton was presented by the Duke of Lancaster to a prebend in the collegiate church of St Mary, Leicester, in

---

[1] DCD. Additional Doc. 107.
[2] *Reg.* nos. 121, 278, 344, 354 & 422.   [3] Above, pp. 53–4.

August 1399.[1] He exchanged this for a prebend in the royal free chapel at Bridgnorth in 1406, and made a further exchange for a stall in the college at Darlington in 1408.[2] Langley first gave him the custody of a hospital at Gateshead in 1407, the rectory of Houghton-le-Spring in 1410, and he was holding this exceptionally rich benefice, the equally valuable hospital at Sherburn,[3] which he had shamefully wasted to his own profit,[4] and prebends at Chester-le-Street and Darlington when he died in 1427.[5] As befitted a man who had enjoyed an annual income of nearly £300, Newton was able to collect a number of pieces of silver and gilt plate and several books, one bearing the interesting title of "Beliall".[6] Nicholas Hulme, who was treasurer of the household before he succeeded Newton as receiver-general, is first known from Durham ordination lists of 1413, but before he became a priest he was given the deanery of Chester-le-Street, which he held for seventeen days in April 1414 and then exchanged it for the church of Great Smeaton in Yorkshire; a second exchange in 1415 made him Rector of Redmarshall in Durham.[7] To this benefice Langley added Greatham hospital and a prebend at Norton, which two benefices he exchanged for a canonry and prebend at Ripon in 1433.[8] Hulme remained in Langley's service after he had been replaced as receiver-general, and was given a licence for an oratory in 1437, when he was a canon of Darlington;[9] after the Bishop's death, he entered the employ- ment of Alice, Countess of Salisbury, the wife of Langley's friend Richard Neville.[10] Richard Buckley's career in the Durham administration can be traced from 1407, and he also received a benefice, the rectory of St Nicholas', Durham, while still in minor orders.[11] He was collated to a prebend at Auckland in 1422, another at Chester-le-Street in 1427, and was also master of the well-endowed hospital at Kepier, where his government was free from blemish.[12] Both Hulme and Buckley received legacies from Langley and were appointed executors of his will.[13]

[1] A. Hamilton Thompson, *The History of the Hospital and the New College of St Mary in the Newarke, Leicester* (Leicester, 1937), p. 251.

[2] *CPR. 1405–1408*, pp. 175 & 389.   [3] Below, p. 178.

[4] Below, p. 192.   [5] *Reg.* nos. 35, 149, 675, 680 & 682.

[6] *Wills and Inventories* (SS. 1835), Vol. I, p. 77; *Reg.* no. 702.

[7] *Reg.* nos. 295, 299, 317, 318, 320 & 355.   [8] *Reg.* no. 1066.

[9] Reg. fo. 240v.   [10] *Testamenta Ebor.* II, p. 219.

[11] *Reg.* nos. 37 & 82.   [12] Ibid. nos. 559 & 675; Reg. fo. 249v.

[13] *Scr. Tres*, Appendix, pp. ccxliii–vii.

The second series of articles recently quoted shows an association between the receiver-general and Buckley, whose precise position in the Bishop's administration at that particular time is a matter for conjecture. His collation to a Durham benefice in 1407 indicates an early entry into the Bishop's service. Bonds made to Buckley and the palatine chancellor in 1411 [1] suggest an official capacity, and he was a member of a commission enquiring into concealments of feudal dues in the summer of that year.[2]   He was keeper of the mint at Durham by 1416,[3] in 1418 was associated with the vicars-general and the official in a commission to array the clergy,[4] and was one of the commissioners who made the survey of the Bishop's estates.[5]   In the following year he was appointed an auditor.[6]   Buckley was only once shown as a witness to diocesan business, at Bishop Auckland, in 1418, when John Newton made a protest concerning the maintenance of parochial chaplains.[7]   This solitary appearance in the Bishop's presence is significant in view of the fact that Newton was also there, and strengthens the presumption, suggested by his joining Newton in preparing articles for the Bishop, that Buckley was the receiver-general's adjutant. After Newton had been replaced in this office by Nicholas Hulme, in 1421, Buckley and one of the Bishop's justices were appointed to levy the debts due to the late sheriff.[8]   Buckley himself became receiver-general in 1422.[9]   Before this date, he was never described as the holder of an office that would account for his apparently responsible position, but although there is no evidence for the use of the title in Durham, in this period, at least, Buckley was probably acting as surveyor. Other great English magnates each had a receiver-general and a surveyor to manage their estates, and it would have been natural for Bishop Langley, when he instituted the office of receiver-general in Durham, also to appoint a surveyor to assist him and presumably to keep watch over his operations.

"Up to the middle of the fifteenth century the steward (*senescallus*) was the most important administrative officer in the palatinate", wrote Lapsley,[10] who did not, however, give any account of the steward's loss of influence or indicate which officer

1 Rot. A. m. 8d.   2 Reg. IPM. ff. 177–8.
3 RG. 189809.   4 *Reg.* no. 498.
5 Rentals and Surveys, 21/29, fo. 2.   6 Rot. B. m. 11.
7 *Reg.* no. 508.   8 Rot. E. m. 2.
9 Rot. E. m. 8.   10 *County Palatine*, pp. 77–8.

usurped his supremacy. This decline can be seen in Langley's pontificate, when the Bishop made the receiver-general the principal agent in his administration and also probably caused the prestige of the stewardship to wane by granting it to a household officer.[1] In the economic sphere, the steward of Durham's major duty was to preside in the courts of the various episcopal manors in the county, when he would have attended to the leasing of farms.[2] His supervision of the collectors is indicated by his statement at one audit that two of the collectors were holding some money to be applied to the upkeep of buildings on certain manors,[3] and his attention to the maintenance of the Bishop's property by a note that he ordered the clerk of the works "to repair the manor of Auckland and Durham Castle in all things before the Bishop's arrival in Lent, God willing".[4] The receiver-general also travelled round the Bishop's estates, for the purpose of inspecting their condition and seeing to the repair of buildings. The accounts of various officers show that allowances were made for sums spent on the receiver-general's instructions, to the clerk of the works, for instance, who had been ordered by Nicholas Hulme to make some repairs to the water-supply at Bishop Auckland. John Newton gave 41s. 2d. to John Dolfanby for building a new moot-hall at Gateshead, and was able to inform the auditors that no profit was made by the coal-mines there in another year.[5] While the administrative duties of the steward of Durham were confined to the estates in the county, the receiver-general would have extended his activity into the Bishop's outlying territories.

The estates in Northumberland and Yorkshire had semi-autonomous administrations. Norhamshire and Islandshire were treated as a single unit, with Norham Castle as the local centre of government. Its constable usually held the offices of steward, sheriff, and escheator, and a receiver ruled over the exchequer of Norham, where the local tenants-in-chief paid their rents.[6] Sir Robert Ogle held the first four offices for nearly all the time of Langley's pontificate, until 1436, when he was succeeded by his son, another Robert, and, under the threat of war, new arrangements were made for the government of this territory.[7] The

1 Below, pp. 101–3.   2 Lapsley, p. 78.   3 RG. 188686.
4 RG. 190043.   5 RG. 189809, 189782 & 190043.
6 Reg. IPM. ff. 168v. & 175v.   7 Below, p. 145.

receivers were clerks: William Caton, appointed in 1406, was master of a hospital in Tweedmouth and Vicar of Woodhorn until he exchanged it for the vicarage of St Oswald's, Durham, in 1412;[1] a move soon followed by his replacement as receiver by John Durham, who later became Vicar of Norham.[2] Both officers rendered accounts at the Durham audit, the first in his capacity of sheriff and escheator, and they were debited with enormous "arrears".[3] Although Ogle made bonds in 1417, 1425, and 1426 to answer for his revenues and commissioners were sent to enquire into concealments of revenues in Norhamshire in 1431,[4] it is unlikely that these deficits were ever substantially reduced. Of Bedlingtonshire, a large manor between the rivers Blyth and Wansbeck, where the Bishop also enjoyed his regality,[5] little is known in this period save that Langley had cause to require some of his serfs to give solemn undertakings not to leave the lordship.[6] A lack of contemporary accounts also prevents a picture being drawn of the Yorkshire estates under Langley's rule. The only officers who can be identified are the receivers of Howden. One, Robert Frend, was a notary, and seems to have been a most active man, not only in the secular sphere, for in addition to his duties as receiver there and as an auditor and occasional commissioner in Durham, he was a resident prebendary and "rector" of the choir in the collegiate church of Howden, where he introduced the use of Sarum. His services were amply rewarded by ecclesiastical promotion.[7] Frend was succeeded as receiver by Richard Burton, who had been clerk of the Bishop's works for seven years.[8] Howdenshire was administered by a steward and four bailiffs beside the receiver, and there were a steward and a bailiff in each of the lordships of Allertonshire, Crayke, and Bedlington.[9]

All officers who handled the Bishop's revenue in any form were required to render an annual account; although the traditional

---

[1] Rot. A. m. 1; *Reg.* nos. 43, 178 & 244.
[2] Rot. A. m. 9; *Reg.* no. 955.
[3] Durham Sheriffs' Accounts, nos. 3 & 4; RG. 190004, 190005, 190007 & 190008.
[4] Rot. B. m. 13, E. m. 11d. & C. m. 4; and see below, p. 84.
[5] Raine, *North Durham*, p. 362.
[6] *Reg.* nos. 158–60.
[7] *Reg.* Vol. I, p. xx; *CPL.* VII, pp. 380 & 386; DCD. Reg. Parvum, I, fo. 35.
[8] *Reg.* no. 967; Rot. A. m. 10 & B. m. 16d.
[9] *Valor Ecclesiasticus*, V, p. 300.

Exchequer date of Michaelmas was observed as the day from which the year was reckoned, it is clear that the auditors met more frequently than at the end of September. Langley's first appointment of auditors was made on 22 September 1408, when those named were: Ralph Eure, the steward; John Burgeys, Dean of Auckland, who had a long record in the financial administration of Durham; [1] John Newton, the treasurer of the household; William Chancellor, the constable, chancellor, and receiver of Durham; and William Mablethorp, an official of the Duchy of Lancaster who was frequently employed by Langley [2] and had the useful status of an "outside assessor".[3] In 1416, a second commission differed from the first only in the replacement of Burgeys by Robert Frend, the receiver of Howden; Richard Buckley was formally associated with these five auditors in 1419.[4] In the third commission, on 14 December 1428, only Buckley, Chancellor, and Mablethorp remained of the previous auditors, and they were joined by Thomas Holden, the new steward; Nicholas Hulme, a former receiver-general; William Proctor, who is otherwise unknown but was to be reappointed by Bishop Neville in 1438; [5] and Richard Burton, the receiver of Howden.[6] Purchases by the receiver permit a glimpse of the auditors at work, comfortably seated on cushions behind their table covered with green cloth, with an abacus to assist their calculations, and their books that were to be kept in a leather bag. The exchequer chamber must have been a gloomy room, or the auditors had to work late, for once fifteen pounds of candles were required for their better illumination. Some of them received payment for their travelling expenses, particularly William Mablethorp, whose usual place of residence was Market Deeping; the journey to Durham took him eight days. Sometimes Mablethorp or Frend went to London and probably to other places where the Bishop was residing to receive the accounts of his treasurer of the household and wardrobe,[7] who, for obvious reasons of episcopal convenience, was excused from personal appearance before the full board of auditors in Durham.

The accounting officers, armed with their rolls and subsidiary

1 Below, p. 185.   2 Below, p. 101.
3 Rot. A. m. 3d.   4 Rot. B. m. 11.
5 *DKR. 34*, p. 167.   6 Rot. E. m. 19.
7 RG. 189809, 189782, 190004, 189810 & 190184.

vouchers, must have approached the audit with dread, for the scrutiny was close and those in default had cause to fear the auditors' severity, which was the more effective because it could invoke the machinery of the Bishop's regalian government.   The bailiff of Darlington who was unable to account for a hundred marks was committed to prison, where he died, still in debt; his lands were then seized until the sum was levied from them.[1] Officers of higher rank, like the forester and coroners, were compelled to enter into bonds in the Bishop's chancery to ensure their payment of arrears,[2] while Robert Ogle made a bond to the Bishop in £1,405 in the royal Chancery under the condition that he would appear before the auditors in Durham to answer for his administration of Norham before 1 July 1426.[3]   William Claxton, who was appointed sheriff and escheator of Durham in 1416,[4] allowed his accounts to fall into sad disorder.   On 24 January 1419, he bound himself to pay the Bishop £78 9s. 9¼d. at Easter and St Peter's Chains, in equal portions, which he did not do, and consequently a writ of *scire facias* was sent to the four coroners of the wards on 13 December, ordering them to summon him to answer for this money.[5]   By this time, moreover, Claxton should have presented his account for the year ending Michaelmas 1419, and this he also failed to do at the appointed term.   He found it wise to stay in Northumberland and on 10 December wrote to Langley to explain his difficulties.   "My right worshopfull lorde, if ye like to here of my degre, like yow understande I am seke and so diseisit that I am impotent to travell at this tyme, and never the lesse yor ministres and auditors within yor Bishoprike of Durham called me dayly to accompt of the tyme that I was yor shiref within yor counte of Durham, supposant to vex me and put me to les be cause forsaide."   He therefore asked for respite until the following October, when he would "apere before yor awen reverent person and thare make ende be yor awen ordinaunce and discrecion, I supposand, gracious lorde, in the mein tyme to amende of sekenes that I may travell and to rayse and gar' rayse yor dettes redy then to pae yow; considerant, gracious lorde, that I am afferde to be demyt be yor stowarde [and] auditours in your forsaid counte in yor absence because yor

1 Below, p. 123.   2 Rot. E. m. 8; and see above, p. 70.
3 *CCR. 1422–1429*, pp. 274–5.   4 Rot. B. m. 8.
5 Rot. B. mm. 16d. & 20d.

stoward I suppose will be to me noght evyn but maliciouse". The receiver-general had also written to the Bishop about Claxton's accounts, and in reply Langley sent him the sheriff's letter with a copy of his warrant to the auditors: Langley did not grant Claxton the respite he had asked for, but directed the auditors, when they had heard his account and if they found him to be in arrears, not to imprison him but allow him to depart after giving security for payment. Robert Eure was to replace Claxton as sheriff, but was not to receive his commission before Claxton had made his account unless the Bishop's council thought that this delay would interfere with the administration of justice.[1] Eure's commission was, in fact, issued on 2 January 1420,[2] but Claxton had apparently refused to make his account before his enemy [3] the steward, for on 12 January 1421 a special commission was appointed to hear his accounts; it was formed by the regular auditors with the exception of the steward. This arrangement satisfied Claxton, who duly accounted, and on 26 January the Bishop appointed Richard Buckley and James Strangways to raise his debts.[4] The accounts of Claxton's successor suggest that the sheriffs of Durham were chronically incapable of collecting the sums with which they were charged: although Robert Eure began in office without any burden of "arrears", he accumulated a deficit of nearly £1,400 within fourteen years.[5]

The auditors were permitted very little discretion in their examination: only once was it stated that allowance was made by the steward, auditors, and others of the council, when the rental for the burgh of Durham was found to be defective.[6] The various accounting officers had equally little latitude in the employment of the revenues they collected beyond the expenditure of a few pence for the purchase of parchment and ink. Although the auditors were empowered to allow officers their expenses within reason, they were sometimes, as the bailiff of Sockburn found, not very generous in this respect; he had to go to prison until the Bishop permitted him to go free if he would find sureties for his debt.[7] The receiver of Durham alone had authority to make disbursements of any proportion, for the items described in his

---

[1] DCD. Additional Docs. 103 & 104.
[2] Rot. B. m. 19.
[3] Below, p. 112.
[4] Rot. E. m. 2.
[5] RG. 189601 & 189604.
[6] RG. 190184.
[7] Rot. D. m. 14.

account as "necessary expenses". Some of these payments were
made on behalf of the auditors[1] or for the purchase of parchment
and the like for chancery; John Palman was paid 2s. for binding
and covering a book called *Le Regestre*, probably of inquisitions,[2]
in 1419–20, and for writing a copy of an account (*compotus*) of the
whole of the Bishopric in 1428–9. As William Chancellor was
constable as well as chancellor and receiver of Durham a good
proportion of these "necessary expenses" went towards the
maintenance of the Castle: 18d. for *Le Bemefillyng* and repair of his
chamber, 23d. for a window in *Le Wardrop*, and sums of similar
size for work on *Le Clok*, the drawbridge, the kitchen, and the
constable's hall. The largest payment for such work, however,
106s. 8d. to make a new fireplace in the constable's hall, was
made by agreement with the receiver-general and on orders from
the Bishop. Some miscellaneous items, rewards for messengers,
the making of an iron sign with a mullet (Langley's armorial
device) to mark measures of wine and other mercantile weights,
11d. for a potell of oil for the chrism at Easter, went to make an
average annual total of £9 10s.[3] A small number of the Bishop's
officers had duties that involved the spending as opposed to the
collection of revenue. Apart from the receiver-general and
household officials, these ministers were the clerk of the Bishop's
works, the keeper of sheep and cattle, the surveyor of lead-
mines and, a temporary office, the surveyor of works in the
manor of Stockton.[4] Their accounts were also subjected to the
auditors' scrutiny.

When the various officers came before the auditors, they
presented a number of subsidiary documents to justify their
statements. All issues from one minister to another, as by a
coroner to the receiver of Durham or by the latter to the clerk of
the works, were supposed to be made under cover of indentures,
and expenditure and payments had to be justified by the production of the Bishop's warrants. The number of these documents
produced at each account must have been considerable: no
vouchers dating from Langley's pontificate survive, but a solitary
file, that of the receiver of Durham for the seventh year of Bishop
Skirlaw, contains seventy-four pieces, mostly indentures relating

---

1 Above, p. 83.   2 Above, p. 70.
3 RG. 189809, 189782, 189810, 190184 & 188686.
4 Below, pp. 89–90, 97.

to receipts in the palatine exchequer but including a small number of warrants under the Bishop's signet to the receiver, collectors, and auditors.[1] Frequent references to Langley's warrants to his ministers appear in their accounts, often with notes of their place-dating: thus the receiver of Norham quotes a warrant dated at Stockton on 17 September 1422 to pay the forester of Fenwick his daily penny,[2] and other issues made pursuant to warrants include payment of miners' wages by the clerk of the works;[3] repayment of two hundred marks to the King's son John, Warden of the East March, and of £100 borrowed from Roger Thornton of Newcastle; delivery to the Prior of Durham, as collector of a clerical tenth, of £33 6s. 8d.;[4] and 100s. given to some merchants of Newcastle in compensation for the loss at sea of wool they had bought from the Bishop.[5] The receiver of Durham did not cite warrants for the delivery of the vast sums that went to the treasurer of the household and receiver-general, only indentures being mentioned, but even the annual payments from the Durham exchequer of their customary fees to the Bishop's officers required a fresh warrant every year.[6]

Other warrants authorized the auditors to make allowances for certain sums the collecting officers were unable to produce: the receiver of Durham quoted a warrant to explain his failure to raise 16s. 4d. from a farm[7] and the sheriff was excused from answering for the issues from the lands of the traitor Thomas Grey and for a farm of 10s. which had been pardoned to the chaplain of a chantry on Tyne bridge. The sheriff also reported that the Bishop had excused him "by word of mouth" in respect of other sums[8] and the receiver reported that when the Bishop was in Durham he had given him orders for the purchase of two cords for Norham Castle.[9] The inability of a minister to produce a warrant for a payment resulted in the refusal of the auditors to make any allowance for the sum involved: thus they did not allow the clerk of the works his wage of 100s. *quia sine warranto*.[10] Sometimes payments were disallowed for lack of warranty and were later allowed when a warrant had been obtained, presumably at another session of the auditors: a payment by the stock-keeper of

[1] RG. 221160. [2] RG. 190004. [3] RG. 189810.
[4] RG. 188714. [5] RG. 190184.
[6] RG. 188714, 189809, 189782, 189810, 190184 & 188686.
[7] RG. 188714. [8] RG. 189601 & 189602.
[9] RG. 189810. [10] RG. 190043.

10s. as tithe to the Dean of Auckland was cancelled, but restored when a warrant was forthcoming,[1] and an issue of 66s. 8d. by the receiver to the official of Durham as part of his fee was at first not allowed for want of a warrant but later permitted by the Bishop's special order.[2]   The receiver once, and perhaps habitually, drew up his list of regular payments before he had received warrants for them all.   In his account for 1424–5 he included the suffragan, as was customary, in this list, with blank spaces left for the date of the warrant and the sum paid; this entry was cancelled as the fee had been paid by the sequestrator by order of the Bishop, and the sum involved was included among the receiver's debts.[3]   A warrant alone was not sufficient: although the receiver of Norham could show a warrant to pay a mason engaged there, the issue was disallowed because he did not produce the mason's receipt.[4]

The Bishop's correspondence with his receiver-general has already revealed the minute attention he paid to all aspects of his financial administration, the maintenance of his property and the expenditure of his revenue.   The numerous references to his warrants on the rolls of accounting officers bear witness to the same close interest in every detail, no matter how small, and the insistence by his auditors that these warrants should be produced reinforced the strength of his personal direction and control.   A payment for the carriage of their books to Bishop Auckland [5] shows that even the auditors were subjected to Langley's surveillance.   From time to time they referred to his personal attention items in officers' accounts that they questioned; thus they made a note to speak to the Bishop about a payment of £30 by the clerk of the works for repairs to two mills and their houses at Darlington which the auditors thought to be excessive.[6]

Less is known of the uses to which Bishop Langley put his revenue than of the methods by which it was collected.   The expenses of his secular government were the first charge on his income and were met from the sums raised by his various officers before any money was set aside for the Bishop's domestic economy.   In addition to his "necessary expenses", the receiver of Durham paid out between £120 and £130 each year in fees: the steward, and William Chancellor as constable, receiver, and chancellor, each received £40; the chief justice of assize had £10, the second

1 RG. 190307.	2 RG. 189809.	3 RG. 189810.
4 RG. 190007.	5 RG. 190184.	6 RG. 190043.

justice £6 13s. 4d., the clerk to the justices of assize £4, and the attorney-general, clerk to the justices of the peace, and chancellor's clerk 40s. each, with smaller sums for other clerks and the keeper of the armoury; while of the diocesan ministers, the suffragan received £13 6s. 8d. and the official was once given part of his fee at the exchequer.[1] The sheriff and escheator of Durham took £10 from his annual receipts and paid £1 to his clerk, known as the clerk of the crown,[2] and other receivers and collectors were similarly rewarded; the receiver-general presumably took his salary from the money in his charge. Langley did not burden his exchequer with pensions and the only additional charges of this nature he imposed were the salaries of the chaplains of his chantry in Durham Cathedral and, for a few years only, an annuity of 106s. 8d. for William Ingleby while he was studying at Oxford.[3] Other bishops of Durham had been accustomed to retain important tenants-in-chief as members of their councils: thus Bishop Fordham had retained John, Lord Neville, for an annual fee of £33 6s. 8d.,[4] and Bishop Neville was to engage William Eure for a fee of £20 [5] as well as to grant his brother the Earl of Salisbury an annuity of £100 at the Durham exchequer [6] and other fees and pensions to a total of £90 from Howden to councillors and members of his family.[7] Langley's parsimony in this respect contrasts strongly with the extravagance of his successor: he had very definite views on the undesirability of grants in perpetuity [8] which his experience as Henry IV's minister must have done much to instil.

Issues by the receiver of Durham for causes other than the payment of fees include a number of sums to be applied to building works of various kinds: £133 7s. 10d. to the governor of the mines at Whickham in 1409; [9] £6 13s. 4d. given by the Bishop for the erection of a bell-tower at Auckland St Andrew and 41s. 2d. towards a new moot-hall at Gateshead in 1416–17, when allowances had to be made for rents from gardens occupied by masons who were building a new tower called "The Northgate" in Durham Castle; £17 4s. 6d. was also paid to the receiver of

---

[1] RG. 189809 & 189810.   [2] RG. 189600.   [3] RG. 189782.

[4] *Hatfield's Survey*, pp. 267–8; see also *Registrum Palatinum Dunelmense* (Rolls Series, 1873–8), Vol. I, pp. 9–10.

[5] Surtees, *Durham* I, p. cxxxiii.   [6] RG. 189811.

[7] RG. 190237.   [8] Below, p. 195.

[9] RG. 188714.

7

Norham in this year for the cost of works there,[1] and £32 19s. 11d. given to the same officer in 1408–9 [2] was probably destined for similar use. A clerk of the works was in regular employment, charged with the duty of building and repairing all castles, manors, and other episcopal property in the Bishopric, whenever necessary and at the Bishop's expense. Thomas Roos, Vicar of Kirk Merrington, was appointed to this office in 1408, and was succeeded by Richard Burton, also a chaplain, in 1414.[3] The account of his successor, Thomas Thornburgh, for the year 1421–2, shows that he incurred expenses totalling £116, which was spent in small amounts on manorial buildings throughout County Durham: a score of mills and their ponds, the common ovens at Chester-le-Street, Sadberge, and Auckland, the enclosures of parks, a new weir, and the water-supply for Auckland manor all received his attention.[4] The task of the clerk of the works was to keep the Bishop's property in a state of general repair and when major repairs or new building were undertaken a special officer was usually put in charge. There was a surveyor of the works at Stockton, where building was carried out throughout the Bishop's lifetime. A payment of £184 was made to this surveyor in 1413–14,[5] and each year he received at least £40, the whole revenue of the bailiwick, and probably other special payments over twenty years and perhaps longer.[6] Other regular payments were made to the officers in charge of the Bishop's mines. The surveyor of the lead-mines in Weardale was paid £112 by the receiver of Durham in 1425–6 [7] and other issues for similar purposes have already been noticed.[8] Major works were undertaken at Norham [9] and Durham Castles and in Durham city, where in addition to the erection of the North Gate and other reinforcements to the Castle, Langley built a new gaol and strengthened the city's defences by the construction of gates on both bridges; [10] moreover, Langley's building expenses in Durham Cathedral must have totalled nearly £1,000.[11] The funds for these operations were not all provided directly from the

---

1 RG. 189809.　　　　　2 RG. 190007.　　　　　3 Rot. A. mm. 2 & 10.
4 RG. 190043.　　　　　　　　　　　　　　　　　5 RG. 188926.
6 RG. 189809, 189782, 189810, 190184 & 188686.
7 RG. 190012.　　　　　　　　　　　　　　　　　8 Above, p. 87.
9 Below, p. 145.
10 *Durham Account Rolls* (SS. 1898–1900), Vols. II, p. 304, & III, p. 621.
11 Below, pp. 196–7.

of this important office can be identified.[1]   There was a wardrobe in the household which may have been in the charge of a separate keeper.[2]   Another clerk held the position of clerk of the kitchen and was thought worthy of a benefice.[3]   The chief office in the household, that of chamberlain, was held by a layman: Thomas Holden, another of Langley's early associates, was his chamberlain throughout his years as Bishop of Durham.[4]   Other lay members of the household, men of armigerous rank, occasionally occur as witnesses to Langley's *acta*,[5] and William Eure, the son of the steward of Durham, spent some of his earliest years, presumably as a page, in the *familia*.[6]   In his will, the Bishop left £5 to each of his esquires, five marks to each yeoman, £2 to each groom, and £1 to each page, while some were further rewarded for their services.[7]

A second expression of the Bishop's wealth that cannot have escaped public attention was the number of his residences.   He possessed two of the greatest fortresses in northern England, the castles of Durham and Norham, though Langley made little personal use of either.   He stayed in his "palace" of Durham [8] on the rare occasions when he passed a night in his cathedral city, and he visited Norham only three times, in 1408 when he was completing his first personal inspection of his estates, and in 1425 and 1429, when he was employed as a commissioner for England in negotiations with Scotland.   In both castles he left his mark by the addition of a new tower.[9]   Of all his episcopal residences, Bishop Auckland was Langley's particular favourite; whenever he came into the Bishopric, he always spent some of his time here, and it was here that he died.   Bishop Auckland was without doubt the fairest of the Bishop's houses, with a fine position in a park set by the River Wear.   The palace had been built by Antony Bek, with a great hall raised on columns of Purbeck marble, a large chapel and a smaller one, and "an exceeding great fair chamber" with a smaller room [10] called "Le Parlour".[11] Langley was content to attempt no major improvement to this

---

[1] Above, pp. 74–5.   [2] Below, pp. 97–8.
[3] RG. 190184; *Reg.* no. 1081.
[4] *Reg.* no. 48; RG. 189782 & 190184; Reg. fo. 238v.; and see below, p. 102.
[5] *Reg.* nos. 48, 133, 159, 220 & 352.   [6] Ibid. 188.
[7] *Scr. Tres,* Appendix, p. ccxliv.   [8] *Reg.* nos. 544 & 546.
[9] Below, pp. 77, 89–90; and above, p. 145.
[10] *Itinerary of John Leland*, I, p. 70.   [11] Reg. fo. 250v.

cost him £60, and his copy of Nottingham *Super Evangelia* was worth £20.[1] No doubt a good number of the Bishop's personal belongings had come to him by the wills of his friends, like the great bed of Robert Waldby, Archbishop of York, who died in 1386, bequeathed to Langley by his predecessor Skirlaw,[2] but the Bishop himself must have been a valued customer of the goldsmiths, drapers, and other merchants of London. Two solitary accounts of his private expenses in the capital include payments to such tradesmen for pearls and blankets, but also 60s. for saltpetre and brimstone for Norham Castle;[3] issues from the Bishop's private coffers were not applied solely to his own comfort or the needs of his household, but could include, as in this case, the requirements of his temporal government. The exercise of charity and hospitality must have accounted for a further proportion of Langley's personal revenue; of his gifts to religious houses there is little evidence save in the case of Durham.[4] One of the accounts of his private expenses records the purchase in 1429 of fifteen hundred pieces of glass of different colours and the cost of their carriage to Hedon, and also payments to a painter living near the Austin friars in London for painting the story of St Cuthbert; the sums spent here totalled £11 5s. od.,[5] and would have been followed by other payments for the same project, which must have been the erection of the St Cuthbert Window in York Minster.[6]

The private expenses of the Bishop, the costs of his household, the upkeep of his residences, and other payments both sumptuary and necessary, must have required considerable annual totals, probably more than half of his annual revenue of approximately £4,000. When the Bishop set out for the Council of Pisa in 1409, he thought it necessary to have a licence to export £1,000.[7] The custody of the household revenue was shared by two officers, the treasurer [8] and the chamberlain, both of whom were required to

---

1 *Wills and Inventories*, I, p. 88.
2 *Testamenta Ebor.* I, p. 325.
3 *Scr. Tres*, Appendix, p. ccccxli.
4 Below, pp. 196–7.
5 RG. 190015.
6 Below, p. 220.
7 *CCR. 1409–1413*, p. 444.
8 It has already been shown that before 1416 the title "treasurer of the household" was given to the officer who after this date was called "receiver-general", while the effective treasurer within the household was known as "clerk of the household". After the introduction of the title "receiver-general", however, this clerk was given the designation "treasurer of the household" (above, pp. 74–5).

provide accounts to the Bishop's auditors, although the treasurer, and probably also the chamberlain, was excused from coming to Durham for this purpose [1] since this would obviously have caused the Bishop inconvenience. Notices of occasional receipts and issues by these two officers provide a very fragmentary picture of their activities and indicate that the chamberlain had the disposal of larger sums than the treasurer of the household. In 1428–9, Thomas Holden received £1,252 at the Durham exchequer, of which sum he gave £40 to the treasurer,[2] and in the same period he also received £474 of the profits from the sale of lead.[3] Holden collected some of the profits of the sheriff of Norham, and made issues to the same officer and the receiver of Norham.[4]

The duties of the treasurer of the household appear to have been confined to the purchase of food for the episcopal *familia*. When the Bishop was in Durham, he was able to live off his estates, but his consumption did not entirely escape the notice of the auditors. The account of the keeper of the Bishop's cattle for the year 1430–1 shows receipts from the sale of herbage and hides and from the receiver-general, chamberlain, and treasurer of the household, and expenditure on the purchase and care of livestock in the Yorkshire estates as well as in County Durham. In addition, the stock-keeper recorded issues of money to the chamberlain and treasurer, who was also shown to have received cattle for consumption: on 15 February 1431, he delivered forty-five beeves priced at 15*s.* each and thirty each valued at 13*s.* 4*d.*, and on 26 December he delivered an even larger number worth £62 17*s.* 8*d.*[5] In 1428–9, the treasurer's account was charged with £45 8*s.* 4*d.* for sixty lambs, one hundred and forty sheep, three large and twelve other beeves and thirty-two quarters of malt delivered to the clerk of the kitchen.[6] In this year, Langley spent only two months outside the Bishopric, but the ten months passed in Durham included Lent, when it may be trusted that fish replaced the household's meat diet. The large consumption in the Bishop's household must have proved more costly when food had to be purchased in London. Another household office,

---

[1] RG. 189782, 190004 & 190307.
[2] RG. 190184. [3] RG. 190015.
[4] RG. 190004; Durham Sheriffs' Accounts, nos. 3 & 4.
[5] RG. 190307. [6] RG. 190184.

the wardrobe, is mentioned in payments to auditors who went to London to receive the accounts "of the treasurer of the household and of the wardrobe".[1] There may therefore have been an officer known as the wardrober, although it is possible that the treasurer was also responsible for this department, which presumably had charge of the Bishop's vestments and other attire, of the hangings, blankets, and other household fittings, and the provision of livery to the Bishop's servants; that the wardrober (or treasurer-wardrober) had the disposal of certain funds is postulated by his requirement to render accounts. Sometimes the Bishop's private expenses were met by payments from an extraordinary fund, such as the profits realized by the sale of lead, when Robert Rolleston, who had carried out this transaction, made a number of small issues on Langley's orders.[2]

The household of Bishop Langley was more than an organization catering for his private comfort: it contained the mainspring of the administration of the palatinate of Durham, as well as the diocesan secretariat. In the same way that the King of England exercised personal control over all departments of his government by means of the Privy Seal Office and, to a lesser extent, of his signet also, the Bishop employed comparable small seals to direct the activities of his officers in County Durham. These seals were taken with him wherever he might go. Thus he is known to have issued a warrant under his privy seal to the constable of Durham, written a letter to the Subprior and Convent sealed with his signet, and, in addition, sent commissions to them and to John Newton under the diocesan seal *ad causas*, all on 6 October 1416 when he was with the King in Calais.[3] Letters issued under the great seal in the Durham chancery, unless of a routine nature, were nearly all authorized by warrants under the Bishop's privy seal and signet [4] and subjects engaged in litigation involving the Bishop had to sue for his writ *de procedendo* under the privy seal.[5] The auditors required accounting officers to produce warrants to explain their issues or might themselves be directed by the Bishop to make allowances.[6] Sometimes the Bishop sent administrative orders direct to the subordinate officials, as to the sheriff, when the

---

[1] RG. 188782 & 190004.   [2] *Scr. Tres*, Appendix, p. ccccxli.
[3] *Reg.* nos. 419–23.   Illustrations of these three Seals are given in Plates III and IV of *Archæologia, 1922*.
[4] Above, pp. 59–60.   [5] Above, p. 67.
[6] Above, pp. 86–8; DCD. 1.11. Pontificalia 12.

signet was employed,[1] and the same seal was also used in some correspondence touching the administration of the diocese.[2] The close attention paid by Langley to all particulars of his temporal government has already been illustrated by his correspondence with the receiver-general, whose articles may be likened to the lists of recommendations submitted to the King by his Privy Council.[3] This ceaseless interest and control persisted during Langley's many and often long absences from Durham, and even when he went abroad he did not, unlike at least one of his predecessors,[4] appoint a lieutenant to take charge of his government though its efficiency must have occasionally been threatened by this retention of full powers. For instance, when Langley was in Italy in 1409, not one letter patent was issued from the Durham chancery.

If the Bishopric had been threatened by a sudden emergency in the Bishop's absence, when he was too distant to be consulted, measures for its protection would doubtless have been prepared by his council. The place of this body in the palatine government had been established in the course of past centuries, although its composition and authority had tended to fluctuate, until from being a feudal body of tenants-in-chief it had become a small, expert, legal, and advisory committee.[5] There are two obstacles to a correct understanding of the position and membership of the council in Langley's pontificate. Firstly, there is the complication caused by his dual status: it is generally possible to distinguish the members of his council for diocesan affairs, the spiritual chancellor and other *jurisperiti*, who witnessed the *acta* recorded in his register,[6] but sometimes laymen appeared on these ecclesiastical occasions, notably Thomas Holden, the chamberlain. Sir Ralph Eure, the steward, and Sir Thomas Surtees were present when a notary was licensed in 1412,[7] and the committal by the Bishop of the administration of the will of the Earl of Westmorland to his executors in 1425 was witnessed by the temporal chancellor, the sheriff, a justice of assize, and the Bishop's attorney in his palatine chancery;[8] as the Earl was the foremost of the Bishop's tenants-in-chief and as his dispositions for his estate were likely to

---

[1] Above, p. 61.
[2] *Reg.* I, p. xli.
[3] Above, pp. 77–8; cf. CPS. 12 and *PPC.* II, pp. 231–2, 363–7.
[4] *Reg. Palatinum Dunelm.* III, pp. 208–10.
[5] Lapsley, *County Palatine*, pp. 136–48.
[6] Below, pp. 170–1.
[7] *Reg.* no. 221.
[8] Reg. fo. 297.

prove contentious,[1] it was natural that Langley should have had a number of his secular ministers present on this occasion. The second obstacle is a dearth of evidence: because of his aversion to grants in perpetuity, Langley did not grant a single charter, so that there are no available lists of witnesses to enable a reconstruction of his council to be made. The practice of some of his predecessors in retaining tenants-in-chief and lawyers to be paid members of their councils [2] was equally repugnant to him and the only indication that Langley retained any of his tenants as councillors is the record of the grant of cloth for robes to two men,[3] one of whom, Thomas Surtees, has just been observed as a witness to some diocesan business.

In addition to the list of witnesses to the grant of administration to the Earl of Westmorland's executors, there are a few scattered references to the members of Langley's palatine council. In 1416, the sheriff of Westmorland was given 66s. 8d. for his expenses in coming to Gateshead "to meet the bishop's council", the councillors being Ralph Eure, the steward, William Chancellor, the temporal chancellor, and William Claxton, the sheriff.[4] When Langley answered his receiver-general's enquiries about Claxton's accounts as sheriff and the appointment of his successor, he wrote that the question of whether or not Robert Eure should be appointed before Claxton presented his accounts should be decided by Ralph Eure and the other justices, the constable (i.e. chancellor), Newton himself, and others of the council.[5] There are two indications that the whole board of auditors were regarded as councillors, as its formation by the chief financial officers would suggest: [6] in 1419–20, 70s. was paid to the steward and others of the council being present at the audit, and in 1428–9 an allowance was made in one account by the steward, auditors, and others of the council.[7] Prior Wessington once referred to the sheriff and others of the council,[8] and there is some reason for supposing that he himself was associated with this body. The composition of Langley's palatine council thus appears to have been almost exclusively official, formed by the leading ministers of his government, namely the steward, chancellor, receiver-general, sheriff,

---

1 Below, pp. 107–8.   2 Above, p. 89.
3 Above, p. 77.   4 RG. 189809; DCD. 3.3. Pontificalia 3.
5 DCD. Additional Doc. 103.   6 Above, p. 83.
7 RG. 189782 & 190184.   8 Below, pp. 103–4.

justices of assize, attorney in chancery, and probably the receiver of Howden. The existence of a healthy corporate spirit among these ministers is revealed by the association of a number of them, including the chancellor and receiver-general, in the establishment of the guild of Corpus Christi in St Nicholas', Durham, in 1436.[1]

Two names may be added to the list of councillors, clerks who held no office in Durham but were given occasional employment by the Bishop: these were William Mablethorp, an official of the Duchy of Lancaster and one of the Bishop's auditors,[2] who assisted in making the survey of the Bishopric[3] and received a number of benefices from Langley, including the rectory of Gateshead and a prebend at Norton;[4] and John Thoralby, once a clerk in the chancery of the Duchy of Lancaster[5] and later a master in the King's Chancery.[6] He was Langley's attorney in his suit there in 1413,[7] a trustee in the foundation of the chantry in the Galilee Chapel,[8] and a member of the commission that made the survey; he is seen to have advised Langley on the preparation of writs,[9] was often in the episcopal household, both in London and in the diocese,[10] and was one of the Bishop's proxies in Parliament in 1428 and 1431.[11] Thoralby was well rewarded for his attendance and counsel, receiving the rich church of Whitburn and prebends at Chester-le-Street, Darlington, and Lanchester. Langley obviously had a strong affection for him.[12]

The presidency of the Bishop's council belonged to his steward of Durham; it was customary for records to refer to "the steward and others of the council". In addition to his duties in the management of the Bishop's estates,[13] the steward was named in all commissions appointing justices of assize and gaol delivery, justices of the peace and auditors,[14] and in occasional commissions of enquiry into the illegal construction of weirs on rivers and other

---

[1] Rot. C. m. 11.
[2] Somerville, *Duchy of Lancaster*, p. 439; and see above, p. 83.
[3] Rentals and Surveys, 21/29, fo. 2.
[4] *Reg.* nos. 169 & 312.
[5] Somerville, p. 477.   [6] Foss, *Judges*, IV, pp. 63 & 261.
[7] Chancery: *Placita in Cancellaria*, file 24, no. 7; and see above, p. 54.
[8] *CPR. 1413–1416*, pp. 206–7.   [9] Above, p. 77.
[10] *Reg.* nos. 159 & 477; *CCR. 1413–1417*, p. 435; *1422–1429*, pp. 274–5, 333, 338, 406 & 412.
[11] *Reg.* nos. 701 & 897.   [12] Ibid. 1072; and see below, p. 224.
[13] Above, pp. 80–1.   [14] Above, pp. 62–3 & 83.

matters requiring investigation.[1]   An illustration of the steward's
political capacity, in which "he represented the Bishop as head
of the civil government of the palatinate",[2] is given by the arrangements made for arbitration between Langley and Sir William
Eure in 1432, when the steward entered into a bond to Eure on
behalf of the Bishop, who could not himself have entered into a
contract of this nature with a subject, while Eure made his
obligation payable to the steward.[3]   On his accession, Langley
retained Skirlaw's steward, Sir Ralph Eure, who already had
fourteen years' experience in his important office.[4]   He was one
of the wealthiest landowners in northern England below the
ranks of the peerage, with estates in Yorkshire and Northumberland as well as lands in Durham worth nearly £100 per annum,[5]
and distinguished himself as a zealous supporter of Henry IV in
the suppression of the rebellions of the Percies in 1403 and
Archbishop Scrope in 1405.[6]   In 1403 he had been recommended
by the royal Council for appointment to the office of steward of
the King's household.[7]   Whatever Langley's feelings were with
regard to Ralph Eure, it would hardly have been politic to dispense
with the services of one so much in royal favour, but after the
steward's death in 1422 he appointed as his successor a man who
owed everything to him.   This was Thomas Holden,[8] who was
one of the few stewards of Durham not a member of one of the
county's leading families.   Like most of the other members of the
Bishop's household, of which he was chamberlain,[9] Holden was
a Lancastrian, from Holden near Whalley,[10] and was attached to
Langley from 1401 at the latest.[11]   His only territorial connection
with Durham was the lease to him for life of the manor of Lud-
worth in 1411; a few months after he became steward, he decided
to fortify his house there,[12] which is rather suggestive.   Holden's
appointment as steward marked a further stage in the process
already seen in the financial administration, now under the
control of the new office of receiver-general, whereby authority

[1] Rot. A. m. 9d; B. m. 17d; E. mm. 11 & 17.
[2] Lapsley, *County Palatine*, p. 78.   [3] Below, p. 119.
[4] *DKR. 33*, p. 55.   [5] Reg. IPM. ff. 214–17.
[6] J. S. Roskell, *The Commons in the Parliament of 1422* (Manchester, 1954),
pp. 178–9.
[7] CPS. 12.   [8] Rot. E. mm. 7d. & 8.
[9] Above, p. 93.   [10] *Reg. Chichele*, II, p. 658.
[11] Reg. Scrope, fo. 5v.   [12] Rot. A. m. 6; E. m. 13d.

was concentrated in the hands of men closely associated with the Bishop, past or present members of his household, whose earlier connections were with his native county of Lancashire rather than Durham itself.

The financial aspect of the work of the Bishop's council has already been indicated; the board of auditors could be described as a select committee of the council.[1] A warrant under Langley's privy seal shows that he had conferred with his council about the Prior of Durham's claim to half the fines imposed on his tenants in the Bishop's courts.[2] Some of the letters on the chancery rolls were warranted *per consilium*, namely the appointment of a receiver of Norham, licences to widows of tenants-in-chief to remarry, the grant of the custody of a ward of the Bishop for three years,[3] and the grant of livery of certain lands. This last was said to have been made with the assent of James Strangways, Christopher Boynton, and others of the council in chancery; although according to the Bishop's rental the tenant should have paid an annual rent of 8s., the inquisition *post mortem* had found the sum to be 4s. 4d. The tenant had shown a charter to confirm the inquisition's report.[4] Obviously this livery was only granted after some discussion in chancery: both Strangways and Boynton were justices of assize in Durham.[5] A bond that a certain man should be brought before the council [6] indicates that, like the King's Council, it was exercising some judicial powers. It was also occasionally permitted to use its own initiative, when the Bishop charged it to take action on his behalf in deciding administrative problems, as in the question of the appointment of a new sheriff.[7] Sometimes the council took action to deal with threatened disorders. In 1432, Prior Wessington excused himself from attendance at the Black Monks' chapter for the reason that he had been requested by the sheriff and others of the Bishop's council to be present when an attempt was made to bring to an end certain disputes then prevailing among leading men of the county.[8] When Langley was in London in January 1434 attending to business touching his palatinate, he wrote to Wessington to inform him of the latest developments; he had

---

[1] Above, p. 83.   [2] Durham Sheriffs' Accounts, no. 2.
[3] Rot. A. mm. 1 & 2; E. mm. 10d. & 11.   [4] Rot. E. m. 5d.
[5] Rot. E. mm. 8 & 18d.   [6] Rot. D. m. 4d.
[7] Above, p. 100.   [8] DCD. Reg. Parvum I, fo. 62v.

already "at diverses tymes writen to my conestable of Duresme, to Sir Richard Bukley my receyvor theer and to other myn officiers" and now charged the Prior "to suche as yow semes necessarye and in especiall to myn officiers at Duresme and to Sir Nichol Hulme gyfe informacion of this my lettre".[1]   In his indenture with the constable of Norham Castle, Langley envisaged a situation when he or his successors might not be readily available in a grave emergency and stipulated that the council should be approached for guidance on such an occasion,[2] but in normal circumstances the Bishop alone exercised the effective direction of his government.   His council was an executive body, deliberative only as he chose, and it had no control over his supreme authority.

4 BISHOP LANGLEY AND HIS SUBJECTS

The ceremonial commencement of Langley's rule in Durham came a year after his consecration, when on 4 September 1407 he was enthroned by the Prior in Durham Cathedral.   The day had been chosen out of respect for local sentiment, for it was the Feast of the Translation of St Cuthbert.   There was a large and distinguished assembly present.   The King's son John, Warden of the East March, the Bishop of Carlisle, and the Abbots of Blanchland, Jervaulx, and Egglestone were there.   The majority were the Bishop's tenants-in-chief—Ralph Neville, Earl of Westmorland, and his son John, Lords Mauley and Dacre, Baron Hilton, Gilbert and Robert Umfraville, John and Marmaduke Lumley, Thomas Grey of Hetton, Ralph Eure, Robert Ogle, and seven other knights.[3]   They had come not only to witness the ceremony, but doubtless also to offer the Bishop homage as their temporal lord.

The majority of the Bishop's tenants-in-chief held their lands of him by "military service", which at this date meant homage, fealty, and suit of court.[4]   Three principal courts were held each year in Durham Castle, Sadberge, and Norham Castle, where certain tenants of the county, wapentake, and shire respectively had to pay their suit, while other tenants had to attend at the common courts in these centres, which were held fortnightly in

---

[1] DCD. Locellus 25, no. 28; and see below, p. 129.
[2] Lapsley, *County Palatine*, p. 151.
[3] DCD. Cartulary I, ff. 118v.–19v.   [4] Reg. IPM. ff. 164v.–5.

Durham and every three weeks in Sadberge and Norham.[1] There was a fourth court for the barony of Coatham Mundeville.[2] Most tenants also had to pay an annual rent in quarterly instalments at the exchequers of Durham and Norham, although it is apparent that this money was in fact collected by the Bishop's coroners,[3] and some estates were charged with services in kind. Thus the tenant of the manor of Aislaby, valued at 100s. per annum beyond its services, had to perform fealty, pay an annual rent of 60s., and guard a fourth part of the gaol in Sadberge; the manor of Henknowl, also worth 100s. to its tenant, was charged with a rent of 8s. and the provision of four oxen for the carriage of the Bishop's wine; and the tenants of the two portions of the manor of Little Usworth each owed military service and an annual rent of 5s., were obliged to pay 5s. towards the common aid (*commune auxilium*) when it was imposed on the Bishopric, 5s. whenever a relief was due, and 2s. 6d. in the case of forfeiture, to provide a greyhound when a chase was publicly announced and the service pertaining to a quarter of a carucate of land if an army were summoned.[4]   Tenants of property in the Bailey of Durham city were charged with the service of "Castelward" in time of war [5] and some tenants in Norhamshire had to assist in guarding Norham Castle; one of these tenants paid 20s. a year for castleguard in addition to the annual rent for his land,[6] and it is likely that this service was usually commuted for money payments. Another charge of a military nature was the annual provision of a catapult,[7] and other services included assistance in the chase; [8] while tenants of the manor of West Auckland held their land in drengage by the servile duties of providing labour for the harvesting of the Bishop's crops.[9]

The good order of the Bishopric rested upon the personal relations of the Bishop and his more powerful tenants.   Foremost among his subjects was the Earl of Westmorland, the most formidable magnate in the north of England now that the Percies had been defeated in rebellion.   The family of Neville had lived in County Durham for centuries, but in recent years had risen to national prominence and acquired lands in many parts of the

1 Reg. IPM. ff. 167, 168 & 208v.   2 Ibid. 228v. & 244v.
3 Above, p. 69.   4 Reg. IPM. 167, 171v. & 216.
5 Ibid. 179 & 199v.   6 Ibid. 230.
7 Reg. IPM. fo. 198.   8 Ibid. 200.
9 Ibid. 172v., 183v., 184v. & 217.

8

country. Its main power was concentrated in south Durham
and north Yorkshire, round its castles of Brancepeth, Raby,
Middleham, and Sheriff Hutton. Ralph was created Earl of
Westmorland by Richard II, but he married Joan Beaufort, a
daughter of John of Gaunt, and he therefore supported Henry IV
from the time of his invasion in 1399.[1] The importance of the
Neville family in Durham is illustrated by a letter written to the
Pope by Henry VI after Langley's death: the King recommended
that Robert Neville, Bishop of Salisbury, a younger son of the first
Earl and Joan Beaufort, be translated to Durham, and it was
pointed out that Robert was a member of the most illustrious
family in that county and his translation would therefore be of
great benefit to Durham.[2] That Langley should be on good
terms with the Nevilles was expedient from a local point of view,
but the connection had wider implications, for Countess Joan was
the sister of Henry, Bishop of Winchester. It has already been
indicated that Langley's relations with Henry Beaufort were not
unfriendly,[3] but, clearly, Langley could not afford to quarrel for
fear of repercussions in his county palatine.

In the lifetime of the first Earl Langley's connection with the
Nevilles was free from complications and their relations har-
monious. Ralph and Langley would have been acquainted for
some years before 1406, as co-executors of John of Gaunt and
members of the King's Council, and in 1405 Henry Beaufort and
Langley were associated in a body of trustees who were to enfeoff
Neville in the honour of Cockermouth after its forfeiture by the
Earl of Northumberland.[4] The Earl headed the commission of
the peace in County Durham.[5] His conventional piety, evidenced
by his foundation of Staindrop college,[6] would have influenced
his attitude to his Bishop. He decided upon a career in the
Church for his son Robert, to whom the Pope granted a dispensation to hold benefices although he was only seven years of age,
in 1411.[7] Three years later, Langley collated Robert to a prebend at Auckland.[8] When Ralph drew up his will in 1424, his
choice of supervisors emphasized the triple relationship between

---

[1] C. W. C. Oman, *Warwick the Kingmaker* (1909), pp. 13–15.
[2] *Correspondence of Thomas Bekynton* (Rolls Series, 1872), Vol. I, pp. 91–3; and
see below, p. 144.
[3] Above, p. 28.   [4] *CPR. 1405–1408*, p. 50.
[5] Rot. A. m. 7; E. m. 8.   [6] Below, p. 188.
[7] *CPL*. VI, p. 247.   [8] *Reg*. no. 307.

himself, the Beauforts, and Langley, for the three he named were the Bishops of Durham and Winchester, and Thomas Beaufort, Duke of Exeter.[1] He died on 21 October 1425.[2] As his son John had died in 1420, leaving a son, Ralph, the Earl's heir was a minor, who became the King's ward,[3] while his lands in Durham were taken into the Bishop's custody.[4]

The first Earl had married twice: Margaret Stafford, his first wife, had predeceased him by some thirty years, the second, Joan, lived until 1440.[5] Margaret had given him nine children, Joan fourteen. The children of the first marriage had been found wives and husbands from the families of north-east England; those of the second made splendid matches, as befitted the kinsmen of the royal house, so that the power of the family was spread throughout the kingdom. Joan's eldest son, Richard Neville, married the sole heiress of the Earl of Salisbury, to whose title and lands he succeeded in 1429.[6] Younger sons became magnates by right of their wives and the daughters married the greatest peers of the realm, the youngest, Cecily, making the most momentous match of all: she married Richard, Duke of York, and was the mother of Edward IV and Richard III.[7] The Earl of Westmorland's provision for his second wife and their family was to prove a bone of contention between the two branches of the Nevilles. In 1404, he had arranged that Sheriff Hutton and other estates in north Yorkshire should be settled on himself and Joan and their heirs male,[8] and thus deprived the heir to his title of part of the family possessions. His grandson Ralph proved his age and received livery of his lands outside Durham in 1429;[9] the separate inquisition to prove his age in the Bishopric was taken in 1432, when livery of his lands in the county was granted.[10] Ralph now began to try to recover what he, not unjustly, regarded as his rightful property, in litigation against Countess Joan and the Earl of Salisbury. The dispute was brought before the King's Council and Parliament.[11] This litigation was carried on for many years, but the parties eventually took to the field.[12] Finally,

1 *Wills and Inventories*, I, p. 73.   2 Reg. IPM. fo. 230.
3 *CPR. 1422–1429*, p. 334.   4 Rot. E. m. 15d.
5 Reg. IPM. fo. 308v.   6 *PPC*. III, pp. 324–6.
7 Surtees, *Durham*, IV, p. 159.   8 *CPR. 1401–1405*, p. 470.
9 *CCR. 1422–1429*, p. 428.   10 Rot. D. m. 6.
11 *Select Cases before the King's Council 1243–1482* (Selden Society, 1918), pp. cix–cx, 101–2.   12 *Excerpta Historica*, pp. 2–3.

the two branches of the family were ranged against each other in the Wars of the Roses, which their quarrel had helped to bring about.

In Langley's day the breach was already open, and there is no doubt which side he favoured: his long connection with the Beauforts made him a partisan of Countess Joan and her children. Langley was one of Richard Neville's feoffees when the latter was preparing to go to France on military service.[1] Richard was first appointed to the commission of the peace for Durham in 1422 and became its leader in 1427; in 1433 he was joined by his brothers George, Lord Latimer, and William, Lord Fauconberg.[2] The second Earl of Westmorland was never appointed to a commission in the Bishopric. The only known occasion of a disagreement between Langley and Prior Wessington arose out of the Neville family quarrel. On 20 September 1434, Langley wrote to the Prior in some displeasure: he had learnt that an earlier will of the first Earl of Westmorland had been delivered to Prior Hemmingburgh in 1400, and Wessington had refused to surrender this will to Countess Joan and the Earl of Salisbury, who were the executors of Ralph Neville's last will. The Prior was threatened with ecclesiastical censure if he continued to withhold the earlier will from these executors.[3] Cardinal Beaufort wrote to Wessington on the same matter,[4] and it is likely that he yielded to this pressure as there is no further evidence of any strain in his relations with the Bishop.[5] As Warden of the West March, Richard Neville was an important figure in the north of England,[6] and Langley undoubtedly relied upon his assistance in the government of the Bishopric. Finally, the Bishop appointed him one of the executors of his will, and when probate was granted at the Earl's castle of Middleham in 1439, he was one of the few executors who immediately undertook the administration of the will.[7] It is clear that there had been affection on both sides.

Langley's relations with the family of Lumley were also cordial. The Lumleys of Lumley Castle were, after the Nevilles, the most important of the Bishop's lay tenants. In County Durham alone their estates were worth nearly £250 a year, and they also had

---

[1] *CPR. 1429–1436*, pp. 122–3.   [2] Rot. E. mm. 8 & 16; C. mm. 7 & 11.
[3] *Reg.* no. 1112.   [4] DCD. Locellus 25, no. 78.
[5] Below, pp. 200–1.   [6] Below, p. 159.
[7] *Scr. Tres*, Appendix, p. ccxlvii.

lands in Yorkshire, Lancashire, Westmorland, and Northumberland. Ralph Lumley was the first member of his family to
receive a writ of summons to Parliament, in 1384. In 1400, he
rebelled against Henry IV and was attainted for treason, his
estates being seized by the King. His son John petitioned for
their restoration in 1405 and was given livery. The success of his
petition was doubtless in part due to his connection with the
Nevilles, for his mother was the sister of the Earl of Westmorland
and he himself was apparently educated in the household of the
Earl's son John. It was naturally desirable for the Bishop to be
on good terms with so important and well-connected a tenant, and
Langley's relations with John Lumley were undoubtedly friendly.
He was godfather to John's first son, Thomas,[1] whose name was
presumably chosen in honour of the Bishop: it was not a Christian
name usually given to a Lumley, at least not to the first son.
Thomas was a minor when his father was killed at the battle of
Baugé in 1421, and his wardship and marriage were granted to a
commission formed by four of Langley's associates, including
John Thoralby and Thomas Holden.[2] Langley had obviously
used his influence in the central government to obtain this grant
and his connection with the transaction is borne out by the
fact that Lumley was married to the daughter of Sir James
Harrington,[3] who was a relative of the Bishop.[4] Thomas Lumley
was given livery of his lands in Durham in 1431 and appointed to
the commission of the peace two years later; on 2 May 1436, he
was granted the office of chief forester of Weardale.[5] John
Lumley's brother Marmaduke also received the Bishop's patronage: he obtained his first benefice from Langley, the deanery of
Lanchester, on 1 May 1417. In 1422, he was collated to the
archdeaconry of Northumberland, and the Bishop also gave him
a prebend at Osmotherley. Marmaduke became Bishop of
Carlisle in 1430.[6]

The report of the inquisition to prove that Thomas Lumley was
of age provides a glimpse of life in fifteenth-century Durham.
The twelve jurors all gave their reasons for remembering when

---

[1] R. L. Storey, "Marmaduke Lumley, Bishop of Carlisle", *Transactions of the
Cumberland and Westmorland Antiquarian and Archaeological Society*, 1955, pp.
113–14.

[2] *CPR. 1416–1422*, p. 443.   [3] *Complete Peerage*, VIII, 273.

[4] *Coram Rege* Roll, Michaelmas 2 Henry V, m. 15d.

[5] Rot. D. m. 3; C. mm. 7 & 11.   [6] Storey, op. cit. pp. 115–18.

Thomas was baptized in the collegiate church of Chester-le-Street by the Dean, Robert Ashburn,[1] on 21 January 1410; the godparents were the Bishop, William, Baron Hilton, and Isabella Claxton, lady of Horden. It must have been a memorable event, for the child was the heir to great estates, and this "proof of age" is therefore likely to be a true account, as the correlation of some of the evidence of different witnesses proves. But even if it were just another example of the "common form" usual in such inquisitions, it does provide examples of the common-place activities of the Bishop's subjects. William Forster and Thomas Burdon said that they had ridden with the Bishop from Auckland to Chester-le-Street, Burdon accompanying his master Thomas Lyes. William Belasis had been in Durham city with his father, the coroner of Darlington ward,[2] and they met the Bishop at Sunderland bridge when they were on their way home. John Esh went into Durham to buy meat; there he met John Newton, the Master of Sherburn hospital, who told him he was about to join the Bishop at Chester. Henry Ravensworth was then living with his father; he went to the church to see the baptism. Baron Hilton had been met by two of the jurors, John Scrutwick, who was coursing a hare in the company of John Hedworth, and John Gilford, who was staying with Sir William Tempest at Washington and invited the Baron in for a drink. John Claxton, a member of the household of the lady of Horden, went with her to Chester-le-Street. Attendance on his master, the Rector of Houghton-le-Spring,[3] took William Norman there. Thomas Boulfleur was at Chester with William Melot; they were hunting a fox, but when he saw the Bishop coming, Boulfleur went with him and held a torch in the church. Robert Marley went to the chapel of Tanfield, in the parish of Chester and John Mason, a chaplain in the parish church, came to celebrate mass and told Marley of the baptism. Robert Horner heard the news in a similar way, from the clerk who brought bread and wine from the parish church to the chapel of Lamesley, where he too had gone to hear mass.[4]

The picture given by this inquisition is a happier one than the

---

[1] He was dean from 1408 to 1413 (*Reg.* nos. 69 & 317).
[2] Robert Belasis, appointed 24 January 1410 (Rot. B. m. 2).
[3] John Newton, the same as the Master of Sherburn.
[4] Reg. IPM. ff. 262v.–3v.

majority of the records provide: the general impression to be derived is of an age of violence and lawlessness. Pardons for murder are not infrequent on the rolls of the Bishop's chancery. In some cases the circumstances are described: there would be a quarrel, and, as most men went armed, death ensued. William Cowherd was guarding Bearpark Moor for his father, its keeper, when he saw John Forster, a skinner, carrying a sack full of nuts. "Where did you get those nuts?" said Cowherd. "What business is that of yours?" retorted Forster. "I think you gathered them in this park, which is in my care, so I will have either them or your pledge," was Cowherd's answer. Forster refused to give either. The men quarrelled, and Cowherd struck Forster with a knife, fatally wounding him.[1]   On a certain night, John Waller of Sunderland exchanged insults with William and Robert Herd in the house of John Piper, probably an ale-house. The disputants went out on to the road, where Waller struck both the Herds with a knife, called a "thwytill"; they died from their wounds two days later.[2]   On two occasions, death was caused by arrows;[3] the murderers must have lain in wait for their victims. The offenders in these cases were generally described as yeomen or labourers.

The landed class was no less violent. On 6 May 1411, Sir Robert Hilton rode into Sunderland with a considerable following, in warlike manner. On Hilton's order, one of his servants fired an arrow at John Duckett, which struck him in the throat; when he lay dying, a second servant hit him with the pommel of his sword. A few days later, Sir William Hilton and others made bonds to the Bishop in a thousand marks that neither he nor his retainers would do any harm to certain men of Sunderland, and a similar bond was made for Robert Hilton. These pledges were presumably honoured, and the reward for this good faith was a pardon for Duckett's murder, granted in 1412.[4]   There was a feud between the families of Marley and Cooper, both of which lived at Langton. On 1 September 1408, the Marleys killed Henry Cooper. Three weeks later, bonds were made in the palatine chancery that the Marleys would not harm William and John Cooper. These recognizances were renewed on 6 September 1410, and the Marleys received a pardon for the murder on

1 Rot. C. m. 6.   2 Rot. B. m. 16.
3 Rot. A. m. 8; E. m. 13.   4 Rot. A. mm. 7d., 8d. & 9.

24 December.[1] There is no further evidence about this quarrel and the two families had presumably been reconciled. Bonds were commonly employed to restrain certain men from attacking others, but, as in these two cases, they were made too late, and followed riotous behaviour.

Even the Bishop's officers engaged in private quarrels. When Sir William Claxton told Langley that he was afraid to submit his accounts as sheriff before Sir Ralph Eure,[2] his fear was not of Eure as steward but as his father-in-law. After several years of marriage to Eure's daughter Elizabeth, who gave him a number of children, Claxton abandoned her and took one Christine Scot to live with him.[3] The receiver-general had told Langley of this scandal at the same time as he asked for instructions about Claxton's accounts and the appointment of his successor,[4] and the Bishop replied that he had written to the vicar-general on this subject [5] as it more properly belonged to his spiritual jurisdiction. Claxton's domestic arrangements were not disturbed by the ecclesiastical authority for several years, but the animosity of the Eures continued to be directed against him by the steward's sons William and Robert after Ralph's death in 1422; they were then each bound in a thousand marks not to do any harm to Claxton.[6] Eventually, in response to a papal bull of 18 November 1423, the Bishop as ordinary cited Claxton to appear before him on 5 April 1424 to answer the charge of adultery. The citation was issued in the parish of Easington and also throughout Northumberland,[7] which indicates that Claxton had thought it safer to live outside County Durham. The absence of records of any further proceedings against him or of bonds with the Eures indicates that Claxton submitted to his diocesan, and was thereby brought to make his peace with his brothers-in-law. He died in 1431. After he had been given livery of his father's lands, his son Robert confirmed the possession by his mother of certain properties, and she in turn renounced all actions against him regarding her husband's estates.[8]

The Convent of Durham did not escape the violence of the Bishop's tenants. In 1410, a dispute had arisen between the

---

[1] Rot. A mm. 4, 6, 6d. & 8.　　　　　　　[2] Above, p. 84.
[3] *Reg.* no. 604.　　　　　　　　　　　　　[4] Above, p. 85.
[5] DCD. Additional Doc. 103.　　　　　　　[6] Rot. E. m. 7.
[7] *Reg.* nos. 604-6.
[8] Rot. D. m. 4d.; DCD. Misc. Charters 6724 & 6725.

Prior and William Billingham; this was submitted to arbitrators, who announced on 20 February 1411 that they found that Billingham owed the Prior homage for lands in Billingham.[1] The matter did not end here, for Thomas Billingham renewed the quarrel with his lord. On 25 June 1419, Billingham and others attacked two monks on the old bridge of Durham, and throughout the following summer he instigated a number of assaults upon members of the Convent. Billingham bore it against the Prior that he had delivered to the sheriff a felon, who had doubtless sought sanctuary in the Cathedral.[2] In one of his attacks, Billingham had been assisted by Thomas Claxton and on 24 August 1419 they were cited to appear before the Bishop's vicars-general to answer a charge of having assaulted the Prior of Coldingham at Chester-le-Street.[3] Claxton's quarrel with the Prior of Durham was at least three years old; in 1416–17, the Prior had brought an action against him for *novel disseisin* at Castle Eden.[4] On 23 September 1421, the Prior agreed to accept the award of Richard Buckley and others in a dispute with Claxton concerning a tenement in Durham city and rents at Castle Eden. On 16 November, the arbitrators decided that the rents belonged to the Convent.[5] The Convent itself, however, was not only the victim of lawlessness. It is a grave commentary on the prevailing attitude to the law that a monk of Durham should have written to the Prior to recommend highway robbery; the object of this enterprise was to prevent a servant of Robert Stanton from delivering papal bulls to his master.[6]

The maintenance of order in England had always depended upon co-operation between the central government and the landed classes, and in Durham, as in the rest of the country, this partnership was dissolving. There was no professional police body to take its place. As has been seen, offenders could be bound over not to pursue a vendetta further, but there was no means of preventing crime, and the administration was often unable to call an evil-doer to account in order to punish him.

---

[1] DCD. Cartulary IV, ff. 142–3.   [2] DCD. Locellus 21, no. 11.
[3] *The Priory of Coldingham* (SS. 1841), pp. 92–3.
[4] DCD. Bursar 1416–17, m. 3d.
[5] DCD. Misc. Charters 5214; Cartulary IV, fo. 131.
[6] DCD. Locellus 25, no. 38. The writer was John Bradbery, ordained acolyte in 1434 (*Reg.* no. 1126). The letter could thus have been written many years after Langley's death.

Thus there was no sufficient deterrent to crime. Bishop Langley's method of tackling the problem is intriguing: he turned to the spiritual arm to remedy the weakness of his secular government. When a crime had been committed, and its perpetrator had escaped undetected, a monition threatening major excommunication was issued against him and all who had aided, favoured, and concealed him, unless he made amends within a limited period, usually two or three weeks.

The use of this threat was quite in order in the cases of thefts from the hospitals of Sherburn and Gateshead, and perhaps even against those sons of iniquity who had poached in the Rector of Sedgefield's fishpond and taken wine from his cellar.[1] The practice of taking arms into the churchyard at Lanchester was obviously undesirable. Thefts of charters,[2] a seal,[3] cattle,[4] and chests from an inn in Durham city [5] were held equally reprehensible. A degree of absurdity was reached, however, when excommunication was threatened against the persons who had set dogs on a cow in calf and had thus caused the death not only of the cow but also, it was gravely added, of her unborn calf.[6] This extraordinary method of combating crime received papal sanction: William Ord obtained a bull from Martin V directing Langley to issue a monition against those who had broken into Ord's house and stolen goods and charters.[7] Parliament also regarded the practice with favour when, in 1433, it petitioned that, in view of the prevalence of crime in the counties of Shropshire, Hereford, York, Nottingham, Derby, and Sussex, the local bishops should be required to threaten the transgressors with excommunication, "so that those who do not fear the justice of human law might dread the sentence of divine vengeance".[8]

The best example of resort being made to the spiritual arm after failure by the temporal administration occurred in 1432. A ship of the Hanse, with which England was on terms of amity, was wrecked on the coast of the county, near Hartlepool, and its goods were seized by the local inhabitants. Following a petition by the merchants to the Bishop for the restitution of their cargo, an order was sent on 26 July from the secular chancery to Robert Jackson,

---

[1] *Reg.* nos. 391 & 883; Reg. fo. 237.   [2] *Reg.* nos. 870 & 596.
[3] British Museum: Additional Charters, no. 66345.
[4] *Reg.* nos. 655–6, 697 & 844.   [5] Reg. fo. 247v.
[6] *Reg.* no. 913.   [7] Ibid. 850.
[8] *Rot. Parl.* IV, p. 421.

the coroner of Easington ward, requiring him to arrest all the goods he could find, no matter into whose hands they had fallen; the merchants or their attornies would identify the goods, which were then to be restored to them, and they would pay compensation for the trouble taken by persons who had rescued the goods. Anyone who refused to surrender them was to come into chancery to give his reason for their retention.[1] Jackson obviously met considerable opposition, and in consequence a monition was issued on 21 August threatening the excommunication of the unknown persons still holding the goods, unless they were restored to the German merchants or Jackson within fifteen days. This threat did not suffice and on 4 October Langley wrote from York to his vicar-general, empowering him to excommunicate the defiant persons who had ignored the monition. The vicar-general issued the sentence of excommunication on 8 October.[2] Four days later, the merchants appointed Jackson their attorney in Durham in all pleas there and to receive their goods.[3] They had, in fact, left Durham, despairing of recovering their cargo.

Several of the monitions concern offences against Langley himself: the destruction of his mills at West Auckland, Wideopen, and Evenwood, of his trees at Ryton, and of the fences of his park at Darlington and the theft of building material and tools from his manor-house there. In 1435, a savage attack was made upon one of his servants by armed men who had disguised themselves and blackened their faces for their fell purpose.[4] The Bishop was particularly troubled by poaching in his forests, which he regarded as an attack upon the franchises of St Cuthbert and therefore a damnable offence. A monition was issued in 1408 against those who had unlawfully set fire to ling in the Bishop's forest of Weardale.[5] In 1436, Langley ordered that two men who had been poaching in Evenwood should be cited to answer for their offence before him, as ordinary. As the Vicar of Gainford alleged that he dared not serve the citation on William Pudsay for fear of death, the Bishop's apparitor was instructed to cite Pudsay.[6] Nicholas Clerionet and others unknown stole some of the Bishop's cattle at Gainford and were summoned to appear in the consistory court.[7] On 23 January 1437, the clergy of Gainford were

1 Rot. C. m. 6.   2 *Reg.* nos. 1002 & 1013; Reg. fo. 300.
3 Rot. C. m. 6.   4 *Reg.* nos. 807, 982, 984 & 1136.
5 Ibid. 80.   6 Ibid. 1190 & 1194.   7 Reg. fo. 236v.

instructed to announce a monition against unknown persons who had poached in Evenwood on the night of 18 January, and four weeks later Langley ordered that the poachers should be denounced as excommunicate since ten days had passed without any sign of repentance.[1] It is difficult to understand how offenders, if unknown, could be debarred from communion, but it is possible that some people who knew the identity of miscreants may have been stirred to give evidence, as they too were comprehended in monitions. The employment of these measures only emphasizes the inability of the Bishop's secular administration to cope with the lawlessness of his subjects.

5 SIR WILLIAM EURE AND THE ATTACK ON THE BISHOP'S FRANCHISE

There were thus two conflicting elements in the body politic of the Bishopric of Durham: on the one side was the Bishop's administration, closely modelled on that of the King both in practice and in the exercise of prerogative authority, and conducted with a hard efficiency for the purpose of securing for its master due recognition of his regalian status and full enjoyment of his sources of revenue; on the other side were the Bishop's tenants, many of them hot-tempered and ready to resort to violence, men of independent spirit who resented the restrictions imposed by a government from whose close surveillance they could not escape and their dislike of which was probably increased by the prominence in it of "foreigners" from Lancashire. The great crisis of Langley's pontificate came in 1433, when on 1 April inquisitions challenging his franchise were taken by royal commissioners at Newcastle-upon-Tyne and Hartlepool. These inquisitions have been described as "an unusually flagrant case of royal encroachment", but this opinion was based solely on the account of subsequent pleadings in Parliament.[2] A totally different interpretation, by which the Crown can be exonerated from any responsibility for this "invasion" and the blame laid upon a group of the Bishop's tenants, is made possible by evidence preserved among the records of the royal and palatine chanceries and the archives of the Prior and Convent of Durham. While this evidence reveals the course and nature of the crisis it is still

---

[1] Reg. ff. 240 & 241v. [2] Lapsley, *County Palatine*, p. 241.

incomplete, for the records available are almost entirely legal and official in nature and therefore to some extent obscure the motives and feelings of the actors in one of the most important chapters in the history of the palatinate.

The inquisition taken at Hartlepool [1] made it clear that several of Langley's subjects had grievances against him, but it is probable that these might have remained unpublished but for the opportunity given by the proximity of the royal commission and for the direction given to the discontented tenants by a man whose social rank, legal ability, and unscrupulous resourcefulness made him a fitting leader for such a movement. This was Sir William Eure, who was driven by litigation from a position of active loyalty to the Bishop to one of extreme and unconcealed hatred. The son of the steward of Durham,[2] Eure spent some of his earliest years in Langley's household, probably as a page, and was at the age of fifteen married to Maud FitzHugh.[3] He thus made a powerful connection, for his father-in-law, an important magnate in Yorkshire, became chamberlain to Henry V and Treasurer of England. Eure accompanied Lord FitzHugh on the King's French expedition of 1415. His father died in 1422, and William must have been disappointed when Ralph's office of steward was given to Thomas Holden, but he was appointed a justice of assize and to the commission of the peace.[4] Also in 1422, Eure went to Westminster as one of the knights for the county of York.[5] In 1424, he was granted a nine years' lease of mines previously demised to his father, at an annual rent of £212 13s. 4d. He was again appointed to the commission of the peace in 1427, and the custody of the Earl of Westmorland's lands in Durham was granted to him and two others, for one year. In 1430, he was one of those appointed to enquire into the state of Sherburn hospital.[6]

Thus far, Eure's relations with Langley had been amicable; in return for his services, he had been rewarded with some favour. After 1431, however, an estrangement set in. Its first known cause was a law-suit of no great moment. Eure alleged that two of his cattle had been seized by Thomas Ferry, and initiated an action by a writ of replevin. When the case was brought before

---

[1] Printed, with references to related records, as Appendix B, pp. 245–62, below.
[2] Above, p. 102.   [3] *Reg.* no. 188; Reg. IPM. fo. 217.
[4] Rot. E. mm. 7 & 8.   [5] Roskell, *Parliament of 1422*, pp. 81 & 178.
[6] Rot. E. mm. 20d., 15d., 16 & 19.

the Bishop's justices on 22 March 1431, Ferry said that he had taken the beasts in a tenement of the Bishop, whose officer he was, but Eure contended that the ground was common pasture in which he was lawfully entitled to graze his cattle. Ferry then pleaded that he should not be prosecuted further and invoked the Bishop's aid; the proceedings were therefore adjourned so that Eure could obtain the Bishop's writ of *de procedendo* directed to the justices.[1] A much more serious dispute opened in the following year. On 24 August 1432, the Bishop had a writ of *scire facias* issued against Eure which stated that it had been found that when he was granted livery of his father's lands on 14 September 1422, William had been allowed, owing to a mistake on the part of the Bishop's chancery, to enter into possession of the manor of Langley and other lands which had been acquired without the Bishop's licence. He was therefore summoned to chancery to show cause why the Bishop should not seize the lands and recover the issues from the day of livery.[2] Consequently, Eure's attorney came into chancery on 11 September, and also William Raket, the Bishop's attorney, but the hearing was adjourned until 17 December.[3] In the interval, a further move was made against Eure. He had fallen into arrears with the payment of the rent due for his lease of the Bishop's mines, and on 8 December the sheriff was instructed to distrain Eure's goods and, if necessary, his lands to the extent of £365 9s. 5d., which was to be paid into the exchequer by 20 December.[4] In view of the concurrent proceedings in chancery, this measure appears as a deliberate attempt to cripple Eure, but as the sum involved represented nearly two years' rent, it can be seen that he had received a fair measure of leniency.

After this full deployment of the Bishop's legal machinery against Eure, events took a turn that gave some promise of an amicable settlement. Eure wished to arrange a marriage between his daughter Marjory and Christopher Conyers, and obtained from the Pope a bull of dispensation, because of their relationship, which Langley, as ordinary, was to execute. This business was performed at Bishop Auckland on 12 December; Eure was represented by a proctor but his brother Robert, the sheriff, was a witness,[5] and it is clear that the occasion was used to ask the

---

[1] Below, pp. 254–5 (c. 14).   [2] Below, pp. 258–9 (c. 19).
[3] Rot. D. mm. 9–10.   [4] Below, p. 256 (c. 16).   [5] *Reg.* no. 1027.

Bishop to moderate his severity against Sir William. On 16 December, it was agreed that the dispute should be settled by arbitration, and Eure and Thomas Holden, the steward, obviously acting for Langley, made bonds to each other in a thousand marks on the undertaking that Langley and Eure would accept the arbitration of Richard Neville, Earl of Salisbury, regarding the arrears of rent, the suit in chancery, an assize pending before the Bishop's justices, presumably concerning the impounded cattle, and other unspecified matters. The award was to be made before 20 January next (1433).[1] That Langley should have taken the unprecedented step of submitting his quarrel with a subject to mediation does suggest that he was anxious for a settlement. In view of the pending arbitration, the hearing in chancery, when the parties met there again on 17 December, was once again adjourned, to 2 April 1433.[2] There is no indication that Earl Richard made an award, but Langley was still in an accommodating humour on 2 February, when he gave permission for the marriage of Eure's daughter to be celebrated in the chapel of his castle at Witton-le-Wear,[3] while Eure made some attempt to placate the Bishop by paying him some £110 of his debt for the rent of the mines. The complete breakdown of all plans for mediation became apparent on 14 March, when a second writ of *fieri facias* was issued, this time to distrain Eure for £298 before 3 April.[4] He must have felt his position to be desperate, for in addition to the impending distraint, the defence he was to make in the suit in the Bishop's chancery was not one that could be substantiated.[5] There was at hand, however, the means not only of retaliation but of possibly bringing about the complete overthrow of the Bishop's power; could this have been achieved, Eure would have been safe from further prosecution.

On 12 February 1433, the Crown had appointed a commission to make enquiries into infringements of royal rights in the counties of Northumberland, Cumberland, and Westmorland.[6] On 1 April, four members of this commission came to Hartlepool, at the instigation, Langley later alleged, of persons "who bore it ill that the Bishop and his church should be endowed with a great

---

1 Rot. D. mm. 5d.–6d.   2 Rot. D. m. 10.
3 *Reg.* no. 1034.   4 Rot. D. m. 7.
5 Below, p. 132.   6 *CPR. 1429–1436*, p. 276.

regality . . . planning to deprive him of his liberty now that he was stricken with age".[1]   Hartlepool lay in the wapentake of Sadberge, which was once part of Northumberland but had been purchased from the Crown in 1189 and incorporated into the palatinate of Durham,[2] although it was always regarded as separate from the county.   This offered the commission a pretext to enter the Bishop's liberty.   Although Durham was not included in its terms of reference, Northumberland was, and in the inquest's report Hartlepool was said to be in the latter county.   The senior member of the commission to sit at Hartlepool was Henry Percy, second Earl of Northumberland.[3]   That he should have been induced to take part in this invasion of the Bishop's franchise may be explained by Langley's part in the quarrel in the Neville family: the second Earl of Westmorland had married Percy's sister, and he doubtless thought this a good opportunity to embarrass the supporter of his brother-in-law's enemies.   This sister had previously been married to John, Lord Clifford;[4] one of the articles presented concerned his lands in Durham.[5]   Moreover, Percy was Eure's lord for certain lands he held in Northumberland.[6]   Another commissioner, Sir William Tempest, had a grievance against Langley.[7]

There were fifteen jurors.   Five of them, Sir Robert Hilton,[8] Sir Ralph Bulmer,[9] John Hedworth,[10] Thomas Billingham,[11] and Robert Marley [12] had each at some time disturbed the peace of the Bishopric.   Hedworth and another juror, William Alwent, both had complaints to make against the Bishop.[13]   William Eure was not one of the jury, but the amount of information supplied at the inquest about his affairs makes it clear that he was present. Of the twenty-four articles presented, four dealt with the points at issue between Langley and Eure: the account of his attempt to recover his beasts from Thomas Ferry; the distraint arising from his arrears of rent; and the suit in chancery.   Touching the

---

[1] *Rot. Parl.* IV, p. 428.
[2] G. V. Scammell, *Hugh du Puiset, Bishop of Durham* (Cambridge, 1956), p. 49.
[3] Appendix B, p. 245, below.   [4] *Complete Peerage, XII*, Part ii, 549–50.
[5] Below, pp. 250–1 (c. 8).   [6] Roskell, *Parliament of 1422*, p. 178.
[7] Below, pp. 249–50 (c. 7).   [8] Above, p. 111.
[9] He had been bound to do certain men no injury, in 1430 (Rot. D. m. 2).
[10] He had been bound to do no harm to the Prior and Convent, in 1419 (Rot. B. m. 18); and see below, pp. 124 & 147.
[11] Above, p. 113.   [12] Above, p. 111.
[13] Below, pp. 259–60 (c. 20) & 260–1 (c. 23).

distraint, accurate details, to the last penny, were given of the lease to Eure, and the writ of *fieri facias* of 8 December 1432 was quoted in full. The plea in chancery was the subject of two articles: the first is expressed in general terms, without any particular instance being quoted, but it obviously applied to Eure's quarrel with the Bishop. In the following clause, the dates of livery to Eure and of the writ of *scire facias* are given correctly; indeed, it seems that this writ was also produced at the inquest, for the report at this stage reads like a paraphrase of it.[1] Two other articles concern William's brother Robert, that he had been appointed the Bishop's sheriff and escheator and had been given a licence to fortify his house at Bradley. As the dates supplied in these two articles are incorrect,[2] it is not likely that Robert supplied the details, rather that William gave this information from memory as part of his indictment of the Bishop.

The report of the inquest at Hartlepool is nothing less than an outright challenge to the existence of the franchises of the Bishopric of Durham, and nearly every aspect of the Bishop's government was described and condemned. The particulars given have a semblance of truth in that they tally with what is already known of the palatine government, although the jurors sometimes appeared to rely on faulty memories, or even on imagination, in their attempt to provide complete details in selected examples. It is difficult to be certain whether the instances they provided of specific administrative and legal practices were isolated, or, as the jurors implied, chosen from a number of cases, but the repeated resort to William Eure's troubles as material for quotation suggests the former alternative. Most of the clauses of the report conclude with a statement that the transactions they recorded were to the King's prejudice and derogated from his prerogatives. In one respect the report is unhistorical, for it generally implies that Langley was the first bishop to assume the exercise of the various regalian privileges. The twenty-first article summarized the charges against him: it was said that during the whole time since he had become Bishop he had exercised every royal privilege, written or unwritten, save the holding of a parliament.[3] Other articles specified the Bishop's regalian powers: he appointed his justices to hold all crown pleas in

[1] Pp. 254–5 (c. 14), 256 (c. 16) & 257–9 (cc. 18 & 19).
[2] Pp. 248–9 (c. 5) & 253 (c. 11).   [3] P. 260 (c. 21).

9

Durham and Sadberge,[1] his sheriff and escheator in the county and wapentake,[2] and his justices of the peace; the arrest of Thomas Claxton and his being bound over to keep the peace were cited as an instance of the powers these justices of the peace unlawfully [sic] exercised.[3] The Bishop was also shown to claim the lands of traitors against the King; the case of Thomas Grey was quoted.[4] Langley was said to compel the tenants-in-chief of the palatinate to do him homage in the same terms as it was proffered to the kings of England, a form of oath that had in fact been offered to the bishops of Durham for many years past.[5] The only points on which the jurors conceded that Langley was not the first bishop to exercise royal prerogatives were in the holding of pleas before his justices of assize and in the use of a great seal in the palatine chancery, with which his writs were sealed: Bishop Hatfield was said, wrongly, to have been the first bishop to have had such a seal. It was further held against Langley that in the writs issued under this seal he employed such phrases as "against the Bishop's peace" and "contrary to the Bishop's crown and dignity".[6]

Other articles in which Langley was shown to have exercised prerogative authority concerned licences he had granted to fortify a house [7] and for the foundation and endowment of a chantry; [8] again in neither case was he the first bishop to have permitted such transactions.[9] The charge of disregarding statutory legislation in Parliament was made in the clause concerning the licence for a chantry and also with regard to the appointment of a sheriff,[10] whose office certainly had features not permitted elsewhere in England.[11] An instance was cited to illustrate how Langley ignored a provision in the Statute of Merton permitting tenants to appoint attornies to pay suit of court; he had exacted fines from tenants who would not pay suit in person.[12] The severity of the Bishop's administration was further illustrated by the accounts of two transactions where no pretence was made that the King was concerned. It was said that Langley had compelled two of his subjects to pay rent for lands they did not occupy and, with an amusing introduction of a second ground for complaint,

---

[1] Pp. 246–7 (c. 2).   [2] Pp. 248–9 (c. 5).
[3] Pp. 247–8 (c. 4).   [4] Pp. 251–2 (c. 9).   [5] P. 253 (c. 10).
[6] P. 257 (c. 17).   [7] P. 253 (c. 11).   [8] P. 254 (c. 13).
[9] DKR. 31, p. 292; DKR. 32, p. 312.   [10] Below, pp. 248–9 (c. 5).
[11] Above, p. 61.   [12] Below, p. 249 (c. 6).

were worth only half the sum he charged.[1] The Bishop's auditors were said to have committed a defaulting bailiff of Darlington to prison in accordance with the Statute of Westminster II, and after his death there his lands were taken into the Bishop's hands until the debt was paid.[2] Two more articles in the inquisition reported the escape from the Bishop's prison for the clergy of three clerks condemned for felony before his justices and committed to him as ordinary.[3] The escape of prisoners was one of the subjects which the royal commission was required to investigate, although presumably when the inmates of the Bishop's spiritual prison escaped he could, as lord palatine, grant a pardon to himself as ordinary, since elsewhere in the realm bishops had to sue the King for pardons for escapes from their diocesan prisons.

The remainder of the clauses concern Langley's relations with his subjects as their feudal overlord and the activities of his palatine chancery; these are the most interesting of all the articles as they indicate the real cause of discontent in Durham. Six articles reported seizures of land by the Bishop's escheator, either after the death of the tenants or because it had been found that they had changed hands without the Bishop's licence. The Bishop was said to claim the custody of all the lands of his wards: the instance given was of his seizure of the estates of John Lumley, including those he had held of Lord Clifford, during the minority of the heir, and as the boy was the King's ward for lands elsewhere in England, the offence was doubly grave.[4] A second example was given of lands being seized after their tenant's death when some were held of an intermediate lord, the example being John Gilford's lands in Gateshead that he held of Sir William Tempest.[5] In the case of lands being acquired without the Bishop's permission, he was said to have seized the lands and taken their issues until the new owner paid him a fine "at his will".[6] The same subject occurs in a second clause, which cites the process against William Eure and gives part of the defence he was to make six months later; [7] this was by way of illustration of the Bishop's vagaries in granting licences for such acquisitions and of his use of writs of *scire facias* to initiate proceedings in his

1 P. 260 (c. 22).
3 Pp. 253-4 & 255-6 (cc. 12 & 15).
5 Pp. 249-50 (c. 7).   6 P. 247 (c. 3).
2 Pp. 260-1 (c. 23).
4 Pp. 250-1 (c. 8).
7 Below, p. 132.

chancery.[1] The same writ was also said to have been used, again to summon tenants to chancery to give cause why the Bishop should not seize their lands, in cases when livery had been given after the death of previous tenants but had been made in a defective form; the lands would then be seized until new writs of livery were purchased.[2] A specific instance of alleged error in the chancery records was furnished by the case of Peter Tilliol, who had entered into his wife's inheritance before livery was formally given and later paid a fine for their release after the Bishop had seized them, but as this fine was imperfectly recorded, the lands were again seized and Tilliol had to pay a second fine for a fresh livery.[3]

The condemnation of Langley's employment of the writ of *scire facias* was accompanied by criticism of three other writs. William Eure's plea of replevin was cited as an instance of a subject being compelled to sue for a writ of *de procedendo*, and the Bishop was said to have exercised this regalian privilege against all his tenants whenever occasion arose.[4] The issue of a writ of *fieri facias* against Eure was said to have been made without any other legal process, to his great injury, contrary to the law of the land and to the prejudice of the King.[5] A writ directed to John Hedworth, one of the jurors, is given in full: the Bishop had learnt that he held six men against their will and on 6 December 1432 ordered him to appear in the Durham chancery within two days, with his prisoners, to explain to the Bishop and his council why he had seized the men.[6] The jurors alleged that Langley used such writs to compel his subjects to answer him in his chancery for matters concerning himself, even though they were triable at common law. In fact, this writ, which is one of *corpus cum causa*, is unique in the rolls of Langley's chancery, nor has any other example been noticed there of its concluding threat, *et hoc nullatenus omittas sub periculo quod incumbit*;[7] but its citation provided another variant in Langley's methods of compelling his subjects to appear in his chancery.

---

[1] Pp. 258–9 (c. 19).   [2] Pp. 257–8 (c. 18).   [3] Pp. 261–2 (c. 24).
[4] Pp. 254–5 (c. 14); and see above, pp. 66–7.   [5] P. 256 (c. 16).
[6] A bond was made on 8 December 1432 that Hedworth would not leave Durham city without the Bishop's licence; he failed to observe this undertaking and a writ of *scire facias* was therefore directed against him on 28 February 1434 (Rot. D. m. 13d.).
[7] Below, pp. 259–60 (c. 20).

Despite the strong undercurrent of private resentment against Langley betrayed in these articles, there was a certain element of constitutional principle in the quarrel. The charter of King John to the "Haliwerfolk", the men of the franchise of St Cuthbert, was quoted as a preface to the articles of the inquest. This charter had been granted in 1208, when the see was vacant. It forbade that the men of Durham should be impleaded touching their free tenements by any process other than by the assizes of the kingdom; these assizes could be taken in the bishop's court. John also granted that if the bishop took pledges from his tenants unlawfully, the sheriff of Northumberland was to cause them to be restored. The charter concluded, however, with a clause saving the liberties lawfully pertaining to the Bishopric; the jurors at Hartlepool thought it preferable to omit any reference to this proviso.[1] The bishop might well maintain that the authority given to the sheriff of Northumberland in respect of pledges was contrary to his liberties. The grant that assizes could be taken in the bishop's court, however, was observed by the bishops of Durham, to their great advantage: the introduction of this procedure into Durham has been remarked upon as a most significant stage in the development of the palatinate, for the bishop's court was now able to offer "to those who resort to it the benefits of the new procedure to be found in the king's courts, to which, however, it denies them access".[2]

Now Langley had very clear ideas on the implications of his regalian prerogatives, and one of these was that he could not be a party to any suit; an assize could not be brought against him, nor would he resort to this procedure, when a dispute regarding the possession of lands arose between himself and a subject, while the justices were not permitted to proceed without his licence in any suit in which he was directly or indirectly involved. In these latter cases, resort had to be made to him for his writ of *de procedendo*. The Bishop's chancery was the only court where pleas touching lands to which he laid claim could be heard. Thus the jurors at Hartlepool could show that the Bishop had failed to observe King John's charter. The citation of this charter makes it apparent that there existed a belief that the liberties of Durham did not mean only the regalian franchise of the Bishopric, but also certain rights of its subjects. A manifestation of this popular

[1] P. 246 (c. 1).   [2] Lapsley, *County Palatine*, pp. 167–8.

idea was seen in 1436, when the men of Durham made fine with the King rather than pay a subsidy, thus preserving the principle of their immunity from parliamentary taxation.[1] It was also later alleged against Langley that he was planning "to have opteigned certayne thinges agains the fraunchises of Goddes Kyrk and Seint Cuthbert of Duresme".[2] The men of the palatinate could take up the position of defending its liberties against the Bishop.[3]

The dispute with Langley was thus raised to one of principle, but the weakness of his opponents' case was betrayed by an important omission. Why did they not cite the "charter of liberties" granted to his tenants by Anthony Bek in 1303? The charter was a renunciation by Bek of various extortionate practices committed by his government. The jurors of 1433 did not accuse Langley of any such abuses and they were wise to make no mention of Bek's charter, for it showed that the Bishop was entitled to seize all the lands of a deceased tenant-in-chief, including those held of an intermediate lord;[4] it was held against Langley that he had done this, but he was obviously acting within his rights. The holding of the inquisition at Hartlepool may be described as a constitutional rebellion. The jurors knew quite well that Sadberge was part of the Bishopric of Durham; that Langley enjoyed no more regalian prerogatives than his predecessors had done; that the Bishop's title to these liberties was well founded, had been maintained as lawful against earlier challenges and had been repeatedly confirmed by the Crown; and that the inquisition itself was therefore illegal.

Those responsible for this seditious act may have spent some thought on the traditional liberties of the "Haliwerfolk", but more immediate preoccupations brought about their revolt. They felt that Langley's administration was unduly severe, and were aware that they had no lawful means of protection against it. The fact that the Bishop claimed the same privilege as the King in his courts of law, namely that he could not be compelled to defend himself without his consent, was strongly resented. Again,

---

[1] Above, p. 55.

[2] DCD. Locellus 25, no. 28; and see below, pp. 129–32.

[3] Henry VIII's act for resuming liberties to the Crown was a cause of the participation of men of Durham in the Pilgrimage of Grace (R. R. Reid, *The King's Council in the North* (1921), pp. 129–30).

[4] *Records of Antony Bek* (SS. 1953), pp. 93–8; Lapsley, op. cit. pp. 132–3.

when the Bishop did become a party, the suit was heard in his own court; in such a plea in the Bishop's chancery there was no jury. The discontented party therefore felt that the Bishop's position at law was so advantageous that redress of grievances would be sought in vain, yet in view of his regalian status, the Bishop was fully entitled to claim these advantages. There could be no parity as long as he was in possession of his franchise, and its destruction therefore became the objective of his enemies. The appointment of the royal commission to make enquiries in Northumberland offered the malcontents a wonderful opportunity, and when some of its members had been persuaded to hold an investigation into the status of the Bishopric, it was presented that the whole fabric of the palatinate, every facet of its administration and judiciary, was unlawful; the acts of Langley's government were said to be illegal, for he was exercising privileges that belonged to the King alone. Such was the case put against the Bishop by his enemies.

The chronology of events accentuates William Eure's part in the attack on Langley. The inquisition was taken on the day immediately before that appointed for the resumed hearing of the Bishop's suit against him in chancery. In the circumstances, the proceedings had to be adjourned to 17 September;[1] Eure's defence had already been prepared—it is partly given in one of the inquest's articles[2]—but Langley's government had to prepare to defend itself. Prior Wessington assisted the Bishop by having a justification of the liberties of the church of Durham drawn up, based upon chronicles and (forged) charters,[3] and helped to prepare his brief for presentation in Parliament by lending him some of the Convent's muniments for production there.[4] Wessington's loyalty in this crisis was the reward for Langley's consistent policy of friendship towards the Convent.[5] Although an old man and living in semi-retirement, Langley set out for London on 15 April and remained there until August. He knew that he could rely upon the aid of his friends in the King's Council in the defence of his franchise. To this favour he must have owed his appointment, for the first time, to the commission of the peace

---

[1] Below, p. 132.   [2] Below, pp. 258–9 (c. 19).
[3] *Scr. Tres*, Appendix, pp. ccxxviii–xxxv.
[4] DCD. 2.1. Archiepiscopalia 13 bears an endorsement to this effect (Mr M. G. Snape kindly supplied this reference).
[5] Below, pp. 199–201.

for Northumberland, on 16 May;[1] the new position must have been of some value to him. On 5 June, Langley obtained from the royal Chancery an *inspeximus* and confirmation of numerous charters relating to the Bishopric that had originally been granted by Parliament in 1422.[2] This was a very valuable concession indeed, revealing that Langley had the support of the government, and it boded well for the success of his cause. When Parliament met at Westminster on 8 July, Langley introduced a petition, protesting against the inquisitions taken at Newcastle[3] as well as at Hartlepool which, he said, had been brought about by the machinations of his enemies. He gave an account of the liberties of the Bishopric, and cited the judgement given in favour of Antony Bek and later royal confirmations in justification.[4]

William Eure now came into the open as the leader of the Durham malcontents. He presented in Parliament a petition to counter that of Langley; he spoke, he claimed, as much for the King as on his own behalf.[5] He made two main points: that the liberties claimed by the Bishop had not been enjoyed from beyond the time of legal memory and had to a large extent been lost to the Crown through the lies of Bek, and that Sadberge was in Northumberland. Eure had moved the line of attack against the Bishop from the particular to the general: while the rebels at Hartlepool had condemned various details of the palatine government, Eure now tried to prove that the whole franchise of Durham had no legal foundation. His concluding prayer that the King would give justice to his subjects reveals the personal aspect of the attack on the Bishop. The two petitions were then examined, and after much discussion and scrutiny of charters, the answer was given that Hartlepool and other places mentioned in the inquest's report lay in the Bishop's franchise, where the King's writ did not run. This was the judgement made in Parliament by the Crown's legal advisers, but another factor was considered by the Council: Langley's long and faithful services to Henry VI and his forbears were recalled when the King granted his petition. The reports of the inquisitions were therefore cancelled in Parliament and

---

[1] *CPR. 1429–1436*, p. 622.   [2] Ibid. 281.

[3] No record of this inquisition remains, if it were a separate inquest and not an adjourned session of the meeting at Hartlepool; if it were separate, it presumably dealt with Norhamshire.

[4] *Rot. Parl.* IV, pp. 419, 427–9.

[5] *Tam pro domino rege quam pro se ipso, ut asseruit.*

placed among its petitions.[1] At Langley's request, an exemplification of these transactions was issued under the Great Seal on 16 August 1433.[2]

Although the liberties of the Bishopric had been preserved, the dispute between Langley and his subjects was not yet settled. The Bishop returned to London for the autumn session of Parliament. While it was sitting, some knights went to the Earl of Warwick to ask him to persuade Langley to submit his quarrel with Eure to arbitration. Consequently Langley chose the Archbishop of York and the Earls of Warwick, Salisbury, and Northumberland,[3] while Eure named the Bishops of London[4] and Carlisle,[5] to mediate between them. The disputants were to give the arbitrators written articles by Easter, and the decree was to be given a fortnight later (11 April 1434). In the event of deadlock, an umpire was to be chosen to give his verdict before 19 June. This information was given by Langley in a letter he wrote to Prior Wessington on 4 January 1434. At the same time, he told the Prior that he had learnt that certain of his subjects had obtained a copy of a petition he was supposed to have delivered in Parliament in order to obtain some things contrary to the privileges of the church of Durham. They had met in the church of St Nicholas', Durham, and had decided to meet again on 2 January when they would determine that some of their number should be sent to the King's Council to oppose the petition. Langley wrote that he would await their coming until 28 January.[6] In the event, he remained in London until late in February, but there is no indication in the records of the Council that the affairs of Durham were discussed there.

The petition referred to in the letter cannot have been Langley's plea against the inquisitions, which could hardly be described as contrary to the liberties of Durham and, moreover, had been granted some four or five months previously. There is no record of Langley presenting a second petition in the Parliament of 1433,

[1] *Rot. Parl.* IV, pp. 429–31.
[2] DCD. Reg. III, ff. 167v.–72v.
[3] Percy's nomination is inexplicable in view of his part at Hartlepool; it can only be presumed that Langley and he had been reconciled. Warwick was to be named as one of the Bishop's executors (*Scr. Tres*, Appendix, p. ccxlvii) and Archbishop Kemp and Salisbury are known to have been friends of Langley.
[4] Robert FitzHugh, Eure's brother-in-law.
[5] Marmaduke Lumley, a member of the Durham family.
[6] DCD. Locellus 25, no. 28.

but two copies exist of a petition that would merit the description, and which, from the content, obviously relates to the dispute between Langley and his subjects. Both copies are entitled "A petition of the lord Thomas Langley, Bishop of Durham, that he and his successors might have causes and matters concerning the rights and liberties of the Bishop of Durham tried outside the county of Durham; but the petition was not granted."

In the preamble, Langley stated that on several occasions in the past the King's escheator in Northumberland and other persons bearing ill-will against the bishops of Durham and seeking to diminish their territory and authority, had taken inquisitions in the county and liberty of Durham lying between the Rivers Tyne and Tees, and in Northumberland, on matters concerning the said liberty; this had been done on the supposition that Durham was part of the county of Northumberland, whereas it was in fact a county in itself, and all the bishops of Durham had appointed their own chancellor, justices, sheriff, etc., and had enjoyed various other liberties. Certain men of the Bishopric who resented Langley's possession of such privileges and their subjection to his rule had now begun to hold assemblies and to form associations with the purpose of destroying his liberties, and were planning to promote legal actions and, *in specie regis*[1] *partem faciendi*, intended to have trials made of the Bishop's liberties, in the belief that any matter touching the Bishop or his government that came into dispute should be tried by a jury of men of the liberty of Durham. It was their obvious intention to destroy the Bishop's franchise.[2]

The circumstances outlined here indicate that this petition was related to the same dispute between Langley and his subjects that led to the inquisition at Hartlepool; indeed, the reference to the taking of inquisitions in Durham was presumably intended to draw the King's attention to that inquest, and the conclusion that this was held as the result of a conspiracy by certain of the Bishop's subjects is borne out. Further, the statement that the malcontents were claiming to be acting on the King's behalf tallied with William Eure's assertion in Parliament that his petition was made *tam pro domino rege quam pro se ipso*.[3]

The substance of this petition of Langley's was that, in order

[1] MS. *regem.*
[2] DCD. Locellus 21, nos. 21 & 21a.
[3] Above, p. 128.

to thwart the plots of his hostile subjects, new arrangements might be made by the authority of the present Parliament for the trial of two classes of cases. Firstly, he asked that if any issue concerning the Bishop, other than treason or felony, arose within his liberty of Durham which also involved the King and was triable according to common law in the Bishop's court before a Durham jury, it might be sent by the Bishop's justices to the King's justices. The case would then be tried in King's Bench, Common Pleas, or another royal court before a jury of men from the county of York. After trial, the case would be sent back to the Bishop's justices for judgement and termination of the plea. On the other hand, the whole business could be conducted in Durham in the Bishop's court, in the accustomed manner, if the Bishop so chose. The second type of case for which Langley asked for special provision was when the question of whether a place lay between Tyne and Tees, that is, in the county of Durham, or in Northumberland (an obvious allusion to Sadberge), arose in any royal court, even though the King was concerned in the matter. Langley requested that instead of having such a case tried before a Durham jury it might, if the Bishop desired, be tried before a jury from Yorkshire or Northumberland.[1]

Langley was apparently offering to surrender part of his prerogative by allowing a case to be sent for trial in a royal court. This, then, could have been the petition by which he was said to be seeking a diminution of the liberties of St Cuthbert. The liberties in question, however, were not those of the Bishop, but those claimed by his subjects, who thought that they should provide a jury in trials arising from disputes in the Bishopric. Langley was not really giving anything away, for he reserved to himself, his executors, and his successors, the right to choose whether they should take this unprecedented step. His concern was to avoid submitting his affairs to the verdict of a jury composed of hostile subjects. His opponents were planning, he said in the preamble, to associate the King with themselves in suits they would bring against the Bishop, and it was only for cases of this sort that the petition requested provision. If such pleas were raised, then the Bishop could choose to have them taken before a jury about whose partiality he would have less reason to be anxious. No mention was made of suits between the Bishop and

[1] DCD. Locellus 21, nos. 21 & 21a.

his subjects: they would still be tried in his courts, most likely in the chancery at Durham. Had the petition been granted, the Bishop's position would have been fortified by having available the facilities to avoid the sort of emergency Langley contemplated. The reason for the rejection of the petition was possibly that the privileges it sought were considered excessive: it would have been a dangerous precedent to have allowed the lord of a great liberty the right to choose from which county a jury should be drawn in a suit in which the Crown was a party, and also prejudicial to the King's prerogative in cases where he was involved.

The legal position thus remained the same as it had been before April 1433. The quarrel with William Eure, however, had not yet run its full course. When the pleadings in the Bishop's chancery were resumed on 17 September 1433, Eure's defence was submitted. His attorney stated that he did not in fact occupy most of the lands in question, and as for the remainder, they should not be seized by the Bishop: it was an ancient custom in Durham that if anyone acquired lands held of the Bishop without his licence a fine was made to him and his pardon was granted; when Eure had offered to pay a fine, Langley had refused to take it but had pardoned Eure the acquisition by word of mouth as a reward for his good services. After the court had heard these submissions, the Bishop's attorney asked for an adjournment, which was granted.[1] In the interval, Langley took another measure to strengthen his government. The commission of the peace for Durham appointed on 1 December omitted Eure and included four influential new justices, the Earl of Salisbury's brothers Lords Latimer and Fauconberg, Thomas Lumley, and Sir Robert Ogle.[2] On 18 December, the Bishop's reply to Eure was given in chancery: the contention that Langley held any of the lands in question was rejected, and as for the supposed oral licence, "the Bishop need not nor by the law of the land could be compelled to answer that plea in the manner and form aforesaid".[3] Langley was invoking his prerogative, and as he doubtless felt that he was obliged to maintain his dignity by giving such an answer it cannot be presumed that he had no alternative and that Eure's plea was true.

---

[1] Rot. D. m. 10.   [2] Rot. C. m. 7.

[3] *Idem episcopus ad placitum illud modo et forma predictis necesse non habet nec per legem terre tenetur respondere.*

As the court was not prepared to give its sentence, it adjourned to 23 March 1434, and from then until 12 August 1435 there was a series of sixteen adjournments.[1] In the meanwhile, the arbitrators appointed at the instance of Parliament in 1433 presumably tried to settle the issue but without success. On 12 August 1435, judgement was given in chancery by the advice of the Bishop's judges and other lawyers: the Bishop could take the manor of Langley into his hands, with the issues from 14 September 1422, but Eure could remain in his other lands. The sentence was thus, to some extent, a compromise, but not a very satisfactory one for Eure. He therefore obtained a writ of error from the royal Chancery on 1 February 1436, and the case was sent to King's Bench on 12 May.[2] Eure's application to the royal court failed. The justices found that the proceedings in the Bishop's court had been legal, and they upheld its sentence. Eure refused to pay the arrears of issues, however, and Langley therefore sought an injunction for payment from King's Bench. On 24 May, the royal justices ordered that Eure should be called before them to answer the Bishop's complaint; this summons was to be delivered by the sheriff of Northumberland, for, as the judicial order said, the King's writ did not run in Durham. The sheriff returned the writ and the parties appeared, but Eure was now engaged in the service of the Wardens of the East March and had royal letters of protection. The proceedings were therefore adjourned to the Michaelmas term.[3] Eure was then employed as captain of Berwick-upon-Tweed, a position he did not relinquish until Easter 1437,[4] and thus had a further respite from prosecution.

It is apparent that Langley was eventually successful in his suit in King's Bench, for Eure was reduced to seeking the final resort of contemplating violence. Upon Langley's petition to the King that Eure was threatening him with death, the Earl of Salisbury and others were ordered, on 12 July 1437, to take from Eure security for keeping the peace.[5] Langley was then a dying man; the conflict of six years ended with his death in the following November. Three years later, Eure received from Bishop Neville a pardon for his acquisition of the disputed lands.[6] He

---

[1] Rot. D. mm. 10–11.

[2] Rot. D. m. 11. Rolls BB & FF Langley are other copies of the proceedings in this suit.

[3] *Coram Rege* Roll, Trinity 14 Henry VI, m. 31.   [4] Below, pp. 161–2.

[5] *CPR. 1436–1441*, p. 89.   [6] *DKR. 34*, p. 168.

had thus been forced to admit defeat; he had abandoned his argument that he had been given a licence by Langley by word of mouth. He might well have submitted to Langley rather than to his successor in suing for this pardon, but it is clear that personal considerations, not disclosed by the records of legal proceedings, made this impossible: the real cause of the dispute must have been private and must remain hidden. There had been bitterness on both sides. The Bishop had raised several charges against Eure simultaneously, while Eure had gone to extraordinary lengths to defend himself, even to instigating a scheme to deprive the Bishop of his regalian prerogatives. He failed completely and the bishops of Durham enjoyed their great liberties for a further hundred years.

III

THE BORDER

THE Romans had regarded the north of England as a frontier district, providing it with a connected line of forts from coast to coast and a system of roads defended by other chains of strong-points. The north retained this character until the seventeenth century, and even to-day the history of the district is revealed by the large number of medieval fortifications still standing. In the rest of England, most castles built after the time of Edward I were not designed primarily for warfare, but to meet a desire for grandeur and comfort. In northern England, great fortresses were still erected and unlike Herstmonceux, Caistor, or Tattershall—imitation castles of brickwork—their contemporaries Raby, Lumley, Sheriff Hutton, and Bolton-in-Wensleydale were massive stone strongholds. At the same time, every man of standing in the north built his own little fort; the number of peletowers in Cumberland and Northumberland is still considerable. In 1415, there were said to be 115 castles and peles in Northumberland alone.[1] In Scotland, the same memorials of an ancient and bitter warfare still remain.

The inhabitants of all border territories were always tempted to make their livelihood by plunder; this occupation appeared less heinous as well as less liable to the penalties of the law when conducted at the expense of people of another kingdom. By the middle of the thirteenth century, however, with amicable relations existing between the rulers of England and Scotland, a body of customs of the march had come to regulate the intercourse of the borderers. The attempt and failure of Edward I to impose the suzerainty of the kings of England over Scotland ended these improved relations. Henceforth, there was no peace between the countries for more than two centuries, but a series of official truces punctuated by periods of open warfare. Scottish invasions were

[1] C. J. Bates, *The Border Holds of Northumberland* (Newcastle-upon-Tyne, 1891), pp. 12–19.

defeated at Durham and Humbledon Hill, but campaigns by English armies in Scotland won no decisive victory. The alliance of Scotland with France obliged England to fight on two fronts during the Hundred Years War. Private raids were incessant, an attack by one side provoking retaliation. Men built castles and towers to protect themselves, but their lands were laid waste, and during the fourteenth century the economic value of Border estates was reduced to a fraction of what it had been before the battle of Bannockburn.[1]

I THE EAST MARCH IN THE EARLY FIFTEENTH CENTURY

The English Border district was divided into two marches, the East March towards Scotland formed by the county of Northumberland, including its franchises, and the West March consisting of the northern parts of Cumberland and Westmorland, the former honour of Carlisle.[2]   There had been a third division, the middle march, in the early years of Richard II's reign, when Northumberland was divided into two parts each under its own warden, but this separation was short-lived and not restored until the time of the Tudors.

The defence of each march was the charge of its warden.   The first warden, appointed in 1309 to guard the West March, and his immediate successors had been military officers only.   From the middle of the century, however, the wardens were also associated with commissions to preserve truces, and these duties soon became part of the wardens' normal functions.   While the scope of the wardens' activities was extended, the nature of their office was also developed, and under Richard II the final stage of the medieval wardenship was reached.   It became the usual practice to appoint one warden only in each march, retained by indenture to serve for a term of years during which he was to keep the town and castle also committed to him—Berwick-upon-Tweed in the east and Carlisle in the west—at his peril, and at the same time to do his best to protect the marches themselves; in return, he was promised payments at a certain annual rate in times of peace or truce and a larger sum for each period of open war.

[1] R. L. Storey, "The manor of Burgh-by-Sands", *Transactions of the Cumberland & Westmorland Antiquarian & Archaeological Society*, *1954*, pp. 123–7.
[2] R. R. Reid, "The Office of Warden of the Marches; its Origin and Early History", *English Historical Review*, *1917*, p. 486.

This practice had the advantage of providing for the permanent maintenance of forces for defensive purposes. There was also a danger, however, that a warden, who was allowed to recruit as many men as he thought necessary, might employ this private army for his own ends. The risk was the greater because it was also desirable that the wardens should have considerable personal authority in their respective marches. In 1391, the Percy family became supreme on the Border, when there were added to its extensive territories in Northumberland and Cumberland the wardenships of both marches. This power was broken in 1403. Ralph Neville, Earl of Westmorland, then gained both the office of Warden of the West March and the forfeited honour of Cockermouth; and John, the King's son, was given the custody of Berwick-upon-Tweed and the East March. The Nevilles established a virtual monopoly over the West March, but the wardenship of the East March changed hands several times before it was recovered by a member of the family which had for many years been popularly regarded as its natural custodian.

The grant of office to a warden was effected by two documents, and occasionally by a third. Firstly, the warden was retained by an indenture, which was the contract with the King setting forth the conditions of service. This was sometimes followed by the issue of the King's letters patent making a grant of the wardenship in accordance with the terms of the indenture.[1] Finally, a commission of his powers was directed to the warden. The form of this commission remained practically unchanged throughout the period under review. The powers granted fell into two main categories: the first section directed the warden to see that certain truces made during the reign of Richard II were observed, and he was empowered to punish English truce-breakers by fine and imprisonment; secondly there were clauses concerning the defence of the country, the punishment of traitors, the setting of watches against invasion, and authority to summon the men of the English marches for military service.[2]

The clauses concerning the preservation of the long-expired truces of Richard's reign were extended in 1412 and 1413 to cover truces made under Henry IV. This additional charge was omitted from the two commissions of 1414.[3] In this year, a

---

[1] Storey, "Wardens of the Marches", pp. 593–603.
[2] *Rot. Scot.* II, pp. 152–291, passim.   [3] Ibid. 200–1, 203–4, 210–12.

statute was made in the Parliament of Leicester declaring all breaches of truces high treason. This enactment was actually directed against piracy on the seas,[1] but it had unfortunate effects on the Border. A year later, the commons of the northern counties complained that the Scots had multiplied their depredations because of the immunity given to them by the statute; the chief form of remedy for the injured had been to sally into Scotland and there make a distraint, but this rough-and-ready form of redress had now been made treason against the King. The petitioners' request that the statute should be repealed was not granted,[2] but after further complaints in 1416, it was enacted that the wardens should be commissioned to hear the complaints of injured subjects and, if application to the Scots for redress was refused, to grant letters of marque.[3] Subsequent commissions appointing wardens restored to them the powers to preserve current truces.[4]

The statute of 1414, however, remained in force. A petition delivered in Parliament in 1429 repeated the complaints and request of that of 1415, but the reply given was that the statute should be kept. It was said by the petitioners that, in the past, conservators of truces and wardens of the marches had power *ex officio* to punish all truce-breakers.[5] This statement is surprising because the wardens still had this authority; moreover, a commission had been appointed to preserve the truce of seven years made in 1424, with power to hear complaints and punish English offenders.[6] If those presenting the petition were unaware of the existence of these powers, the reason must have been that they were not effectively employed. What the borderers really wanted, as they had indicated in 1415, was to be freed from restraint on the ancient practice of self-help. This traditional method of redress was still practised, however: in 1435, a man was charged before the justices of gaol delivery with having given warning that a fellow-countryman was about to lead a party into Scotland "to take a distraint there for goods of his own that had previously been stolen by Scots".[7] Despite the unpopular statute and the prevailing truce, such disloyalty was considered an indictable offence in Northumberland.

---

[1] *Rot. Parl.* IV, pp. 22–4.   [2] Ibid. 68.   [3] Ibid. 105.
[4] *Rot. Scot.* II, pp. 221, 226, 237–8, et seq.   [5] *Rot. Parl.* IV, p. 351.
[6] *Rot. Scot.* II, pp. 253 & 256; Reid, op. cit. pp. 434–5.
[7] GD. 208, m. 34d.

The wardens of both marches had their courts.   In 1436, when there was no warden of the East March, the captain of Berwick-upon-Tweed was authorized to hear pleas and do justice in the warden court.[1]   Although no records of the activities of these courts in this period survive, it is apparent that their jurisdiction in cases concerning both English and Scots was being encroached upon from two sides.   The occasional appointment of conservators of truces clearly led to the temporary diversion from the warden courts of suitors alleging depredations by the Scots and of English subjects charged with similar offences.   On the other hand, the common law court of the justices of gaol delivery also tried persons charged with offences lying in the warden's jurisdiction.   One of the duties of the warden was to make enquiries concerning subjects who conspired with Scots to treasonable ends, and to try and punish them.[2]   Several cases have been noticed of such offences being brought before the King's justices.[3]   In another case, a man was tried before the justices on a charge of conspiring with certain Scots in defiance of an ordinance which put this offence in the warden's jurisdiction.[4]   The truce of 1424 had provided for the trial of subjects of England and Scotland arrested after the commission of a felony in the other country in accordance with its laws.[5]   References to the trial of Scots at Newcastle-upon-Tyne are frequent in the gaol delivery rolls.

The territory committed to the Warden of the East March was in a desperate condition, for the troubled state of Anglo-Scottish relations had had a deplorable effect upon the society of Northumberland.   It is obvious that frequent raids would have taken toll of both life and property, but the consequences of this petty warfare went much further.   The feeling of apprehension that had prevailed in the minds of the people of the county for generations past tended towards the demoralization of their character.   The occupation of many of them in the pillaging of their Scottish enemies gave rise to a disregard for the laws of their own country. These professional robbers knew little distinction of nationality: in fact, there was a freemasonry of Border reivers.   Many Scottish thieves lived in Northumberland and received assistance and shelter from natives of the county.

[1] *Rot. Scot.* II, p. 296.

[2] Ibid. 152 et seq.

[3] Below, pp. 141–2.

[4] GD. 208, m. 26.

[5] *Foedera*, X, p. 330.

Northumberland was without doubt the most lawless part of England. The records of gaol deliveries in the two counties of the West March show that conditions there were far from being as serious; Cumberland and Westmorland were less populated with resident Scots, nor did their inhabitants co-operate with their enemies. A petition delivered in Parliament for the commons of Northumberland in 1411 said that the county was "so far distant from the law" that the King's justices failed to visit it regularly. Another petition, in 1414, laid the cause of the evil on the existence of the franchises of Hexhamshire, Tynedale, and Redesdale. These were said to harbour Scots and other robbers, who could live there without fear of retribution, for the King's writ did not run in the first two liberties, while the men of Redesdale were so lawless that the sheriff of Northumberland dared not enter to execute writs without the support of a small army. In 1421, it was said that the greater part of those living in these three liberties were robbers and felons called "intakers" and "outputters", and their "maintainers".[1]

The complaint made in the petition of 1411 is borne out by the gaol delivery rolls. Since 1401, the royal justices had visited Newcastle-upon-Tyne only five times.[2] The rolls for most of the reign of Henry V are not available, but under his son sessions were more regularly held, usually in the second week of August.[3] Each year, between fifty and a hundred prisoners stood their trial, most of them indicted of the theft of sheep or cattle, and a considerable proportion were charged with aiding felons to escape from justice. There were rarely more than three convictions. The most severe jury for many years was that of 1427, when seven men were found guilty and hanged; three were natives of Redesdale, a fourth was described as a "Scotisman".[4] Men so designated were often tried at Newcastle, but rarely condemned, for there were legal difficulties when a foreign national was concerned. John Coltherd, a Scot of Annandale, whose occupation was recorded as "thefe", was indicted of the theft of over a thousand sheep, but he was discharged because the indictment did not give the name of his vill.[5] Another Scot, recently living in Northumberland, was appealed of homicide and convicted; the

---

[1] *Rot. Parl.* III, p. 662; IV, pp. 21 & 143. [2] GD. 191, mm. 45–52.
[3] GD. 199, mm. 16–24; 208, mm. 20–37.
[4] GD. 199, m. 17d. [5] GD. 208, m. 26 (in 1432).

crime had taken place in the county, but the jury said that the murdered man was a Scot, who had been sometimes residing in Scotland and at other times in England. The justices were therefore uncertain as to how they should deal with the murderer, and sent him back to prison so that they could take counsel.[1]

Charges of co-operating with Scots in the commission of felonies in Northumberland were frequent. There were many cases like that of William Davison, who met certain Scots at Ingram and helped them to steal a horse. He received from the Scots his share of its price.[2] Simon Hilton of North Shields, who was convicted of a theft committed in Newcastle, was said to be a notorious "trewbreker" and to have associated for some time with a certain Scot in robbing English subjects.[3] Scottish robbers were also assisted in making their escape across the Border; indictments of harbouring them were common. William Obilson, described as a notorious robber, was said to have given shelter to a Scot who had robbed a house in Redesdale, and later conducted him into Scotland.[4] English thieves also found it convenient to sell stolen cattle to Scots. Yet another form of lawless enterprise much in vogue was to kidnap fellow-countrymen, take them into Scotland, and then exact ransom for their release. At times, this business was also conducted with the aid of Scots: Thomas Fletcher and others were accused of helping to capture six men in Redesdale who were taken across the Border and ransomed.[5]

The association of thieves of both countries sometimes went beyond co-operation in robbery. The horse-thief, William Davison, was also accused of meeting Scots at Lowick on 6 October 1408 to betray to them the castle of Roxburgh; the plot failed, but he was hanged.[6] Robert Kendal was said to have conspired with Scots on 13 May 1409 to assist them to take Jedburgh Castle.[7] The castle was, in fact, captured by the Scots that summer; it was taken by surprise, in time of truce, and razed to the ground.[8] Scottish agents also received assistance from English thieves. In 1428, two men of Newcastle who were indicted of various robberies were in addition said to be notorious

1 GD. 211, m. 28d. (in 1441).
2 GD. 191, m. 51.　　　　　　　　　　3 GD. 208, m. 32.
4 Ibid. m. 25d.　　　　　　　　　　　 5 GD. 199, m. 23.
6 GD. 191, m. 51.　　　　　　　　　　7 Ibid. m. 51d.
8 *Scotichronicon of J. Fordun*, ed. W. Goodall (Edinburgh, 1759), Vol. II, p. 444.

receivers of Scots called "spyers".[1]   In 1421, Robert Shortrede
of Newcastle was accused of receiving and concealing in his house
on 20 May 1413 two Scots called "spyes", "knowing that they
were commonly and notoriously reputed to be engaged in
exploring and detecting the secrets of the King and kingdom, in
time of war".   His fellow-citizen, John Gilling, was said to have
harboured spies on 1 August and 25 December 1415, "in time
of war".[2]

The condition of Northumberland was thus not only gravely
disturbed by lawlessness, it was also dangerous.   The defence of
the realm was threatened by constant intercourse between the
unruly men of England and Scotland.   English robbers owned
as little loyalty to their country as they showed respect for its laws.
The situation was such that it gave rise not only to common
brigandage but to occasional private warfare.   An instance of the
latter was reported in Parliament in 1410, and the answer given
to the petition of complaint shows that its allegations were
accepted as proven.   On 1 November 1409, Sir Robert Ogle
laid siege to Bothal Castle, the property of his brother John
Bertram.   After four days' encirclement, the castle was taken by
assault and sacked.   Two justices of the peace had tried to
prevent the attack, but their protests were received with contempt
and they fled, fearing personal injury.   It is significant that some
of Ogle's two hundred soldiers were Scots.[3]   He would have had
little difficulty in recruiting his army: there were plenty of the
kind of men he required in Northumberland.

Ogle's attack on Bothal Castle was a notorious example of the
feuds that prevailed between certain leading families of the
English Border.   The Anglo-Saxon tradition of the *weregild*
remained in force here until the sixteenth century: the relatives
of a man killed in a feud preferred monetary compensation to the
King's justice, or, failing payment, tried to take private vengeance.
Bishop Langley was once concerned in such a dispute.   On
20 January 1428, William Heron of Ford entered the village of Etal
in northern Northumberland and there he and his company were
attacked by John Manners and his followers; as Etal was Manners'
home, it is likely that he was provoked to violence.   He maintained that Heron was responsible for the ensuing affray, alleging
that his men drew their bows and that Manners' retainers raised

[1] GD. 208, m. 20.   [2] Ibid. m. 24.   [3] *Rot. Parl.* III, pp. 629–30.

their swords in self-defence and thus killed Heron. Manners was not himself guilty of the fatal blow, although he was later accused of killing Heron's servant Robert Atkinson with a "Scotte ax" and a sword.[1] The Crown appointed a commission on 8 February[2] to enquire into the cause of Heron's death, but it was left to the local magnates and the friends of Manners and Heron to settle the dispute. Sir Robert Umfraville was the principal supporter of Heron's widow Isabel, and Sir Robert Ogle led Manners' friends. The Bishop and the Prior of Durham urged the parties to peace, and when Cardinal Beaufort visited the Border early in 1429[3] he used his influence to the same purpose. Consequently, Umfraville wrote to the Prior on 3 April that if Manners would give security for the payment of four hundred marks, he would write to London to put an end to proceedings begun there on behalf of the Herons. The Prior informed Manners of this proposal and he replied that he could not find such a large sum without his friends' assistance but he would come to Durham to seek Wessington's advice on 15 April. On the 23rd, Manners made an indenture at Durham by which he bound himself to pay Heron's debts and to establish chantries with annual revenues of twelve marks and forty shillings for the souls of Heron and his servant. Heron's widow was not satisfied with this settlement and in consequence negotiations between the friends of both parties continued for another two years. On 18 September 1430, the Priors of Durham and Tynemouth, who had been chosen as umpires, decreed that Manners should come to Newcastle in the following year to be formally reconciled with Umfraville and the Herons, cause five hundred masses to be said in the next twelve months for the relief of William Heron's soul, and pay a sum of two hundred and fifty marks. The reconciliation was effected on 24 May 1431 in the presence of the Bishop of Durham and the Earl of Northumberland.[4] Finally, Manners was brought before the justices of gaol delivery at Newcastle on 25 August 1432 and charged with Atkinson's murder; his acquittal[5] marked another triumph of Border custom over the law of the land.

---

[1] GD. 208, m. 27d.; DCD. Locellus 5, no. 53.
[2] *CPR. 1422–1429*, p. 467. [3] Below, p. 157.
[4] DCD. Locellus 5, nos. 45–53; Raine, *North Durham*, pp. 210–11.
[5] GD. 208, m. 27d.

2 THE BISHOPRIC OF DURHAM AND THE BORDER

Before Edward III created great franchises for members of his family, the kings of England had not permitted the growth of such privileged temporal lordships except on the borders of the realm.   The marcher lords had special powers as it was their duty to contain the Welsh.   Likewise in the north of England, the Bishopric of Durham was a major part of the defences against Scotland, and it is probable that King William II had a similar purpose in mind when he created the short-lived honour of Carlisle, that it should be to the western march what Durham was to the eastern.   Between Cumberland and Durham lay the liberties of Tynedale and Redesdale, and the Archbishop of York's franchise of Hexhamshire.   The extensive privileges of Durham were tolerated because they gave stability and strength to a vital frontier district.   The military responsibilities of the bishop were admitted by Edward II when he recommended Louis Beaumont to the Chapter of Durham, for "he would be a wall of brass between the King and his Scottish enemies".[1]   Likewise, when Henry VI wrote to the Chapter of Durham in 1437, to bid it elect Robert Neville, he said that he was particularly concerned for that see

as wel for it is oon of the grettest and moost notable chirches of oure patrounage within this our royaume as for hit is nygh unto the marches of Scotlande, for the whiche cause namely hit is right necessary and expedient booth for the wele of that countrey and for the said church to set and pourvey of suche a notable and myghty personne to be heed and bisshop thereof, as am and may puissantly kepe thayme best to the honour of God and defence of this our royaume.[2]

A consequence of the strategic importance of the see of Durham was that it was allowed to remain under the rule of a bishop so long as nature permitted him; long episcopates were not rare at Durham, and the only two medieval bishops to be removed by translation [3] had to go elsewhere because their loyalty to the government of the day was very much in doubt.   While the King was anxious for the administration of the Bishopric to be disturbed by a change of ruler as infrequently as possible, the Bishop undoubtedly took consolation for his exclusion from further

---

[1] *Scr. Tres*, p. 98.   [2] DCD. Locellus 25, no. 96.
[3] John Fordham, to Ely in 1388, and Laurence Booth, to York in 1476.

ecclesiastical promotion in the thought that only at Winchester could he enjoy richer temporalities.

The outlying parts of the Bishopric, Norhamshire and Islandshire, lay on the south side of the Tweed, for ten miles westwards from its mouth.[1] Their government was largely separate from that of County Durham: the chancery at Durham was their administrative headquarters, but they had their own sheriff and escheator, justices of the peace and gaol delivery, and receiver.[2] Norham Castle was the local centre of government. It was also the largest English castle on the south bank of the Tweed, and thus held an important place in the defences of the Border. It was greatly strengthened by Langley, who had its west gate rebuilt, great iron-bound gates put in, and a new tower erected.[3] The constable of Norham Castle usually also held the offices of steward, sheriff, and escheator of Norhamshire and Islandshire. On 23 August 1436, Langley took the unprecedented step of granting all four offices to Sir Robert Ogle for twenty years; he was to receive local issues during times of peace and truce, and an additional £200 per annum from the bishop in times of war.[4] This arrangement was made in wartime;[5] the Bishop obviously preferred that the responsibility for the upkeep and supply of the castle should be taken by a resident commander, and had adopted the practice employed by the King in retaining wardens of the marches. The accounts of the sheriff were previously rendered annually at Durham. Apart from the usual items, the Bishop's share in the ransom of Scottish prisoners[6] emphasizes the peculiar position of these territories. Being so close to Scotland, the district was exposed to Scottish raiders, and the value of lands was adversely affected.[7] The revenues drawn by the Convent of Durham from its estates in Islandshire revealed the same tale of destruction.[8] The sessions of the justices had to be postponed occasionally, the cause presumably being that Scottish raids prevented their being held in safety.[9]

Owing to Scotland's adherence to the Avignonese party in the Great Schism, the Bishop was also involved as ordinary in the

---

[1] Raine, *North Durham*, pp. 15–16.

[2] Above, pp. 61, 63–4, 69, 72, 81–2.   [3] Raine, p. 287.

[4] DCD. 3.3. Pontificalia 1; Rot. C. m. 11; Raine, pp. 7–8.

[5] Below, pp. 160–1.

[6] Durham Sheriffs' Accounts, nos. 3 & 4.   [7] Reg. IPM, fo. 173v.

[8] Below, p. 193.   [9] Below, p. 159.

politics of the Border. The English town of Berwick-upon-Tweed, the castle of Roxburgh, and the Durham cell of Colding-ham, lay in the diocese of St Andrews, and were thus under the jurisdiction of a supporter of the "anti-pope". In 1390, Boniface IX granted to Skirlaw powers of episcopal jurisdiction in Berwick, Roxburgh, and whatever other parts of the diocese of St Andrews the English king might conquer. Langley exercised the same powers by virtue of this bull. He mediated in a dispute between the Prior of Coldingham and Vicar of Holy Trinity, Berwick, in 1408, and in 1411 issued a monition against those responsible for violations of sanctuary in Berwick.[1] He exercised this jurisdiction until 1423.[2]

The diocese of Durham entered into the pattern of Border defence and the clergy were occasionally arrayed for military service. The record of a muster in 1400 shows the share each beneficed clerk had to provide. The Rector of Sedgefield brought five men-at-arms and ten archers; the Dean of Auckland four men-at-arms and ten bowmen; and the remainder smaller contributions.[3] A vicar of Gainford who died in 1412 bequeathed his bows and plate-armour to his chamberlain.[4] The payment of royal captains was sometimes made by assignment on the clerical subsidies of Durham. In 1419, £100 collected by the Prior of Durham as part of a clerical tenth was paid to Sir John Bertram, keeper of Roxburgh Castle[5] and the Prior paid £60 to Bertram in 1420.[6] Part of the Bishop's contribution to a clerical subsidy was paid to the wardens of the marches in 1436.[7] In 1412, Langley and William Chancellor paid Sir Robert Umfraville a hundred marks for the repair of the walls of Berwick.[8] Langley also sent money to Roxburgh; in 1418, he lent a hundred marks for the repair of the castle, and for some years payments were made to the captain of Roxburgh "by the hands of Thomas Houden", once described as receiver of the Bishopric of Durham.[9] This would have been Langley's steward,

---

[1] *Reg.* nos. 96 & 210.
[2] Reg. fo. 279v. (undated, but recorded between entries of 17 February and 25 April 1423).
[3] *Scr. Tres*, Appendix, pp. clxxxv–clxxxvii.   [4] *Reg.* no. 265.
[5] Receipt Roll 686, m. 17.   [6] Ibid. 693, m. 13.
[7] Ibid. 747, m. 4.   [8] Rot. A. m. 9d.
[9] *Calendar of Documents relating to Scotland*, ed. J. Bain (Edinburgh 1881–8), Vol. IV, pp. 177–82.

Thomas Holden, which suggests that the Bishop had undertaken to advance money for the costs of Roxburgh, being reimbursed at the royal Exchequer later.

Throughout the years of Langley's rule in Durham, the history of the Border was one of constant raids, threats of invasion, and frequent exchanges of embassies. The laymen of the palatinate were frequently called out for military service, on orders from the Bishop, while Langley himself had an important part in Anglo-Scottish diplomacy. Being so closely concerned with the state of Border relations, the Bishop of Durham was inevitably called upon from time to time to join in negotiations for their amelioration. There was no question of his taking an independent part in view of his palatinate, as some of his predecessors had done.[1] He was, however, responsible for the observation of truces by his subjects. In 1434, John Hedworth, who had been impleaded in the court of the Warden of the East March for breaches of the truce then existing, was bound over to answer to the Bishop or his officers for this offence.[2]

3 BORDER DEFENCE AND DIPLOMACY

In the year that Langley became Bishop, good fortune gave England a valuable prisoner—James, son of the King of Scots. His father died that same year and James was recognized as King, while the government of Scotland was committed to his uncle, the Duke of Albany. Albany seems to have entertained the hope of completely supplanting his nephew, by converting his position of governor to that of king of Scotland, and he was therefore only too willing that James' captivity should be a long one.[3] At the same time, he had no wish to be troubled by English attacks, as he was sufficiently occupied in maintaining his hold on Scotland. The prospect for some understanding between the two countries was thus fair. The current truce was due to expire at Easter 1407. It was at this stage that Langley began to take part in Anglo-Scottish diplomacy. Henry IV was in some doubt about Albany's title to the regency; he was not sure of the Duke's correct style of address. The Bishops of Durham and London were consulted, and advised that two forms of commission should

---

[1] Lapsley, *County Palatine*, pp. 36–9. [2] Rot. D. m. 8d.
[3] E. W. M. Balfour-Melville, *James I, King of Scots* (1936), pp. 31–5.

be prepared for the English representatives in the coming talks: one to empower them to treat for a truce with the ambassadors of the Duke of Albany, governor of Scotland; the second to treat with the commissioners for Scotland. Archbishop Arundel wrote to Henry IV about this time, saying that he believed that the copy of the previous truce with Scotland was in the hands of Langley and others of the council.[1]

Truces were frequently made and renewed for short terms. Nevertheless, the hostility and predatory instincts of the inhabitants of the marches prevented any real state of peace from being restored. The Earl of Northumberland found shelter in Scotland until he departed early in 1408, to meet his death at Bramham Moor.[2] Negotiations were usually conducted for England by men holding no outstanding positions: north-country gentlemen and clerks were generally employed. Richard Holme, Langley's spiritual chancellor, was sometimes appointed to these diplomatic commissions.[3] On 4 April 1411, John of Lancaster and the Earl of Westmorland—the Wardens of the Marches—were instructed to negotiate for a truce. A more powerful commission was appointed on 23 May, including the Bishops of Durham and Bath and Wells, and the Earls of Warwick and Westmorland.[4] Their instructions were to conclude a truce for two or three years, with limitations of the frontier zones round every town and castle; if the Scots would not agree to the fixing of these bounds, the English commissioners had to report back to the King before concluding any truce.[5] The duration of the truce sought was longer than usual. The King's Council, then directed by Prince Henry, wished for peace in the north in order to be free to pursue an aggressive policy in France. There is no trace of the movements of this embassy. Hawdenstank was the place appointed for its meeting with the Scottish ambassadors, who were granted safe-conducts up to 1 July.[6] Langley took no part in these negotiations: he

---

[1] S. B. Chrimes, "Some Letters of John of Lancaster as Warden of the East Marches towards Scotland", *Speculum*, *1939*, pp. 21–2.

[2] Langley spent the spring and summer of that year in the north, and was at Norham Castle on 28 June. His business seems to have been private: he wished to see his Border castle and lands, and one result of his inspection was the initiation of works to strengthen his fortress (Raine, *North Durham*, p. 287).

[3] *Rot. Scot.* II, pp. 192, 214 & 215.

[4] Ibid. 195–6; *Foedera*, VIII, p. 686.

[5] Chancery Misc. (Diplomacy, etc.), file 12, no. 12.

[6] *Rot. Scot.* II, p. 196.

passed the summer in County Durham, continuing his episcopal visitation.   If the meeting did indeed take place, it achieved little or nothing, for a smaller commission was appointed on 24 September following.   On 1 November, a truce until Easter 1418 was arranged.[1]

This truce, however, was not to run its full course.   Henry V's Council, meeting on 29 June 1413, advised that the Wardens should be reinforced, and it was decided on 10 July that additional forces should be engaged.[2]   Apart from the usual negotiations for short truces, exchanges were also made concerning the release of notable prisoners.   In 1413, Scottish embassies were permitted to come to treat for the release of James I, and on 5 August 1415 an English commission, appointed to treat for truces, was also empowered to discuss the exchange of Murdoch, the Duke of Albany's son, with Henry Percy, grandson of the Earl of Northumberland.[3]   The fact that Henry V was about to invade France made him disinclined to release the King of Scots.   The last commission appointed before his departure from Southampton had more desirable objects.   A truce was particularly necessary, because Henry could well expect Scottish attacks as a consequence of his invasion of France.   There was an Elizabethan tradition that, when the Council was debating the proposed invasion, the Earl of Westmorland opposed it, pointing out the danger of repercussions on the northern frontier.[4]   In April, the Council had made arrangements for its defence and commissions of array were appointed.[5]   Langley went to Durham after seeing the English fleet sail for France in order to be at hand during the expected emergency.   There was some activity on the West March, but no major Scottish attack.[6]

Meanwhile, there had been changes in the office of Warden of the East March: John, Duke of Bedford, was replaced by Edward, Duke of York, who was retained as Warden for three years from 29 September 1414.   Henry V required York to take part in his invasion of France, however, and his place was taken by Richard, Lord Grey of Codnor, on 16 May 1415.[7]   The importation of

1 *Rot. Scot.* II, p. 197; *Foedera*, VIII, pp. 737–8.
2 *PPC.* II, pp. 125–6, 132–3.
3 *Rot. Scot.* II, pp. 204 & 214; *Foedera*, IX, pp. 302–3.
4 Shakespeare, *Henry V*, Act I, Scene II.
5 *PPC.* II, pp. 157–8; *Foedera*, IX, p. 255; Rot. A. m. 11d.
6 *Scotichronicon*, II, p. 448.   7 Storey, "Wardens", p. 613.

these "foreign" wardens was not considered satisfactory however. The King was anxious to have a warden who enjoyed the favour of the people of Northumberland, and for this reason negotiations for the release of Henry Percy were resumed. The Duke of Albany was equally eager to recover his son, who had been a captive in England since the battle of Humbledon Hill. On 21 May, John Hull and William Chancellor were instructed to take Murdoch to Newcastle, whence he was to be conducted to Berwick when the time of Percy's arrival there was learnt.[1] Nothing came of these plans, but a second English commission was appointed on 11 December to continue the discussions; its composition was entirely of Durham men—Sir Ralph Eure, Sir William Claxton, Richard Holme, and John Huntman, Dean of Auckland.[2]　As Langley was at Bishop Auckland from 18 December to 24 January 1416, it is probable that he had some part in the negotiations. The exchange was effected. Percy came to Parliament to do homage to the King and was created Earl of Northumberland,[3] and on 10 December was retained as Warden of Berwick and the East March for two years from 11 April 1417. Percy held the wardenship continuously until 1434.[4]

Further negotiations for the release of James I were carried on in 1416, and safe-conducts were issued for Scottish embassies on 26 April and 8 December. On the second date, Langley and the Earls of Northumberland and Westmorland were commissioned to hold discussions regarding bonds and hostages offered by James in an indenture for his release, and to determine whether these were adequate.[5]　They later wrote to Henry V that James wished to go to the north of England to await the Scottish commissioners, and Henry agreed that the Bishop and Earls should take James to Raby Castle where he might remain until Easter 1417, if necessary.[6]　On 12 March, the Earl of Northumberland was empowered to grant safe-conducts to Scottish ambassadors coming to Raby.[7]　Langley had been in the north since December 1416 but returned to London in March. This diplomatic activity proved fruitless, for Henry wanted the Scots to admit his sovereignty as a condition of James' release and this they would

1 *PPC.* II, pp. 160–4.　　2 *Rot. Scot.* II, p. 215; *Foedera*, IX, p. 323.
3 *Rot. Parl.* IV, p. 71.　　4 Storey, loc. cit.
5 *Rot. Scot.* II, pp. 217 & 219; *Foedera*, IX, pp. 417–19.
6 *PPC.* II, pp. 221–2.　　7 *Rot. Scot.* II, p. 220.

not do.[1]   The subject was again considered in 1421,[2] but while Henry lived James remained his prisoner.

The danger to England was more serious in 1417, when Henry began the conquest of Normandy.   The Duke of Albany had received French envoys and was planning to send Scottish soldiers to France.   Henry is said to have prevented the early departure of this expedition by putting about the rumour that he intended to attack Scotland; the Scots therefore remained at home to await this nebulous invasion while the English army crossed the Channel.[3]   The hostility of the Scottish government was certainly not concealed, and in addition there was disaffection in England. In March, commissions had been sent out to enquire into treasons in Northumberland, Yorkshire, Cumberland, and Westmorland.[4] The Lollard, Sir John Oldcastle, was still at large, and was supposed to have conspired with the Scots, urging them to invade England and bring with them the "mammet", *alias* "King Richard II".[5]   How grave the danger of treason was is shown by an account of the capture of Oldcastle's confederate, Thomas Pain, who was taken outside Windsor Castle on the night he had planned to enter it to rescue James of Scotland; a copy of the itinerary by which James was to have been taken to Edinburgh was said to have been found in Pain's possession.[6]

One day after Henry had sailed for France, the Earl of Northumberland learned, on 31 July, that the Duke of Albany proposed to attack Berwick by land and sea, and on 3 August Sir Robert Umfraville, the captain of Roxburgh and chamberlain of Berwick,[7] heard that Albany, with sixty thousand men, would lay siege to Berwick within twenty days.   The Council issued letters of Privy Seal on 14 and 24 August to order various men to join the Lieutenant, the Duke of Bedford, at Leicester; he would go further north if necessary.[8]   Bedford was too late to take part in the repulse of the Scots.   The Duke of Exeter was then in the north, visiting the shrines of St John of Beverley and St Cuthbert,

---

[1] *Henrici Quinti Gesta* (English Historical Society, 1850), pp. 81–2.
[2] *Rot. Scot.* II, p. 229.
[3] *Metrical Chronicle of Scotland* (Rolls Series, 1858), Vol. III, p. 501–3.
[4] *CPR. 1416–1422*, p. 85.
[5] Walsingham, *Historia Anglicana*, II, p. 325; *Ypodigma Neustriae* (Rolls Series, 1876), p. 482.
[6] *Excerpta Historica*, pp. 145–6; *PPC.* V, pp. 104–5.
[7] *Rot. Scot.* II, pp. 167 & 197.   [8] CPS. 31; *Foedera*, IX, pp. 307 & 310.

and gathered an army of north-countrymen, of whose fighting qualities he formed a very high opinion. The Earls of Northumberland and Westmorland also collected forces, and the Archbishop of York called out his clergy. The combined force was said to have been one hundred thousand strong; this figure, like that given for the Scots, is fantastic, but it does indicate that the numbers involved were a great deal larger than was usual in Border warfare. As the English army advanced, the Scots learned of its approach. The Earl of Douglas, who was besieging Roxburgh Castle, hastily broke camp, and Albany likewise abandoned the siege of Berwick, burning the town of Norham as he retreated.[1] John Hardyng attributed the English success to the inspiration given by the leadership of the Earl of Northumberland, "for trust it is true, there is no lorde in Englande that may defend you agayn Scotlande as well as he, for they have the hertes of the people by north and ever had".[2]

The English King apparently hoped that the Border would now be more quiet, for on 25 September 1417 he wrote to Langley, who was then Chancellor, to bid him arrange for the Duke of Exeter to join him in France.[3] Henry was soon of a different opinion: early in 1418, he wrote to Exeter to ask him to confer with Bedford, Langley, and the northern earls "to set a gode ordinance for my north marches". The King was anxious about his French prisoners, for he had learnt that a servant of the Duke of Orleans had been in Scotland to talk to Albany, so that in the following summer the Scots would again take hostile action; there was a plan to rescue King James, Orleans, and other Frenchmen.[4] Exeter passed the King's instructions to Langley on 2 March.[5] Commissions of array for the defence of the realm were issued in April and in July arrays were ordered in Durham, while the clergy were called out in August,[6] but the danger does not appear to have

---

[1] T. Otterbourne, *Chronicle*, ed. T. Hearne (Oxford, 1732), p. 278; *Henrici Quinti Gesta*, p. 121; *Memorials of Henry V*, p. 152; *Ypodigma Neustriae*, pp. 482-3; *Historia Anglicana*, II, pp. 325-6.

[2] J. Hardyng, *Chronicle*, ed. H. Ellis (1812), p. 378.

[3] *Original Letters illustrative of English History*, ed. H. Ellis, Series III (1846), Vol. I, p. 74.

[4] *Original Letters*, Series I (1824), Vol. I, pp. 1-2. (The addressee's name is not given, but the following reference provides it.)

[5] *Lettres des Rois, Reines et Autres Personnages* (Coll. des Docs. Inédits, 1839, 1847), Vol. II, pp. 396-7.

[6] *CPR. 1416-1422*, pp. 196-7; Rot. B. m. 15d.; *Reg.* nos. 497-8.

materialized and the Wardens were empowered to treat for short truces.[1] In 1419, there was a typical Border incident: Wark Castle was taken by some Scots by a trick and its inmates put to the sword. Langley's sheriff of Norhamshire, Sir Robert Ogle, shortly afterwards retook the Castle and massacred the enemy garrison. From this event one Scottish chronicler drew a lesson:

> Now to conclude, as richt weill ma be kind,
> Crudelitie with cruelnes dois end.[2]

In these same years, Sir Robert Umfraville, who was known to the Scots as "Robin Mendmarket" for his exploit in burning Peebles on market-day and because "his measures were so large and pleyn", thought it was a shame that all the martial fame of his day should be won in France and therefore for the space of two years "made the warre on Scottes to have a name".[3]

Negotiations for the release of King James were resumed after the death of Henry V. An English commission led by the Bishops of Durham and Worcester and the Wardens of the Marches was appointed on 12 July 1423. The Scots appointed an embassy to meet it on 19 August [4] and the talks were conducted at York in the second week of September. The English representatives had been given their instructions on 6 July. Firstly, they were to make difficulties if the Scots wished to see James before Langley's arrival, but not to refuse if pressed. If the Scots' credentials were sufficient, a treaty of release was to be made, when the sum of £40,000 was to be demanded to repay the costs of James' imprisonment, but this figure might be reduced to £36,000; securities for payment were to be taken. Whether or not the Scots asked for a treaty of peace or truce, the English were to ask for a peace treaty; if one could not be arranged, then truces were to be concluded in order that time to make peace could be obtained. Every method was to be used to persuade the Scots to recall their soldiers from France. Should the Scots suggest the marriage of their King to an English lady, the point might be developed, but it would be unseemly for the English to raise such a delicate matter.[5] The Scottish embassy, however, was only

---

[1] *Rot. Scot.* II, pp. 222, 223 & 226; *Foedera*, IX, p. 913.
[2] *Scotichronicon*, II, p. 458; *Metrical Chronicle of Scotland*, III, pp. 499–500.
[3] Hardyng, pp. 366–7, 380.
[4] *Foedera*, X, pp. 298–9; *Rot. Scot.* II, p. 238.   [5] *Foedera*, X, pp. 294–5.

empowered to negotiate for James' release. On 10 September, articles were agreed to by Bishops Langley and Morgan (of Worcester), the Earl of Northumberland, and Master John Woodham on the English side, and by the Scottish ambassadors on the other. The Scots agreed to pay £40,000 within six years of James' return to Scotland, but as they had not been instructed as to the names of hostages to be given as security for payment, it was decided that James should go to Brancepeth or Durham on 1 March following to treat with his subjects on this matter. The commissioners agreed that a royal marriage was to be desired, and the Scots promised to send another embassy to the English Council before 20 October to come to a conclusion.[1]

The Scottish embassy did not arrive in London until December, when the English representatives to meet it were led by the Bishop of Worcester; neither Langley nor the Wardens took part.[2] On 4 December, a further set of articles was agreed upon, more detailed than those made at York but not very different in substance. James was to arrive at Durham or Brancepeth by 10 February, instead of 1 March; the hostages and bonds were to be handed over in Durham Cathedral on 1 March, or before 31 March at the latest.[3] The Scottish embassy had also discussed the question of James' marriage, and before he left London he married Joan Beaufort, niece of the Bishop of Winchester and the Duke of Exeter; in consequence, as had been agreed at York, ten thousand marks were remitted from the ransom.[4] The treaty of peace which the English Council was so anxious to obtain had not yet been made, nor had its desire for the recall of the Scottish contingent in France been realized, for the Scottish embassies had not been authorized to discuss either topic, nor had they even been empowered to conclude a truce. A third English commission was appointed on 14 February 1424, when the Bishops of London and Durham, the Earls of Westmorland and Northumberland, the Keeper of the Privy Seal, and four north-country magnates were empowered to treat with James himself or with his representatives for a final peace or a truce.[5]

There was again a slight delay in the proceedings: James did not arrive at Brancepeth until 1 March and had to wait there for

---

1 *Foedera*, X, pp. 299–300.   2 Ibid. 301; *Rot. Scot.* II, p. 240.
3 *Foedera*, X, pp. 302–5; *Rot. Scot.* II, pp. 241–3.
4 Ibid. 246; *Foedera*, X, pp. 322–3.   5 *Rot. Scot.* II, p. 246.

most of the month,[1] for although Bishop Kemp of London was able to set out for Durham on 18 February,[2] Langley was still in London on 28 February and did not reach Durham much before 20 March. On 28 March, at Durham, James gave his bond for £40,000 and made an indenture with the English representatives by which he gave over to them a number of hostages and bonds in security. On the same day, a second indenture was sealed to testify the conclusion of a truce to last for seven years from 1 May following.[3] James then departed for Scotland. As had been arranged on 4 December, he made letters under his great seal confirming these agreements after his entry into his kingdom, and he also took an oath to observe the various treaties; this was received at Melrose on 5 April by Sir William Bowes, Master William Doncaster, and William Park.[4] James had been a captive for eighteen years, and the early reversal of the policy of Henry V and his father that brought about his release was due to the urgent desire of the English Council to make peace with Scotland. It was disappointed in this object, but had secured the longest truce made with Scotland since Henry IV's accession. As for the Council's second aim, the recall of Scottish troops from France, all it obtained was James' promise to send no further forces there, but as most of the Scottish contingent was killed at Verneuil five months later, the problem ceased to be important.[5]

The presence of King James in Durham gave Prior Wessington a good opportunity to seek his favour for Coldingham; the interest taken by the Convent in the diplomatic exchanges is attested by the entry of a copy of the treaty of truce in the Prior's folio register.[6] The Duke of Albany had ordered the English monks to leave Coldingham in 1409, when the Abbot of Dunfermline appointed a prior.[7] This was in the time of the Schism, however; Scotland had now fallen into line with the rest of Christendom, and Langley had recently surrendered the powers conferred by the Papacy to exercise episcopal jurisdiction in the diocese of St Andrews.[8] After James had returned to Scotland, the claims of Durham and Dunfermline were heard in a parliament at Perth on 26 May, and it was decided that William Drax, the Prior of Coldingham

1 Balfour-Melville, p. 102.
2 British Museum: Cleopatra C. IV, fo. 156.   3 *Foedera*, X, pp. 327–32.
4 DCD. 2.5 Regalia 2; *Foedera*, X, pp. 332–3; *Rot. Scot.* II, p. 247.
5 Balfour-Melville, p. 103.   6 DCD. Reg. III, ff. 6v.–8 (first foliation).
7 DCD. Reg. Parvum I, fo. 12.   8 Above, p. 146.

appointed by Durham, was in lawful possession; as the priory was in ruins, said to have been caused by the English, Drax was ordered to repair it and maintain divine services.[1] This affirmation of the Convent of Durham's rights was apparently referred to in a commission of Henry VI to Langley on 26 February 1425: James had asked that the English King should show the same favour to Scottish houses deprived of their property in England, and Langley was appointed to hear their claims and report to the Council.[2] Whether he did hear such complaints cannot be ascertained, but he supported a like claim by the Convent of Durham, writing to James on 10 March to ask that certain lands taken from the Prior of Coldingham should be restored to him.[3] Coldingham's position remained an unhappy one and Henry VI took the cell into his protection in 1436, as it was still suffering from the depredations of both Scots and English.[4]

After the Treaty of Durham, and as he gradually withdrew from his place in the King's Council, Langley became increasingly engaged in Anglo-Scottish relations; indeed, in the seven years following his resignation of the Great Seal in 1424, his participation in Border diplomacy was his chief part in national affairs. On 14 July 1425, he was the first-named of an embassy appointed to discuss breaches of the truce and reparations; all those with complaints were told to come before the English commissioners at Berwick on 16 August.[5] Before this meeting, Langley inspected his own Border territories, visiting Holy Island on 12 August and Norham two days later. He went to Berwick for the negotiations, and on 20 August was staying in the house of the Rector of Berwick, where he granted an indulgence for a Scottish chapel.[6] The meeting of ambassadors was not very fruitful, and on their return southwards Langley and his colleagues, Lord Scrope and William Alnwick, wrote to the Council from Warkworth on 23 August, complaining of the obstructive tactics of the Scottish representatives, who had refused to come to any conclusion without consulting their King. The English side of the dispute, concerning the bounds of the foraging areas of the garrisons of

---

[1] *Acts of the Parliaments of Scotland* (Record Commission, 1814–75), Vol. II, p. 25; Raine, *North Durham*, Appendix, pp. 20–1.

[2] *Rot. Scot.* II, p. 251.

[3] DCD. Registrum Papireum Diversarum Litterarum Cancellarie Dunelmensis, fo. 24.

[4] *Rot. Scot.* II, p. 298.   [5] Ibid. 253.   [6] *Reg.* no. 650.

Berwick and Roxburgh, had been presented, and Sir Robert Umfraville was sent to James to repeat these arguments,[1] with what success is not known.

Cardinal Beaufort was now making preparations for his crusade against the heretics of Bohemia, and proposed to hold a personal meeting with King James in order to ask him for recruits. James was granted a safe-conduct to permit him to come to Durham or Newcastle, but the meeting took place at Coldingham, early in 1429.[2] On his way north, the Cardinal visited the Prior of Durham,[3] and apparently also the Bishop; on 16 January, Langley appointed commissions to proclaim the crusade in Durham which were dated at Crayke,[4] where he presumably had gone to meet Beaufort. On 10 February, the English Council gave the Cardinal permission to meet James in order to discuss affairs of state as well as of the Church, but on 15 February a separate commission headed by Langley was appointed to treat with James regarding the unpaid balance of his ransom, his hostages, breaches of the truce, and also the possibility of its extension.[5] There is no record of the outcome of all this impressive diplomatic activity. Later in the year, on 15 June, two further English embassies were appointed. One of these, formed by the Bishops of Durham and Carlisle, the Earls of Salisbury and Northumberland, and six others, was to treat regarding the ransom and hostages, and to ask for a treaty of final peace, possibly linked with a marriage alliance, or further truces. The second was smaller, but all its members belonged to the large embassy; Langley was not a member. Its object was the less important one of discussing breaches of the truce.[6] The Prior of Durham had excused himself from attendance at the Black Monks' chapter as he wished to speak to these ambassadors,[7] probably on behalf of Coldingham. The smaller commission met the representatives of Scotland on 12 July, and concluded articles for the better observation of the truce and reparations.[8] Langley was at Norham on 13 July, but he and his colleagues were not successful.[9]

The English Council was becoming alarmed at the Scottish

1 *PPC*. III, pp. 171–4.

2 *Foedera*, X, pp. 408–9; *Rot. Scot*. II, p. 264; Balfour-Melville, p. 168.

3 DCD. Bursar 1428–1429, m. 3d.   4 *Reg*. nos. 797–800.

5 *Rot. Scot*. II, pp. 264–5; *Foedera*, X, pp. 410–11.

6 *Rot. Scot*. II, 266–7.   7 *Priory of Coldingham*, p. 103.

8 *Foedera*, X, pp. 428–31.   9 *PPC*. IV, pp. 347–8.

situation, for the "auld alliance" with France had been renewed in 1428, and the truce was due to expire in 1431. The marriage alliance the Council was considering was that of Henry himself to a Scottish princess. It had received an envoy from James who expressed his own desire for peace.[1] On 24 January 1430, two commissions similar to those of 15 June 1429 were sent to Langley and other ambassadors;[2] their instructions referred to James' message to the Council, and they were required to listen to the Scottish proposals for peace. If no such overtures were made, the English desire for a settlement was to be declared in general terms. Should the Scots ask for the marriage of Henry to a Scottish princess, their offers were to be heard with favour but no conclusion was to be reached until after a treaty of peace had been made. The English instructions also required some discussion of the non-fulfilment of the conditions of James' release, but the payment of the balance of the ransom might be deferred if this made the conclusion of a truce more likely.[3] The English embassy wrote to James on 5 April, and his reply was brought to the Earl of Northumberland at Warkworth on 21 April, but the Earl would not open the letter in the absence of his colleagues, and the Scottish messenger then retired with unseemly haste. Northumberland wrote to Langley to suggest that the commissioners should meet in Newcastle on 1 May, and Langley, who was then in Lumley Castle, passed this message on to the Earl of Salisbury on 25 April. The meeting took place on 28 April, however, when a letter was written to James to protest at the precipitate retreat of his envoy, which had prevented the arrangement of a meeting of representatives of both countries.[4]

Despite this fiasco, the English Council continued its efforts to make peace, and appointed another commission, once more headed by Langley, on 15 November; it was to negotiate on the same matters as previously with the exception of the marriage, which was not mentioned. Two members of the embassy, Lord

[1] *PPC.* IV, pp. 19; C. Macrae, "The English Council and Scotland in 1430", *English Historical Review, 1939,* pp. 415–17.
[2] *Rot. Scot.* II, pp. 268–9.   [3] PPC. IV, pp. 18–27.
[4] Macrae, p. 418. Two letters printed in his appendix (nos. II & III, pp. 423–4) were obviously written by Langley, although the writer's name is not given. They are dated 25 and 26 April, at Lumley Castle. Their tone indicates that the writer was one of the leaders of the embassy, and their content that he was neither of the Earls. Elimination leaves Langley, who was then at Lumley.

Scrope and Master John Stokes, went to Edinburgh, where a truce
was concluded on 15 December, to last for five years from the
expiry of the current truce.[1] Langley's participation in Border
diplomacy now became more and more nominal. On 14 August
1432, he was asked by the Council to surrender a number of
documents in his possession; one was the Treaty of Troyes, but
most related to the Border.[2] He was empowered to grant safe-
conducts to Scots coming to England, on 7 June 1434,[3] but he
was not a member of the commission that was appointed later
that year to treat for peace and on other subjects.[4] On 20 July
1435, he was appointed to an embassy to discuss the fulfilment of
James' agreements at Durham in 1424, as well as to treat for an
extension of the truce.[5] Langley did not move from Stockton,
leaving the business to his younger colleagues. When another
embassy was appointed on 5 February 1436, he was not one of
the stipulated *quorum*.[6] Once more, he did not leave his diocese.

During these last years, the marches were still in a troubled state
and their inhabitants continued to raid each other. Instructions
by the Council to the English commanders failed in their object,
the preservation of the truce. Large bodies of Scots had plun-
dered round Berwick and in Glendale during July 1433,[7] the
sessions of the Bishop's justices at Norham had to be adjourned in
April 1432, April and September 1433, and March 1434,[8] and the
greater part of Alnwick was burnt by the Scots.[9] On 28 May
1435, commissions of array were issued in Durham, and although
it was believed that the Scots were planning to invade in force,
the orders were ignored and had to be repeated on 16 September.[10]
The lack of any feeling of urgency on the part of either the Bishop
or his subjects suggests that this was a false alarm.

The Earl of Northumberland gave up the custody of the East
March when the term of his last indenture expired in 1434. The
Council had decided on 6 July that the custody of both marches
should be given to the Earl of Salisbury, who had been Warden of
the West March since 1420, and now entered into separate
indentures for each march, the term set being one year in each
case. He was able to make a number of conditions, including

1 *Foedera*, X, pp. 482–7.   2 *PPC*. IV, pp. 127–8.
3 *Rot. Scot.* II, p. 287.   4 Ibid. 288.
5 Ibid. 291–2; *Foedera*, X, pp. 621–2.   6 Ibid. 629–30; *Rot. Scot.* II, p. 294.
7 *PPC*. IV, pp. 169–70.   8 Rot. D. mm. 5, 7d. & 8d.
9 *CPR. 1429–1436*, p. 345.   10 Rot. D. mm. 11d. & 13d.

provision for the payment of arrears of sums due for the custody
of the West March and for the supply of Berwick and the repair
of its fortifications: [1] that the Council assented to these terms
indicates the difficulty encountered in persuading Salisbury to
undertake the two wardenships. Early in 1435, however, he
asked that he should be discharged as he was unable to bear the
costs of his offices. On 12 July, the Earls of Northumberland and
Huntingdon were retained jointly as Wardens of both Marches,
for one year in each office.[2] The plan of uniting the wardenships
was not new, although it had not been attempted for many years.
It had the advantage of promoting a more efficient handling of the
defensive forces by placing them under a single command. It
soon broke down, however, on the usual Lancastrian stumbling-
block, inadequate revenue. Salisbury should have received
£3,750 for his year in both offices if the truce lasted, and payment
at double that rate in war-time. His desire to be relieved of his
command was undoubtedly due to the failure of the government
to pay him in full. The Wardens had for several years been
unable to receive the sums for which they had contracted.[3]

The financial failure of the government had serious consequences in 1436 which might well have proved disastrous. The
truce with Scotland expired in that year and James' daughter was
married to the Dauphin of France, despite the despatch of an
English herald to dissuade him.[4] James decided to support
France openly and to assist his ally by invading England. The
English Council believed this attack imminent on 27 June, when
it ordered the sheriffs of the northern counties to call out the local
forces to join the Wardens in resisting the Scots. A similar order
was sent to the Bishop of Durham,[5] but Langley did not appear to
be very alarmed, and waited for some six weeks after receiving it
before he issued a summons to his subjects. The term of the two
Earls as Wardens of the East March expired on 25 July and the
Council had made no arrangements for retaining them any
longer or for a new appointment. The soldiers of the garrison of
Berwick began to desert, as they did not know who would pay
their wages. Thomas Elwick, the Mayor of Berwick, hastened

1 PPC. IV, pp. 268–77.   2 Storey, "Wardens", pp. 604–5.
3 A. Steel, The Receipt of the Exchequer 1377–1485 (Cambridge, 1954), p. 190.
4 Metrical Chronicle of Scotland, III, p. 552.
5 CCR. 1435–1441, p. 66.

to Durham, where he reported this information to the Archbishop of York, the Bishops of Durham and Carlisle, and the Earl of Northumberland. Presumably he knew that he would find them there: this small body of notables was apparently acting as a branch of the Council to supervise the defences of the marches. They

charged the saide Thomas to ride in all haste possible to oure [i.e. the King's] saide toune of Berewyk to thentente for to trete the saide souldeours that were last therinne to abide and to acquite thaim so namly in that article of nede as thei myght deserve thanke of us for a tyme til that thei myght be better ordened fore. The which Thomas after that he hadde soo doon, conceyvyng the grete scarcite of peple at that tyme left in oure saide toune and also the simple kepyng of the wacthes therynne, hired wacthes for viij days and viij nyghts and paied thaim of his owne monay.[1]

This unsatisfactory arrangement was a temporary expedient only and a week later Archbishop Kemp persuaded Sir William Eure to undertake the defence of Berwick.[2] The lack of a warden to lead the English forces was remedied by the appointment of a commission headed by Kemp and his three colleagues. On 10 August, the lay members were ordered to relieve Roxburgh,[3] and on 15 August Langley's sheriff was told to proclaim that the men of Durham were to prepare to set out whenever required by these magnates.[4] It was fortunate that James had decided to try to take Roxburgh Castle rather than Berwick. The size of his army was said to have been enormous, the lowest contemporary estimate being one hundred thousand, the largest over double that figure; he had called out all the men of military age. Their attacks were resisted by the small garrison of Roxburgh under the command of Sir Ralph Grey, but when the Scots heard of the approach of a relieving army led by the Earl of Northumberland they rapidly abandoned the siege, leaving their artillery behind. There was unrest in their camp: in fact, the disaffection against James that led to his murder in the following year was the chief cause of England's bloodless defensive victory.[5] The English

---

[1] Warrants for Issues, 53/131. [2] Ibid. 53/132.
[3] *Rot. Scot.* II, pp. 294-5. [4] Rot. D. m. 5.
[5] *Scotichronicon*, II, p. 502; *Metrical Chronicle*, III, pp. 554-5; Hardyng, p. 397; *Three Fifteenth Century Chronicles* (Camden Society, 1880), p. 165; *Incerti Scriptoris Chronicon Angliae*, Part 3, p. 16; C. L. Kingsford, *English Historical Literature in the Fifteenth Century* (Oxford, 1913), p. 322.

then retaliated with a raid in force; according to the Scots, the Earl of Northumberland was defeated with heavy losses at Piperden, on 10 September, but an equally biased chronicler on the other side of the Border claimed that "he made a nobylle jorney".[1]

The danger of invasion had passed, but the problem of the wardenships had not been settled; Huntingdon and Northumberland ceased to act in the West March after 12 September. Their place was taken after an interval of three months by Marmaduke Lumley, Bishop of Carlisle, whose offer to guard the West March for seven years at a rate of pay lower than had usually been promised was accepted by the King's Council with relief. The wardenship of the East March remained vacant until the Duke of Norfolk was persuaded, on 12 March 1437, to accept the office for one year.[2] In the meantime, some of the duties had been carried out by Sir William Eure, who remained in charge of Berwick until Norfolk relieved him on 31 March, at the heavy charge to the Exchequer of a hundred marks a week.[3] Thus for some eight months, even though there was a state of war all the time, the East March was without a warden to organize its defence. The introduction of Norfolk did not solve the problem; he left the marches after his short term was spent, being replaced by Robert Ogle, the constable of Norham, and Ralph Grey. They undertook the office for one year and later renewed their indentures for a similar term. Henry Percy, the heir of the Earl of Northumberland, succeeded them in 1440 and held the office until 1461,[4] so that the government of the East March was again established in the hands of its traditional ruler. The war had already been brought to an end in 1438 with the conclusion of a truce for eight years.[5]

Langley had died before this return to normal conditions. Throughout the years of his rule over Durham, the subjects of the Bishopric had been prominent in Border warfare: in the two years spent by Robert Umfraville in harrying the Scottish march,

> . . . none helpe had but of his countre men,
> Of the Bishopryke and of Northumberland then.[6]

---

1 *Scotichronicon*, II, pp. 500–1; *Historical Collection of a Citizen of London*, p. 179.
2 Storey, "Wardens", p. 605.
3 Warrants for Issues, 53/132 & 179; *Rot. Scot.* II, pp. 296–7.
4 Storey, p. 614.
5 *Foedera*, X. p. 688.   6 Hardyng, pp. 381–2.

Langley had himself been the leading English diplomat in Anglo-Scottish relations for many years, but the achievement of this diplomacy had been far from spectacular, a sorry tale of making and ineffectively attempting to preserve truces.   Langley's work in strengthening Norham Castle was, in effect, his most permanent contribution to the stability of the English Border.   On the other hand, a less tangible factor has to be taken into account: the English position on the Border would have been gravely imperilled had Durham been under a feeble and inefficient administration.   Northumberland was "far distant from the law",[1] but behind it lay the compact government of the Bishopric.   Langley's administration was undoubtedly weakened by the lawlessness of his subjects, but it was strong compared with the influence of the central government in Northumberland.   Durham was the bulwark of the East March, and its value to the kingdom in this rôle was implicitly recognized by Edward IV.   When he created a new principality in the West March in 1483, he took the Bishopric as his model.[2]

[1] *Rot. Parl.* III, p. 662.   [2] Storey, p. 608.

IV

THE DIOCESE OF DURHAM

WHEN Thomas Langley became Bishop of Durham he was about forty-five years of age. He had held a number of benefices, but his interest in them was almost solely financial. As Archdeacon of Norfolk, however, he had undertaken some of the responsibilities of ecclesiastical office, conducting visitations of his archdeaconry, whereas his contemporaries generally preferred to have this done by deputy.[1] Otherwise his knowledge of Church affairs would have been confined to such matters as were brought to his notice in the course of his public duties, especially as Chancellor. He had not studied at a university, so that his knowledge of canon law could not have been extensive, although he would have become familiar with its functions. The practical ability that had taken Langley to the office of Chancellor and his experience of the ways of mankind were not spiritual qualities, but they would have been of value in his administration of the diocese.

The circumstances of his election to Durham are well-documented; this is the more fortunate because the records reveal that, even in the fifteenth century, the election of a bishop could still be contested. The see had become vacant by the death of Walter Skirlaw on 24 March 1406 and, as the archbishopric of York was also vacant, the custody of the spiritualities of Durham devolved upon the Prior and Chapter. On 30 March, two monks were appointed by their brethren as keepers of the spiritualities. The Chapter of York protested, claiming for itself the right to this custody but the Durham Chapter was able to maintain its title; the King's son John, Warden of the East March, to whom the keeping of the temporalities had been assigned,[2] gave his support against York. The register of John Ripon, the Subprior, and John Barton, as keepers of the spiritualities, records their exercise of authority throughout the vacancy, mostly in the

[1] Above, pp. 16 & 20. [2] *CFR. 1405–1413*, p. 30.

admission of clerks to benefices. The Chapter had given them full jurisdictional powers and these they exercised in the excommunication of persons practising witchcraft.[1] A suffragan bishop was appointed and the keepers also called a synod of the clergy of Durham.[2]

The practice generally observed in the appointment of bishops in the later middle ages was that of provision by papal bull, but the Pope's choice of English bishops was usually guided by the King. Henry IV must have lost little time in informing Innocent VII of his wish for Langley's promotion to Durham. Indeed, the Pope must have been well aware of the King's desire to advance Langley, since he had twice refused to grant his provision, firstly to London and later to York. On this occasion he raised no objection and the bull of provision was issued on 14 May.[3] It had presumably been delivered before 8 June, when Langley received the royal licence to pay the first-fruits of Durham to Rome.[4] With the choice of bishop being determined in this manner, the formal election by the Cathedral Chapter "was simply an act of consent to the king's choice".[5] The Chapter of Durham had sent two monks, Thomas Rome and William Barry, to the King on 2 April. The royal licence to elect a bishop was granted on 25 April[6] and the writ was laid before the Chapter on 3 May, when it was decided to call a full meeting a fortnight later to make the election.[7]

The King had presumably informed the two proctors of his wishes: the Pope's provision was made three days before the election by the Chapter. Even so, there was a second candidate for the see. This was Thomas Weston, Archdeacon of Durham, who had been Skirlaw's spiritual chancellor.[8] That he was regarded with some favour by the Convent is indicated by their presentation of him to a prebend in their collegiate church of Howden, in 1401.[9] It would also appear that he enjoyed some popularity among the leading laymen of the county. His candidature was supported by John of Lancaster, who wrote to his father the King on behalf of Weston. This intrigue must have

---

[1] *Scr. Tres*, Appendix, pp. cxciv–vi.
[2] DCD. Misc. Charters 5723; Cartulary III, ff. 145–50.
[3] *CPL.* VI, p. 83; *Reg.* no. 1.   [4] *CCR. 1405–1408*, p. 40.
[5] Hamilton Thompson, *The English Clergy*, p. 17.
[6] *CPR. 1405–1408*, p. 166.   [7] DCD. Misc. Charters, 5723.
[8] *Scr. Tres*, Appendix, p. clxvi.   [9] DCD. Reg. III, fo. 2.

been in train from the time Skirlaw died, for Weston saw John's letter to Henry IV on 11 April. He wrote about this to the monks Rome and Barry, protesting his ignorance of his nomination until that day. He professed that he was unwilling to press for election if the King intended to promote either Langley or Nicholas Bubwith, the Keeper of the Privy Seal, to Durham. It was possible, Weston thought, that Langley might continue to prosecute his promotion to York, or that these two royal ministers would be advanced to other sees; if this were the case, he would spare neither trouble or expense to procure his own promotion to Durham, even though this would cause the exclusion of Henry Bowet, Bishop of Bath and Wells. Weston was most reluctant, however, to oppose Langley, and would send a messenger to London to learn what his intentions were.[1]

Weston's aspirations were vain. When the Chapter met on 17 May, forty-seven of the fifty-seven monks present voted for Langley. The Master of the cell of Jarrow gave his vote for Henry Bowet. The remaining nine, who included the Master of Wearmouth, the chamberlain, and the precentor, gave their support to Weston. The result was foregone, even though the election had not been a mere formality. It is probable that John Wessington, who had been one of the majority, remembered the circumstances of Langley's election in 1438. He was then Prior, and secured the agreement of the monks to accept the person he named as bishop. Thus Langley's successor received the Chapter's assent without the hazard of a contested election.[2]

Langley's election completed the canonical requirements. On 1 July, after he had paid £600 into the King's chamber, the temporalities of Durham were committed to his agents.[3] As the archbishopric of York was still vacant, he had been given licence by the Pope to seek consecration at the hands of any catholic bishop and to select other bishops to assist at the ceremony. This took place in St Paul's Cathedral, London, on 8 August. The Archbishop of Canterbury consecrated the new Bishop of Durham.[4] On the following day, the King formally released the temporalities.[5] Langley's first commission as ordinary was to appoint the Prior of Durham and Thomas Weston his vicars-

1 DCD. Locellus 6, no. 2.
2 DCD. Reg. III, ff. 22–5, 213–15.　　3 *CPR. 1405–1408*, p. 208.
4 *Reg.* nos. 8 & 10.　　5 *CPR.* p. 222.

general *in spiritualibus*; [1] he was still Chancellor of England and unable to leave London.

I DIOCESAN ADMINISTRATION

The Lancastrian episcopate was notorious for its absenteeism, for its neglect of spiritual duties for secular business. Such is the character given to it by the censorious Thomas Gascoigne.[2] Langley was thus no worse than his contemporaries in that he spent the greater part of his time in London, or elsewhere, on affairs of state. He was not, however, as constantly non-resident as some of his fellow-bishops: in only one year, 1419, did he fail to visit the diocese. He usually contrived to come on two occasions annually, in the summer and for Christmas. His longest period of absence was from October 1418 to August 1420, but it was exceptional. In the last ten years of his life, his absences were less frequent and generally short.[3]

The routine of diocesan administration had by this time been sufficiently developed to function of its own accord. The long absences of a bishop gave rise to abuses, but as long as he made sure that the various administrative and judicial offices were held by men of ability and sound canonical training, he could feel certain that the machinery would operate without much danger of a breakdown. A second feature of ecclesiastical government, leading from the first, was that there was a class of clerks who specialized in administrative work. They formed, in fact, the Church's "permanent civil service". Some of these men found employment in episcopal households, but others resided and worked in the dioceses, continuing in employment under succeeding bishops: [4] Langley's first two officials had both been ministers of his predecessor.[5] The interesting career of William Doncaster was begun as an advocate in the Durham consistory court. He was a bachelor of laws and a notary-public and was employed by the Prior of Durham, by the two archdeacons of the diocese, and eventually by the Bishop as sequestrator-general

---

[1] *Reg.* no. 12.

[2] *Loci e Libro Veritatum*, ed. J. E. T. Rogers (Oxford, 1881), pp. 21 & 37.

[3] Appendix A, pp. 226–44.

[4] R. L. Storey, "Diocesan Administration in the Fifteenth Century" (York, 1959), pp. 20–2.

[5] *Reg.* Vol. I, p. xii.

and official; nor did any of these masters ever have a monopoly of his services.[1] Men like Doncaster could only hope to pursue such a career when the system of administration was stabilized, but they in turn gave to the system its continuity.

The Bishop's government was two-fold. Close at hand, in his household, was his secretariat and, whenever he chose to constitute it, his court. Secondly, there were the local officers in the diocese. Many of the duties of an absentee bishop were delegated to his vicar-general *in spiritualibus*, but for the sacerdotal functions of the episcopal office a suffragan bishop was employed. Archdeacons were no longer, by virtue of their office, ministers of the bishop, but they exercised a theoretically subordinate jurisdiction. The diocese of Durham had two archdeacons, one for each of its counties of Durham and Northumberland. In addition, there were in these counties a number of jurisdictional peculiars. Hexhamshire lay directly under the Archbishop of York, and the Prior of Durham claimed, and in Langley's day fully enjoyed, the position of archdeacon in all churches appropriated to his convent in both counties. The archdeacons continued to contest these claims, but without avail.[2] Langley himself effected a further reduction in the archdeacons' influence by excluding them from the churches in his gift, all of which lay in his temporal franchise. During the episcopate of Thomas Hatfield (1345–81), the archdeacons inducted newly instituted incumbents into every benefice in the diocese,[3] and in 1406 both Bishop Skirlaw and the keepers of the spiritualities after his death ordered the archdeacons to induct to benefices in the Bishop's patronage.[4] From the very beginning of his episcopate, however, Langley committed the induction to such benefices to his own officers and *ad hoc* commissaries,[5] and the only churches to which he ever instructed the archdeacons to induct were those in the gift of persons other than the Bishop and the Prior and Convent, apart from those churches of the Convent which it had not appropriated.

[1] A. B. Emden, *A Biographical Register of the University of Oxford to A.D. 1500* (Oxford, 1957–9), Vol. I, p. 585.

[2] Below, pp. 197–8.

[3] DCD. Reg. Hatfield, *passim*.

[4] DCD. Reg. III, fo. 20; Cartulary III, ff. 145–9. I am indebted to Mr M. G. Snape for providing this information.

[5] This practice was still observed in the sixteenth century (*The Registers of Tunstall and Pilkington* (SS. 1952), nos. 17, 21, 36, 73–6, 475, 489, 503, 532 & 538).

The two principal officers of the Bishop's household, on its diocesan side, were the spiritual chancellor and the registrar. In former times the chancellor had been the Bishop's secretary, but by the fifteenth century he had ceased to act in this capacity. Langley's three chancellors were all lawyers. Richard Holme had been employed by Bishop Skirlaw and became his successor's first chancellor. He was a Yorkshireman and had taken the bachelor's degree at Cambridge. He had been an abbreviator of letters at the Roman Curia, the chancellor of John Waltham, Bishop of Salisbury, and a royal clerk and diplomat; he continued occasionally to serve the King on embassies to France and Scotland while he was employed by Langley. He was succeeded in 1422 by Thomas Hebden, a native of the same diocese as Langley, the son of a knight, and a doctor of laws. John Bonour, doctor of laws in the University of Bologna, was appointed chancellor in 1433. Although the seal *ad causas*, under which all formal diocesan letters were issued, was committed to the chancellor's keeping, the grant of its custody seems to have been no more than a traditional practice, surviving from a time when his duties were of a secretarial nature. The chancellor was the Bishop's chief legal counsel, the foremost of his *jurisperiti*; he was constantly attendant on the Bishop to give advice on matters of law, particularly when the Bishop acted as judge. Langley's chancellors were often engaged as his commissaries in legal causes and in conducting visitations, and they sometimes deputized for him in the transaction of routine business.

The preparation of the Bishop's diocesan commissions and letters was the responsibility of the registrar. Langley had five successive registrars; the first, Thomas Lyes, rose to become the Bishop's vicar-general and Dean of Auckland, while his successors, although their subsequent careers were less eminent, received benefices in reward for their services. The registrar did not himself usually do the actual written work, although, being a notary, he was required to append his sign and subscription to formal instruments; Richard Brancepeth, the third registrar, was the exception, for he did not employ a clerk to write for him. The registrar was also the custodian of the Bishop's archives; he saw to the preservation of letters and reports received, and drafts of letters despatched, which were kept in files unless they were too large. From time to time, this correspondence was copied into the Bishop's register, which was the final record of his official *acta*, of letters and commissions of appointment, wills and ordination lists. Sometimes the Bishop caused to be enregistered records of certain matters of a non-diocesan nature, personal to him or arising from his position in other capacities, as Chancellor of England for instance. Langley's register is a very imperfect record, however, for much business went unrecorded. The drafts and originals which were to be copied into it were sometimes lost or displaced, probably as a result of his constant journeying, so that no record was ever made of their content. A certain amount of the Bishop's correspondence regarding his spiritual administration, as of his temporal government, appears to have been despatched under his signet, and letters of this sort, with a solitary exception, were never recorded in his register.[1]

The register shows a few reports of legal proceedings before the Bishop. This jurisdiction, exercised by the Bishop in person, stood in approximately the same relation to the consistory court as did the King's Council or Chancery to the courts of common law. The proceedings took place in a court that seems to have been somewhat informal. It was held in that one of his manors in which the Bishop happened to be residing in the diocese; he delegated this judicial power to his vicar-general while absent. Most of the causes shown were of matrimonial disputes, and Langley occasionally delegated such cases to commissions. On 5 February 1433, at Bishop Auckland, he gave judgement concerning the fraudulent resignation of a benefice. A suit regarding the carrying of consecrated water in the parish of Lanchester was entrusted to a commission. Once, Langley had before him a Carmelite friar accused of preaching false doctrines, heard his confession, and received his submission.[2] When the Bishop held his informal court, a number of *jurisperiti* was always present. These were the ecclesiastical lawyers who formed the Bishop's council for diocesan affairs. On 13 March 1436, John Heyworth, who had on the previous day become Master of Gateshead Hospital by exchange, declared to the Bishop that he could not accept the collation unless he was granted a dispensation from residence. Langley replied that he could not alter the form of the collation but he would consult his council regarding a dis-

---

[1] *Reg.* Vol. I, pp. xiii–xlii.
[2] Ibid. nos. 185, 257, 291, 510, 613 & 1035.

pensation. This was subsequently granted, *viva voce*, in the presence of the chancellor, the registrar, and a doctor of theology.[1]

The composition of the Bishop's diocesan council is to be deduced from his penitentiary commissions. These empowered the grantee to receive confessions and grant absolution even in cases reserved to the Bishop, with certain exceptions, including violation of the liberties of the church of Durham. The earliest of Langley's commissions were granted to individual members of religious orders.[2] In 1412, three commissions were issued on one day: John Ripon, Subprior of Durham, John Huntman, Dean of Lanchester, and Robert Ashburn, Dean of Chester-le-Street, were appointed to the first; the Abbot of Alnwick and John Brigg, Vicar of Corbridge, to the second; and Huntman and Ashburn to the third, in which no exceptions were made to their powers. Ashburn was the official of Durham and Brigg the sequestrator in Northumberland.[3] Later commissions tended to be larger; two bodies were appointed at the one time, one for each archdeaconry. Appointments were made regularly, with the usual exceptions and were to last during the Bishop's pleasure. Between 1428 and 1436, commissions were appointed on six occasions; for Northumberland, the average membership was eight, and for Durham, nine. The former commission included the Abbots of Alnwick and Newminster, the Prior of Holy Island, the sequestrator and the Vicars of Newcastle, Bedlington, and Embleton; it may be presumed that these Vicars were the deans of the three rural deaneries of Northumberland. The Subprior and a monk of Durham headed the other commission, and the vicar-general, spiritual chancellor, official, and sequestrator were also members; the balance was formed by clerks holding some of the best benefices in the Bishop's gift, who were generally all graduates.[4] The secular clerks on the Durham commission were undoubtedly the members of the Bishop's diocesan council; from time to time, they were present to witness his *acta*. It is apparent that Langley's experience of secular government had led him to develop in his spiritual administration a system parallel to that of commissions of the peace.

1 *Reg.* nos. 1199 & 1200.
2 Ibid. 17, 26, 42, 44 & 131.
3 Ibid. 154, 156, 242 & 243.
4 Ibid. 709, 802, 901, 968, 1144 & 1189; and see below, pp. 179–80.

The local organization of the diocese centred on the consistory court, which, in Durham, was held in the Galilee Chapel of the Cathedral. Here sat the official-principal, to dispense justice according to canon law. The registrar of the court attended to supervise the making of its records, which the court itself kept.[1] It was thus only when the official had to appeal to the Bishop that any traces of the court's activities made their way into the episcopal register. For instance, the Bishop had to cite Margaret Marley to appear before him or his commissaries; she had been suspended from attendance at church for ignoring a summons from the official.[2] On another occasion, the official informed Langley that John Ram of Newcastle had been excommunicated, yet refused to submit. Langley therefore wrote to the King to invoke the secular arm.[3] The position of the church courts with regard to the inhabitants of the County of Durham was much stronger, because of the Bishop's temporal franchise, than in Northumberland or elsewhere in England.

The best evidence for the activities of the consistory court is to be found in the records of the Prior and Convent of Durham. On 23 July 1415, the official gave judgement in their favour against Thomas Blakiston, in a suit they had brought for non-payment of tithes of coal.[4] Sentence was given for the Convent on 10 January 1419 in a suit against a parishioner of Bywell St Andrew, who was shown to have refused to pay tithes on two hundred sheep. The defendant gave notice of appeal to York, but failed to lodge it in the term given.[5] Fees were paid for litigation in the Durham consistory. In 1419–20, the sacrist of the Convent paid 3s. 4d. for a sentence against the Abbot of Blanchland. In 1436–7, the almoner paid 2s. to a notary for making an instrument concerning the recovery of tithes of coal at Fulforth, and 2s. to William Doncaster, the official, for attaching his seal to the instrument;[6] 2s. was also paid to the official for a letter of excommunication.[7] At the instance of the Prior the official issued a monition, on 4 March 1432, against unknown persons who had stolen goods

---

1 *Reg.* Vol. I, pp. xvii–xviii.   2 Ibid. no. 751.
3 *Reg.* no. 561; Chancery: Significations of Excommunication, file 199, no. 11.
4 DCD. Cartuarium Evidenciarum Communarii, fo. 51.
5 DCD. Cartulary IV, ff. 33v.–34.
6 *Durham Account Rolls*, Vol. II, pp. 233 & 407.
7 DCD. Bursar 1414–1415, m. 3d.

from the Master of Farne, and on 4 August following, a citation to seven men who had stolen the Prior's fishing-nets to appear in the court.[1] At times, the official was asked to have copies made of documents. Thus an exemplification of the (alleged) charter of Bishop William I was made in the court on 12 February 1419; the official attached his seal in testimony, and notarial marks were made by William Doncaster, then an advocate of the court, and Robert Berall, the registrar of the court, whom the official referred to as "our scribe".[2]

The official's commission empowered him to act in proceedings brought about by the exercise of his office or at the instance of parties.[3] According to canon law, the Bishop should have conducted a visitation of his diocese every three years. This rule was no longer observed, but a major object of visitations, investigations into misdemeanours by clergy and people, was adequately catered for by the system of church courts. The consistory court was the centre to which various local officers sent reports of *crimina et excessus*. Rural deans and parish priests would inform the official of alleged offences. It was also open to individuals to denounce suspected persons. On 6 March 1431, four chaplains and three male and two female parishioners met in Gateshead church to make charges against John Bolton, lately curate of that church. He was accused of incontinence and abuse of the confessional office; he spent well-nigh every night in taverns, eating and drinking with laymen, and lay so long abed in the mornings that it was doubtful if he ever said matins. The notary examined the parishioners and recorded their evidence in an instrument.[4] This report was presumably sent to the official.

The operations of the two sequestrators-general, one for each archdeaconry, also ensured that a close watch was kept over the behaviour of the clergy and people of the diocese. Duties arising from sequestrations, however, accounted for only a fraction of their activities. They were given powers to grant probate of wills and exercise other testamentary jurisdiction in respect of all persons except nobles and knights and their wives and widows. They also had to take charge of any benefices which fell vacant and to collect all pensions due to the Bishop from

---

1 DCD. Reg. Parvum I, ff. 55v. & 64.
2 *Scr. Tres*, Appendix, pp. ccviii–ccix.
3 *Reg.* nos. 15 & 59. 4 DCD. Locellus 10, no. 18.

churches in the archdeaconry. The sequestrator made an account for his receipts annually, at Michaelmas; it was usual for sequestrators to be appointed about this time. The similarity with the terms of a sheriff's service is explained by the fact that the pensions from churches were delivered to the receiver of Durham, whose year of account ended at Michaelmas. The account rendered by a sequestrator for Northumberland during the vacancy of the see, for the period 25 April to 24 August 1406, shows the extent of his activities. He accounted to the keepers of the spiritualities for the receipt of probate charges and for fines taken from laymen convicted of incontinence; in his four months of office, he made six circuits of the whole county and two of Newcastle.[1] The sequestrator's routine duties were certainly heavy, and in addition he was frequently required to perform other tasks, such as holding inquisitions into titles to present to benefices and the state of church buildings, or inducting new incumbents and supervising the purgation of defamed persons.[2]

The operations of the sequestrators must have made considerable inroads into the sphere of archidiaconal jurisdiction; as officers of the Bishop, they would have been in a favoured position against the archdeacons. The Archdeacons of Durham and Northumberland were generally absentees, leaving their responsibilities to officials. At one time, the ubiquitous William Doncaster was the official of both archdeacons.[3] The only notice of any judicial activity by either of the archdeacons in the Bishop's register is an inhibition directed to the official of the Archdeacon of Northumberland, who was prosecuting a woman for an offence of which she had purged herself in the presence of the Bishop's official.[4] Occasionally, Langley would direct certain commissions to an archdeacon, or his official, similar to those enjoined upon the sequestrator in addition to his usual duties. There is more evidence of the activity of the Prior of Durham as archdeacon in the appropriated churches. Visitations were made by his commissioners of the Convent's churches in Northumberland in 1409, 1417, and 1422, and in Durham in 1433 and 1434. Two monks of Durham visited Billingham in 1418 or 1419.[5] The

---

[1] Storey, *Diocesan Administration*, pp. 13–14.
[2] *Reg.* nos. 105, 108, 336, 362, 390, 756, 787 & 1024.
[3] Emden, loc. cit.   [4] *Reg.* no. 928.
[5] DCD. Reg. Parvum I, fo. 73; Reg. III, fo. 155v.; 2.2. Archidiaconalia Northumbr' 3–9; Bursar 1418–1419, m. 3d.

court of the Prior, as archdeacon, was held in the church of St Oswald's, Durham; an official was employed for this work, and Doncaster once numbered it among his occupations. A record of the court's proceedings from 1435 to 1456 survives.[1]

As Langley spent so much of his time outside the diocese, his vicars-general were almost constantly active. The Prior and Archdeacon of Durham were appointed on 10 August 1406, but as Archdeacon Weston soon left England to seek his fortune at the Roman Curia, Prior Hemmingburgh must have acted alone until 1411.[2]   Robert Ashburn, the official, succeeded him on 1 September, but the Prior was re-appointed after Ashburn's death in January 1413.[3]   In 1414, John Huntman, Dean of Lanchester, became Hemmingburgh's colleague; Thomas Lyes joined Huntman after the Prior's death.[4]   When Huntman died in 1417, Lyes continued to act alone. Although Langley resided in the diocese a score of times during Lyes' period of office, only one further commission is recorded, in April 1432.[5]   A new commission was not necessary every time the Bishop was absent: the vicar's activities ceased when the Bishop was in the diocese and recommenced after his departure. The vicar-general had authority to transact all routine diocesan business that would be carried out in the Bishop's presence when he was in the diocese, including the informal jurisdiction of the "audience", but he was not empowered to fill vacancies in livings in the Bishop's gift. Langley kept a tight hold over his rights as a patron, although very occasionally, as when he went to Pisa in 1409, he did appoint commissioners to exercise episcopal patronage for the duration of his possibly long absence.[6]

Langley had a suffragan bishop continually in his employment. The first was Oswald, styled Bishop of Galloway, a see *in partibus infidelium* during the Schism; he had been Skirlaw's suffragan.[7] Langley's other three suffragans were bishops of Irish sees;[8] one of them, Robert Foston, Bishop of Elphin and a Minorite friar, was probably the same as the Robert Foston who was a member of the Minorite house at Hartlepool in 1408. The Pope deprived him

[1] *Depositions and Ecclesiastical Proceedings*, pp. 26–37.
[2] *Reg.* no. 12.   Weston died at Pistoia, near Florence, on 29 August 1408 (Reg. Bowet I, fo. 14).
[3] *Reg.* nos. 154, 266 & 317; DCD. 1.2. Archidiaconalia Dunelm' 67.
[4] *Reg.* nos. 337 & 425.   [5] Ibid. 983.   [6] Ibid. 121.
[7] Ibid. 14 & 101.   [8] Ibid. 530, 531 & 1166; Reg. fo. 287.

of his see because of his non-residence, but permitted him to adopt the style of "bishop in the universal church".[1] Both Foston and Oswald obtained papal dispensations to hold benefices, obviously necessary for their support, and these they received in Durham.[2] An annual salary of £13 6s. 8d. was paid to each suffragan from the Bishop's palatine exchequer.[3] The task of the suffragan was to carry out the Bishop's sacerdotal duties, principally in the ordination of clergy and confirmation of the laity, but also to bestow the episcopal benediction on newly elected heads of religious houses and to consecrate churches, graveyards, and the like. The suffragan's work was not light, and must have caused him to undertake many journeys about the diocese.[4] Langley's regular employment of a suffragan was appreciated beyond the boundaries of the diocese of Durham: both religious and secular clergy of the diocese of Carlisle, where no suffragan seems to have been engaged,[5] and canons of Hexham and Guisborough in the diocese of York, frequently came into Durham to receive their orders.

2 THE SECULAR CLERGY

The diocese of Durham comprised a total of nearly one hundred and thirty parishes, of which number slightly more than half were in County Durham. Here, because this was the patrimony of St Cuthbert, there was a great concentration of ecclesiastical patronage in the hands of the Bishop and the Prior and Convent of Durham, who between them held the advowsons of more than forty churches, almost equally divided; while the Masters of the hospitals of Sherburn, Greatham, and Kepier, who were the patrons of six other churches, were themselves appointed by the Bishop. In addition, there were in the five collegiate churches of Auckland, Chester-le-Street, Darlington, Lanchester, and Norton some three dozen prebends also in the Bishop's gift. In Northumberland, the Prior and Convent of Durham was the most considerable patron, but other religious houses in the county and outside, with the Bishops of Durham and Carlisle, and nine or ten lay patrons, mostly in the franchises, formed a much more hetero-

---

1 *Reg.* nos. 42 & 884; *CPL.* VIII, p. 175.
2 *Reg.* nos. 495 & 884.
3 Above, p. 89.   4 Below, pp. 201–2.
5 Storey, "Marmaduke Lumley", p. 122.

geneous pattern of patronage.[1] By the fifteenth century, the conventual patrons had appropriated nearly all the benefices at their disposal; this practice may now have proved itself advantageous to the clergy of Northumberland, for as vicars they received fixed stipends which in several cases must have exceeded the revenues drawn by the appropriators from benefices subject to the hazards of Scottish raids. A number of the vicarages in this county were held by regular canons; the Premonstratensians of Alnwick[2] and Blanchland[3] supplied vicars to eight churches, and Austin canons from Hexham[4] and Brinkburn[5] held five other vicarages. In 1422, the lay patron presented the Prior of Carlisle to the rectory of Kirkhaugh, and another canon of this house became Vicar of Whittingham in 1428.[6] It is unlikely that any other English county had a quarter of its churches served by members of religious orders.

Bishop Langley appears to have enjoyed almost complete freedom in the exercise of his ecclesiastical patronage; no instance is known of any effective papal provision during his episcopate, and his objection to Henry IV's presentation to a church in Durham[7] seems to have put a stop to any tendency to royal encroachment in this direction. Only in the case of the archdeaconries was he unable to resist the Crown's pretensions, which by this time had been generally established; even the Bishop of Durham had been obliged to submit to these claims, for he could not reply that the right to present to an archdeaconry was an appurtenance of his temporal franchise. In 1419, Henry V presented Robert Gilbert to the archdeaconry of Durham. Langley did not readily accept the royal nominee, and the King had to send him two "reminders" in 1420. The Bishop then appointed a commission to enquire into the King's title to present.[8] Its report was not recorded in the Bishop's register, but Gilbert was Archdeacon of

---

[1] R. N. Hadcock, "A Map of Medieval Northumberland and Durham", *Archaeologia Aeliana*, *1939*, pp. 159–207.

[2] Alnham, Chatton, Lesbury and Shilbottle (*Reg.* no. 322; Reg. ff. 247v., 274v. & 249v.).

[3] Bolam, Bywell St Andrew, Heddon-on-the-Wall and Kirkharle (Ibid. 280 & 303; *Reg.* nos. 1038 & 1051).

[4] Ovingham, Stamfordham, and Warden (Ibid. 973; Reg. fo. 277v.).

[5] Felton and Longhorsley (Ibid. 273 & 286v.).

[6] Ibid. 277v.; *Reg.* no. 720.

[7] Above, pp. 53–4.

[8] *Reg.* nos. 537–40.

Durham in 1425. He was then succeeded by Robert Rolleston, the Keeper of the Great Wardrobe.[1] Gilbert's predecessors since 1406 had been Thomas Weston and Alan Newark, both of whom served Bishops Skirlaw and Langley;[2] John Hovingham, protonotary of Chancery, who also performed some duties in the diocese;[3] and John Kemp, subsequently Chancellor of England and Archbishop of York.[4] Langley gave some benefices to the kinsmen of his influential friends[5] and to some of his acquaintances and subordinates in the King's service,[6] but the number of these was small.

In 1437, only one of the Durham benefices in the Bishop's gift was held by a man appointed before 1406. This was the rectory of Ryton, worth £40 per annum in 1535,[7] which was held by Robert More, who had been the sequestrator in Durham.[8] Among the clergy reported to have been non-resident on 14 January 1438 were Thomas Asteley, Rector of Houghton-le-Spring (£124); Robert Rolleston, the Archdeacon, who also held the church of Easington (£100); John Heyworth, Rector of Sedgefield (£74); and Thomas Tanfield, Rector of Gateshead (£27).[9] Heyworth had become Rector of Sedgefield by exchange with George Radcliffe, doctor of canon law, a former sequestrator and a member of the Bishop's diocesan council, who was to end his career as Treasurer of Lichfield and vicar-general of the Bishop of Coventry and Lichfield.[10] Another stranger had been imported when Nicholas Hulme exchanged the mastership of Greatham hospital (£80) with John Saulby for a prebend at Ripon; Hulme had been the treasurer of Langley's household and receiver-general of Durham, and was still serving the Bishop in 1437.[11] Sherburn hospital (£124) was held by John Marshal, an officer of Archbishop Kemp.[12] Thomas Buckley had become Rector of

---

[1] *Reg.* no. 659. [2] *Reg.* I, p. xii & no. 105.
[3] Ibid. 115, 306, 319, 451 & 454; *CPR. 1413–1416*, p. 142.
[4] Below, p. 209. [5] Above, pp. 106 & 109.
[6] E.g. William Kinwolmarsh, collated to a prebend at Auckland in 1415 (*Reg.* no. 347); *Reg. Chichele*, II, p. 660.
[7] Values are taken from the *Valor Ecclesiasticus*, V, pp. 307–18.
[8] First mentioned 1408, last 1431 (*Reg.* I, p. xxxix, n. 6, & nos. 43 & 931).
[9] York: Register of Archbishop Kemp, fo. 490v.
[10] Storey, *Diocesan Administration*, pp. 23–4.
[11] Above, pp. 74 & 79.
[12] *Reg.* nos. 1061 & 1209. The collation was made on 23 July 1433, a time when Langley would wish to be assured of Kemp's goodwill (Above, p. 128).

St Nicholas', Durham,[1] by arrangement with his namesake Richard, the previous incumbent.[2] The deanery of Chester-le-Street ($£41$) was acquired by Rowland Thornburgh in an exchange in 1415.[3] No more is known of him, nor of Thomas Butler, M.A., the Rector of Boldon ($£24$),[4] but they were not absentees at the time of the Bishop's death.

The principal officers of Langley's two administrations were all well-rewarded: Richard Buckley, the receiver-general in 1437, was Master of Kepier hospital ($£145$);[5] William Doncaster, LL.B., the official, Dean of Auckland ($£100$); [6] Thomas Lyes, the former vicar-general, Rector of Bishop Wearmouth ($£100$); and Dr Thomas Bonour, the spiritual chancellor, Rector of Whitburn ($£40$).[7] The churches of Haughton-le-Skerne ($£53$) and Stanhope ($£67$) were held by Richard Pennymaster, B.THEOL., and William Blackburn, LL.B., both members of the diocesan council.[8] The Vicar of Darlington ($£36$), Richard Witton, M.A., had been appointed to the penitentiary commission in 1431 and was resident in 1434.[9] Stephen Austell, James Oculshaugh, and Richard Kelloe were all members of the Bishop's household; Austell was Dean of Lanchester ($£40$),[10] Oculshaugh Rector of Wolsingham ($£31$),[11] and Kelloe Vicar of Norton ($£31$).[12] Thus half of the twenty wealthiest benefices at Bishop Langley's disposal were held by men who had been actively engaged in his service, while some of the remainder had only passed into strange hands by exchange with other ministers. The clerks employed by the Bishop were often pluralists, holding prebends in one or more of his collegiate churches in addition to their rectories and hospitals.[13] Langley's exercise of patronage was eminently practical, used to maintain his ministers and please influential connections. Although Convocation had decreed in 1422 that bishops should give a share of their patronage to university graduates,[14] Langley continued to give benefices as he had done

1 The value in 1535 is not known, as this church was then appropriated to Kepier hospital.

2 Reg. fo. 253.

3 Reg. no. 489.

4 Ibid. 905.

5 Above, p. 74; and see n. 1, above.

6 Emden, *Register of Oxford*, I, p. 585.

7 Reg. I, pp. xv & xix.

8 Ibid. 1189.

9 Ibid. 901 & 1115.

10 Ibid. 287, 398 & 758.

11 Ibid. 754, 1060, 1133 & 1222.

12 Ibid. 867 & 887; CCR. *1417–1422*, pp. 31 & 211.

13 Reg. I, pp. xv & xix–xxii; and see above, pp. 78–9.

14 Ibid. no. 558.

before: a number of graduates, chiefly lawyers, did receive Durham benefices, but they were employed in the Bishop's diocesan administration.

The wealthiest Durham benefice of which the Bishop was not patron was the vicarage of Gainford, said to be worth £40 a year in 1535;[1] its patrons were the Abbot and Convent of St Mary's, York. Pope Boniface IX provided William Heworth to this vicarage in 1389 or 1390, but the papal candidate was disappointed by the institution of Roger Kirkby. After Kirkby's death in 1412, Heworth entered into possession and speedily obtained the King's pardon for so doing,[2] but St Mary's presented Master Richard Arnall, whom the Bishop instituted after an enquiry had established St Mary's title to present.[3] The two claimants now resorted to litigation in at least three courts; it was probably Heworth who first appealed to the Roman Curia, while Arnall instituted proceedings in the court of York, where he was the official's commissary-general,[4] and in King's Bench. Heworth continued to occupy the vicarage, however, where he defied the Bishop's order for its sequestration in 1414.[5] He was outlawed for his failure to answer Arnall in King's Bench, and the King appointed a commission to arrest him.[6] As he was then in the liberty of Durham, Heworth was safe from the King's officers, but the Bishop's second commission of sequestration, strengthened by the inclusion of his palatine steward and chancellor and the authority to invoke the secular arm, was a more formidable threat, and when the Archbishop informed Langley of Heworth's excommunication by the court of York,[7] the period of his successful defiance was brought to an end. He must have made his peace with the ecclesiastical authorities at least, for later in 1415 he was able to obtain from the Bishop a copy of an instrument relating to his claims.[8] This copy was probably required to support his suit in Rome, but this was now decided against him: on 6 April 1416, the Bishop was informed of sentences in favour of Arnall, whose reinstatement as vicar he ordered.[9] The tenacity shown by Heworth in fighting his claim deserves some measure of admiration; he must have enjoyed the support of the parishioners

[1] *Valor Ecclesiasticus*, V, p. 318.
[2] *CPR. 1408–1413*, p. 455.
[3] *Reg.* nos. 282–6.
[4] Ibid. 345 & 361.
[5] Ibid. 341 & 345.
[6] *CPR. 1413–1416*, p. 294.
[7] *Reg.* nos. 345 & 349.
[8] Ibid. 376.
[9] Ibid. 404.

of Gainford, for he was a local man,[1] and this factor must have been largely responsible for his ability to hold the vicarage for three years. Arnall remained Vicar of Gainford until 1428, and at one stage of his distinguished career, in 1425, held the position of official of Durham.[2]

To men like Richard Arnall, benefices were of interest principally as sources of revenue; the Bishop's officers also, although their work in his temporal and diocesan administrations cannot have led them far afield, would not have been able fully to attend to their parochial cures, and they employed chaplains to perform their routine duties. The class of clergy exercising the cure of souls was thus largely one of stipendiary priests, of vicars in the case of appropriated churches, and of curates on behalf of secular rectors. Very little is known of this ecclesiastical proletariat; its members were mostly ordained on titles provided by religious houses, and they progressed from being chaplains of chantries to employment as parish priests, with a vicarage as the summit of their practicable ambitions. The recruitment of curates sometimes had to be effected by compulsion; several incumbents told the Bishop that they were unable to obtain the services of parish priests, and he appointed commissions to compel priests, usually already serving chantries, to enter the service of rectors.[3] One priest who had been engaged by the Rector of Gateshead refused to complete the period of his contract, and had to be ordered to serve until the end of the agreed term.[4] The need to resort to these measures suggests that the supply of priests in the diocese of Durham was not sufficient for its needs. It has been observed that such large numbers of priests were ordained in England in this period that there should not have been any difficulty in filling vacancies,[5] but petitions in Parliament in 1402, 1414, and 1419, showing that the statutory scale of clerical stipends was not being respected,[6] indicate that this opinion may be mistaken. It certainly was not true of Durham, where the number of secular clerks ordained to the priesthood did not often exceed twelve in a year; it seems improbable that many priests were attracted by the conditions of the Border diocese to come from southern

[1] *Reg.* no. 349.   [2] Ibid. 619 & 700.
[3] Ibid. 390, 661, 919 & 1031; Reg. ff. 283v. & 287v.
[4] *Reg.* no. 1003.
[5] Hamilton Thompson, *The English Clergy*, p. 143.
[6] *Rot. Parl.* III, p. 501, & IV, pp. 51–2, 121.

England, while the grant by Langley and his vicars-general of at least [1] one hundred and thirteen letters dimissory shows that many clerks left the diocese to pursue their careers in less troubled parts of the country.

The lives and work of the clergy and, to a lesser degree, of their parishioners, were subject to the constant surveillance of the Bishop's permanent administration, but its activities were to a large extent purely mechanical, and his unsleeping interest and occasional intervention were essential for the well-being of the religious life of his diocese. In no way, however, could his influence be brought to bear more closely than through the method of personal visitation; thus only could he see for himself how matters stood in the various parishes of the diocese. Langley's record in this respect is not good and he seems to have relied almost entirely upon his local officers to watch over the people in his charge. In this he was no worse than most contemporary bishops. Even in visitations, he often delegated the work to commissions. Their appointment, however, shows that he was well aware of the need for reform in certain quarters, and wished to remedy abuses. Records of visitations, whether by Langley or his deputies, are regrettably scanty; such as do remain show that measures were taken to correct the defects that were discovered.

On 28 June 1408, Langley sent to the Archdeacon of Durham his citation of visitation; certificates were to be laid before him by 24 July. On 23 July, he visited the Convent of Durham.[2] Shortly afterwards, the visitation of the archdeaconry was begun; Langley was at Auckland on 29 July, Stanhope on 10 August, Darlington on 14 August and 20 September, and back at Auckland on 22 September, before his return to London; he had visited all five of the collegiate churches.[3] Much was found to be amiss, for many fines were imposed, to be paid into the building funds of the Cathedral and other churches. Many of the fines had not been paid by the end of the year, when a commission was appointed to order their payment.[4] While at Norton, Langley observed the ruinous condition of the chancel, and ordered each prebendary to pay 40s. towards its repair.[5] The visitation was not completed, but was continued three years later. The citation was then

1 See *Reg.* I, p. xl.   2 Below, pp. 194–5.
3 *Reg.* nos. 88, 89, 92–95, 103 & 113; cf. 88 & 202.
4 Ibid. 108.   5 Ibid. 148.

issued on 22 June and the returns ordered for 4 July.[1]   Langley
went to Sherburn on 6 July, was at Auckland on 31 July, Stockton
on 8 August, and again at Auckland on 24 August; by 3 September
he was on his way to London.   He found cause for complaint at
Sedgefield and Staindrop, where markets were held on Sundays,
and on 15 April 1412 he issued monitions against this practice.
The people of Sedgefield were unaffected by the episcopal
censure, and the monition was repeated in 1430;[2] indeed, this
was an offence of long standing, for Bishop Richard de Bury had
forbidden Sunday markets at Sedgefield in 1344.[3]   The amount
of time spent by Langley in this visitation of County Durham—
four months—indicates that he was conscientious: other prelates
were more hasty.[4]

This was Langley's only full-scale visitation in the diocese,
although he did appoint commissions in 1411 and 1435 to make
enquiries into the behaviour of his subjects and to correct and
punish offenders.[5]   There are also indications that the Bishop
made informal visitations while travelling through the diocese.
Thus when he went to Berwick to meet Scottish ambassadors in
1425, he visited Holy Island on his way there and issued monitions
against the unknown thieves of animals belonging to two of its
parishioners; on his return, he granted an indulgence for a chapel
at Belford,[6] which he had presumably noticed to have been
ruinous.   When at Norham four years later, he observed that the
church of Carham needed repair, which he ordered.[7]   In 1432,
he issued a citation for the visitation of Gainford,[8] where he was
so much troubled by the poaching of his game.[9]   Langley later
proposed to visit the collegiate church of Darlington, on 31 May
1434;[10] as he was at Auckland on that day and at Stockton from
4 June it is likely that he carried out the visitation, since he would
have passed through Darlington.

Other local visitations were conducted by commissioners.   In
1415, a commission was appointed to visit Newcastle-upon-Tyne
and the hospital of West Spital[11] on 14 September; one of its acts

---

[1] *Reg.* no. 202.   [2] Ibid. 254 & 847.
[3] *Reg. Palatinum Dunelm.* IV, pp. 297–8.
[4] See, for instance, proposals for visitations by Archbishop Kemp of York
and Bishop Lumley of Carlisle, in C. M. L. Bouch, *Prelates and People of the Lake
Counties* (Kendal, 1948), pp. 114, 150–2.   [5] *Reg.* nos. 203 & 1172.
[6] Ibid. 655–6, 665.   [7] Ibid. 811.   [8] Ibid. 978.
[9] Above, pp. 115–16.   [10] *Reg.* no. 1099.   [11] Below, p. 190.

was the suspension of a priest for one year. The Bishop sent another commission to visit Newcastle in 1436.[1] The visitation by commissioners of the church of Eglingham, in 1430,[2] was followed by some lively litigation. Shortly after the visitation, some parishioners brought a suit against the vicar in the consistory court, alleging that he refused to pay the stipend of a curate who should have been maintained in the chapel at Brandon, in the parish. Judgement was given against the vicar, William Bamburgh, who then appealed to Rome. Langley wrote to William Swan about this on 14 January 1432. He had learnt that Swan was a proctor of the parishioners, whose cause he commended. Swan was asked to try to have the case delegated to the Archbishop or another person in the diocese of York.[3] On 4 July, the Pope referred the appeal to the Prior of Durham.[4] The court of appeal assembled in Durham Cathedral on 9 January 1433. The official, William Doncaster, acting as the Bishop's proctor, rehearsed the earlier proceedings. The Prior then called for Bamburgh, and informed him "in sweet and loving words" that he was going to settle the dispute. "Then the vicar, scarce deigning to approach, said openly, with much opprobrious language, that he would do nothing before him (the Prior), nor would he obey him or consent to such a judge; and so he contemptuously and contumaciously withdrew from the judge's presence, dragging with him one William Kirby, of the diocese of Carlisle, his so-called notary, who in truth, as it is said, was no notary at all." At Doncaster's instance, the Prior sent his apparitor to the Vicar's house to cite him to appear in eight days time to give cause, if he could, why he should not be excommunicated because of his contumacy.

The court thus met again, on 16 January. Bamburgh was called two or three times "before he chose to reply, although he was not standing far away and could hear quite well. At length, standing at a distance and not condescending to come nearer, he cried out in a derisory manner, 'What do you want?'." The judge then explained to him the reason for his summons. "The Vicar replied openly, 'I don't want you for my judge', and thrust upon him a closed paper schedule. Warned by the judge to wait

---

[1] *Reg.* nos. 370, 371, 384, 1236 & 1237.   [2] Ibid. 857.
[3] British Museum: Cleopatra C. IV, fo. 161.
[4] DCD. 1.3. Papalia 5; Cartulary III, fo. 195.

until he had opened the schedule and learnt what it contained, the Vicar refused, and displaying even more contempt than on the previous day, if that were possible, he left the court." At the request of the Bishop's proctor, the Prior then excommunicated the Vicar.[1] Bamburgh had already, on 12 April 1432, been ordered to resume residence in his vicarage. Despite this warning, he remained absent and farmed the issues. On 28 February 1436, Langley ordered the issue of a formal monition that he was to return.[2] Here the story seems to end. It is remarkable that Bamburgh had not been deprived earlier, for his contumacy as well as for his non-residence.

The failure of beneficed clergy to reside in their livings was a common abuse, but few cases of absenteeism by incumbents of churches occur in Langley's register. In 1411, the Bishop ordered the Rector of Boldon to abandon his intention of going on a pilgrimage.[3] John Burgeys was a notorious offender whose services to the secular government of Durham had earned him preferment and gave him a privileged position. He was Bishop Fordham's treasurer in 1386, and had become Dean of Lanchester and Master of Sherburn hospital before 1392;[4] he later exchanged the deanery for that of Auckland. Bishop Skirlaw took proceedings against Burgeys on account of his bad administration and non-residence, depriving him of the custody of Sherburn Hospital and ordering him to resume residence at Auckland under a similar penalty in January 1404.[5] In the previous year, however, the Dean had obtained a papal licence to be absent for the duration of his life.[6] He must have returned to Durham by 1408, when Langley appointed him as an auditor of the accounts of the palatine officials,[7] but there is no further notice of his presence in the diocese; he may have joined his previous master, Fordham, at Ely. In 1414, Langley threatened to sequestrate the deanery of Auckland unless Burgeys returned to it, and the Dean appealed to the court of York, which inhibited the sequestration. Since he did not appear at York on the day appointed for his appeal it was dismissed, the inhibition was revoked, and the Bishop

---

1 DCD. Misc. Charters, no. 2613.
2 *Reg.* nos. 985 & 1195.   3 Ibid. 211.
4 *Hatfield's Survey*, p. 273; *DKR. 33*, pp. 47 & 81.
5 *CPR. 1401–1405*, p. 475; DCD. Locellus 17, no. 3.
6 *CPL.* V, p. 555.
7 Rot. Langley A. m. 3d.

13

sequestrated the deanery.[1] Burgeys now proposed to appeal to Rome, but Langley forestalled him and secured the withdrawal of his indult for non-residence.[2] The Bishop was spared from taking further proceedings by Burgeys' death three months later.[3] Another absentee Dean, William Pelleson of Lanchester, was ordered to reside by the vicar-general in 1417; he wisely made his escape by a timely exchange with the rector of a church in York.[4] He had undoubtedly been impressed by Langley's success against Burgeys, but its effect on the practice of non-residence generally was short-lived: in 1438, it was reported to the keeper of the spiritualities of Durham that seventeen rectors and vicars were absent from their benefices.[5]

Another general problem was the neglect of church buildings; commissions to enquire into reports of dilapidations were all too common. Sometimes Langley ordered repairs under pain of suspension, as in 1429 when the parishioners of Pittington were told to restore their belfry.[6] The chantry of "Le Close" at Heddon-on-the-Wall was utterly wasted by its lay patron, a factor that accounts for the inability of the Archdeacon of Northumberland to induct a chaplain in 1416.[7] It was usually the clergy, however, and not the laity, who earned the Bishop's displeasure for this negligence; absentees like Robert Gilbert, Archdeacon of Durham,[8] were the most obvious offenders, but some of the resident clergy could not afford to keep the chancel, rectory, and other property in a good state of repair.[9] It is probable that some new incumbents sought an inquisition for defects as a matter of course, to safeguard themselves. William Brown, Dean of Lanchester, complained to the Bishop of the deterioration of the deanery's property in the time of his three predecessors, and when an inquisition was taken it was estimated that £44 would hardly suffice to make good the damage to the Dean's house and buildings held by his tenants.[10] On the other hand, Thomas Hebden, who became Dean of Auckland on 29 December 1431, was by no means justified in the complaint he made three months later that there were dilapidations in the deanery dating from the time of

[1] *Reg.* no. 326; Reg. fo. 259.
[2] *CPL.* VI, p. 458.
[3] *Reg.* no. 348.
[4] Reg. ff. 284v.–5.
[5] Reg. Kemp, ff. 490v.–1.
[6] *Reg.* no. 815.
[7] *CCR. 1413–1419*, p. 161; *Reg.* no. 417.
[8] *CPL.* VIII, pp. 44–5.
[9] E.g. *Reg.* no. 392.
[10] Ibid. 499 & 500.

his predecessor Thomas Lyes,[1] for the ensuing inquisition fully exonerated Lyes: there were some trifling defects in a few buildings, but it was estimated that he had spent £229 5s. 2d. on repairs to the deanery and £100 in food for workmen; the house of the chapel of St Helen could have been restored at little cost, yet he had had it wholly rebuilt. It was reported that Lyes had given continuous hospitality at Auckland throughout the sixteen years that he had been Dean.[2]

Thus if some churches had been allowed to become ruinous, there was also some new building. Langley himself offered a magnificent example in Durham Cathedral, and his vicar-general Lyes had seconded him. Not only the deanery of Auckland, but also the collegiate church, had been extensively repaired, the latter by the Bishop.[3] Most of the oratories licensed by Langley were rooms in private houses, but licences show that chapels were built for public use in the parish of Bywell St Andrew, where floods prevented some parishioners from reaching their church, and at Archdeacon-Newton and Bishop Auckland.[4] A remarkably large number of new foundations testifies to the strength of conventional religious feeling in Langley's day. The Bishop founded a chantry in the Galilee Chapel of the Cathedral, the two chaplains of which were to teach grammar and song to poor children free of charge; this foundation was the origin of the present Durham School.[5] Roger Thornton, the princely merchant of Newcastle, founded a hospital there in 1412.[6] Chantries were established by John Cockin, Dean of Lanchester, and John Belasis, in the churches of St Nicholas and St Mary in the North Bailey, Durham, in 1408 [7] and 1418 [8] respectively; by Sir Robert Umfraville in his manor of Farnacres, in 1429; [9] and in the churches of Newcastle and Gateshead, in 1406 [10] and 1421,[11] by inhabitants of these towns; while grants of lands by William Hutton, the Prior's steward, William Doncaster, the official of

---

1 *Reg.* nos. 951 & 975.
2 DCD. Locellus 17, no. 12.
3 J. F. Hodgson, "The Church of St Andrew Auckland" (*Archaeologia Aeliana, 1899*), pp. 148–51; Hutchinson, *History of Durham*, I, p. 335.
4 *Reg.* nos. 147, 327 & 600.
5 *VCH. Durham*, I, pp. 371–86. 6 *CPR. 1408–1413*, p. 412.
7 Rot. A. mm. 2 & 3. 8 Above, p. 254 (c. 13).
9 Rot. E. m. 18; *CPR. 1422–1429*, p. 454; *CPR. 1436–1441*; p. 53.
10 *CPR. 1405–1408*, p. 262.
11 Rot. E. m. 6d.

Durham, and two chaplains, augmented the endowments of chantries already existing in the churches of Sedgefield,[1] Auckland,[2] and St Nicholas, Durham.[3]   A group of Langley's palatine ministers founded the guild of Corpus Christi in this last church.[4] The most important new foundation of Langley's time was the erection in 1412 of the collegiate church of Staindrop by Ralph Neville, Earl of Westmorland; the college was formed of a warden, eight chaplains, four clerks, six esquires, six yeomen, and six other poor men.   The Earl must be credited with the common desire of furthering his spiritual welfare by the augmentation of divine service, but he was also making provision for those retainers of his family who had to be retired from active service, and that he should do this by the appropriation of three parish churches to the college was a deplorable abuse of ecclesiastical practice.[5]

The most outstanding feature of Langley's episcopate was his work to reform the secular foundations; he showed particular concern for the three greater collegiate churches of County Durham, Auckland, Lanchester, and Chester-le-Street. The canons were mostly absentees who generally neglected to provide suitable, if any, deputies; in 1410, the three deans were ordered to warn the canons to remedy this state of affairs.[6]   In the course of his visitation of the archdeaconry of Durham Langley learnt that the founder's statutes were not being observed at Lanchester, and at the request of the Dean, ministers, and parishioners, commanded that if any absent canon failed to maintain a vicar, the revenues that should have been applied for this purpose were to be taken and half paid towards the upkeep of the fabric of the church and the other half divided among the resident ministers. In 1429, the Bishop was informed that four farmers of prebends were ignoring this ordinance, and they were summoned to the consistory court to answer for their neglect. Five years later, the Dean of Lanchester and the sequestrator of Durham were authorized to admonish those absentee canons, or their agents, who did not maintain vicars and otherwise disobeyed Langley's decree; they were empowered to sequestrate the prebends whenever necessary, and cause the offenders to appear in an eccle-

---

[1] Rot. C. m. 9.   [2] Ibid. 13.
[3] Rot. E. m. 18.   [4] Above, p. 101.
[5] Reg. no. 256; CPR. 1408–1413, p. 35; Valor Ecclesiasticus, V, p. 311.
[6] Reg. no. 153.

siastical court.[1] The prebends of Chester-le-Street were sequestrated in 1408, as their buildings had become ruinous. No
impression was made on the canons, who received a further
monition in April 1415. The warning was ignored. Two
months later, Langley wrote that he had learnt and seen for himself that no canon of Chester was in residence, divine service was
neglected, and no hospitality given; the prebends were therefore
sequestrated for a second time.[2]

Anthony Bek had ordered, in his statute of 1293, that the
canons of Auckland who did not reside were to maintain vicars;
the vicars of sacerdotal prebends were to be paid five marks per
annum, the deacons 40s., and the subdeacons or clerks 30s.; if a
canon failed to provide a vicar within a month, the dean was to
appoint one for the remainder of the year. Thomas Lyes, the
energetic Dean of Langley's time, petitioned the Bishop for a
reform of the college. He said that the stipends fixed for vicars
were obviously inadequate, although four canons who kept priests
as vicars had paid them eight marks per annum. Despite Bek's
decree, no houses or canonical habits were provided for the
vicars. Langley was urged to provide a remedy immediately,
for only five vicars were then maintained, and they were disposed
to leave unless their position was improved. The value of some
prebends was quite insufficient to enable their holders to support
vicars, and the Bishop was advised to divide those prebends that
had increased in value and to join together those that had become
poorer.[3] In consequence, on 20 March 1428, Langley ordered
an inquisition into the value of the prebends.[4] On 20 September
following, he gave the college new statutes, when Lyes' recom-
mendation for the redistribution of the prebends was adopted.
The position of the vicars was greatly improved; their stipends
were doubled and the dean was empowered to sequestrate the
the prebends of canons who did not pay them. The canons were
to provide houses for the vicars and they were given security of
tenure, for even those appointed by the dean on the failure of the
canons could only be dispossessed for disciplinary reasons or if the
canons came into residence; in the latter case, the canon had to

---

[1] *Reg.* nos. 819 & 1097.   [2] Ibid. 81, 350 & 365.
[3] Durham Chancery Miscellanea, bundle 206, no. 6, fo. 2v.; and see *Reg.*
Vol. I, p. xxxiii.
[4] *Reg.* no. 714.

give his vicar adequate warning, so that he could look for employment elsewhere.[1]

The condition of hospitals was generally unsatisfactory in this period, and was the subject of complaints in Parliament in 1414 and 1416. With the decline in the incidence of leprosy, the original purpose of hospitals was to some extent removed, and the endowments, often generous, gave large surpluses to their custodians; the office of master thus often became a valuable sinecure whose holder, bent on securing a handsome profit, paid little heed to the duties of his charge. Langley's interest in this problem appears to date from the presentation of these parliamentary petitions, to which the King had replied that the Bishops had undertaken to provide remedies.[2] The Bishop of Durham's commissioners who conducted a visitation of Newcastle-upon-Tyne in 1415 found that William Carlisle, the Master of West Spital, a house of the Augustinian order, was absent from the hospital, and they ordered him to resume residence within a month and present the Bishop with an account of his administration.[3] Carlisle had been in trouble before, for Bishop Skirlaw had excommunicated him in 1398,[4] but he was appointed a papal chaplain in the following year and dispensed to hold a benefice.[5] When the previous master of the hospital died in 1412, Carlisle and the one other canon surrendered their right to elect his successor, and Langley appointed Carlisle.[6] Two years after the visitation of 1415, Langley learned that the hospital badly needed reform: divine service was neglected, the revenues had decreased, the buildings were ruinous, and the Master had ignored the order to appear before the Bishop. Langley therefore appointed two formidable commissions: one, headed by the sheriff of Northumberland,[7] was to take charge of the hospital's property, and had power to invoke the aid of secular authority; the second, which was to visit the hospital, was formed by the Archdeacon of Durham, the spiritual chancellor, and three other members of the Bishop's "diocesan council". The outcome of this visitation

---

[1] *Reg.* no. 782; *Monasticon Anglicanum*, ed. W. Dugdale (1817–30), Vol. VI, pp. 1334–7; *CPR. 1429–1436*, p. 182.

[2] *Rot. Parl.* IV, pp. 19–20, 80–1.   [3] *Reg.* no. 372.

[4] DCD. Locellus 17, no. 29 (also supplied by Mr Snape).

[5] *CPL.* IV, p. 308; & V, p. 159.

[6] *Reg.* nos. 452 & 453.

[7] *List of Sheriffs* (Public Record Office Lists and Indexes, no. IX, 1898), p. 98.

was that William Carlisle "freely" resigned his office of master. Langley looked elsewhere for his successor, and appointed John FitzHenry, a canon of Newburgh.[1] The Bishop's satisfaction with his nominee is suggested by his regular appointment to the penitentiary commission for Northumberland,[2] and it may be presumed that in his long term of office [3] FitzHenry strove hard to restore the fortunes of West Spital.

The custody of the hospital of St Edmund and St Cuthbert in Gateshead was granted to John Walkington in 1410.[4] In 1421, the hospital was visited by commissioners who ordered a number of measures to improve its administration. Ten years later, however, in 1431, the Bishop was informed that Walkington had disregarded these injunctions, and accordingly sent a second commission to visit the hospital. The sequel was similar to that to the second visitation of West Spital: Walkington was deprived of his office, and a new master was collated early in 1432.[5] Langley received information that Walkington went to Rome, and wrote about the matter to William Swan, his agent in the Curia: he said that Walkington had for many years ignored orders to repair the hospital and amend his way of life, but since he had allowed the buildings to become ruinous and remained incorrigible, the Bishop's commissioners had expelled him and sequestrated the hospital; Langley had not learnt of any appeal being made in Rome against the deprivation, and asked Swan to discover what action Walkington had taken and to initiate such measures as he himself thought expedient.[6] Swan consequently obtained a bull appointing the Prior of Durham and the Treasurer of York to ascertain why Walkington had not lodged an appeal within one year of his deprivation.[7] Here the matter ended; the new master remained in possession until he exchanged the hospital for another benefice in 1436.[8] The hospital maintained its separate existence for only twelve more years, until 1448, when it was granted to the nuns of St Bartholomew's, Newcastle.[9]

Two large and wealthy hospitals in the immediate vicinity of

---

[1] *Reg.* nos. 450, 451, 454, 481 & 482.
[2] Ibid. 520, 542, 709, 802, 901, 968, 1144 & 1189.
[3] J. Brand, *History of Newcastle-upon-Tyne* (1789), Vol. I, p. 77.
[4] *Reg.* no. 135. [5] Ibid. 909 & 958.
[6] Cleopatra C. IV, fo. 162. [7] DCD. 1.3. Papalia 2.
[8] *Reg.* no. 1199. [9] *VCH. Durham*, II, p. 119.

Durham city also received the Bishop's attention. Kepier hospital was visited by a commission in 1436, and Richard Buckley, the Master, who was Langley's receiver-general, was given a full acquittance for his conduct of its affairs.[1] Sherburn hospital, a twelfth-century foundation, was held for sixteen years by John Newton, one of Langley's most trusted ministers. In 1429, a commission was appointed to enquire into reported dilapidations, grants of corrodies, and similar wastage of the hospital's revenues during the time that Newton was its master.[2] In fact, Newton was not the first to abuse this trust, for his predecessor, Alan Newark, had in 1409 leased some of the hospital's lands for a period of forty-seven years,[3] and the previous master had been removed for maladministration.[4] Langley received the Pope's licence to make new statutes, which the depletion of the revenues made necessary. Where Bishop Puiset's ordinance made provision for sixty-five lepers, the statutes enacted by Langley on 22 July 1434 provided for only two lepers and thirteen poor men; they also included rules for the government of the hospital and the observance of divine service. Langley's statutes for Sherburn hospital remained in force until the following century.[5]

3 THE RELIGIOUS AND MENDICANT ORDERS

The history of the medieval diocese of Durham is dominated by a single foundation, the Benedictine Convent of the Cathedral Church of St Cuthbert of Durham; its magnificent buildings, notorious wealth, and often turbulent annals have secured for it a degree of attention that has led to the neglect of the other monastic houses of the diocese. Apart from the Durham cells of Finchale, Jarrow, Monkwearmouth, Holy Island, and Farne, there were in Langley's day nine other convents of religious in the counties of Durham and Northumberland, all but one of them in the northern county. Tynemouth Priory, a cell of St Albans, was a house of considerable proportions, said to be worth nearly £400 a year in 1535. Second to it in wealth, although but half its annual value, came the abbey of Premonstratensian

---

[1] Reg. ff. 248 & 249v.; *Memorials of St. Giles's, Durham* (SS. 1895), pp. 224-7.

[2] Rot. E. m. 19.   [3] Rot. B. m. 2.   [4] Above, p. 185.

[5] Reg. ff. 244-6; *CPL*. VIII, pp. 44-5; *VCH. Durham*, II, p. 116.

canons at Alnwick, which, like the much poorer house at Blanchland, owed obedience to the ruler of Newhouse, in Lincolnshire,
as its father-abbot.   There were also houses of Cistercian monks
at Newminster and Austin canons at Brinkburn: Hexham Priory,
also of the order of St Augustine, lay outside the Bishop's jurisdiction and in the Archbishop of York's temporal and ecclesiastical
franchise of Hexhamshire.   The diocese of Durham had four
nunneries, in Newcastle-upon-Tyne, at Holystone in Redesdale,
Lambley on the South Tyne, and Neasham in County Durham.
While it is true that the revenues of the Convent of Durham more
than equalled those of the nine other monastic houses of the
diocese, Durham [1] was by any account an exceptionally great
foundation: at the Dissolution, only six houses—Christ Church,
Canterbury, Bury St Edmunds, St Albans, Glastonbury, Westminster, and St Mary's, York—could show larger incomes.[2]

In the early fifteenth century, the monks of Durham could look
back upon fatter years: estates yielding £1,000 in 1293 produced
only £400 in 1430.   This severe fall in revenue could be attributed
to the complete loss of rents derived from Coldingham and other
lands in Scotland, and the reduction to a fraction, because of the
wars, of issues from northern Northumberland; in County
Durham, where rents had fallen by half, one of the principal
causes was the conversion of arable land to pasture.   In 1436,
the rent received from these lands was £353, but as not all the
extensive Yorkshire estates were included in this figure, nor
spiritual sources, the total is not complete.[3]   If the number of
monks were an indication of the Convent's financial condition, it
would appear that its fortunes gradually improved during the
years of Langley's episcopate: fifty-seven monks were present at
his election in 1406; [4] ten years later, the figure was sixty-nine; [5]
and when Langley's successor was elected on 27 January 1438,
the total number of monks was seventy-three.[6]   In the thirty
years that John Wessington was Prior, a total of £6,123 8s. 7½d.
was spent on repairs to the Cathedral, the buildings of the
Convent, and other property.[7]   In the same period, the Convent

---

1 *Valor Ecclesiasticus*, V, pp. 303, 310, 327–30.
2 Ibid. I, pp. 16, 147, 424 & 451; III, p. 465; & V, p. 9.
3 *Scr. Tres*, Appendix, pp. ccxlviii–ccliii.
4 DCD. Reg. III, fo. 22.   5 *Reg.* no. 432.
6 DCD. Reg. III, fo. 213.
7 *Scr. Tres*, Appendix, pp. cclxxii–cclxxvi.

sacrificed any additional revenue it might have gained by the appropriation of its church of Hemingbrough, in Howdenshire, by converting it, in 1426, into a college for a warden, three canons, six vicars, and six clerks. The warden was to receive £40 per annum and each canon ten marks.[1] That the Convent felt able to deny itself this potential income is a sign that it had few misgivings about the state of its finances.

The Bishop, as ordinary, was concerned with the general condition of life in the Convent. On 11 June 1408, Langley sent the Prior his citation to announce that he was going to conduct a visitation, commencing on 23 July.[2] On 16 June, the Prior, John Hemmingburgh, wrote to the Prior of Finchale, and doubtless to the priors of the other cells, warning him of the visitation and ordering him to attend.[3] The Prior of Durham acknowledged the Bishop's citation on 12 July, stating that he had summoned all members of the cells, save those who had to remain in order to administer services; he appended a list giving the names of fifty-seven monks. On the appointed day, the visitation was carried out in the established manner. In accordance with the constitution of Boniface VIII, Langley brought with him, as assessors, John Henton, a monk of St Mary's, York, Master Richard Holme, the spiritual chancellor, Master Alan Newark, canon of Lanchester, and Master Thomas Lyes, a notary and the Bishop's registrar.[4] Although the Convent had obtained a bull from Boniface IX, in 1397, decreeing that the Bishop should have as assessors two or three clerks, one being a notary, and a monk of Durham,[5] no protest was made against the composition of Langley's entourage.

The Prior and monks came before the Bishop. The Prior presented his acknowledgement of the citation, and took an oath of obedience to the Bishop. Then John Wessington, on behalf of the Convent, asked that this oath might be recorded in a notarial instrument; this was made by Thomas Lyes. After the issue of a threat to excommunicate all entering into any conspiracy to hinder the visitation, the monks all left the chapter house, except for the Prior. He was then examined by the Bishop and his

---

1 DCD. 1.3. Archiepiscopalia 6; *CPR. 1422–1429*, p. 382.
2 *Reg.* nos. 86 & 87.
3 DCD. Reg. Parv. I, fo. 7: 2.7. Pontificalia 2.   4 *Reg.* no. 89.
5 DCD. Cartulary I, fo. 21v.

assessors on sixty-six articles; these were most comprehensive, covering all aspects of monastic life and the administration of the Convent's property. After the Prior had been examined, the monks were questioned singly by the assessors.[1] No record of any *comperta* survives. There had been some apprehension as to the Bishop's course of action. The Prior had written to a lawyer of York, on 2 July, asking that he should be present at the visitation: the Prior did not know whether Langley intended to inflict any punishments or do anything prejudicial to the Convent's privileges, although he did not expect him to.[2] Thomas Lythe, the third prior, had anticipated the Bishop's censure: on 21 July, he had made an appeal to Rome.[3] In 1439, one of the Bishop's injunctions was still remembered, namely that the convent was not to grant any office for term of life.[4] Langley also visited some of the Convent's appropriated churches. Procurations were paid to him at Pittington and Aycliffe. This was a breach of custom: Bishop Beaumont had conceded, in 1328, that procurations should not be paid by the Convent in respect of its appropriated churches. This grant was confirmed by succeeding bishops,[5] though not by Langley. Apparently no protest was made, a clear indication that the visitation at Durham had passed comfortably.

This was Langley's only visitation of the Convent of Durham, although during his episcopate six visitations were made by visitors appointed by the chapters of Benedictine monks in England,[6] but in no case have *comperta* been left. There is sufficient evidence elsewhere, however, that monastic life at Durham was not without its scandals. At the time of Wessington's election, it was reported that John Bonner could not be allowed to have any part in it on account of his infamous behaviour and disobedience. Two other monks, John Fishwick and Adam Durham, had run away and therefore been excommunicated.[7] Adam had cast off his monk's garb many years earlier, and had roamed abroad as a layman. In 1407, the Prior had learnt that he was being sheltered at Burton, in Lindsey,

---

[1] *Reg.* no. 89. [2] DCD. Reg. Parvum I, fo. 7.
[3] DCD. Locellus 21, no. 49.
[4] *Priory of Coldingham*, pp. 109–10, 114.
[5] DCD. 4 & 3 Pontificalia 6; 1.9. Pont. 4.
[6] DCD. Reg. Parvum I, ff. 15 & 57v.; Reg. III, ff. 53v., 100v. & 195; Cellarer, 19 April–17 May 1430.
[7] *Reg. Langley*, Vol. II, p. 119.

and he asked for the Bishop's aid in suing a royal writ for Adam's capture.[1] In 1422, a third monk, John Marley, abandoned the Convent; it was later learnt that he had gone into Hexhamshire.[2] A letter from the Duke of Bedford probably referred to Marley: he had recently been told "that oon of the monkes of youre convent was nit longe ago proved and founde gylte of the horrible synne of sodomye". He had been imprisoned, but had escaped and apostasized. Bedford was concerned for the honour of the Convent, "sithen that we be brothir therof", and charged the Prior to seek the monk and punish him "sharpely".[3] In 1434, Thomas Nesbit successfully maintained his innocence against a charge of adultery; he was purged by the oaths of twelve brother-monks.[4] Violence was inevitable in those times: in 1407, Thomas Esh, in the course of a quarrel with a second monk, Richard Stockton, struck and wounded him with a knife. They were reconciled. The Prior gave Esh licence to go to Rome to seek absolution, but he met a papal nuncio in London, who absolved him there and then, as he was too old and feeble for the journey.[5] Both monks were fairly senior: Stockton had died by 1416, but Esh was then Master of Farne.[6] In 1420, one monk actually killed another. John Tynemouth was indicted before the Bishop's justices of the murder of William Warner; he confessed, and was put in prison. Langley felt that it was indecent that a monk should be shut up with common robbers, and gave Esh into the Prior's custody, observing that this transfer was not to be held as a precedent.[7] The Convent was visited by Bishop Neville in 1442; although he found that some matters were in need of reform, he declared that the morals of the monks of Durham and its cells were without blemish.[8]

In these years a great amount of work was done on the buildings of the Cathedral and Convent. The dormitory and a large part of the cloisters were completed before 1406, most of the expense being borne by Bishop Skirlaw. The work on the cloisters was not completed until 1418. In 1416, Langley engaged a mason to build the fourth side, and he gave some £240 towards the total cost. In the church, a number of repairs were made to the main

1 *Scr. Tres*, Appendix, p. cc.   2 Reg. III, fo. 98v.; Misc. Charters, 6565.
3 DCD. Locellus 25, no. 115.   4 *Scr. Tres*, Appendix, pp. ccxxxix–ccxli.
5 DCD. Locellus 3, no. 19.   6 *Reg. Langley*, Vol. II, p. 118.
7 DCD. Locellus 27, no. 3.   8 DCD. Cartulary III, fo. 307.

structure and its windows.[1] Two at least of the windows were provided by the Bishop: one over the north door to the cloisters depicted Langley beneath the Virgin, with Saints Cuthbert and Oswald on either side; and the central window in the Chapel of the Nine Altars, over the altar of Saints Oswald and Laurence, also portrayed the Bishop.[2] In 1424, the Convent acquired lands to the annual value of ten marks which were to be devoted to the maintenance of its buildings.[3] A number of the monks contributed towards the cost of work on their solar and lavatory. On the night of 25 May 1429, the central tower of the Cathedral was struck by lightning, and although the fire was prevented from spreading, the repairs cost over £230.[4] In 1428, work had been begun on major alterations to the Galilee Chapel; the cost was borne by the Bishop, whose chantry had been founded there in 1414. The roof was completed in 1432, and work on the windows commenced in the following year. The four large west windows that had just been made were filled with pictures mostly of Anglo-Saxon saints and kings, with portrayals of Henry VI and Langley in one of them. The work was completed in 1435; it had cost the Bishop nearly £500, which was paid from his exchequer by Richard Buckley, the receiver-general.[5]

The Prior and Convent were frequently engaged in litigation.[6] There was a dispute with John Rikinghall, Archdeacon of Northumberland, concerning the Prior's claim to archidiaconal jurisdiction. This had been established for many years, but on a doubtful title,[7] and challenges continued to be made. In 1410, the Prior warned the clergy of his churches in Northumberland not to admit Rikinghall,[8] who had apparently proposed to visit them. The case was first heard at York, where John Wessington was the Convent's attorney.[9] The issue was not settled there, however, for on 28 February 1413, Rikinghall and Wessington came to Langley, in London, and swore to accept his arbitration.[10]

---

[1] *Scr. Tres*, pp. 145–6, and Appendix, pp. cciv–ccv, cclxii–cclxiv.
[2] *The Rites of Durham* (SS. 1902), pp. 110, 118–19; *Wills and Inventories*, I, p. 88.
[3] Cartulary III, fo. 293v.
[4] *Scr. Tres*, Appendix pp. ccxvii–ccxviii, cclxiii, ccccxlii–ccccxlv.
[5] DCD. Misc. Charters, 5713–21; *Rites of Durham*, pp. 47–51; *Scr. Tres*, p. 146.
[6] See also below, pp. 172–3.
[7] F. Barlow, *Durham Jurisdictional Peculiars* (Oxford, 1950), pp. 43–50.
[8] Reg. Parvum I, ff. 11v.–2.   [9] Bursar 1412–1413, m. 3d.
[10] 3.1. Archidiaconalia Northumbr' 16; Cartulary III, ff. 143–4.

Wessington prepared a formidable list of twenty-eight articles for the Bishop's edification.[1] The whole story of the Convent's privileges, from the foundation of a community of monks by King Oswald in A.D. 635 right up to the present time, with numerous confirmations by popes, kings, and bishops of Durham, testified to the justice of the Convent's claim,[2] as well as to Wessington's skill as a legal antiquary. It may be presumed that the Convent's case was proved in full. In the archdeaconry of Durham, John Hovingham contested the Prior's title, but agreed, on 22 September 1411, to cease taking legal action. He also promised to accept the award made by Langley, as arbitrator, who had inspected the Convent's records on this subject; in compensation, Hovingham was retained as legal counsel by the Prior and Convent.[3] Langley had obviously settled the dispute during his recent visitation of the diocese.

At the same time, the Prior and Convent were engaged in a suit with Archbishop Bowet of York. Bowet had held visitations of Howdenshire in July 1409 and of Allertonshire in July 1410.[4] He learned that the Prior of Durham took pensions from certain churches in those districts without, as Bowet said, any canonical title; he also disputed the Prior's right to hold visitations there. On 26 July 1410, the Archbishop commissioned his chancellor, Master Richard Pittes, Canon of York, to conduct legal proceedings in this matter.[5] The cause was heard before Pittes on 28 July. The Convent's attorneys established that it had legally appropriated the churches of Northallerton, Eastrington, and Giggleswick; that the churches of Roddington, Bossall, and Fishlake were legally appropriated to Durham College, Oxford; and that the Convent had a clear title to the pensions it drew from ten other churches. In addition, the Prior's claims to hold visitations and levy procurations, administer wills, and exercise other jurisdictional powers in Howdenshire and Allertonshire were upheld. Pittes admitted the claims, and granted a demise. A confirmation of this sentence was obtained from Pope John XXIII on 7 December 1412.[6] The Convent's expenses had been heavy.

---

1 *Scr. Tres*, Appendix, p. cclxix.
2 I.I. Archidiaconalia Northumbr' 5 & 8; Cartulary I, ff. 144–7v.
3 DCD. I.I. Archidiaconalia Dunelmensia 16; Cartulary I, ff. 132v.–3.
4 York: Reg. Bowet, I, ff. 270 & 273.
5 Ibid. 273v.; DCD. 3.2. Archiepiscopalia 3.
6 Ibid. 2; *CPL*. VI, pp. 389–91.

The Archbishop's demise cost £20 and the papal bull £4 8s. 10d.[1] As early as 6 July 1410, the Prior had written to a friend for financial assistance: he had already spent large sums and lacked the means to continue in the suit.[2]

The relations between Langley and the priors of Durham were amicable throughout his episcopate, and afforded a remarkable contrast to the history of Durham a century earlier, when the enmity shown to each other by bishops and priors was most bitter. Prior Hemmingburgh was Langley's vicar-general for nearly ten years.[3] He was occasionally the Bishop's guest; he spent Christmas with him at Bishop Auckland in 1409, and again in 1412.[4] In 1407, he told Langley that neither he nor the Convent, although summoned, could attend Parliament, and asked that if there were any unfortunate repercussions Langley would make excuses for them.[5] Hemmingburgh again sought the Bishop's aid in 1412. He had been appointed collector of a clerical half-tenth, but had not had the time to collect it in full. A royal writ had ordered the sheriff of Yorkshire to distrain the Prior's goods in that county. Langley was asked, when he was with the King, to use his influence to persuade the Exchequer to grant a longer term for the collection of the subsidy and to cancel the order for distraint.[6]

Hemmingburgh died on 15 September 1416.[7] The Subprior and Convent met to consider how they were to procure a licence to elect their next prior, because the Bishop was abroad. It was debated whether the licence should be sued from the vicar-general, but finally decided that it would be safer to send a messenger to the Bishop.[8] Thomas Ryhale, a notary, was therefore sent to Calais to speak to Langley.[9] On 6 October, Langley sent his warrant of privy seal to his temporal chancellor for a licence under the great seal of the palatinate; he appointed John Newton guardian of the Priory during the vacancy and wrote to the Chapter, under his signet, to exhort the monks to elect a worthy prior. The licence for the election was issued on 17 October.[10] The election was held on 5 November, when John Wessington, the sacrist and chancellor, was unanimously chosen. On

1 Bursar 1410–1411, m. 3d., & 1412–1413, m. 3d.
2 Reg. Parv. I, fo. 13v.   3 Above, p. 175.
4 DCD. Bursar 1409–1410, m. 3d., & 1412–1413, m. 3d.
5 Reg. Parv. I, ff. 4v.–5.   6 Ibid. 14v.
7 Reg. no. 432.   8 Above, p. 56.
9 Durham Account Rolls, III, p. 614.   10 Reg. nos. 419–23.

26 November, the Bishop appointed Thomas Lyes to examine the election proceedings. The examination was, however, merely a matter of form, for a week before he received Lyes' report, the Bishop, as temporal ruler, gave his assent to the election, on 7 December. With the permission of Archbishop Bowet, the election was canonically confirmed by the Bishop at his Yorkshire manor of Howden, on 22 December, and William Barry, a monk of Durham, proffered obedience as the proctor of Wessington, who was suffering from some indisposition. Another commission was sent to Thomas Lyes, this time to induct the Prior, and the ceremony was performed on 24 December.[1]

Langley was as friendly with Wessington as he had been with his predecessor. The Prior, as he once wrote, often went to the Bishop for advice, and was always treated with kindness; he had liberty of access to Langley as often as he wished, nor did he ever fail to obtain the counsel he sought.[2] In 1418, he sent a monk to explain to Langley the grave financial condition of the Convent's cells, particularly Jarrow and Monkwearmouth.[3] When the central tower of the Cathedral was damaged by fire, Wessington lost no time in sending Langley a report of the disaster.[4] He once went hunting with the Bishop in his park.[5] The Bishop's lavish expenditure on the Convent's buildings could not have failed to earn its good-will, and he was also considerate as its temporal overlord, showing respect for its privileges: unlike the King elsewhere in the realm, the Bishop did not burden the religious houses in his palatinate with corrodians. The Prior for his part made some return for Langley's favour: he provided the Bishop's suffragan and spiritual chancellor with benefices,[6] and the scholarship of John Wessington more than once provided Langley with information concerning his temporal franchise.[7] In the critical events of 1433, Wessington stood by the Bishop.[8] Whether Langley's cordial association with the priors arose from political design, a sense of episcopal duty, or mere human affection, the fruit it bore in that year was invaluable: a prior in the days of Bek or Beaumont would have sought to extract the utmost advantage from the Bishop's embarrassment. Wessington gave

---

1 *Reg.* nos. 432–41.   2 DCD. Reg. Parv. I, fo. 29.
3 DCD. Reg. III, fo. 62.   4 *Scr. Tres*, Appendix, pp. ccxvii–ccxviii.
5 DCD. Bursar 1418–1419, m. 4d.
6 *Reg.* nos. 885; Reg. Parv. I, fo. 67.
7 *Scr. Tres*, Appendix, pp. cclxx–cclxxi.   8 Above, pp. 127 & 129.

Langley cause for displeasure in 1434,[1] but the disagreement was short-lived, and in the following year the Bishop gave him a mitre as a gift.[2] In Langley's will, he left money to the Prior and monks so that they should pray for his soul, books for their library and that of Durham College, and jewels, ornaments, and vestments.[3]

The Bishop's relations with the Convent were influenced by considerations of his temporal as well as of his spiritual estate, for the Prior was one of the most important of his tenants-in-chief: he was not beset by this double relationship in his dealing with the other houses of his diocese. Little information is available with regard to his relations with them, or of their private histories. Langley did not make a visitation of any one of the houses in Northumberland; he was excluded from most by the privileges of their orders, and had to leave investigation into their internal condition to the superiors of each order. Tynemouth is known to have been visited by the Abbot of St Albans, John Wheathamstead, in 1426.[4] Two years earlier, Langley's suffragan, the Bishop of Elphin, had come to Tynemouth to conduct a general ordination service, four of those ordained being monks there.[5] Between 1414 and 1437, a total of nineteen monks of Tynemouth received orders,[6] and there are other indications that the economy of this house was in a healthy state. Prior John Macrell, whose long period of office ended in 1419, raised a gatehouse and put new windows into the priory church; Abbot Wheathamstead found it necessary to warn the monks against the perils of over-eating; and the house was enriched by the presence of a Subprior whose life of Prior Macrell aroused the wonder of his nephew the verbose Abbot.[7]

Tynemouth was happy in its distance from the Border and the strength of its castle-guarded headland; the other houses of Northumberland were more exposed. The nuns of Holystone in Redesdale were the most dangerously placed, and they had pleaded their losses from Scottish raids when they sought leave to appropriate the church of Alwinton in 1375;[8] their circumstances were

---

[1] Above, p. 108. [2] *Wills and Inventories*, I, p. 88.
[3] *Scr. Tres*, Appendix, pp. ccxli–ccxlvii.
[4] *History of Northumberland* (Newcastle-upon-Tyne & London, 1893–1940), Vol. VIII, p. 101. [5] Reg. fo. 290.
[6] Ibid. 251v., 265, 265v., 276v., 289, 290, 293v., 296 & 302v.
[7] *Northumberland*, VIII, pp. 101–3. [8] *CPL*. IV, p. 214.

further straitened by the persistent refusal of the chamberlain of Berwick to pay their annuity of eight marks.[1] There were seven nuns here in 1432.[2] The Abbey of Alnwick, shrine of that therapeutic relic the foot of Simon de Montfort,[3] cannot have escaped molestation in 1434, when the Scots burnt the town.[4] When an abbot of Alnwick was elected in 1437, one of the canons came to Langley to explain that for various reasons, including the expense and the dangers of the road owing to Scottish raids, the Abbot could not come to Bishop Auckland to receive Langley's benediction; the Bishop therefore agreed to the request that his suffragan should be sent to Alnwick to give his benediction there.[5] The revolts of their patron, the first Earl of Northumberland, would have alarmed the canons, one of whom was sufficiently implicated to seek refuge in Scotland until he had received the King's pardon.[6] Between 1415 and 1433, a total of seventeen canons were ordained,[7] and in 1424 the Pope's licence to send one of them to study at a university was obtained,[8] but three years passed after the sack of Alnwick town before another canon was admitted.[9]

The small priory of Brinkburn was clearly undergoing a crisis in its affairs in 1418 when ill-health obliged John Brigg to resign his office of Prior on 16 September. On the same day, Brigg and a second canon surrendered their title to elect the next prior to Bishop Langley, and a third canon made a similar submission in the following week. Although Langley presumed that he had received the submission of all the canons, and then proceeded to appoint a prior, it would seem that unless the Bishop's registrar had been careless, there were at least four other canons who had not agreed to this arrangement.[10] The circumstances do point, however, to dissension in the Chapter of Brinkburn, and Langley wisely selected a canon of another house, the Augustinian priory of Hexham, as the new Prior.[11] When this Prior resigned in 1424, the canons elected one of their number to succeed him.[12] The

---

[1] CPR. 1422–1429, p. 242.   [2] Reg. no. 987.
[3] G. Tate, History of Alnwick (Alnwick, 1866–9), Vol. II, pp. 14–15.
[4] CPR. 1429–1436, p. 435.   [5] Reg. fo. 247.
[6] CPR. 1401–1405, p. 428.
[7] Reg. nos. 750 & 1030; Reg. ff. 260v., 273v., 275, 289–92v.
[8] CPL. VII, p. 369.   [9] Reg. fo. 251v.
[10] Cf. Reg. no. 229; Reg. ff. 264 & 281.
[11] Reg. nos. 501–4.   [12] Reg. fo. 290v.

Bishop's register shows the ordination of only eight canons, and that the last admission was in 1432;[1] this suggests that Brinkburn also suffered from the Scottish raid in 1434. The Abbey of Newminster was farther from the Border than Alnwick and Brinkburn, but another kind of disaster befell it in 1435. The central tower had recently been repaired at great expense, but the work was badly executed: the masons were not sufficiently skilful, and no attention was paid to the tower's old supports, with the result that the structure collapsed, damaging the nave and choir. The Bishop granted an indulgence to all persons who contributed to the cost of repairs in the next four years.[2] The ordination of at least nineteen monks of Newminster between 1408 and 1437 [3] does not suggest that the house was in a depressed condition, although the causes of the downfall of the tower reveal that the Convent's administration was not directed by particularly competent hands. The Abbots of Newminster and Alnwick were regularly appointed to the Bishop's penitentiary commission for Northumberland, and were sometimes given other diocesan business, as in 1432, when the Abbot of Newminster was sent to Holystone to assist the nuns in their election of a new prioress.[4] The three houses of canons had a useful part in the ordinary life of the diocese, for they supplied ten churches with vicars.[5]

Poverty was the common lot of houses of religious women; the northern Convocation always exempted them from liability to pay subsidies. In the diocese of Durham at least, the basic cause of this condition was the meagreness of their endowments. The wealthiest of the four nunneries, St Bartholomew's in Newcastle, was said to be worth £36 a year in 1535; it owed some of this revenue to a grant made ten years after Langley's death.[6] The valuation of Holystone's revenue at £11 is not remarkable in view of its situation, but Neasham, at the very opposite end of the diocese, had less than twice this income. The figure for Lambley, which had a reasonably safe position in relation to the Border, is not known, but it appears that the total income of the four houses of nuns exceeded only that of the canons of Blanchland.[7] Little

[1] *Reg.* nos. 229 & 974; Reg. ff. 264, 273v., 280v., 281 & 293.

[2] *Depositions and Ecclesiastical Proceedings,* pp. 24–5; *Reg.* no. 1143.

[3] *Reg.* nos. 102, 258, 295, 630, 890 & 1068 ; Reg. ff. 242, 263v., 274v., 280 & 293v.

[4] *Reg.* no. 977.　　　　　[5] Above, p. 177.

[6] *VCH. Durham,* II, p. 119.　　　[7] *Valor Ecclesiasticus,* V, pp. 310, 327–9.

is known of Bishop Langley's dealings with the nuns in Northumberland; he issued one monition against persons who had unlawfully taken possession of property belonging to the Convent of Lambley, and a second at the instigation of the Prioress of St Bartholomew's, where a nun had been persuaded by the evil counsels of some unknown but wicked people to cast off her habit and wander abroad.[1]   A second nun left this house for another in 1427 with the Pope's licence; she had found the Tyneside climate insupportably inclement.[2]   In the following year, the Prioress permitted Margaret Danby, "notwithstondyng that she is ful necessarye and profitable to us both in spirituell governance and temporell", to go to Neasham on her postulation by the seven nuns of that house as their new Prioress.   Dame Margaret died after little more than twelve months in office, and the nuns, now six in number, chose one of themselves to succeed her.[3]

Neasham lay on the north bank of the Tees, close to the Bishop's manor of Darlington on the west side and not far from Stockton on the other; news of its fortunes had not far to travel to reach the Bishop's ear, as they did in the last year of his life. When he was at Darlington on 5 June 1436, he appointed the Abbot of Blanchland and Master Richard Pennymaster, Rector of Haughton-le-Skerne and one of the Bishop's *jurisperiti*, to conduct a visitation of the nunnery.   Three months later, the Bishop decided to visit the house in person, on 12 October;[4] his injunctions indicate that he found much at fault.   The Prioress was ordered, under pain of deprivation of her office, to see that the nuns were called to all the canonical services and to attend them herself; impose silence at the required hours; treat her nuns in a kindly spirit, and refrain from accusations and upbraiding language, but to correct their faults in a charitable manner and in accordance with their rule; seek the consent of the nuns in the business of the house; permit no secular persons to eat or sleep in the Convent, and require the nuns to dine in the refectory and pass the night in their dormitory; and to have the conventual buildings repaired, the nuns decently clad and the Convent's plate redeemed from its creditors before 24 June 1437.   The nuns for their part were admonished to live in a state of charity, show reverence to their prioress, and cease from communication with

1 *Reg.* nos. 790 & 1091.   2 *CPL.* VII, p. 516.
3 *Reg.* nos. 770–3, 840–3.   4 Ibid. 1213 & 1228.

the laity.[1]   The nuns' liking for secular company had given rise
to scandal: two months after the visitation, a layman asked the
Bishop that he might be purged of a charge of adultery with one
of the nuns.[2]   The Bishop's desire for the reform of Neasham
persisted; on 17 July 1437, he appointed his spiritual chancellor
and the sequestrator of Durham to visit the house and find
whether his injunctions were being obeyed.   The commissioners
must have given the Bishop an unfavourable report, for the
resignation of the Prioress speedily followed.   There were now
only five nuns, the majority of whom voted for Agnes Tuddow
as their next prioress.   When she appeared before the Bishop on
10 November, Agnes received his dispensation for incontinence
before she was admitted as prioress.[3]   This was Langley's last
episcopal act.

The fortunes of the mendicant orders of the diocese are even
more difficult to follow than those of the religious in this period.
The four largest orders of friars, Austin, Carmelite, Dominican,
and Minorite, all had houses in Newcastle-upon-Tyne, and there
was a second house of Friars Minor at Hartlepool, but despite this
characteristic concentration in the two mercantile centres, the
total number of friars was sufficient to suggest that their influence
extended to larger areas of the diocese.   In 1539, there were in
the four houses of Newcastle thirteen Dominicans, eleven
Minorites, the same number of Austin friars, and ten Car-
melites; [4] while at Hartlepool, where the Minorites had recently
been replaced by Friars Observant, there were eighteen friars.[5]
The lists of ordinations by Langley and his suffragans indicate a
similar total, of about fifty friars all told, in his day, although it is
probable that the number at Hartlepool was smaller, while the
Dominicans of Newcastle seem to have been more numerous.
The Order of Preachers also appears to have been the most active
in the diocese, for the Bishop granted licences to receive confessions
to six of its members; [6] three Minorites of Hartlepool were
licensed on one day, in 1407, and another member of this house
in 1424.[7]   Only one Austin friar received a licence,[8] although
John Bamburgh, who was Prior-Provincial of his order in 1417

1 Reg. ff. 255v.–6.   2 Margaret Witton (Ibid. 237v.).
3 Ibid. 248v., 249, 252v. & 254.
4 Brand, *Newcastle*, I, pp. 130, 336, 348 & 63.
5 Surtees, *Durham*, III, p. 119.   6 *Reg.* nos. 387, 447, 582, 610 & 775.
7 Ibid. 42 & 610.   8 Ibid. 925.

and 1419, was appointed to the Bishop's penitentiary commissions between 1416 and 1420.[1] The Bishop was entertained in the house of the Austin friars when he visited Newcastle in 1428 and 1431.[2]

As the Carmelite Order was at this time enjoying a certain vogue in England, with the promotion of two of its members from the office of royal confessor to the bishoprics of Hereford and Chichester,[3] it is worthy of notice that Langley issued a penitentiary commission to only one Carmelite friar, in 1408;[4] later events suggest that the Bishop may have had reservations about this mendicant order. In 1425, the Vicar of Newcastle-upon-Tyne came before the Bishop to accuse William Boston, Prior of the Carmelite house in that town, of having propounded certain false opinions in a public sermon, which were summarized in seven articles. Boston denied most of these articles and undertook to vindicate himself, but on the day appointed for this purpose he admitted his inability to do so and submitted to the Bishop's pleasure. He was then required to read a formal renunciation of his error, which had been to say that the customary gift by the laity of candles in their parish churches at the Feast of the Purification was not obligatory. The gravity of the Carmelite's offence lay not so much in the deviation of his opinion from accepted doctrinal teaching but in the fact that it was directed against the interest of the secular clergy, and in his retraction Boston had to express his regret "that I have in this matire any worde of hastinesse or malice saide or movet agein[st] any curet (*curate*) that more shewet steryng to debate thanne norysshyng of love and charitee".[5] These proceedings made another episode in the intermittent strife between the friars and the secular clergy.

4 THE BISHOP AS SUFFRAGAN

The Bishop of Durham possessed no franchise in spiritual jurisdiction to parallel his temporal estate; while he was the most privileged of the King's tenants-in-chief, he owed to the Arch-

---

[1] *Reg.* nos. 396, 464, 484, 520 & 542.   [2] Ibid. 775 & 925.
[3] David Knowles, *The Religious Orders in England* (Cambridge, 1948–59), Vol. II, pp. 145 & 148.
[4] *Reg.* no. 44.
[5] Ibid. 613; *Depositions and Ecclesiastical Proceedings*, pp. 21–3.

bishop of York the same measure of respect and obedience that any suffragan owed to his metropolitan. The belief that the diocese of Durham enjoyed in the northern province a degree of immunity similar to that once supposed to have been the privilege of *Ecclesia Anglicana* in the Universal Church is as fallacious as Maitland has shown the latter doctrine to be. Bishops of Durham previous to Langley, desiring a spiritual authority to match their temporal regality, had tried to exclude the Archbishop from any influence in Durham; these constitutional disputes had often been embittered by the conflict of personalities. Bishop Langley is not known ever to have taken exception to his metropolitan's supremacy, and his acceptance of the polity of the province of York can be exemplified by his respect to its two central institutions: the Archbishop's mandates requiring the Bishop to cause his clergy to send representatives to the Convocation of York were executed, and Langley himself occasionally took part in the assembly; [1] while his regard for the court of York is indicated by his appointment of an attorney there [2] and the suspension of a sentence of sequestration in response to an order from the court's commissary-general.[3] Langley's attitude offers a strong contrast to that of Antony Bek, who disregarded both summonses to Convocation and mandates from the court of York.[4]

The see of York was without an archbishop for more than two years after the execution of Richard Scrope in 1405, until Henry Bowet was translated from Bath and Wells. The King's attempt to have Langley advanced to the archbishopric, and the provision by Innocent VII of a second candidate, have already been noticed.[5] The disputed provision of Robert Hallam has left faint echoes in Langley's register: papal letters of 13 August 1407 charged Langley to dispense persons of the diocese of York because Archbishop Robert was said to be *in remotis*; while English disregard of his advancement is illustrated by records of the Chapter of York acting as keepers of the spiritualities of York in the vacancy of the see.[6] The Chapter also made a claim to exercise episcopal jurisdiction in Durham when that see was vacant simultaneously; the archbishop was entitled to this

---

[1] Below, pp. 215–17.   [2] *Reg.* no. 120.
[3] Reg. fo. 259.
[4] C. M. Fraser, *A History of Antony Bek* (Oxford, 1957), pp. 111–14.
[5] Above, pp. 181–9.   [6] *Reg.* nos. 30, 47 & 65.

authority, which he employed after Langley's death, but the Prior and Convent of Durham were able to uphold their title to act in the dual vacancy. It has already been seen that they did not lack influential support in their dispute with the Chapter of York,[1] and it may be supposed that Langley, as Dean, tried to restrain his colleagues in an action which must have embarrassed him as bishop-designate.

There were two archbishops of York during Langley's period at Durham. Both Henry Bowet (1407–23) and John Kemp (1426–52) were the sons of knightly families, had proceeded to the degree of doctor of both laws, and made their careers by different paths in the secular administration of England.[2] Bowet is reputed to have been famed for his wealth, lavish hospitality, and generous benefactions to York Minster, but he might equally well be celebrated for his courage and military exploits; he had accompanied Bishop Despenser of Norwich on his "crusade" in 1383, provided a contingent in Henry IV's Welsh campaign in 1403,[3] and is said to have been carried in a litter at the head of his clergy when they were arrayed against the Scots in 1417. Bowet was for some time in the service of Richard II, but passed to that of John of Gaunt; his loyalty to the House of Lancaster occasioned his condemnation for treason in 1399, but soon brought its reward after Henry IV's accession in his election to the see of Bath and Wells. He continued in royal service, as councillor and occasional ambassador, until his translation to York in 1407; apart from a brief period four years later, he now ceased to take a prominent part in royal affairs, and spent most of his time in the diocese of York. His visitations of Howdenshire and Allertonshire brought him into collision with the Convent of Durham,[4] but did not involve the Bishop. There is good reason to suppose Langley's relations with the Archbishop to have been friendly: they shared a common loyalty to the House of Lancaster. Henry IV had called on Bowet to join his Council in 1411, after the dismissal of Prince Henry, and appointed him an executor of his will; Langley was his colleague in both these duties.[5] The Archbishop is also known to have entertained his suffragan of Durham at Cawood in October 1410.[6]

[1] Above, p. 164.
[2] *Dictionary of National Biography.*
[3] Warrants for Issues, 18/604.
[4] Above, p. 198.
[5] Above, pp. 29–30.
[6] *Reg.* no. 168.

Bowet's successor was a less pleasant character. John Kemp began his career in the court of Canterbury, whence he easily passed into royal service as a diplomat and went on to become Keeper of the Privy Seal. Among the benefices he received at this stage were the archdeaconry of Durham and a prebend at Norton.[1] His ascent of the episcopal ladder was indecently fast: beginning at Rochester in 1419, he went on to Chichester two years later, was Bishop there a few months only before his translation to London, and within five years won the see of York, not without intrigue by his agents at the Roman court. As Archbishop of York, Kemp has long stood condemned by the assertion of Thomas Gascoigne that he remained almost a complete stranger to his see throughout his twenty-six years as its ruler, spending perhaps two or three weeks there once in every dozen years.[2] This allegation is grossly untrue with regard to Kemp's first ten years at York: the Chancery rolls show that when he was Chancellor of England, from 1426 to 1432, the Archbishop spent at least one month of each of the first five summers in his diocese; he was there when Convocation met in 1428 and 1429, and he also presided over later meetings in 1432 and 1436.[3] He was at Durham in this last year, although his business there was the defence of the Border.[4] Again there is no evidence of any friction between Langley and his Archbishop, and the Bishop's appointment of Kemp as one of his referees in the attempted arbitration of his dispute with William Eure,[5] and his bequest of a cup and St Augustine's *De Civitate Dei*,[6] testify to a mutual esteem between two distinguished statesmen.

Between 1406 and 1436, the Convocation of the northern province was called to assemble twenty times, and several of these sessions were prorogued, so that it met at least twice in every three years. The usual purpose of its assembly was to grant subsidies to the King, who by his writs ordered the Archbishop to cause his clergy to meet. On six occasions, the archbishops ordered assemblies without such prompting, when they wished purely ecclesiastical matters, usually the representation of the province in general councils of the Church, to be arranged. Two Convocations called for this purpose, however, were induced to

---

[1] *Reg.* nos. 480 & 491.   [2] *Loci e Libro Veritatum*, p. 37.
[3] *CFR. 1430–1437*, pp. 180 & 309.   [4] Above, p. 161.
[5] Above, p. 129.   [6] *Scr. Tres*, Appendix, pp. ccxlv & ccxlvi.

vote taxes to the King,[1] while those meeting at the royal behest presumably also attended to business more congenial to the clergy.

The financial difficulties of Henry IV, and the need of Henry V for money to wage war in France, caused both monarchs to make resort to Parliament and the two Convocations for subsidies with unpopular frequency. It was customary for the King's writs to be sent to both archbishops almost simultaneously, an equitable practice that was later discontinued in the face of gradually increasing resistance by the northern clergy. York granted Henry IV tenths in 1406, 1408 and 1410, and a half-tenth in 1412, all to be paid in halves, two in both 1407 and 1409 and one in the November of the three succeeding years.[2] No subsidy was raised in 1413, when Convocation granted its first tenth to Henry V; it was paid in the following year, in February and August.[3] In this year, Parliament made the King a large grant to finance his preparations for war against France,[4] the southern clergy voted him two tenths,[5] and in the following January (1415), their brethren of York made a similar concession; a whole tenth was to be paid on 14 April, and the second tenth, in halves, in 1416.[6] Before it had been fully paid, however, the northern Convocation was assembled to grant another tenth, and in 1417 it met yet again for the same purpose; this last request for a subsidy inevitably met strong protest, for in 1415 the clergy had stipulated as a condition of their concession then that they should not be called upon to make a further grant for two years.[7] After a week of debate, however, they consented that the tenth granted in the previous Convocation should be paid two months earlier, on 11 April 1417, and conceded a second tenth to be collected in the following November.[8]

This payment of two whole tenths in 1417, the year of Henry V's invasion of Normandy, marked the peak of clerical taxation in the province of York. It gave rise to a mounting and by no means ineffective opposition, and led to an increasing disparity between

[1] Below, p. 213.

[2] *Reg.* nos. 111, 172 & 271. The 1406 Convocation was held by the Chapter of York as keepers of the spiritualities (K. R. Memoranda Roll, 7 Hen. IV, *Recorda*, Michaelmas, rot. 26).

[3] *Reg.* no. 309.   [4] *Rot. Parl.* IV, p. 35.

[5] *CFR. 1413–1422*, p. 90.   [6] *Reg.* no. 400.

[7] Ibid. 400.   [8] Ibid. 455.

the contributions of the two Convocations to the royal revenue. The clergy of Canterbury made a grant of two tenths in December 1417,[1] but at its meeting in the following January, the northern Convocation conceded one tenth only, again after lodging many complaints; to the usual plea of poverty were added the more specific excuses of their array against the Scots twice in the previous year, and the losses incurred by Scottish attacks; this tenth was to be paid on 2 February 1419,[2] thus giving a year free of taxation. The next writ ordering a meeting of the Convocation of York showed that the government was aware of this opposition, for instead of the usual vague reason for its assembly there was the statement that the King could not maintain his wars without financial support.[3] When Convocation met on 13 January 1420 the clergy again complained about the burden of military service: they had been frequently arrayed against the Scots in 1419, and had also suffered from their attacks. The extent of the damage caused by the Scottish attacks is to be gauged by the complete exception from liability to taxation of all benefices and religious houses in Northumberland, Cumberland, and Westmorland; hitherto, benefices in these counties had been exempted only when the bishops could provide the Exchequer with certificates of impoverishment as a result of enemy action. The total exemption of all clergy in the three counties became the rule from this year.[4] Despite these protests by Convocation, and other complaints of drought and murrain among the cattle, one half-tenth, to be paid on 1 May, was granted.[5]

The last five Convocations held at the instance of Henry V had met in the month of January; the next writ did not allow the Archbishop the usual latitude in the choice of date but specifically ordered the assembly to be convened on 22 September 1421.[6] This departure from current practice must have been made to enable Bishop Langley, the Chancellor, to attend the meeting by breaking his journey to London after his summer vacation in Durham. This year the clergy made the weather the mainstay of their excuses: excessive rain, bringing floods, had ruined the crops and—like the drought of 1419—caused murrain among the

[1] CFR. 1413–1422, p. 218.   [2] Reg. no. 492.
[3] CCR. 1419–1422, pp. 59–60.
[4] Storey, "Marmaduke Lumley", loc. cit., pp. 120–1.
[5] Reg. no. 533.   [6] Ibid. 555.

cattle. They eventually granted the King one tenth, however, to be paid in halves in 1422 and 1423;[1] as the Convocation of Canterbury had granted the same tax in the previous May,[2] Langley cannot have been dissatisfied with the outcome of his intervention. With the death of Henry V in 1422, the period of heavy clerical taxation came to an end: in less than ten years, the clergy of York had voted him eight and a half tenths, two tenths less than Canterbury. The weight of this burden is better appreciated by comparison with the amount paid to Henry IV; he was conceded six and a half tenths in his somewhat longer reign, and although this was not a low incidence, its average annual yield was half the yearly payment to his son.[3] While a growing number of religious houses and the benefices in the marches were wholly or partially exempted, the liability to taxation was extended to the poorer clergy: until 1415, benefices with an annual value of £6 13s. 4d. and under were excluded, but from that year the figure was lowered to £5, and again to £4 in 1418, while in 1420 no limitation was made; in the following year, the level for exemption was £5 6s. 8d.

The Dean and Chapter of York, as keepers of the spiritualities after Bowet's death, were once ordered to summon Convocation,[4] but neither at the first meeting on 6 October 1424 nor at the second session on 1 December[5] would the clergy grant a subsidy.[6] Barely a month after John Kemp's accession, he was required by the Crown to order a meeting of Convocation.[7] This was opened on 12 August 1426 with Langley acting as president in the absence of the Archbishop. The first few days were given to ecclesiastical business,[8] and after its conclusion on the 16th, the Convocation's spokesman asked for its dissolution. Langley refused this request out of hand, and again when it was repeated on the following day; it would seem that the commissioners appointed by the King to ask for a subsidy had been delayed, and the clergy conceived the

---

[1] CFR. 1413–1422, pp. 410–11.
[2] Ibid. 401.
[3] J. H. Ramsay, Lancaster and York (Oxford, 1892), Vol. I, pp. 152, 310 & 314.
[4] CCR. 1422–1429 p. 147.
[5] I am much indebted to Canon Eric Kemp for providing this information from the York Sede Vacante Register. It indicates that Langley attended the meeting on 6 October.
[6] The Repertory to the L.T.R. Memoranda Rolls, 1–20 Henry VI, and printed sources have been consulted.
[7] Reg. Kemp, fo. 27.   [8] Below, p. 216.

ingenious stratagem of procuring their dismissal before the arrival of the commission. These commissioners did come into Convocation on 17 August, and after their withdrawal Langley urged the assembly to make the requested grant. The clergy answered that they wished to know the value of their tithes from the present harvest. Langley then appointed his proctors and presumably departed from York. After further unsuccessful attempts to persuade it, Convocation was prorogued to 5 October. As Langley had not returned to York on that day, the session was adjourned until the 7th, when the Bishop resumed his exhortations, which were unavailing, and although he would not dissolve the assembly, he was obliged to announce its adjournment on 9 October.[1] No record has been found of a further session of this Convocation, and it certainly made no grant to the King.

The success of the clergy's opposition caused the King's Council to alter its approach; at the instance, it may be supposed, of Archbishop Kemp, who was then Chancellor, more discreet tactics were employed. Kemp ordered his second Convocation to meet on 2 August, for the purpose of considering the nefarious activities of certain heretics, doubtless those of Bohemia, and other matters concerning the peace of the Church, King, and kingdom.[2] The Archbishop was in York throughout this session,[3] and obtained a grant to the King of a half-tenth without any recorded protest.[4] This Convocation was prorogued to the following July, and again to February 1430,[5] when a whole tenth, to be paid in halves in the next two years, was conceded, again without any note of complaint.[6] In 1432, Kemp repeated his tactics; when Convocation met on 3 October to arrange for its representation at the Council of Basle,[7] the Archbishop asked for a grant to the King. His diplomacy was less fruitful on this occasion, for after several days all he could persuade the clergy to concede was a meagre quarter of a tenth, to be paid in February 1434, and even this amount they described as a burden greater than they could support because of the floods and pestilence that had diminished their tithes.[8] The strength of the resistance by the northern

---

1 *Records of the Northern Convocation* (SS. 1906), pp. 153–60.
2 *Reg.* no. 735.
3 *CCR. 1422–1429*, pp. 377, 395 & 406; *CPR. 1422–1429*, pp. 496 & 546.
4 *CFR. 1422–1430*, pp. 255–6.
5 *Reg.* no. 845.   6 *CFR. 1430–1437*, pp. 23–4.
7 *Reg.* no. 1006.   8 *CFR. 1430–1437*, pp. 180–1.

clergy can be measured by the parallel taxation of the southern province: in the first ten years of Henry VI's reign, York had granted a tenth and three-quarters, as against Canterbury's four and a half, and the latter were to grant a further two and a quarter tenths before the next meeting of the Convocation of York.[1] This was held on 11 June, consequent to a royal writ. Again the Archbishop spent several days answering protests with exhortations, but he eventually negotiated a grant. The clergy were well aware of the imminent danger of a Scottish invasion,[2] and were afraid lest they might be arrayed, but they also appreciated the government's need for funds to resist the attack. Convocation therefore granted a half-tenth, to be paid in the following February, which they commended for use in the defence of the marches, and a second half-tenth, which would be paid a year later if they were not arrayed before then. In the event, the clergy's money was preferred to their military services, and in 1438 they were required to pay the remainder of the subsidy.[3]

The taxation of the clergy of York has left more documentary evidence of this aspect of Convocation than any other, but a smaller number of records give occasional notices of other activities; these nearly all concern the appointment of ambassadors to the General Councils of the Church at Pisa, Constance, Pavia, and Basle. The assemblies convened for this purpose tended to be larger than those whose principal business was to grant the King subsidies. Archbishop Bowet, for instance, issued two mandates for Convocations in 1408: for the first, which had been called in response to the King's writ, he required from Durham the personal attendance of the Bishop and Prior, the Archdeacons and other abbots and priors, one proctor from every chapter and two for the secular clergy; for the second, when the forthcoming council of Pisa was to be discussed, he asked that in addition to these persons men distinguished for their learning should be invited to attend.[4] There survive among the archives of Langley's registry two returns to his orders to the archdeacons to execute such archiepiscopal mandates. One of these, from the official of the Archdeacon of Durham, concerns the Convocation called by

---

[1] *CFR. 1422–1430*, pp. 105–7, 149–50, 269–71, 306–8; *1430–1437*, pp. 62–4, 159–61, 227–9, 269–71.
[2] Above, p. 160.
[3] *Reg.* no. 1239.; *CFR. 1430–1437*, pp. 309–310; *1437–1445*, pp. 8–9.
[4] *Reg.* nos. 75 & 91.

Kemp in 1428 to consider ecclesiastical matters and to which he wished the heads of collegiate churches as well as the usual priors and other representatives to be summoned.[1] The return shows that the Deans of Auckland, Chester-le-Street, and Lanchester had been cited, and that Master George Radcliffe, Rector of Sedgefield (Durham), and John Brigg, Vicar of Corbridge (Northumberland), would represent the clergy.[2] The second return is for the archdeaconry of Northumberland in 1436, when a convocation of the more common kind was to be held, and states that the Abbots of Newminster and Alnwick and the Priors of Tynemouth and Brinkburn had been summoned, and that the Archdeacon's official would be the proctor for the clergy.[3] If these returns are typical, they suggest that the clerical proctors usually belonged to the ministerial class, for the two representatives in 1428 had both been sequestrators in their respective archdeaconries.[4]

Although the Archbishop's mandates told the Bishop he could not be excused from personal attendance in Convocation, he does not seem to have been much moved by this warning. Appointments by Langley of proctors to represent him were occasionally recorded in his register,[5] but his registrars must have omitted several others and his itinerary offers more dependable evidence of his attendance. Langley was absent from both Convocations held in the summer of 1408; these were prorogued to the following December, when the business of the first was despatched on the 10th with a grant to the King,[6] and of the second on the following day, when the Bishop of Durham, the Abbots of St Mary's, York, and Jervaulx, Richard Coningston, Richard Holme (Langley's chancellor), and Thomas Rome, a monk of Durham, all of whom were present in Convocation, were appointed to represent it at Pisa.[7] The Convocation called to meet on 15 February 1410 [8] appears to have been prorogued twice, to 24 May, when it granted a tenth to Henry IV,[9] and again to 3 October. Langley was then in York and probably gave an account of the General Council. Convocation was informed that the half-tenth it had voted for the expenses of its ambassadors was insufficient, but it was so well

[1] *Reg.* no. 735.
[2] DCD. Locellus 20, no. 11g.
[3] Locellus 20, no. 14.
[4] *Reg.* I, p. xxxix, n. 6, & no. 156.
[5] E.g. Ibid. 95, 407 & 556.
[6] *Reg.* no. 111.
[7] Reg. Bowet I, ff. 219v.–2.
[8] Ibid. I, fo. 284.
[9] *Reg. Langley*, no. 172.

pleased with their conduct that it "cheerfully" [1] granted another quarter of a tenth; Langley lost little time in arranging for its collection.[2]   It is possible that he made appearances in the Convocations of 1412, 1413, and 1417, and his presence at the assembly in 1421 has already been observed.[3]   It seems likely that he intended to take his place in the Convocation called for 22 September 1422 to appoint a delegation to the Council of Pavia,[4] but was obliged to make an earlier return southward from Durham when he was informed of the death of Henry V.[5]

As Archbishop Kemp was unable to preside in his first Convocation in 1426, he appointed the Bishops of Durham and Carlisle and the Abbot of St Mary's to act in his place.   When Langley took his seat as president on 13 August, an accusation of preaching heretical doctrines was made against Thomas Richmond, a Minorite friar, who had previously been charged before the Archbishop's vicar-general.   Richmond denied all the articles of his impeachment, but on examination admitted that he had uttered the words quoted in the first of these, namely that a priest fallen into mortal sin was no priest.   He then produced three fellow-friars, "to help him, as it seemed, in the defence of the said articles"; these witnesses were questioned by Langley, and agreed that they had heard the words spoken.   When they also said that they would not defend Richmond's opinions, he showed himself utterly confounded [6] and after some thought confessed his guilt on all the articles, renounced the privileges of his order, and placed himself at the Archbishop's pleasure. Langley accepted this statement and ordered Richmond to appear before the Archbishop at a later date.[7]   The collapse of Richmond's defence had been hastened by Langley's examination of his supporting witnesses; clearly the Bishop of Durham, with his long experience as Chancellor, knew how to handle such a situation: he was less successful in the further proceedings of this assembly.[8]   Langley attended the first sessions of the next three Convocations: the meeting in 1428 was prorogued to the following year, and again to 1430, when Langley appointed his proctors, stating that he was occupied on the King's affairs,[9] a reference

---

[1] *jocundo spiritu.*
[2] *Reg.* no. 166.
[3] Above, p. 211.
[4] *Reg.* no. 572.
[5] Above, p. 44.
[6] *ad cor ut apparuit reversus.*
[7] *Records of the Northern Convocation*, pp. 148–52.
[8] Above, pp. 212–13.
[9] *Reg.* no. 845.

to his appointment to a diplomatic commission;[1] in 1432, he was present when the embassy of the northern province to the Council of Basle was appointed, and was probably responsible for the nomination of his chancellor, John Bonour;[2] he made his last appearance in Convocation in June 1436 and appointed proctors for a second session in November with the excuse that he was detained by pressing business.[3]

Langley's record as a member of the Convocation of York is a respectable one, although it is difficult to be sure of his motives for attending some of its meetings. He certainly went to York in September 1421 in his rôle of Chancellor of England, rather than as suffragan, in order to secure a grant of taxation; and his representation of the province at Pisa, which accounts for his presence in convocation in December 1408 and October 1410, would have been undertaken at the instance of Henry IV. Whenever he did attend, however, he played an important part in the proceedings: as the senior suffragan, he acted as president in the absence of the Archbishop, and his experience as Chancellor, in the King's Council and in the court of Chancery, must have been invaluable. After his resignation of the Great Seal in 1424, his attendance became most regular; as he had declared before the Council, he intended to devote his last years to his church,[4] and he regarded his duty to attend the Convocation of York as an integral part of his responsibilities as Bishop of Durham.

1 Above, p. 158.
3 Ibid. 1238.

2 *Reg.* nos. 1022 & 1041.
4 *PPC.* III, p. 197.

V

CONCLUSION

THE dominating issue in the last five years of Langley's life was the defence of his secular franchise against the conspiracy of Sir William Eure and his associates, and the Bishop spared no pains in meeting the attacks of his enemies, travelling to London to answer them in Parliament and the King's Council and successfully combating Eure's appeal to King's Bench, while in Durham he pressed his suit against Eure to a conclusion and took further measures to fortify his government. Yet despite this great preoccupation and also the fear that his enemy had it in mind to do him personal injury, Langley continued his active administration of the diocese; in the midst of his troubles, he carried out a visitation of Darlington and gave Sherburn hospital its new statutes.[1] In 1434, he went as far as Cirencester to join the royal Council in its discussions on the young King's conduct, attended Parliament at Westminster in the autumn of the following year and Convocation at York in June 1436, and gave assistance in the preparations made for the defence of the Border against the Scots in July; but after his visitation of the Convent of Neasham on 12 October, he retired to his favourite manor, Bishop Auckland, and never again left it. That he was now seriously unwell is evident, for his will was sealed on 1 December,[2] and when he excused himself from attendance of Parliament on 10 January 1437, he said that he was broken by old age and his frame stricken with illness.[3] He remained in this state for twelve months, but was able to maintain his interest in his diocese; the last five ordinations of his episcopate were all conducted in the major chapel of Auckland manor by the suffragan,[4] and Langley's desire to be present at these services explains their being held here rather than in Durham city. His feebleness is indicated by the grants for life of two offices, one

[1] Above, pp. 183 & 192.   [2] *Scr. Tres*, Appendix, p. ccxlvii.
[3] Reg. fo. 238v.   [4] Ibid. 238, 242, 243, 246 & 251v.

being the appointment of his godson Thomas Lumley as chief forester; [1] this was Langley's only departure from his rule against perpetuities. On 10 November he was able to examine the new Prioress of Neasham.[2] Ten days later, in the third hour of the morning, he died in the inner chamber of his manor.[3] He was probably seventy-five years of age.

Langley had outlived nearly all his notable contemporaries: he was the last surviving executor of John of Gaunt [4] and of the bishops who were holding office at the time of his consecration there remained only Henry Beaufort of Winchester. Langley's longevity can only be attributed to a remarkable physique. He appears to have been ill for a few months in 1425,[5] but he fully recovered and was able to resume his vigorous activities until the last year of his life. Nothing is known of his appearance save that he was bearded,[6] but he was undoubtedly possessed of excellent health as well as extraordinary energy. His itinerary is ample witness to this, and there is further evidence in the fact that when he visited Durham in a brief intermission from his heavy duties as Chancellor, in 1418, he chose so vigorous a form of relaxation as hunting.[7] This was a quality that must have commended Langley to Henry IV, who himself displayed remarkable energy in his campaigns against his foreign and domestic enemies, and obviously required a similar spirit in the Secretary or Keeper of the Privy Seal who accompanied him. When Henry confirmed the liberties of the Bishopric of Durham in 1407, he gave among his reasons for granting the charter the special affection he bore towards the Bishop,

who had, from the days of his youth, laudibly served our dear father John, late Duke of Lancaster, and ourself in our affairs and those of our realm, and still is, towards us, tirelessly dutiful.[8]

Another quality common to both King and Bishop, one often associated with energy, was courage. Langley displayed this early in his career, when he went into the rebel camp at Shrewsbury, but also in his later years: he may have feared Eure's

[1] Rot. C. mm. 13 & 14. His previous appointment was "during pleasure" (above, p. 109).   [2] Above, p. 205.
[3] Reg. fo. 257.   [4] *Reg.* no. 1187.   [5] Above, p. 46.
[6] Fowler, "The St. Cuthbert Window", p. 260.
[7] DCD. Bursar 1418–1419, m. 4d.
[8] Hutchinson, *History of Durham*, I, p. 332.

violence, but he did not take refuge from it, and though he had houses in Yorkshire and London he remained in his county palatine.

Throughout his long career of public service, Langley was constant in his loyalty to the House of Lancaster, and he left a memorial to his devotion in the St Cuthbert Window he gave to York Minster in 1429.[1] In the lowest panes appear figures representing the donor and the four generations of the house he had served. The presence there of figures of Humphrey of Gloucester and Cardinal Beaufort is a record of Langley's neutrality in their deplorable quarrel.[2] He was no time-server: he had stood beside Henry IV in the King's last years and did not desert him in order to make sure of favour in the next reign, obviously not far distant as Henry's health declined. Nor did Henry V hold this loyalty to his father against Langley: he was well aware of the high nature of Langley's character and abilities, and took him into his confidence from the beginning of his reign. In the minority of Henry VI Langley's devotion was given primarily to the infant King. Despite his reluctance to continue as a member of the Council and his desire to devote himself to his diocese, he came to give his counsel when the strife of Beaufort and Gloucester reached a crisis or when the young King's education was to be considered. This service was given freely: other councillors took salaries, a charge the country could ill afford, but Langley did not take anything. It was a bitter irony that, in the north, he had given his friendship and support to one so prominent among those who were to overthrow the house to which Langley had been so devoted: Richard Neville, Earl of Salisbury, was the father of Warwick "the Kingmaker" and uncle of Edward IV.

These qualities of energy, courage, and loyalty only partially explain Langley's distinguished career as a royal servant, for no other servant of the Duchy of Lancaster rose so high as he in the service of the state, or to such prominence in the Church. Langley's advancement from Secretary to Henry IV to Chancellor of England within the space of six years, and his later tenure of the Great Seal for a period of seven years—a longer span than any Chancellor had served since the death of Edward III—is remark-

---

[1] Above, p. 96.
[2] Fowler, "The St. Cuthbert Window", pp. 259–63; Harrison, *Painted Glass of York*, p. 219.

able in view of his earlier career. The other Lancastrian Chancellors of England began their careers with greater advantages than he: Thomas Arundel, Henry Beaufort, and Edmund Stafford had the benefit of noble family connections, while John Kemp and John Stafford came from that nursery of diplomats, the court of Canterbury. Langley owed his success to his outstanding administrative ability. He had the faculty of being able to attend to a great variety of subjects simultaneously, and to give to each a degree of care that extended to its smallest detail. This is evident in the records of his correspondence with the receiver-general of Durham in December 1419, but it must be recalled that at this time Langley was Chancellor of England, when the absence abroad of Henry V and most of his other councillors, the additional business falling on the few members of the Council remaining in England and an increase in the judicial activities of Chancery, all imposed upon him an almost overwhelming burden of employment. Langley's talents made him an extremely efficient civil servant but there is no evidence that he possessed a mind of conspicuous originality.

On the other hand, Langley left no uncertain mark on the government of Durham. The contrast between his character as a royal minister and his work as temporal lord of the Bishopric is not inexplicable, for the innovations he made in the administration of Durham were the fruits of his experience in Duchy and royal service. He had the imagination to see that it was necessary to improve the secretarial methods of his palatine chancery and to remodel his financial organization, and his knowledge of the governments of England and the Duchy suggested to him practices that might be adopted. The same practical sense can be observed in his work as diocesan: the object of his reforms at Auckland and Sherburn was to adapt these old foundations to meet new circumstances and to adjust their finances so that they should be able to continue to carry out their appointed functions, while his ordinances for the new college at Manchester, which made it necessary for the fellows to reside, proved his wisdom a century after his death.

The statutes for Auckland, Manchester, and Sherburn were Langley's most constructive achievements in the ecclesiastical sphere. His measures at Lanchester, Neasham, and in the hospitals of his diocese also show him to have been a reforming bishop, but here his concern was to enforce respect for established rules. This attitude was a most notable feature in all his work, especially in his secular government. As Chancellor of England he had become fully acquainted with the extent of regalian prerogatives, and, as an old servant of the Duchy of Lancaster, he had learnt how far these could be applied in the government of a palatinate. Thus he carried into Durham a fully developed sense of the nature of his authority, particularly in the matter of suits at law against himself, when he insisted that he should have the same consideration in the Bishopric as the King had in England. This extreme interpretation of his privileges was an innovation that provoked the resentment of a number of his subjects, but he successfully defeated their challenge; Parliament admitted his title and the judges of King's Bench upheld his practice. His achievement in this respect, as in his successful claim to the forfeitures of traitors against the Crown and in the recovery of his portion of the Tyne bridge, enabled him to leave to his successors a far stronger position than he had inherited from the feeble Walter Skirlaw. Langley was equally anxious to uphold the rights of his royal masters. The monks of Meaux grumbled at his refusal to make them a charter of perpetual exemption from taxation on certain property, but his attitude was due to his reluctance that the Crown should lose any revenue.[1]

If Langley was resolute in demanding of others that they should observe established laws and privileges, he was also conscientious in carrying out his own duties. He was often an absentee from his diocese, yet he visited it frequently and never neglected his responsibilities as ordinary. Before he became Bishop, when he was Archdeacon of Norfolk, he showed an interest in his ecclesiastical charge unparalleled in his contemporaries. He undoubtedly enjoyed a considerable reputation for integrity, for his services as a supervisor or executor of wills were constantly in demand; he was appointed to these offices by kings, bishops, great magnates, and men who had served with him in the royal and Duchy administrations.[2] One of the most interesting of these appointments was that as supervisor of the will of Thomas Weston, Archdeacon of Durham: although he had hoped to be

---

[1] *Chronica Monasterii de Melsa* (Rolls Series, 1866–8), Vol. III, pp. 297–305.
[2] *Reg. Chichele*, II, pp. 66, 76, 87, 236, 314, 383 & 473; *Testamenta Ebor.* I, pp. 314 & 375, & III, pp. 25 & 42.

elected Bishop of Durham in 1406, Weston had been employed by Langley as his vicar-general.[1] Langley might well have regarded his unsuccessful rival with suspicion, but instead treated him with a confidence that was reciprocated.

Despite the rigidity of his attitude in matters of principle, Langley displayed great patience in his relations with individuals. In the affairs of both diocese and county palatine he was reluctant to take severe measures in haste. The custodians of the hospitals of Gateshead and West Spital were not dismissed until after second visitations of their houses, and the same restraint was shown towards the Prioress of Neasham. The offenders were given an opportunity to mend their ways, but their failure to comply with the Bishop's injunctions was punished. Likewise in the dispute with Sir William Eure, Langley let the suit in his chancery be protracted so that an opportunity for a more amicable settlement might be found; his anxiety for such a solution was sufficient to make him abandon his regalian position, in that he twice submitted his quarrel to arbitration. Langley's conduct in Convocation in 1426 reveals his patience and skill in dealing with men: he caused the heretical friar's brothers to abandon him and the accused man himself to confess, and although he was unable to persuade the clergy to grant a subsidy, it was not for want of solicitation on his part. Here he showed those qualities that gave him so much employment in diplomatic affairs. These, with the equally essential characteristic of discretion, are well exemplified by his part in the negotiations with the French prisoners in 1417: they were to be persuaded to assist their captors, and the whole business conducted in the utmost secrecy. Henry V wrote to his ally the Emperor to report Langley's success and told him that no one else knew of these transactions. At the very outset of his career, Langley's talent for diplomacy had given him access to John of Gaunt's confidence.

In his dealings with Priors Hemmingburgh and Wessington, these qualities of the Bishop—and his generosity—enabled him to establish terms of friendship in remarkable contrast to the bitter hostility between the Convent and previous bishops. It was, of course, sound policy on Langley's part to seek a cordial understanding with the Prior, if it firstly be presumed that the Bishop was more concerned for his temporal government than his

[1] *Reg. Langley*, nos. 12 & 112.

spiritual authority; but there is good reason to suppose that feelings of episcopal duty and personal instinct also prompted him, for there are indications that he was capable of warm feelings. He took particular pleasure in the company of men from his own county of Lancashire, and in his will showed himself considerate for each member of his large household. His grief at the sad condition of his old friend, John Thoralby, is noticeable in even an official letter.[1] A great capacity for compassion was one of Langley's more prominent characteristics. His register contains many grants of indulgences for the benefit of people who had suffered severe losses, for local merchants and seamen captured by enemies or men whose homes had been destroyed by fire.[2] The best illustration of the Bishop's sympathy for the helpless appears in his ordinance for Sherburn hospital: the clause concerning the thirteen poor men on the foundation decreed that they were to say their hours, but those who were feeble were to sit up in bed at the times of the canonical hours and masses, and say their hours there, "and those who are weaker still, so that they cannot even sit up, may lie in peace and say what they can".[3] Even those persons who had merited his displeasure were regarded with consideration: Langley's concern for the errant Vicar of Eglingham deterred him from proceeding to extreme measures.[4]

The records offer few other indications of Langley's character. He was not a learned man,[5] but his will shows that he possessed a small library, consisting mainly of theological works, but also including a complete text of the canon law, the *Corpus Juris Civilis* and, perhaps for lighter reading, *Polichronicon* and *Bestiarum Figurationes*.[6] The notice of his having gone hunting with Prior Wessington and his monitions against those who poached his game suggest a liking for outdoor sports. Langley shared the desire for worldy splendour common to the princely bishops of Durham, and his tomb in the Galilee Chapel, blocking the great west door of the Cathedral, is impressive although not pretentious.

---

[1] *Reg.* no. 1072.   [2] Ibid. 138, 194, 252, 622, 693, etc.
[3] Reg. fo. 245v.
[4] Hamilton Thompson, "Thomas Langley", p. 16.
[5] Langley's handwriting, to judge from a unique example, a letter addressed to his receiver-general, was that common to clerks of his day and known as bastard secretary hand (DCD. Additional Doc. 108). His signature, which appears in many acts of the Privy Council, was equally restrained (CPS. 45–51).
[6] *Scr. Tres*, Appendix, pp. ccxlv–ccxlvi.

There were other memorials, military as well as ecclesiastical buildings in various parts of the Bishopric, the tally of which is so long that Langley has been remembered chiefly as a builder and philanthropist. His two religious foundations had a more valuable purpose than the perpetuation of his memory, for both at Durham and Middleton schools were attached to his chantries, where education was to be given free to poor children, and he also had placed in the Galilee Chapel a font, where, by papal licence, the children of excommunicated parents could be baptized.[1]

Langley holds a high place among the bishops of Durham, for his achievements as lord of the county palatine no less than for his record of reform in the diocese. His chief title to fame, however, rests on his work as a minister of the House of Lancaster, and his epitaph may therefore best be taken from the tribute paid to him when his petition against the attack on his franchise was granted in Parliament in 1433: among the considerations said to have moved Henry VI to show favour to Langley were

the countless magnificent and fruitful services, profitable to himself and all his realm of England, diligently and faithfully shown and given by the said Bishop in the time of our lord the King, as well as in that of his noble forbears, without stint of toil, cost or expense, nor without grievous bodily hurt.[2]

[1] *Scr. Tres*, p. 147.   [2] *Rot. Parl.* IV, p. 431.

APPENDIX A

OUTLINE OF BISHOP LANGLEY'S ITINERARY FROM HIS CONSECRATION ON 8 AUGUST 1406

THIS is not an exhaustive record of Langley's movements because the amount of relevant information is very great indeed, and his full itinerary has been abridged in three respects: when three or more days in a month are known that are not more than five days from each other, the intermediate days have been ignored, although references are given, and the whole period is shown as an unbroken sequence at the one place; only one reference is given for each day even though more are sometimes available; and all notices of Langley's presence in London, Westminster, Old Ford, and elsewhere in the immediate vicinity of the capital are given as at London only. The unwarranted letters on the Chancery rolls are cited as evidence of Langley's movements when he was Chancellor. The Bishop's residences may be identified by reference to pp. 93–4.

1406

August 8–24	London	*Reg.* nos. 10–13; *CFR. 1405–1413*, p. 3.
26	Leicester	Ibid. 19.
September 3, 4	,,	Ibid. 3.
8	Huntingdon	*CCR. 1405–1409*, p. 148.
8, 9	Pishiobury	*CCR.* p. 147; *CPR. 1405–1408*, p. 212.
12–24	London	*CFR.* p. 3.
October 15, 29	,,	*Reg.* no. 21; CPS. 23.
November 3–30	,,	*Reg.* nos. 11, 14–19; Chancery Warrants, 1543/24.
December 8–24	,,	*PPC.* I, p. 295; *Reg.* no. 20; *Rot. Parl.* III, pp. 581, 585 & 603; RG. 188714.

1407

January 1, 22	London	*Reg.* nos. 22–4.
30	„ —*Resignation as Chancellor*	*CCR.* p. 250.
February 19	London	*Calendar of Letter Books of the City of London,* ed. R. R. Sharpe (1899–1912), Vol. I, pp. 58–9.
March 13, 21	„	*Reg.* nos. 25–6.
April	—	
May 5, 7	London	Ibid. 27–8.
June 11	„	Ibid. 30.
July 2	„	Ibid. 29.
16	Wheel Hall	Ibid. 30.
August	—	
September 4	Durham—*Enthronement*	DCD. Cartulary I, fo. 118v.
8	Bishop Wearmouth	*Reg.* nos. 31, 33–4.
13	Bishop Auckland	Ibid. 35–6.
21	York	RG. 188714.
October 23	Gloucester	Stubbs, *Reg. Sacrum,* p. 84
November	—	
December 6 & 7	Gloucester	*Reg.* no. 37; *Foedera,* VIII, pp. 507–9.
27–29	Bishop Auckland	*Reg.* nos. 39–41.

1408

January 1	Bishop Auckland	Ibid. 43–4.
6	Wheel Hall	Ibid. 45.
7	Selby	Ibid. 48.
30 & 31	London	Ibid. 49; CPS. 23.
February 7–28	„	*Reg.* nos. 50–8.
March 2	„	*PPC.* I, p. 308.
26, 30	Howden	*Reg.* nos. 59–61.
April 4–16	„	Ibid. 62–8.
21	Pontefract	Ibid. 83.
May 1	Howden	Ibid. 69.
23, 30	Northallerton	Ibid. 71, 72 & 84.
June 5–11	Stockton	Ibid. 76–80, 86.
26	Durham	Ibid. 96.
28	Norham	Ibid. 88.
July 18, 20	Bishop Auckland	Ibid. 99; RG. 188714.
23	Durham—*Visitation of the Convent*	Above, pp. 194–5.
	Visitation of the archdeaconry of Durham, as follows:	Above, p. 182.
27, 29	Bishop Auckland	Ibid. 98: RG. 190007.

1408 (continued)

August 10	Stanhope	Reg. no. 92.
14	Darlington	Ibid. 94.
September 18	Bishop Auckland	Ibid. 100.
20	Darlington	Ibid. 113.
22	Bishop Auckland	Ibid. 103.
October 8	Swineshead [1]	Ibid. 105.
18, 24	London	Ibid. 117 & 104.
November 7	,,	Ibid. 107.
December 11	York—Convocation	Above, p. 215.
31	Wheel Hall	Reg. no. 108.

1409

January 3, 4	Wheel Hall	RG. 188712; DCD. Locellus 18, no. 108.
10	Grantham	Reg. no. 109.
21	Greenwich	Testamenta Vetusta, I, pp. 17–18.
27	London	Reg. no. 111.
February 15, 16, 25	,,	Ibid. 114–16.
March 8, 10	,,	Reg. no. 118; RG. 188714.
10	Greenwich	CCR. 1405–1409, p. 498.
21, 26	London	Reg. nos. 119–21.
April–October	Embassy to the Council of Pisa	Above, pp. 26–7.
November	—	
December 3, 5	Wheel Hall	Reg. nos. 125–6.
9	Northallerton	Ibid. 127.
25	Bishop Auckland	DCD. Bursar 1409–1410, m. 3d.

1410

January 1–6	Bishop Auckland	Reg. nos. 128–30.
9	Durham	Ibid. 132.
21	Bishop Auckland, Chester-le-Street	Above, p. 110.
February 12–20	London	Reg. nos. 133–7.
March 8	,,	Ibid. 138.
April 25	,,	Ibid. 139 & 219.
May 5	,,	Ibid. 140.
June 13–19	,,	Ibid. 141; PPC. I, pp. 331–8.
30	Wheel Hall	Reg. no. 142.
July 12	,, ,,	Ibid. 217.
28	Durham	DCD. 1.13. Pontificalia 14.

[1] Six miles west of Boston, Lincolnshire. Professor Hamilton Thompson has suggested that Langley's visits here and to Long Sutton on 21 July 1424 were made on his return from the shrine of Our Lady of Walsingham (*Durham University Journal*, *1945*, p. 4). There is no evidence that Langley had any particular veneration for this shrine and another explanation for these journeys can be made (above, p. 7).

1410 (continued)

August 15–18	Bishop Auckland	*Reg.* nos. 143 & 234.
21	Jarrow	Ibid. 144.
26, 27	Bishop Auckland	Ibid. 149, 151 & 219.
September 8–26 [1]	„ „	Ibid. 148, 152–65, 218.
29	Crayke	Ibid. 167.
October (3	York—*Convocation*)	Above, p. 215.
6	Cawood,[2] Wheel Hall	*Reg.* nos. 166 & 168.
20–26	London	Ibid. 169, 170 & 218.
November 12	„ [3]	Ibid. 218–19.
December 1, 2	Leicester	Ibid. 172–3.
7, 8	Wheel Hall	Ibid. 174–5.
25	Bishop Auckland	Ibid. 177.

1411

January 2–14	Bishop Auckland	Ibid. 178–83.
20	Howden	Ibid. 217.
24, 25	Bishop Auckland	Ibid. 186 & 196.
29	Crayke	Ibid. 189.
30	Sheriff Hutton[4]	Ibid. 190.
February 1	Howden	Ibid. 218, 220 & 234.
March 9, 11, 20	London	Ibid. 193, 194 & 217; *PPC.* II, pp. 6–7.
April 27, 28	Howden	*Reg.* nos. 195, 217 & 220.
May	—	
June 7, 9, 17–23	Bishop Auckland	Ibid. 198, 199, 202–5, 220.
July 2	„ „	Ibid. 201.
	Visitation of the arch-deaconry of Durham, continued, as follows:	Above, pp. 182–3.
6	Sherburn hospital	Ibid. 207.
31	Bishop Auckland	Ibid. 209.
August 8	Stockton	Ibid. 226.
24, 26	Bishop Auckland	Ibid. 208 & 212.
September 1	„ „	Ibid. 226.
3	Northallerton	Ibid. 222.
20, 28	London	Ibid. 223–4.
October 8–30	„	Ibid. 217, 219, 232–4; Durham Warrants 1, e.
November	—	
December 10	London	*Reg.* no. 234.
27	Howden	Ibid. 236–7.

[1] Nos. 145 & 147 are dated 1 and 7 September "*ut supra*"; this would strictly be Jarrow, the place of no. 144.
[2] The Archbishop of York's castle.
[3] Cf. no. 217, giving Leicester.
[4] A castle of the Earl of Westmorland, 9 miles north-east of York.

1412

January 12–14	Bishop Auckland	*Reg.* nos. 220, 238–9.
(20	York—*Convocation*)	Above, p. 210.
24–28	Howden	*Reg.* nos. 217, 240–2.
February 6, 15	London	Ibid. 244–5.
March 4	,,	Ibid. 218.
13, 14	Wheel Hall	Ibid. 246–8.
25, 26	Durham	Ibid. 249 & 252.
April 2	,,	Ibid. 250.
14–18, 28, 29	Bishop Auckland	Ibid. 220, 251, 254–7.
May 10, 17	London	Ibid. 268–9.
June	—	
July 9, 10, 24	London	*PPC.* II, p. 31; *Reg.* no. 272.
August 19	York	Ibid. 274.
24, 26	Howden	Ibid. 278–9.
September (?	Middleton 1)	Ibid. 276.
October 13, 14, 20	London	Ibid. 217; *PPC.* II, p. 36.
21	Merton 2	Ibid. p. 38.
November	—	
December 4–25	Bishop Auckland	Ibid. 217, 221, 263, 266, 267, 284, 286–7; DCD. Bursar 1412–1413, m. 3d.

1413

January 9–14	Bishop Auckland	*Reg.* nos. 288–91.
22	Wheel Hall	DCD. 1.2. Archidiaconalia Dunelm' 67.
February 3, 10, 28	London	*Reg.* nos. 292 & 317; DCD. Cartulary I, fo. 143.
March	—	
April	—	
May	—	
June	—	
July 2, 9–16	London	*Reg.* nos. 217, 294 & 316; *PPC.* II, p. 131.
(27, 28?	York—*Convocation*)	Above, p. 210.
August 25	Stockton	*Reg.* no. 304.
30	Gateshead	Ibid. 306.
September 1	Durham	Ibid. 302.
23	Bishop Auckland	Ibid. 299.
October 1	York	Ibid. 453.
6, 8	Howden	Ibid. 352; RG. 189602.
November 11, 15	London	*Reg.* nos. 307–8.
December 12, 14, 28	,,	Ibid. 312–14.

1 Five miles north of Manchester.
2 Eight miles south-west of London.

1414

January	—	
February	—	
March 5–22	Bishop Auckland	*Reg.* nos. 321–7.
April 3–7	,, ,,	Ibid. 331, 333 & 341.
May 12, 26	Leicester	Ibid. 336–7.
June 3	,,	Ibid. 315.
17	London	Ibid. 338.
July 8, 10	,,	Ibid. 339.
	Embassy to France	Above, p. 31.
October 2, 7	London	*Reg.* no. 340.
November 13, 28	,,	Ibid. 342 & 382.
December 12, 14	,,	Ibid. 343.
	Embassy to France	Above, pp. 31–2.

1415

March 29	London 1	
April 2, 10–28	,,	*Reg.* nos. 344–8, 350 & 353; *PPC.* II, pp. 154–8.
May 17, 18	Darlington	*Reg.* nos. 356–8.
22, 27, 30	Bishop Auckland	Ibid. 359–62.
June 2, 5	Stockton	Ibid. 364 & 369.
19	London	*PPC.* II, p. 170.
30	Winchester	Above, p. 32.
July	—	
August *1, 4*	*Southampton*	Charter Roll 186, m. 21.2
21	Howden	*Reg.* nos. 367–8.
September 6, 7	Stockton	Ibid. 370–1.
27	Durham	Ibid. 374.
October 9	York	Ibid. 375.
11–15	Wheel Hall	Ibid. 220, 376–8.
November 8, 25	London	*Le Cotton Manuscrit Galba B.1*, ed. G. van Severen (Brussels, 1896), p. 363; *PPC.* II, p. 184.
December 28, 31	Bishop Auckland	*Reg.* nos. 379–81.

1416

January 1–13, 23, 24	Bishop Auckland	Ibid. 384, 386–91, 393–6.
February 22, 25	London	Ibid. 398; *PPC.* II, p. 191.
March 21, 22	,,	*Reg.* nos. 399 & 403.

1 This is the day of Langley's return from Paris according to the account for his embassy (see note 1, p. 32), but other sources show him to have been in London in February, on the 4th, 12th, and an unknown day (*Reg.* nos. 401 & 402; *PPC.* II, p. 145).

2 This source is demonstrably unreliable and has previously been ignored; but in this case it has been cited as offering the most probable position of Langley, who is shown by the vicar-general's register to have then been absent from the diocese (*Reg.* fo. 260v.).

1416 (continued)

April 6–14, 22, 24	London	*Reg.* nos. 404, 406–9.
May 1	,,	Ibid. 410.
June 13	,,	Ibid. 412.
July 12–26	Stockton	Ibid. 413–17.
29	Wheel Hall	Ibid. 418.
August	—	
September 4	Sandwich	*CCR. 1413–1419*, p. 368.
	Calais	Above, p. 33.
October 6–11	,,	*Reg.* nos. 419–23, 425 & 427.
November 11, 16, 26	London	Ibid. 428, 430 & 433.
December 22–24	Howden	Ibid. 436–40, 443–4.

1417

January	Pontefract	*Foedera*, IX, pp. 425–7.
(5–12?	York—*Convocation*)	*Reg.* no. 455; above, p. 210.
12	Howden	*Reg.* no. 445.
16–18	Pontefract	Above, pp. 33–4.
19	York	Ancient Correspondence, Vol. LVII, no. 79.
31	Bishop Auckland	*Reg.* no. 448.
February 2–28	,, ,,	Ibid. 220, 446–7, 449–51, 454, 456–60, 462–5.
March 1, 10	Howden	Ibid. 466 & 471.
22	Huntingdon	Ibid. 467.
April 21, 27	London	Ibid. 468; *Reg.* fo. 284.
May 2	Mortlake	*PPC.* II, p. 232.
13	London	*Reg.* no. 486.
14	Reading	Ibid. 474.
20, 22	London	Ibid. 472–3.
June 8	Titchfield [1]	*PPC.* II, p. 233.
July 23	Southwick [1]—	*CCR. 1413–1419*, p. 435.
	Appointed Chancellor	
23, 24	Wickham [1]	Ibid. 435; *CPR. 1416–1422*, p. 110.
29	Lewes	Ibid. 138.
(30 or 31?	Hastings)	*Reg.* no. 475.
August 3–14	London	*CPR.* pp. 113 & 115; Chancery Warrants, 1542/3.
17	Guildford	*CCR.* p. 436.
21	Winchester	*CPR.* p. 120.
September 29	London	*Reg.* no. 476.
October 13, 20–30	,,	Ibid. 480–2, 506; *PPC.* II, pp. 218 & 239.
November 10–20, 28	,,	CPS. 32; *Reg.* nos. 477–9, 483 & 487; *Rot. Parl.* IV, p. 106.
December 2, 10	,,	Ibid. 111; *Reg.* no. 485.

[1] All near Portsmouth.

1418

January 4	Esher	*Reg.* no. 490.
21	London	Lyte, *Great Seal*, p. 191.
February 24	,,	*CCR.* p. 457.
March 19	,,	*Reg.* no. 489.
April 4, 5	,,	Ibid. 491 & 493.
7	Windsor	Chancery: French Roll no. 101, m. 9.
16–22	Southampton	Ibid. 9–10.
24	London	*Reg.* no. 494.
May 4	,,	Chancery Warrants, 1364/53.
June 2, 18	,,	DCD. Hunter MSS. Vol. III, p. 26; *Reg.* no. 495.
July 20	,,	Ibid. 496.
28	Grantham	*CPR.* p. 173.
August 1	Howden	Chancery Files (*Brevia Regia*), Series C, file 124.
6–15	Stockton	Ibid.; *CCR.* p. 507; French Roll 101, m. 4; *Reg.* nos. 498–9.
18, 19	Durham	Chancery Files, C. 124; *CFR. 1413–1422*, p. 239.
25	Bishop Auckland	French Roll 101, m. 4.
September 16, 22	,, ,,	*Reg.* nos. 501 & 508.
24	Durham	Ibid. 503 & 509.
30	Howden	*CPR. 1416–1422*, p. 177.
October 11, 16	London	*London Letter Books*, I, p. 205; *Reg.* no. 511.
November 15	,,	CPS. 32.
December 17	Stepney	*Reg.* no. 513.

1419

January 5, 6, 14, 20, 28	London	Ibid. 516–20; *Foedera*, IX, p. 669.
February 6, 10, 23	,,	*The Brut* II, p. 444; *Reg.* no. 507; Durham Warrants 1, a.
March 1, 6	,,	*PPC.* II, p. 246; Duchy of Lancaster Misc. Book 17, fo. 146v.
17	Sevenoaks	*CPR.* p. 458.
22	Canterbury	*CFR. 1413–1422*, p. 274.
April 20	London	*Reg.* no. 521.
May 17, 28	,,	RG. 189782; Reg. fo. 270.
June 16	,,	*Reg.* no. 522.
July 5	,,	Ibid. 218.
August 3–12	Southampton	Chancery Warrants, 1543/13; *CPR.* pp. 214, 219 & 268.
23, 31	London	Chancery Warrants, 1543/14; *PPC.* II, p. 261.

16

1419 *(continued)*

September 2	London	*Reg.* no. 524.
October 12, 16, 23, 24	„	CPS. 33; *Rot. Parl.* IV, p. 116; RG. 189782.
November 3, 9, 12	„	CPS. 33; *Reg.* nos. 525–6.
December 24	„	Ibid. 528.

1420

January 6	London	Ibid. 529.
February 1, 6, 16	„	Ibid. 532, 534–5.
March 14	„	RG. 189782.
April 6	„	*CCR. 1419–1422*, p. 104.
23–30	Southampton	French Roll 103, mm. 6–8.
May 1–14	„	Ibid. 6–8.
	London [1]	
June 28	„	CPS. 33.
July 13–15	„	Ibid. 33; *CPR. 1416–1422*, p. 298.
21	Wakerley [2]	Chancery Files, C. 126.
August 5–10	York	*CPR.* pp. 298 & 312.
20	Newcastle-upon-Tyne	Ibid. 312.
24, 28	Bishop Auckland	Chancery: Gascon Roll, no. 118, m. 3; Chancery Files, C. 126.
September 4, 10	„ „	*CPR.* p. 312.
12	York	Originalia Roll 185, m. 44.
20, 22	Stockton	Ibid. 44; RG. 189601.
26	York	*CPR.* p. 312.
30	Howden	Reg. fo. 274.
October 5	Saffron Walden	*CPR.* p. 312.
13, 18	London	*CCR. 1419–1422*, p. 84; Reg. fo. 274v.
November	—	
December 2, 12, 20	London	*Rot. Parl.* IV, p. 123; *Reg.* no. 541; Reg. fo. 274v.

1421

January	—	
February 18, 24	London	CPS. 33; *The Chronicle of Fabian* (1559), p. 402.
March 18, 19, 25	Durham	*Reg.* nos. 541 & 546; *CCR.* p. 195.
29	Stockton	Reg. fo. 275.
April 5, 6	York	*CFR. 1413–1422*, p. 377; Chancery Files, C. 127.

[1] On 12 and 13, according to *Reg.* nos. 536 & 540.
[2] A manor 7 miles south-west of Stamford in which Langley and others were enfeoffed by his friend Thomas de la Warre in 1414. After the Bishop's death, the manor reverted to De la Warre's heir (*CCR. 1422–1429*, pp. 301–2; *1435–1441*, p. 154).

1421 *(continued)*

April 8, 11	Howden	Chancery Files, C. 127; *CPR.* p. 384.
15	Lincoln	Ibid. 337.
May 1–16	London	*Rot. Parl.* IV, p. 129; CPS. 34; *PPC.* II, p. 315.
June 1	Canterbury	French Roll 104, m. 10.
10, 17	Dover	*CCR.* p. 201; Chancery Files, C. 127.
July 1–15, 28	London	*CCR.* p. 206; CPS. 35; *PPC.* II, pp. 287, 293 & 300; *CPR.* p. 391.
August 2	Daventry	*CFR.* p. 378.
7	Macclesfield	*CPR.* p. 395.
8–10	Manchester	Ibid. 393 & 395; Originalia Roll 186, m. 63.
13	Skipton-in-Craven	*CPR.* p. 395.
September 1	Durham	*CPR. 1416–1422*, pp. 451 & 461.
2	Lumley Castle	*Reg.* no. 551.
2–4	Gateshead	*CCR. 1419–1422*, p. 226; Rot. E. m. 4d.
4–15	Bishop Auckland	*CFR. 1413–1422*, p. 378; *CPR.* pp. 394 & 418; *Reg.* nos. 552, 554, 563–4.
19	Stockton	Ibid. 909.
19	Crayke	*CFR.* p. 406.
20–24	York—*Convocation*	Ibid. 378; *CCR.* p. 204; above, p. 211.
24–28	Wheel Hall	*CFR.* p. 378; Originalia Roll 186, m. 63; Durham Warrants 1, c.
October 2	Blyth	Chancery Files, C. 127.
9–13	London	*CPR.* p. 394; CPS. 35; *PPC.* II, p. 303.
November 12–17	,,	*CCR.* p. 215; *PPC.* II, p. 309.
December 1, 14, 18, 23	,,	Chancery: Significations of Excommunication, 199/11; Chancery Warrants, 1543/49B; *Rot. Parl.* IV, pp. 150 & 153.

1422

January 4	London	*Reg.* no. 556.
February 7	,,	CPS. 36.
March 27	,,	*Reg.* no. 567.
April 6–29	Southampton 1	*CCR.* p. 246; *CFR.* p. 425; *CPR.* p. 426; French Roll 105, mm. 1–3.
31	Southwick	*Reg.* no. 569.

1 Including Southwick on 8 and 16, and Wickham on 23.

1422 (continued)

May 1, 2	Southwick	French Roll 105, m. 2.
16	London	*Reg.* no. 568.
June 3	,,	Ibid. 571.
July 1	,,	*CPR. 1422–1429*, p. 117.
August 6	York	French Roll 105, m. 1.
7	Northallerton	*CPR. 1416–1422*, p. 442.
8, 11, 18–27	Stockton	*CCR.* pp. 250 & 265; *CPR.* p. 443; *Reg.* nos. 573, 575; Chancery Files, C. 128.
September 9, 10	,,	*Reg.* nos. 576, 577, 580.
15	Crayke	Ibid. 579.
28	Windsor Castle— *Resignation as Chancellor*	*CCR. 1422–1429*, p. 46.
October 12	Dover	*PPC.* III, p. 5.
November 5	London	Ibid. 6.
16	London—*Appointed Chancellor*	*Rot. Parl.* IV, p. 171.
19, 27	London	*CCR.* p. 49; *Reg.* no. 583.
December 20, 21	,,	*PPC.* III, pp. 10–12.

1423

January 14–26	London	*CPS.* 39; *PPC.* III, pp. 18–22.
February 1–28	,,	*CPS.* 39; *PPC.* III, pp. 23–45.
March 1–7	,,	*CPS.* 39; *PPC.* III, pp. 48–65.
14	Doncaster	*CFR. 1422–1430*, p. 3.
26	Durham	Chancery Files, C. 129.
April 2	,,	*CPR. 1422–1429*, p. 99.
6	York	Originalia Roll 188, m. 49.
11	Blyth	Chancery Files, C. 129.
19–30	London	*CPS.* 40; *PPC.* III, pp. 66–9.
May 1–30	,,	*CPS.* 41; *PPC.* III, pp. 69–101.
June 9–30	,,	*CPS.* 42; *PPC.* III, pp. 102–8.
July 3–18	,,	Ibid. 110–16.
30	Howden	*CPR.* p. 10.
August 1	,,	Ibid. 10.
5	Middleham	*CCR.* p. 76.
8, 24	Stockton	*Year Books of Henry VI. 1 Henry VI* (Selden Society, 1933), p. 56; Chancery Files, C. 129.
September 11–16	York	*CCR.* pp. 130 & 134; *CPR.* p. 178; *Rot. Scot.* II, p. 239.
18	Bishop Auckland	*CFR.* p. 50.
20	Raby	Chancery Files, C. 130.
22	Bishop Auckland	*CPR.* p. 139.
28	Howden	Chancery Files, C. 130.

1423 (*continued*)

October 7	Wakerley	Chancery Files, C. 130.
18–29	London	*PPC.* III, pp. 116–18; *Rot. Parl.* IV, p. 197.
November 5–29	,,	CPS. 43; *PPC.* III, pp. 121–9.
December 17, 18	,,	Ibid. 130; *Rot. Parl.* IV, p. 200.

1424

January 14–31	London	CPS. 43; *PPC.* 131–4.
February 1–28	,,	CPS. 44; *PPC.* III, pp. 135–46.
March 10	Huntingdon	*Reg.* no. 560.
11, 12	Howden	Chancery Files, C. 130.
12	York	Ibid.
20, 31	Durham	*Reg.* nos. 592, 604.
31	Bishop Auckland	Ibid. 605.
April 5	,, ,,	Ibid. 602.
9	Durham	Ibid. 601.
15, 18	Bishop Auckland	*CPR.* p. 189; Chancery Files, C. 130.
22	Durham	*Reg.* no. 593.
May 6	Huntingdon	*CPR. 1422–1429*, p. 194.
26, 28	London	Early Chancery Proceedings, 5/1; *PPC.* III, p. 147.
June 8	,,	Ibid. 147.
July 2–15	,,	CPS. 45; *PPC.* III, pp. 154.
16	Hertford Castle— *Resignation as Chancellor*	*CCR. 1422–1429*, p. 154.
21	Long Sutton [1]	*Reg.* no. 597.
August 29	Newcastle-upon-Tyne	Ibid. 609.
September 11	Bishop Auckland	Ibid. 598.
16, 29	Stockton	Ibid. 599, 600.
October 1	Durham	Ibid. 610.
6	York—*Convocation*	Above, p. 212, note 5.
20–28	London	*Reg.* nos. 607, 608, 614.
November 8–28	,,	CPS. 46; *PPC.* III, pp. 161–3.
December 11	York	*Reg.* no. 612.

1425

January 5, 14, 18	Bishop Auckland	Ibid. 625, 626, 633.
February 2, 9, 16–23	,, ,,	Ibid. 613, 618–24.
March 1, 6, 25	,, ,,	Ibid. 603, 613, 629.
April 5–12	,, ,,	Ibid. 639–42, 645.
May 3, 15–17	London	Ibid. 643, 646–8.
June 1	,,	*Rot. Parl.* IV, p. 275.

[1] Eighteen miles south-east of Swineshead (see above, p. 228, n. 1).

1425 *(continued)*

July 1	London	*Reg.* no. 644.
30	Howden	Ibid. 638.
August 5	Stockton	Ibid. 658.
12	Holy Island	Ibid. 655.
14	*In Scotland*	Cf. nos. 658 & 659.
20	Berwick-upon-Tweed	Ibid. 650.
23	Warkworth	*PPC.* III, p. 174.
25	Newcastle-upon-Tyne	*Reg.* no. 665.
27, 28	Bishop Auckland	Ibid. 636, 649, 666.
31	Stockton	Ibid. 661.
September 7	Bishop Auckland	Ibid. 634.
7	Durham	*Reg.* fo. 292.
18	Newcastle-upon-Tyne	*Reg.* no. 635.
October 4	Bishop Auckland	Ibid. 654.
11	Stockton	*Reg.* fo. 292.
November 6, 12	,,	*Reg.* no. 663; *Reg.* fo. 292.
14	Bishop Auckland	Ibid. 297.
20	Raby	Ibid. 297v.
December 4	London	*Reg.* no. 653.

1426

January 14, 31	London	*PPC.* III, p. 480; *Reg.* no. 667.
February	—	
March 7–12	Leicester	*PPC.* III, p. 190; *Rot. Parl.* IV, p. 297.
30	Bishop Auckland	*Reg.* fo. 292v.
April	—	
May 1–28	Leicester	*CPS.* 47; *PPC.* III, pp. 193 & 196.
June 1, 2	,,	*CPS* 47; *PPC.* III, pp. 197–8.
15	London	*CPS.* 47.
July 4–26	,,	*CPS.* 47; *PPC.* III, pp. 201–8.
August 12–17	York—*Convocation*	Above, pp. 212–13, 216
September		
October 7–9	York—*Convocation*	Above, p. 213.
November 24	Reading	*PPC.* III, p. 221.
December 6–8	London	*CPS.* 48; *PPC.* III, p. 226.

1427

January	—	
February	—	
March 6	London	*PPC.* III, p. 253.
April 7, 14	Bishop Auckland	*Reg.* nos. 698, 725.
May 16–23	London	*CCR. 1422–1429*, p. 337; Chancery Warrants, 1544/69; *PPC.* III, pp. 268–9.

1427 *(continued)*

June 24–27	London	Chancery Warrants, 1544/70 & 72; Reg. fo. 295.
July 2–8, 16	,,	Chancery Warrants, 1544/74; *PPC.* III, pp. 270–5, 356.
August *or* September } ?	Stockton	*Reg.* no. 941.
October 3	Howden	RG. 190013.
November 8–12, 20–30	London	*Reg.* nos. 672–82, 734.
December 6	,,	Ibid. 685.
15	Howden	Ibid. 687.
19	Darlington	Ibid. 688.
23, 29, 30	Bishop Auckland	Ibid. 690, 692, 693.

1428

January 2–10	Bishop Auckland	Ibid. 694–8.
12	Darlington	Ibid. 699, 700.
21–31	Bishop Auckland	Ibid. 701, 703–8.
February 14	,, ,,	Ibid. 709.
28	Durham	Ibid. 710.
March 8, 12, 20	Bishop Auckland	Ibid. 712–15.
April 1–10	,, ,,	Ibid. 716, 718–20.
14	Leconfield [1]	Ibid. 721.
18	Howden	Ibid. 686.
28	Stockton	Ibid. 722.
May 13	,,	Ibid. 727.
17	Bishop Auckland	Ibid. 729.
20, 22	Stockton	Ibid. 730–2.
June 1, 15, 20, 22, 27	London	CPS. 50; *PPC.* III, p. 298; *Reg.* nos. 733, 736; *Rot. Parl.* IV, p. 334.
July 1–14	,,	CPS. 50; *CPR. 1422–1429*, p. 519; *Reg.* no. 738.
August (2–7	York—*Convocation*)	Above, p. 213.
12–18	,,	*Reg.* nos. 742–3.
28	Stockton	Ibid. 745.
September 9–11	Bishop Auckland	Ibid. 746–8.
16, 20	Stockton	Ibid. 749, 751, 782.
October 5, 25, 31	,,	Ibid. 752, 753, 756.
November 3, 10–12	,,	Ibid. 757–62.
17, 19	Bishop Auckland	Ibid. 763–5.
December 1–6	,, ,,	Ibid. 766–9.
15	Newcastle-upon-Tyne	Ibid. 773, 775.
18	Durham	Ibid. 774.
19–30	Bishop Auckland	Ibid. 776–9, 783–7; RG. 190184.

[1] A castle of the Earl of Northumberland, two miles north of Beverley.

1429

January 5, 6	Bishop Auckland	*Reg.* nos. 788–90.
14–16	Crayke	Ibid. 791, 792, 797.
24	Bishop Auckland	Ibid. 792.
February 5, 9, 17–19	,, ,,	Ibid. 801–6.
March 3, 27	,, ,,	Ibid. 807, 809.
April 17	London	*PPC.* III, p. 323.
May 3, 10	,,	Ibid. 326; Chancery Warrants, 1545/8.
June	—	
July 13	Norham	*Reg.* no. 811.
19	Durham	Ibid. 812.
22, 25	Stockton	Ibid. 810, 813.
August 16	,,	Ibid. 816.
20	Bishop Auckland	Ibid. 817.
21	Stockton	Ibid. 818.
September 6	,,	Ibid. 822.
12	Howden	Above, p. 49.
October 10, 18, 25	London	Chancery Warrants, 1545/10; *PPC.* IV, pp. 4 & 6.
November 2–7, 20	,,	Ibid. 7; CPS. 51; *Reg.* nos. 825, 826; and above, p. 49.
December 20, 22	Bishop Auckland	*Reg.* nos. 829, 830.

1430

January 8–30	Bishop Auckland	Ibid. 832–4, 837–44.
February 3, 13–23	,, ,,	Ibid. 845–9.
March 1–3	,, ,,	Ibid. 850, 851, 862.
5–11	Durham	Ibid. 852–7.
April 1, 15	Bishop Auckland	Ibid. 858, 859.
26	Lumley Castle	Ibid. 860.
28	Newcastle-upon-Tyne	Above, p. 158.
29	Durham	*Reg.* no. 861.
May ?	Bishop Auckland	Ibid. 864.
June 10	,, ,,	Ibid. 865.
July 6–14	,, ,,	Ibid. 866–74.
15	Durham	Rot. C. m. 1.
19	Ryton	*Reg.* no. 876.
24, 31	Bishop Auckland	Ibid. 877, 878.
August 1	Darlington	Ibid. 880.
14	York	Ibid. 881.
25	Bishop Auckland	Ibid. 882.
September 2–6, 16, 23	,, ,,	Ibid. 886–9.
October *c.* 1	Durham	*Durham Account Rolls*, I, p. 61.
November 6	London	*PPC.* IV, p. 70.
30	Northallerton	*Reg.* no. 891.

1430 (continued)

December 11, 14	Bishop Auckland	*Reg.* nos. 892, 893.
c. 15	Durham	*Durham Account Rolls*, I, p. 61.
20, 23, 29	Bishop Auckland	*Reg.* nos. 894–6.

1431

January 2, 8	Bishop Auckland	Ibid. 897, 901.
11	York	Ibid. 898.
14, 22	Howden	Ibid. 898–900.
February 5, 11	,,	Ibid. 902–4.
18, 24	Bishop Auckland	Ibid. 905, 906.
March 17–20, 28	,, ,,	Ibid. 907–10.
April 11	,, ,,	Ibid. 913.
11	Durham	Ibid. 914.
17–28	Stockton	Reg. Kemp, fo. 356v; *Reg.* nos. 915, 918, 919.
May 7–18	,,	Durham Warrants 1, f; *Reg.* nos. 920–4.
24, 25	Newcastle-upon-Tyne	Above, p. 143; *Reg.* no. 925.
June 21	Stockton	Ibid. 928.
July 1, 20–31	,,	Durham Warrants 1, d; *Reg.* nos. 929–32.
August	—	
September 6–15, 30	Stockton	Ibid. 933–8; DCD. Reg. III, ff. 144–5v.
October 1–13	,,	*Reg.* nos. 939–43.
20	Howden	Ibid. 944.
November 4, 6, 20, 28–30	London	Ibid. 945, 948; CPS. 53; *PPC.* IV, pp. 100, 104–8.
December 3	Dunstable	*Reg.* no. 946.
16	Howden	Ibid. 949.
22, 29, 30	Bishop Auckland	Ibid. 950–2.

1432

January 3, 4, 13, 22–30	Bishop Auckland	Ibid. 954–60; RG. 190005.
February 22–29	,, ,,	*Reg.* nos. 961–6.
March 1–24	,, ,,	Ibid. 967–76, 978.
April 2, 9–23	,, ,,	Ibid. 187v.–92; 977, 981–6, 988, 992–6.
May 12, 26	London	Ibid. 997, 999.
June 14	,,	Ibid. 1001.
July (24	*Outside diocese)*	Reg. fo. 299v.
August (5	,, ,,)	Ibid. 299v.
21, 22	Stockton	*Reg.* nos. 1002, 1003.

1432 (continued)

September 12	Durham	*Reg.* no. 1004.
15	Bishop Auckland	RG. 189604.
16–19	Stockton	Reg. ff. 193v.–4; *Reg.* nos. 1005, 1008, 1009.
23, 28	Bishop Auckland	Ibid. 1011; DCD. 1.11. Pontificalia, 12.
October 1	Crayke	*Reg.* no. 1012.
4	York—*Convocation*	Ibid. 1013.
9	Crayke	Ibid. 1015.
27	Stockton	Ibid. 1016.
November 5, 6, 13, 16, 21, 22	Bishop Auckland	Ibid. 1017–23.
December 6–13, 24–31	„ „	Ibid. 1024–7, 1029, 1031–3.

1433

January	—	
February 2–23	Bishop Auckland	Ibid. 1034–42.
March 13–23, 31	„ „	Ibid. 1044–7, 1049.
April 1–15	„ „	Ibid. 1050–3, 1055–6.
18	Crayke	Ibid. 1057.
May 8, 12, 24	London	Ibid. 1058–9; *PPC.* IV, p. 163.
June 20	„	Baldwin, *King's Council*, pp. 525–9.
July 10, 16, 22–31	„	Ibid. 529; Chancery Warrants, 1545/45; *PPC.* IV, p. 172; *Reg.* nos. 1060–3.
August 8, 12	„	CPS. 54; *Reg.* no. 1064.
31	York	Ibid. 1065.
September 11, 13, 20–27	Stockton	Ibid. 1066–7, 1069–72.
October 6	Howden	Ibid. 1073.
19	Grantham	Ibid. 1074.
November 3, 4, 14–23, 31	London	Ibid. 1075, 1077–8; *PPC.* IV, p. 184; *Rot. Parl.* IV, p. 422.
December 6, 8, 15, 21	„	Chancery Warrants, 1545/51; *Reg.* no. 1080; *Rot. Parl.* IV, p. 446.

1434

January 4–30	London	*Reg.* nos. 1081–5; and above, p. 129.
February 1, 24	„	*PPC.* IV, p. 196; *Reg.* no. 1086.
March 18	Bishop Auckland	Ibid. 1090.

1434 *(continued)*

April 9	York	*Reg.* no. 1089.
19, 20, 27, 29	Bishop Auckland	Ibid. 1091–6.
May 1, 22, 31	,, ,,	Ibid. 1097–9.
June 4, 5, 14, 15, 30	Stockton	Ibid. 1101–5.
July 22	Durham	Reg. fo. 246.
27	Stockton	*Reg.* no. 1106.
August 21	Durham	Ibid. 1107.
23	Newcastle-upon-Tyne	Ibid. 1120.
25	Durham	Ibid. 1108.
26	Stockton	Ibid. 1109.
September 14, 20	,,	Ibid. 1110, 1112.
23	Durham	Ibid. 1122.
25	Bishop Auckland	Ibid. 1117.
October 2	Crayke	Ibid. 1116.
6	Howden	RG. 189604.
November 6, 8	London	CPS. 55.
10	Abingdon	*Reg.* no. 1118.
12	Cirencester	*PPC.* IV, p. 289.
26	Howden	*Reg.* no. 1120.
December 8–20, 27	Bishop Auckland	Ibid. 1123–5, 1127–30.

1435

January 8–11, 27, 31	Bishop Auckland	Ibid. 1131–6.
February 1–10, 21–28	,, ,,	Ibid. 1137–42.
March 7–12, 21, 29	,, ,,	Ibid. 1143–7.
April 7, 8	,, ,,	Ibid. 1148–9.
12	Durham	Ibid. 1150.
20	Bishop Auckland	Ibid. 1151.
29	Newcastle-upon-Tyne	Ibid. 1152.
May 5	Bishop Auckland	Ibid. 1154.
10	Howden	Rot. D. m. 13.
June 11	Bishop Auckland	*Reg.* no. 1155.
16, 29, 30	Stockton	Ibid. 1157–9.
July 3, 18, 22	,,	Ibid. 1160, 1162, 1165.
August 4, 6, 24, 27	,,	Ibid. 1166–9.
September 8	,,	Ibid. 1172.
12	Northallerton	Ibid. 1175.
16	Crayke	Ibid. 1174.
24	Howden	Ibid. 1176.
October 24, 26	London	CPS. 56; RG. 188686.
November 8–26	,,	*Reg.* nos. 1179–83; *Rot. Parl.* IV, p. 488.
December 16	York	*Reg.* no. 1185.
16	Crayke	Ibid. 1185.

1436

January 10	Bishop Auckland	*Reg.* no. 1186.
February 1–14	,, ,,	Ibid. 1187–91.
18	Durham	Ibid. 1192.
25	Bishop Auckland	Ibid. 1193.
27, 28	Durham	Ibid. 1194–5.
March 1–20	Bishop Auckland	Ibid. 1196–7, 1199–1204.
April 11, 17, 18	,, ,,	Ibid. 1207–9.
May 17, 28, 29	,, ,,	Ibid. 1210–11.
June 5	Darlington	Ibid. 1213.
9	Crayke	Ibid. 1214.
(11	York—*Convocation*)	Above, p. 217.
25	Bishop Auckland	*Reg.* no. 1215.
July 25	Durham	Above, p. 161.
27	Bishop Auckland	*Reg.* no. 1216.
August 1–12	Stockton	Ibid. 1217–20.
September 10–14, 23	,,	Ibid. 1221–3, 1226.
October 4	,,	Ibid. 1228.
12	Neasham—*Visitation of the Convent*	Above, p. 204.
16	*From this day until his death on* 20 November 1437 *the Bishop is not known to have left* Bishop Auckland.	Reg. ff. 234–57.

APPENDIX B

REPORT OF THE INQUISITION TAKEN BY ROYAL COMMISSIONERS AT HARTLEPOOL ON 1 APRIL 1433

THE text given here is that of the original report which was cancelled in Parliament (see pp. 128–9). Its Public Record Office reference is Chancery: Parliamentary and Council Proceedings, roll 23.[1] The Prior of Durham made a copy of the report in the contemporary folio register of the Convent (DCD. Reg. III, ff. 159–64v.); this text has been collated with the original report and significant variations, excluding those in the names of persons and places, have been noted. The contemporary records of the government of Durham have been consulted with the object of determining the accuracy of the statements made at the inquest, and such information as is available is given in footnotes.

For the sake of convenience, the text has been broken into numbered paragraphs, and other editorial departures from the original are disregard of its capital letters and punctuation, the replacing of "u" and "i" by "v" and "j" where these are used as consonants, and the extension of all contractions save those of place-names.

The contents of this report are discussed on pp. 120–6.

Inquisicio capta apud Hertelpule infra comitatum Northumbr' die mercurii proximo ante dominicam in Ramispalmarum anno regni regis Henrici sexti post conquestum Anglie undecimo coram Henrico comite Northumbr' Willelmo Tempest Johanne Cartyngton et Johanne Horsley, commissionariis dicti domini regis virtute litterarum suarum patencium eisdem Henrico comiti Willelmo Johanni et Johanni ac aliis commissionariis domini regis in litteris dicti domini regis patentibus quarum tenor huic inquisicioni est consutus specificatis, per sacramentum Roberti Hilton chivaler Radulphi Bulmer chivaler Thome

[1] Unpublished Crown Copyright material in the Public Record Office is reproduced by permission of the Controller of H.M. Stationery Office.

Lambard chivaler Willelmi Lomley chivaler Willelmi Lomley armigeri Johannis Trollop Johannis Hedworth Thome Billyngham Roberti Merley Willelmi Heron Willelmi Berntoft Henrici Tailbois Willelmi Alwent Radulphi Kirkby et Johannis Jentyll.

(1) Qui dicunt super sacramentum suum quod Johannes nuper rex Anglie progenitor domini regis nunc per litteras suas patentes, quarum datum est apud Kirkeby in Kendale xxj° die Augusti anno regni sui decimo,[1] concessit liberis tenentibus episcopatus Dunelmensis per domen militum et liberorum tenencium de Halywerfolk quod, si ponantur in placitum de liberis tenementis suis, possint se defendere secundum communem et rectam assisam regni sui Anglie; et si quis eorum velit rectum suum petere[2] secundum communem et rectam assisam per brevia originalia, capiantur in curia domini regis,[2] et si ipsi vel heredes sui implacitentur de aliqua re in curia episcopi Dunelmensis, quod possint[3] se defendere secundum communem et rectam assisam regni; et quod non implacitentur de liberis tenementis suis nisi per breve regis et heredum suorum seu capitalis justiciarii domini regis, sicut fieri consuevit toto tempore regis Henrici patris predicti Johannis nuper regis;[4] et cum in forisfacturam episcoporum inciderint,[5] deducerentur de amerciamentis secundum assisam ejusdem episcopi,[6] et quod si episcopus Dunelmensis ceperit averia eorum et tenuerit contra vadium et plegia, vicecomes Northumbr' faciet eis illa replegiari et eis inde juste deduci; et quod ipsi et heredes sui habeant decetero libertates et asiamenta in foresta episcopi Dunelmensis que ipsi et antecessores sui habuerunt temporibus Henrici patris dicti Johannis et tempore[7] Johannis predecessoris predicti episcopi.[7] Et dicunt quod predicti liberi tenentes libertates predictas habere debent virtute litterarum predictarum dicti domini regis Johannis patencium.

(2) Dicunt eciam dicti juratores quod Thomas episcopus Dunelmensis nunc ut in jure ecclesie sue Dunelmensis et predecessores sui ab antiquo usi fuerunt libertatibus subscriptis, videlicet habere cognicionem

---

[1] Enrolment printed in *Rotuli Chartarum, 1199–1216* (Record Commission, 1837), p. 182. There is a copy in DCD. Cartulary I, fo. 184.

[2-2] *Enrolment has* quod possit illud petere secundum communem et rectam assisam regni.   [3] *MS.* possunt.

[4] *This omits* et omnium antecessorum suorum et quod breve placiti sit ejusdem forme cujus fuit tempore regis Henrici patris nostri.

[5] *MS.* incederint.   [6] *For* episcopatus.

[7-7] *For* Hugonis episcopi predecessoris episcopi Philippi. *The enrolment concludes here with* quare volumus et firmiter precipimus quod predicti milites et liberetenentes de Halwarefolc et heredes eorum habeant inperpetuum predictas assisas et libertates et usus et aisiamenta ita quod non impediantur eis uti pro aliqua consuetudine vel aliquo usu qui hucusque fuerit in Haliwarefolc qui non sit rectus et communis in regno, salvis libertatibus ad episcopatum de jure pertinentibus. Teste [*etc.*].

omnium placitorum coram justiciariis ipsius episcopi apud Dunelm'
emergencium infra libertatem Dunelmensem aceciam cognicionem
omnium placitorum emergencium infra wapentagium Sadberg' [in
predicto comitatu Northumbr'[1]] coram justiciariis ipsius episcopi apud
Sadberg' a tempore regis Henrici tercii post conquestum usque nunc.

(3) Et dicunt quod idem episcopus colore libertatum predictarum de
injuria sua propria usurpavit super dictum dominum regem nunc et
super Henricum iiij^{tum} avum ipsius regis ac Henricum v^{tum} patrem
suum nuper reges Anglie, utendo libertatibus et franchesiis subscriptis
infra libertatem et wapentagium predicta, videlicet quod ubi quidam
Nicholaus de Lindeley perquisivit[2] sibi et heredibus suis unum mesuagium et centum quadraginta acras terre cum pertinenciis in Shirburn
infra dictam libertatem Dunelmensem de quodam Percivallo de
Lyndley armigero, que quidem mesuagium et terre tenentur de dicto
episcopo in capite et valent per annum ultra reprisas centum solidos,
predictus episcopus dicta mesuagium et terram cum suis pertinenciis
post perquisicionem predictam, videlicet vicesimo die Maii anno regni
regis Henrici iiij^{ti} duodecimo, per ministros suos in manus suas seisivit
et inde[3] exitus et proficua a dicta vicesima die usque diem jovis
proximo post festum sancti Michaelis archangeli anno regni regis
Henrici quinti primo percepit, pro eo quod dictus Nicholaus dicta
mesuagium et terram licencia dicti episcopi inde non obtenta perquisivit,[4] quousque dicto die jovis dictus Nicholaus cum dicto episcopo
finem pro deliberacione mesuagii et terre predictorum de manibus
dicti episcopi habenda occasione transgressionis predicte facte pro
centum solidis cum eodem episcopo in cancellaria sua apud Dunelm'
persolvit.[5] Et quod dictus episcopus fecit seisire in manus suas diversa
terras et tenementa per diversos homines sic perquisita[6] infra libertatem
et wapentagium predicta temporibus eorundem regum, et inde percepit
exitus et proficua ad valenciam centum librarum quousque tenentes
terrarum et tenementorum illorum graves fines cum dicto episcopo in
forma predicta ad voluntatem suam fecerint, in domini regis contemptum et populi sui in hac parte dampnum non modicum et
gravamen.

(4) Item. Dicunt dicti juratores quod dictus episcopus per litteras
suas patentes sub sigillo suo signatas, quarum datum est apud Dunelm'
die lune proximo post festum sancti Mathei apostoli anno regni domini

---

1 Reg. III, fo. 159v.   2 MS. perquesivit.
3 MS. seisivit dicta mesuagium et terram et inde.
4 MS. perquevisit.
5 These transactions cannot be traced in the records of the Bishop's chancery.
6 MS. perquesita.

regis nunc undecimo,[1] assignavit et constituit Willelmum Chauncellar armigerum Thomam Holden Robertum Jakson et Ricardum Bukley clericum justiciarios suos ad pacem suam tam infra dictam libertatem Dunelmensem quam infra wapentagium predictum conservandam et omne id faciendum quod ad justiciarios pacis domini regis pertinet faciendum;[2] qui quidem justiciarii ad querimoniam et requisicionem Johannis Spence vicesimo die Januarii anno supradicto domini regis nunc undecimo apud Dunelm' quemdam Thomam Claxton armigerum arrestaverunt colore dictarum litterarum patencium, et eum ibidem tunc imprisonaverunt et in prisona detinuerunt quousque idem Thomas securitatem pacis coram dictis Willelmo Thoma Holden Roberto et Ricardo justiciariis etc. invenerit, videlicet recogn[ovit quod[3]] se debere dicto episcopo centum libras sub condicione quod si idem Thomas non conservaret pacem dicti episcopi erga cunctum populum dicti episcopi et precipue erga dictum Johannem Spence, quod tunc dicta summa centum librarum de terris et catallis suis ad opus dicti episcopi deberet levari;[4] qui quidem Willelmus Thomas Robertus et Ricardus colore earundem litterarum patencium dicti episcopi ex mandato dicti episcopi die et anno supradictis tam apud Dunelm' quam apud Sadberg' fecerunt inquisiciones et ceperunt indictamenta coram eis secundum quod alii justiciarii domini regis ad pacem conservandam assignati in aliis comitatibus Anglie faciunt, et indictamenta illa audiverunt et determinaverunt[5] et omnia alia que ad dictos justiciarios pacis pertinent auctoritate diversorum statutorum domini regis nunc et progenitorum suorum inde confectorum [fecerunt], qua auctoritate dicti juratores ignorant, [in derogacionem et prejudicium corone domini regis[6]].

(5) Item. Dicunt quod predictus episcopus per litteras suas patentes per viginti annos proximo jam elapsos ad libitum suum fecit et constituit unum vicecomitem et unum escaetorem in libertate et wapentagio predictis ad exercendum et faciendum ibidem omne id quod ad officia vicecomitis et escaetoris domini regis alibi in Anglia pertinebat faciendum. Et dicunt quod dictus episcopus sic assignavit et constituit per litteras suas patentes Robertum de Eure vicecomitem et escaetorem suum in libertate et wapentagio predictis in crastino sancti Michaelis archangeli anno regni domini Henrici nuper regis

---

1 This was not the manner of dating employed in the Durham chancery: it gave the day, month, and pontifical year.
2 There is no record on the chancery roll of a commission of the peace dated 22 September 1432. The last commission issued before this date was on 26 September 1427, when the four justices named above were among those appointed (Rot. C. m. 7).
3 Erased.
4 This recognizance does not occur on the contemporary chancery roll.
5 *MS.* audire et determinare.   6 Reg. III, fo. 160.

Anglie patris domini regis nunc septimo;[1] qui quidem Robertus virtute litterarum predictarum et per mandatum ipsius episcopi officia illa continue a predicto crastino hucusque fecit et occupavit et adhuc facit et occupat in libertate et wapentagio predictis, in enervacione corone domini regis et in contrarium statutorum domini regis de vicecomitibus et escaetoribus faciendis editorum et in contemptum domini regis. Et quod idem episcopus a dicto crastino sancti Michaelis hucusque aliquem vicecomitem seu escaetorem domini regis in dicto comitatu Northumbr' officium pro proficuo regis in libertate Dunelmensi et wapentagio predictis facere non permisit, set eos ad hoc faciendum omnino per idem tempus impedivit.

(6) Dicunt eciam dicti juratores quod cum in statuto apud Merton quondam edito provisum sit quod quilibet liber homo qui debet sectam ad comitatum thrythyngum hundredum et wapentagium vel ad curiam domini sui libere facere possit attornatum suum ad sectam illam pro se faciendam;[2] quidam Henricus Ravinsworth qui sectam nuper debuit ad curiam dicti episcopi, quam idem episcopus [pro] comitatu Dunelmensi nuncupare facit de quindena in quindenam apud Dunelm' tenendam, pro uno mesuagio et centum acris terre cum pertinenciis que idem Henricus tenet de dicto episcopo in Gatessyd per sectam, xxiiij° die Novembris anno domini regis nunc undecimo apud Dunelm' in cancellaria dicti episcopi peciit de eodem episcopo breve suum pro attornato suo recipiendo ad sectam predictam pro eo faciendam, quod quidem breve idem episcopus adtunc et ibidem eidem Henrico omnino negavit, et ipsum tunc ibidem ad finem xl d. cum ipso episcopo pro secta predicta facienda compulsit. Et dicunt quod idem episcopus in hujusmodi casu per spacium viginti annorum jam proximo elapsorum diversis tenentibus suis infra libertatem Dunelmensem et wapentagium predicta hujusmodi brevia negavit, et tenentes suos per idem tempus compellebat facere sectam vel finem ad voluntatem ipsius episcopi pro hujusmodi sectis suis sic faciendis, statuto predicto non obstante, in domini regis contemptum et legiorum domini regis grave dampnum ac contra formam statuti predicti.

(7) Item. Dicunt dicti juratores quod ubi Johannes Gilforth armiger jam defunctus fuit seisitus in dominico suo ut de feodo die quo obiit de iij mesuagiis et centum acris terre cum pertinenciis in Gatesyd et quod Johannes Gilforth filius[3] et heres ejusdem Johannis Gilforth armigeri

---

[1] Robert Eure was in fact appointed sheriff and escheator on 2 January 1420 (Rot. B. m. 19), not on 30 September 1419; although he presumably accounted from the earlier date.   [2] *Statutes of the Realm*, I, p. 4.

[3] *MS.* consanguinius. Reg. III, fo. 160v., and other records (see next note) state that John was the son of John senior.

17

tempore mortis ejusdem Johannis, videlicet primo die Septembris anno regni domini regis nunc sexto, fuit plene etatis, scilicet triginta annorum et amplius, et quod dicta mesuagia et terre tenebantur de dicto episcopo in capite per servicium militare, et quod idem Johannes Gilforth armiger obiit seisitus de uno mesuagio et decem acris terre in eadem villa que tenentur de Willelmo Tempest chivaler, que quidem terre et tenementa in Gateshed valent per annum centum solidos; que quidem terre et tenementa tam illa que de dicto episcopo quam de dicto Willelmo Tempest sic tenentur per Robertum Eure escaetorem dicti episcopi infra libertatem et wapentagium predicta primo die Octobris anno regni dicti domini regis nunc septimo seisita fuerunt in manus ejusdem episcopi, et quod idem episcopus exitus et proficua inde percepit a dicto primo die Octobris usque ad festum sancti Michaelis anno octavo regni ejusdem domini regis, quo festo apud Dunelm' predictus Johannes Gilforth fecit finem cum ipso episcopo pro quatuor libris pro deliberacione predictarum terrarum et tenementorum predictorum de manibus ejusdem episcopi habenda.[1] Et dicunt quod dictus episcopus in omnibus hujusmodi casibus seisire facere solet in manus suas omnia terras et tenementa post mortem tenencium suorum infra libertatem et wapentagium predicta, et inde exitus et proficua percepit quousque heredes hujusmodi tenencium breve de diem clausit extremum et brevia de liberacione terrarum et tenementorum hujusmodi extra manus episcopi habenda prosequantur, et exitus et proficua illa inde ad valorem mille librarum ad usum suum proprium de diversis tenentibus suis diversis temporibus per spacium viginti annorum proximo elapsorum percepit infra libertatem et wapentagium predicta, in magnam depauperacionem eorundem tenencium.

(8) Item. Dicunt juratores predicti quod quidam Johannes Lomley chivaler nuper seisitus fuit die quo obiit, videlicet in vigilia Pasche anno regni domini regis Henrici patris domini regis nunc octavo, in dominico suo ut de feodo de uno mesuagio et centum acris terre in Seton Carrowe infra wapentagium Sadberg' et dicta terras et tenementa tenuit de dicto episcopo in capite per servicium militare, que quidem terre et tenementa occasione mortis predicti Johannis et racione minoris etatis Thome filii et heredis ejusdem Johannis seisita fuerunt in manus dicti episcopi; et postea, videlicet die martis proximo ante festum sancti Gregorii pape anno regni dicti domini regis nunc sexto, compertum fuit per quandam inquisicionem coram Roberto

---

[1] There was doubt about the tenure of Gilford senior's land in Gateshead; according to the inquisition *post mortem*, he had granted it to William Tempest and others before his death. He was said to have died on 23 December 1428, not 1 September, and his son was given livery on 28 January following, when he did homage to the Bishop at Bishop Auckland (Reg. IPM, ff. 243v.-4; Rot. E. m. 18d.).

Eure tunc escaetore dicti episcopi in wapentagio Sadberg' apud Sadberg' captam quod dictus Johannes Lomley obiit seisitus in dominico suo ut de feodo de manerio de Stranton cum pertinenciis in wapentagio predicto, quod tenebatur de domino de Clyfford et valuit per annum ultra reprisas centum marcas,[1] quod quidem manerium virtute inquisicionis illius seisitum fuit in manus dicti episcopi, eodem episcopo usurpando et clamando prerogativam dicti domini regis nunc sibi pertinere in hac parte eo quod idem episcopus clamavit custodiam dicti manerii quod de alio sic tenetur sibi pertinere, pro eo quod alia terre et tenementa in Seton predicta in quibus idem Johannes seisitus fuit fuerunt in custodia dicti episcopi racione minoris etatis dicti Thome Lomley in eodem wapentagio Sadberg', quod manifeste sonatur contra dignitatem domini regis nunc et jura corone sue in hac parte tam ex causa predicta quam pro eo quod idem Thomas racione minoris etatis sue fuit in custodia domini regis,[2] pro eo quod dictus pater suus alibi tenuit de domino rege in capite per servicium militare die quo obiit. Et [dicunt] quod predictus episcopus toto tempore domini regis nunc usurpavit super dictum dominum regem nunc et utitur in wapentagio et libertate predictis omnibus prerogativis avauntagiis et privilegiis que ad dictum dominum regem nunc et in jure corone et dignitatis [3]sue que a persona domini regis separare non possunt, in [3] derogacionem et detrimentum corone domini regis predicti et dignitatis sue et populi dicti domini regis ibidem oppressionem et exheredacionem manifestam, qua auctoritate ignorant.

(9) Item. Dicunt dicti juratores quod Thomas Gray chivaler quondam fuit seisitus in dominico suo ut de feodo talliato de manerio et villa de Conset infra dictam libertatem Dunelmensem, que valent per annum decem marcas ultra reprisas, qui quidem Thomas Grey postea, videlicet primo die Augusti anno regni regis Henrici v[ti] post conquestum Anglie tercio, commisit altam prodicionem erga dictum regem Henricum quintum patrem domini regis nunc, unde quinto die Augusti eodem anno convictus est et morti adjudicatus fuit, prout in curia ipsius nuper regis liquet de recordo; et postea coram dicto Roberto Eure escaetore dicti episcopi infra dictam libertatem Dunelmensem primo die Novembris anno dicti domini regis patris domini regis nunc octavo apud Dunelm' per inquisicionem coram eodem escaetore captam compertum fuit quod dictus Thomas Grey fecit prodicionem erga dictum regem Henricum quintum in forma predicta

---

[1] This inquisition *de melius inquirendo* was taken on 13 May 1430, not 16 March 1428, and was unable to prove of whom John Lumley had held the manor of Stranton (Reg. IPM, fo. 248).

[2] Above, p. 109.

[3]–[3] Omitted in Reg. III, fo. 161.

et tempore cujus prodicionis facte idem Thomas seisitus fuit de manerio et villa predictis in dominico suo ut de feodo, colore cujus inquisicionis dictus escaetor seisivit terras et tenementa predicta in manus dicti episcopi ut terras et tenementa eidem episcopo et successoribus suis occasione prodicionis predicte forisfacta,[1] ac idem episcopus injuste clamando forisfacturam illam inde exitus et proficua a tempore inquisicionis predicte usque diem veneris proximo post festum sancti Martini in hyeme anno regni dicti domini regis nunc quinto [percepit]; quo die quidem Radulphus Gray filius dicti Thome Gray clamando dictum manerium et villam de Conset virtute cujusdam scripti talliati facti cuidam Thome Gray militi patri predicti Thome Gray chivaler et heredibus de corpore suo procreatis ut consanguineus et heres dicti Thome Gray militis per formam donacionis predicte, videlicet filius dicti Thome Gray chivaler filii predicti Thome Gray militis, venit coram dicto episcopo in cancellaria sua apud Dunelm' et peciit manerium et villam predicta virtute tallii predicti sibi liberari, qui quidem episcopus post peticionem [2] predicti Radulphi Gray eidem episcopo sic factam per litteras suas patentes apud Dunelm' fecit inquiri de titulo ipsius Radulphi in peticione predicta contento, per quam quidem inquisicionem in cancellaria dicti episcopi retornatam dictus titulus pro eodem Radulpho compertus fuit,[3] ac idem episcopus manerium et villam predicta dicto Radulpho cum pertinenciis habenda et tenenda sibi secundum formam tallii et donacionis predictorum extra manus suas liberavit, reservando eidem episcopo et successoribus suis quod si contingat dictum Thomam Grey militem sine herede de corpore suo exeunti obire quod tunc dicta manerium et villa cum pertinenciis dicto episcopo et successoribus suis reverterent imperpetuum, prout in cancellaria dicti episcopi liquet manifeste,[4] in domini regis nunc et corone sue dampnum non modicum et exheredacionem manifestam. Et dicunt quod dictus episcopus eodem modo clamat et usurpat super dominum regem nunc habere sibi et successoribus suis forisfacturam tam terrarum et tenementorum quam bonorum et catallorum omnium tenencium in libertate et wapentagio predictis prodicionem erga dominum regem faciencium de quibus convicti fuerint, in exheredacionem dicti domini regis nunc et heredum suorum.

[1] There is no record of this inquisition, but one was taken at Durham on 27 January 1416 before William Claxton, then escheator (Reg. IPM, fo. 182v.).

[2] MS. petecionem.

[3] A commission of enquiry was appointed on 23 March 1430 and on 3 April established that Consett was held in the form stated above (Rot. D. m. 2; Reg. IPM, ff. 248v.–50).

[4] Livery was granted in April 1432. In the enrolment only the first three words of the clause of reservation are recorded, indicating that it was common form (Rot. D. m. 5).

(10) Item. Dicunt dicti juratores quod idem episcopus compellit omnes tenentes suos de eo tenentes per homagium infra libertatem Dunelmensem et wapentagium Sadberg' predicta facere sibi homagium regale in hec verba: Je deveigne vostre homme de vie et de membre et de terreyn honour etc. sub eadem forma que homagium domino regi per legios suos fieri deberet.[1]

(11) Item. Dicunt quod dictus episcopus infra libertatem Dunelmensem et wapentagium Sadberg' predicta usurpavit super dictum dominum regem nunc et progenitores suos, videlicet super predictum dominum Henricum avum suum et dominum Henricum patrem suum, dando et concedendo cuicumque de populo domini regis qui castra seu forcelletta edificare voluerint infra libertatem Dunelmensem et wapentagium Sadberg' predicta licencias per litteras suas patentes ad edificanda batallanda et machecollanda forcelleta castra muros et alia domos et edificia defensabilia infra libertatem et wapentagium illa, et quod idem episcopus die sabbati vicesimo die Septembris anno regni regis Henrici quinti nono apud Aukeland concessit Roberto Eure per litteras suas patentes quod ipse possit apud Bradley infra libertatem Dunelmensem predictam quo[d]dam castrum batellare edificare et machecollare,[2] in derogacionem dicti domini regis et corone sue.

(12) Item. Dicunt dicti juratores quod Willelmus Stowere de Norton in libertate Dunelmensi laborer nuper coram justiciariis dicti episcopi apud Dunelm' legaliter indictatus fuit de eo quod ipse apud Norton felonice furatus fuit unum bovem precii x s. de bonis et catallis Johannis Osbarn, prout in dicto indictamento satis liquet, et postea, videlicet die mercurii proximo post festum sancte Lucie virginis anno regni domini nunc regis sexto, apud Dunelm' coram dictis justiciariis idem Willelmus de felonia predicta in forma juris arrectatus fuit et per juramentum patrie tunc ibidem inde convictus, et postea eisdem die et anno ibidem idem Willelmus coram dictis justiciariis peciit privilegium clericale, et pro eo quod idem Willelmus coram eisdem justiciariis examinatus legebat ut clericus, idem Willelmus per eosdem justiciarios tunc ibidem dicto domino episcopo ut loci illius ordinario commissus fuit ad salvo custodiendum sub periculo incumbenti, et postea, videlicet primo die Maii anno regni dicti domini regis nunc septimo, predictus Willelmus ex prisona dicti domini episcopi apud

---

[1] This was the traditional form of oath to the bishop (*Reg. Palatinum Dunelm.* I, p. 92).
[2] The licence was in fact dated at Durham on 20 January 1432 and its warrant at Stockton on 1 July 1431 (Rot. C. m. 5; Durham Warrants 1,d). On 20 September 1421, which was a Saturday, the Bishop was in York.

Dunelm' pro defectu bone custodie et in defectu predicti nunc episcopi evasit et ad largum ivit.

(13) Item. Dicunt dicti juratores quod dictus episcopus decimo die Octobris anno regni regis Henrici sexti post conquestum tercio apud Dunelm' per litteras suas patentes, injuste et sine titulo assumando super se potestatem regalem et prerogativam domini regis, pro fine xl s. eidem episcopo in cancellaria sua predicta soluta concessit et licenciam dedit Johanni Bellasis quod ipse secundum avisiamentum disposicionem et ordinacionem sua quandam cantariam unius capellani ad altare beate Marie in ecclesia sancte Marie Dunelm' divina imperpetuum pro anima dicti Johannis et animabus omnium fidelium defunctorum celebraturi de novo creare fundare et stabilire [1] possit, et quod idem Johannes dicto capellano et successoribus suis capellanis cantarie predicte terras [2] et tenementa in libertate Dunelmensi predicta ad valenciam x li. per annum dare et concedere possit, et quod idem capellanus eadem terras [3] et tenementa ab ipso Johanne Bellasis recipere habere et gaudere possit habenda et tenenda sibi et successoribus suis capellanis cantarie predicte imperpetuum; [4] qui quidem Johannes xx° die Januarii proximo tunc sequentis cantariam predictam de novo creavit fundavit et stabilivit [5] et Johannem Stillington capellanum cantarie predicte constituit et ordinavit, ac eidem capellano virtute dictarum litterarum patencium decem mesuagia et centum acras terre cum pertinenciis in Dunelm' que valent per annum decem marcas dedit et concessit habenda et tenenda eidem capellano et successoribus suis capellanis cantarie predicte imperpetuum, virtute quorum doni et concessionis idem Johannes Stillington inde seisitus fuit et adhuc existit colore juris cantarie predicte, statutis domini regis in contrarium factis non obstantibus, in contemptum domini regis et corone sue lesionem manifestam.

(14) Item. Dicti juratores dicunt quod cum Willelmus Eure chivaler nuper in cancellaria dicti nunc episcopi apud Dunelm' quoddam breve de replegiari de averiis suis injuste captis, videlicet duobus bobus in uno loco vocato Southmoreden in villa de Shaldeford infra libertatem Dunelmensem, versus Thomam Fery de Shaldeforth apud Dunelm' prosecutus fuisset retornabile coram justiciariis ipsius episcopi die jovis proximo ante diem dominicam in Ramispalmarum

---

[1] MS. stabelire.   [2] MS. terre.   [3] MS. terre.
[4] The licence was actually granted on 28 June 1418 and other details are wrong: the licence was granted to John Holderness and Alan Hayden (as trustees of Bellasis) and the chantry was to be at the altar of St Katherine (Rot. B. mm. 15–16; and above, p. 187).   [5] MS. stabelivit.

anno regni domini regis nunc nono; et idem Thomas coram eisdem justiciariis tunc ibidem bene cognovit capcionem averiorum predictorum, et dixit quod locus in quo supponebatur capcionem predictam fieri fuit solum et liberum tenementum predicti episcopi ut de jure ecclesie sue sancti Cuthberti Dunelmensis, et dixit quod ipse fuit ballivus ipsius episcopi et quod invenit boves predictos herbam ipsius episcopi depascentes et ipse eos cepit et imparcavit, prout ei bene licuit; et predictus Willelmus dixit quod ipse seisitus fuit tempore capcionis predicte de uno mesuagio et decem acris terre cum pertinenciis in Shaldeforth in dominico suo ut de feodo et quod ipse et omnes alii quorum statum ipse tunc habuit in tenemento predicto habuerunt communem pasturam cum omnimodis averiis suis omni tempore anni in loco predicto a tempore quo non extat memoria tanquam pertinentem ad eadem tenementa et quod ipse boves predictos in eodem loco posuit, prout ei bene licuit; et predictus Thomas dixit quod ipse non potuit ulterius inde sine dicto episcopo respondere, et peciit inde auxilium de dicto episcopo; et super hoc dies datus fuit partibus predictis coram prefatis justiciariis apud Dunelm' usque in crastinum sancti Laurencii tunc proximo sequentem, et dictum fuit prefato Willelmo quod interim sequeretur erga dominum episcopum si sibi videret expedire; et sic predictus Willelmus per eundem episcopum in curia sua compulsus fuit ad prosequendum breve predicti episcopi de procedendo prefatis justiciariis suis directum ¹ ubi talem prerogativam nullus habere potest nisi dominus rex. Et dicunt quod dictus episcopus in forma predicta compulsit diversos residentes et tenentes infra libertatem et wapentagium predicta in hujusmodi casibus prosequi brevia de prosequendo et peticiones prout domino regi in curia sua prosequi debent, in maximam derogacionem juris domini regis et in contemptum dicti domini regis et populi sui dampnum manifestum.

(15) Item. Dicunt dicti juratores quod ubi Johannes Breiser et Walterus Whitewain die jovis proximo post festum sancte Lucie virginis anno regni regis Henrici quinti secundo apud Dunelm' coram justiciariis ipsius episcopi nunc arrectati fuerunt pro certis feloniis sibi impositis unde indictati fuerunt, de quibus quidem feloniis iidem Johannes et Walterus coram eisdem justiciariis tunc ibidem de bono et malo posuerunt se inde in exitum patrie, per quem triati in forma juris tunc ibidem convicti fuerunt, et pro eo quod iidem Johannes et Walterus coram eisdem justiciariis tunc clamaverunt privilegium ² clericale et per ordinarium examinati legerunt, per predictos justiciarios dicto episcopo nunc ut ordinario loci illius tunc ibidem

---

¹ Above, p. 118.   ² *MS*. priviligium.

commissi fuerunt salvo et secure custodiendi sub periculo incumbenti; qui quidem Johannes et Walterus postea, videlicet decimo die Octobris anno regni dicti domini Henrici nuper regis Anglie quinti post conquestum quarto, apud Dunelm' ob defectum bone custodie a prisona ejusdem episcopi et in ejus defectu evaserunt et sui juris ad largum iverunt, in contemptum dicti domini regis.

(16) Item. Dicunt juratores predicti quod cum per quandam indenturam inter prefatum episcopum ex parte una et Willelmum Eure militem ex parte altera apud Dunelm' vicesimo die Aprilis anno regni regis Henrici sexti post conquestum secundo factam idem episcopus dimiserit prefato Willelmo mineras suas carbonum in Raby et in baronia de Evynwod habendas usque ad finem novem annorum extunc proximo sequencium, reddendo inde dicto episcopo annuatim durante termino predicto Cxij li. xiij s. iiij d.; predictus episcopus pro CCClx et v li. ix s. et v d. quos sibi a retro fore supposuitur de firma predicta misit breve suum clausum de fi[e]ri facias vicecomiti suo Dunelmensi in hec verba: Thomas dei gracia episcopus Dunelmensis vicecomiti Dunelmensi salutem. Precipimus tibi quod de bonis et catallis Willelmi Eure chivaler in balliva tua fieri facias trescentas sexaginta et quinque libras novem solidos et quinque denarios quos nobis debet de firma minerarum nostrarum carbonum et ferri subtus eosdem carbones in Raby Caldhirst Hertkeld Hathereclogh alias vocato Tollawe et Wollaws et in baronia de Evynwod, quas quidem mineras idem Willelmus de nobis tenet ad firmam per centum et duodecim libros tresdecim solidos et quatuor denarios per annum, prout nobis constat per inspeccionem rotulorum cancellarie nostre,[1] ita quod denarios illos habeas ad scaccarium nostrum Dunelm' vicesimo dic Dccembris nobis solvendos. Et si forte bona et catalla ipsius Willelmi in balliva tua non sufficiant ad solucionem debiti predicti, tunc pro eo quod inde defuerit capias in manum nostram omnia terras et tenementa ipsius Willelmi in balliva tua et ea salvo et secure ad opus nostrum custodies, ita quod de exitibus eorundem nobis respondeas quousque nobis de debito predicto plenarie fuerit satisfactum. Et quid feceris in premissis nobis ad dictum scaccarium nostrum ad dictos diem et locum distincte et aperte constare facias. Et habeas tunc ibi hoc breve. Teste Willelmo Chaunceller [cancellario] nostro octavo die Decembris anno pontificatus nostri vicesimo septimo.[2] Absque alio processu inde versus predictum Willelmum in hac parte facto, ad grave dampnum ipsius Willelmi, contra legem terre et in derogacionem domini regis.

---

[1] The indenture is enrolled on Rot. E. m. 20d.
[2] The writ is enrolled on Rot. D. m. 6d.; and see above, p. 118.

(17) Dicunt eciam quod ubi dominus Thomas Hatfeld quondam episcopus Dunelmensis predecessor predicti nunc episcopi tempore domini Edwardi nuper regis Anglie tercii post conquestum fieri fecisset sibi quoddam magnum sigillum clausum ad similitudinem sigilli regii in cancellaria sua usitati,[1] et quod dictus episcopus nunc toto tempore suo habuit et usus fuit hujusmodi sigillo et cum eo brevia sua sigillari fecit, et in brevibus de transgressione utitur hujusmodi terminis: contra pacem ipsius episcopi; et in brevibus de recordis suis de appellis in curia sua prosecutis utitur talibus terminis: contra coronam et dignitatem ipsius episcopi; in exheredacionem domini regis et corone sue lesionem manifestam. Et dicunt quod omnes usurpaciones predictarum libertatum [et] franchesiarum predictarum usurpate sunt et fuerunt per dictum episcopum nunc et predecessores suos tempore predicti regis Edwardi tercii et deinceps infra libertatem et wapentagium predicta, in magnam oppressionem populi domini regis in hac parte ac exheredacionem corone sue.

(18) Item. Dicunt dicti juratores quod cum idem episcopus deliberacionem fecerit tenentibus suis post mortem antecessorum suorum de terris et tenementis suis in manibus ipsius episcopi seisitis per brevia sua de terris liberandis, idem episcopus postmodum per breve suum de scire facias prosequitur et sepius prosequebatur versus eosdem tenentes ad ostendendum et respondendum dicto episcopo in cancellaria sua predicta quare dicta terre et tenementa de manibus suis sic deliberata in manus suas reseisire[2] et de exitibus eorundem respondere non debeant pro defectu forme et aliis omissionibus et mesprisionibus per ministros suos proprios in hujusmodi brevibus de liberacione et inquisicionibus coram escaetore suo super brevibus de diem clausit extremum factis et habitis, et per eadem brevia de scire facias dicta terras[3] et tenementa reseisire fecit et exitus et proficua inde percepit a tempore liberacionis predicte quousque hujusmodi tenentes suos de novo liberacionem extra manus dicti episcopi de terris et tenementis illis prosecuti fuerint, et sic extorcionaliter compellit dictos tenentes suos de novo prosequi deliberacionem de terris et tenementis hujusmodi, non obstante dicta prima liberacione; et istam prerogativam dictus episcopus nunc usurpavit super dictum dominum regem et super tenentes suos infra libertatem et wapentagium predicta

---

[1] Although many bishops had seals before Hatfeld's time, Richard de Bury was probably the first to have had a great seal made for the sole use, and therefore kept, in the temporal chancery in Durham Castle (*Reg. Langley*, I, p. xiii). Hatfeld's great seal was the first to resemble the King's in that it showed him enthroned on the obverse and mounted on the reverse (C. H. Hunter Blair, " Medieval Seals of the Bishops of Durham ", p. 16).

[2] *MS.* reseisere.

[3] *MS.* terre.

ubi nullus predecessorum ipsius episcopi ante ipsum illam prerogativam unquam habuit nec clamavit.

(19) Dicunt eciam dicti juratores quod cum coram escaetore ejusdem episcopi in libertate et wapentagio predictis compertum fuerit quod si aliquis tenens perquisivit [1] aliqua terras et tenementa de ipso episcopo tenta in capite infra libertatem et wapentagium predicta, licet idem perquisitor [2] optuleret eidem episcopo racionabilem finem pro transgressione illa sic facta et pecierit litteras patentes dicti episcopi de perdonacione sibi in hac parte faciendas, idem episcopus illam perdonacionem facere recusat et postea perquisitores[3] hujusmodi de exitibus terrarum et tenementorum sic perquisitorum [4] sibi respondere et eos prosequi hujusmodi perdonacionem et finem pro eisdem facere compellit, in derogacionem populi domini regis in hac parte. Et ulterius dicunt quod ubi Radulphus Eure chivaler perquisivit [5] sibi heredibus et assignatis suis manerium et villam de Langley ac diversa terras et tenementa cum pertinenciis in Neweland cum Ladley Park et Faweleyes in Wulsyngham cum pertinenciis, que tenentur de dicto episcopo in capite per servicium militare, post quam perquisicionem [6] idem episcopus oretenus apud Dunelm' perdonavit dicto Radulpho transgressionem factam in hac parte et finem sibi in hac parte contingentem et pertinentem eidem Radulpho in vita sua, ac prefato Willelmo Eure filio et heredi dicti Radulphi post mortem ejusdem Radulphi separatim dedit et concessit ac ipsos inde separatim plenarie [7] exoneravit ibi dictus episcopus post mortem dicti Radulphi; et postquam idem episcopus xiiij⁰ die Septembris anno pontificatus sui xvij⁰ ceperit homagium et fidelitatem predicti Willelmi Eure chivaler filii et heredis predicti Radulphi Eure chivaler defuncti pro omnibus terris et tenementis que idem Radulphus de ipso episcopo tenuit die quo obiit, et predicto quartodecimo die Septembris per breve suum omnia terras et tenementa illa prefato Willelmo reddiderit et ei inde plenarie liberacionem fecerit; [8] quoddam breve de scire facias vicecomiti Dunelmensi directum cujus datum est vicesimo quarto die Augusti anno pontificatus dicti episcopi xxvij⁰ retornabile coram ipso episcopo in cancellaria sua Dunelm' die jovis proximo post festum nativitatis beate Marie proximo sequentem versus ipsum Willelmum prosecutum fuit, ad premuniendum ipsum Willelmum ad ostendendum si quid pro se habeat vel dicere sciat quare predicta manerium et villa de Langley ac terre et tenementa cum pertinenciis

---

[1] MS. perquesivit.
[3] MS. perquesitores.
[5] MS. perquesivit.
[7] MS. ceparatim perdonar' (plenarie occurs in Reg. III, fo. 163).
[8] Enrolled Rot. E. m. 8.

[2] MS. perquesitor.
[4] MS. perquesitorum.
[6] MS. per inquisicionem.

in Neweland cum Ladley Parke et Faweleys in Wolsyngham cum pertinenciis parcellis dictorum terrarum et tenementorum unde idem episcopus predictam liberacionem prefato Willelmo fecerat occasione perquisicionis [1] ac non solucionis [2] et satisfaccionis finis predicte in manus suas resumi et reseisiri non deberent, idemque Willelmus Eure de exitibus inde medio tempore perceptis eidem episcopo respondere et satisfacere non deberet, prout in eodem brevi plenius continetur; [3] virtute cujus brevis Robertus Eure tunc vicecomes Dunelmensis retornavit super breve illud quod ipse scire fecit prefato Willelmo quod esset in dicta cancellaria ad diem illum ad faciendum et recipiendum quod breve illud in se exigit et requirit per Willelmum Malet Johannem Spence Hugonem Forster et Willelmum Mordon,[4] per quod predictus Willelmus Eure ad comparendum ad diem illum in cancellaria predicta cum eodem episcopo super breve illud placitare injuste et contra legem terre compulsus fuit, quod quidem placitum adhuc ibidem inter eos pendet indiscussum.[5]

(20) Item. Dicti juratores dicunt quod dictus episcopus, assumendo super se et usurpando prerogativam que ad coronam et dignitatem domini regis pertinet, die lune proximo post festum sancti Martini ultimo preteritum mandavit Johanni Hedworth armigero per Robertum Dalton coronatorem ipsius episcopi infra libertatem Dunelmensem [6] [per] breve ipsius episcopi clausum quod ipse compareret coram prefato episcopo in cancellaria sua apud [Dunelm [7]] certo die in dicto breve limitato ad respondendum dicto episcopo de hiis que tunc sibi ex parte dicti episcopi obicerentur et ad recipiendum et faciendum quod curia predicta consideraret in hac parte, cujus brevis tenor sequitur in hec verba: Thomas dei gracia episcopus Dunelmensis dilecto sibi Johanni Hedworth armigero salutem. Quia datum est nobis intellegi quod tu Robertum Richardson Willelmum [Leman Geo]rgium Scot Henricum de Ogle Johannem Forman et Willelmum Correx cepisti et absque causa racionabili sub custodia tua injuste detinuisti [8] et adhuc detines, quibuscum certis de causis nos specialiter moventibus tibi precimus firmiter injungentes quod sis coram nobis in cancellaria nostra Dunelm' die lune proximo futuro, tecum ducendo predictos Robertum Willelmum Georgium Henricum [Johannem

---

1 MS. perquesicionis.   2 MS. soluciones.
3 The writ is enrolled on Rot. D. m. 5, where it is misdated 14 August (other records of these proceedings confirm the date given in the inquisition.)
4 Confirmed by records of the placita.
5 Above, p. 118.
6 Dalton was coroner of the ward of Chester (Rot. E. m. 8d.).
7 From this point the bottom left-hand corner of the MS. has been torn off, and the words lost (given here in square brackets) have been supplied from Reg. III, ff. 163v.–4v.   8 MS. detenuisti.

Forman] et Willelmum, ad [1] faciendum ulterius et recipiendum quod curia nostra consideraverit in hac parte. Et hoc nullatenus omittas sub periculo quod incumbit. Et habeas ibi hoc breve. Datum die lune per manus Willelmi Chauncellar cancellarii nostri vj° die Decembris anno pontificatus dicti episcopi xxvij°. Per ipsum episcopum.[2] Quod quidem breve eidem Johanni Hedworth eodem die lune apud Chestre [in le Street deliber]atum fuit. Et dicunt quod idem episcopus ligeos domini regis infra libertatem et wapentagium predicta commorantes ad libitum suum compellit per hujusmodi brevia respondere dicto episcopo in cancellaria sua predicta de materiis que negocia ipsius episcopi concernunt ad libitum ipsius episcopi, licet materie ille ad determinacionem legis communis terre pertineant, in contemptum [domini regis dignitatis] sue derogacionem et prejudicium manifestum, quo titulo predicti juratores ignorant.

(21) Item. Dicunt quod predictus nunc episcopus toto tempore ex quo ipse in episcopum Dunelmensem creatus fuit omnes et singulas prerogativas domini regis tam scriptas quam non scriptas injuste usurpavit et super se assum[p]sit [et usurpat [3]] et usus fuit colore libertatis sue [Dunelmensis infra libertatem et] wapentagium predicta tam toto tempore domini regis nunc quam toto tempore domini Henrici nuper regis Anglie patris sui et tempore domini Henrici nuper regis avi sui, preterquam quod idem episcopus non tenet parliamentum suum ibidem, in magnum prejudicium et derogacionem [4] domini regis et corone sue et populi sui dampnum non modicum et gravamen, [quo titulo dicti juratores ignorant].

(22) Item. Dicunt dicti juratores quod ubi Willelmus Alwent et Johannes de Morton habent et tenent villam de Morton sibi et heredibus suis imperpetuum, exceptis xlvj acris terre que sunt dicti episcopi ut de jure ecclesie sue Dunelmensis in eadem villa et jacent in decasu in manibus dicti episcopi et jacuerunt per vj annos ultimo elapsos, idem episcopus extorsive per eosdem sex annos [compulsit dictos Willelmum et Johannem con]tra suam voluntatem per duriciam [5] districcionis solvere annuatim ibidem dicto episcopo xl s. pro dictis quadraginta sex acris terre, ubi dicte xlvj acre terre non valuerunt xx s. per annum, ad grave dampnum ipsorum Willelmi et Johannis.

(23) Item. Dicunt dicti juratores quod dictus episcopus decimo die Novembris anno regni regis Henrici v[ti] patris domini regis nunc nono apud Dunelm' assignavit Willelmum [Chaunceller Willelmum Malber-

---

1 MS. et ad.
3 In Reg. III, fo. 163v., only.
5 MS. duriciciam.

2 Enrolled Rot. D. m. 6.
4 MS. dirogacionem.

thorp et Robertum] Frende auditores ad audiendum compotum Thome Ferrour de tempore quo idem Thomas fuit ballivus et receptor denariorum ipsius episcopi apud Derlyngton,[1] coram quibus idem Thomas adtunc et ibidem computavit de balliva et recepcione predictis, super quo compoto idem Thomas inventus fuit et remansit in arreragiis dicto episcopo in centum [marcis, pro quibus arreragiis dictus Thomas Ferrour per au]ditores predictos secundum formam statuti in hujusmodi casu provisi[2] per agreamentum et preceptum dicti episcopi gaole ipsius episcopi castri Dunelm' commissus et Roberto Eure custodi ejusdem gaole liberatus fuit, ibidem custodiendum in execucionem pro debito predicto quousque idem Thomas debitum illud eidem episcopo plenarie persolvisset, in qua [gaola idem Thomas sic in execucionem existens] obiit; post cujus mortem dictus episcopus diversa terras et tenementa, videlicet decem mesuagia et ducentas acras terre cum pertinenciis in Consclyff et Derlyngton, que fuerunt ipsius Thome tempore mortis sue, pro eodem debito decimo die Aprilis anno regni domini regis nunc primo injuste et extorsive seisivit et illa in manibus suis extunc tenuit, et exitus et proficua inde percepit quousque ipse [dictas centum marcas de eisdem terris et tenementis plene lev]avit et percepit,[3] dicta execucione corporis ipsius Thome pro eodem debito non obstante.

(24) Item. Dicunt dicti juratores quod cum quedam Isabella Claxton sexto die Decembris anno regni regis Henrici quinti nono obiit seisita de viginti mesuagiis quingentis acris terre centum acris prati et mille acris cum pertinenciis in Lumley [Moreslawe et Hetton infra dictam libertatem Dunelmensem, que va]llent per annum xx li. et que tenentur de episcopo Dunelmensi per servicium militare,[4] post cujus mortem quidam Petrus Tillioll miles et Elizabeth uxor ejus etatis xl annorum et amplius in predictis terris et tenementis cum pertinenciis intraverunt ut in jure ipsius Elizabethe filie et heredis ipsius Isabelle, que quidem terras et tenementa predictus episcopus decimo die Marcii [anno regni dicti regis Henrici nono in manus su]as racione ingressus predicti seisire fecit, et illa sic seisita in manibus suis tenuit et omnia exitus et proficua inde percepit, scilicet a dicto decimo die Marcii usque ad ultimum diem Aprilis anno decimo ejusdem regis

---

1 There is no record of a special commission being appointed to audit Ferrour's accounts, as this item suggests; a commission associating Richard Buckley with the auditors of accounts of all officers was issued on 10 November 1419 (Rot. B. m. 11), the day quoted above.

2 Statute of Westminster II, c. 11 (*Statutes of the Realm*, I, pp. 80–1).

3 The chancery records indicate that Ferrour died four years later, as the issue of a writ of *diem clausit extremum* on 13 April 1427 testifies (Rot. E. m. 14d.). There is no inquisition *post mortem* in Reg. IPM.

4 According to the inquisition *post mortem*, taken on 5 May 1421, she died on 1 February 1421 (Reg. IPM, fo. 207).

Henrici quinti, quo die dictus Petrus antequam deliberacionem inde extra manus [dicti episcopi habere poterit finem cum dicto episcopo pro deliberacione il]la habenda in cancellaria sua apud Dunelm' pro xxv li. fecit, et easdem xxv li. dicto episcopo adtunc et ibidem persolvit; post quam quidem deliberacionem et solucionem dictarum xxv li. predictus episcopus, scrutatis rotulis cancellarie sue, invenit dictum Petrum eidem episcopo in quadam recognicione de predictis [xxv li. ex causa predicta sibi in dicta cancellaria obligatum], ac idem episcopus predicta terras et tenementa causa recognicionis et trans- gressionis predictarum, non obstantibus liberacione et solucione predictis, in manus suas de novo rese[i]sire fecit, videlicet quarto die Maii anno regni domini regis nunc secundo, absque aliquo processu versus dictum Petrum ea de causa faciendo, et ea sic seisita in manibus suis extunc tenuit et exitus et proficua inde percepit [quousque predictus Petrus de novo cum ipso episcopo pro ingressu et recogni- ci]one predictis antequam deliberacionem inde extra manus suas habere poterit finem pro xxxv li. pro deliberacione illa habenda fecit, et easdem xxxv li. idem episcopus per ministros suos ad opus suum tercio die Decembris anno regni ejusdem domini regis nunc quarto ibidem extorsive fecit levari,[1] in magnum detrimentum ipsius Petri.

In cujus rei testimonium tam sigilla juratorum predictorum per [quos facta fuit hec inquisicio [2] quam sigilla predictorum comitis Willelmi Tempest Johannis Cartyngton] et Johannis Horsley commission- ariorum unde in tenore litterarum domini regis patencium huic inquisicione indentata annexarum fit mencio eidem inquisicioni sunt appensa. Datum apud Hertelpule predicta die mercurii proximo ante diem dominicam Ramispalmarum anno regni regis Henrici sexti [undecimo].

[1] The only record on the chancery rolls referring to these transactions is of the grant of livery on 23 August 1423 (Rot. E. m. 7). The roll of the receiver of Durham for 1424-5, however, shows that Tilliol paid £16 13s. 4d. (25 marks) in this year in full payment of a recognizance (RG. 189810).

[2] The text in Reg. III ends at this point and the remaining words printed in brackets here are conjectural.

BIBLIOGRAPHY

I MANUSCRIPT SOURCES

The British Museum

Additional Charters, no. 66345 (Act of the official of Durham, 1410).
Campbell Charters, VIII, 2 (Act of Privy Council, 1435).
Cottonian MSS.: Cleopatra C. IV, ff. 124–229 (Letter-book of William Swan, part II).
Harleian MSS., no. 431 (Letter-book of John Prophet).

The Dean and Chapter of Durham

(i) *MSS.*
Register of Bishop Hatfield.
Register of Bishop Langley.
Hunter MSS., Vol. III.

(ii) *Archives*
Records in volume form:
Cartularies I–IV.
Folio Register III.
Registrum Parvum I.
Documents listed in the *Magnum Repertorium*:
Papalia, Regalia, Archiepiscopalia, Pontificalia, Archidiaconalia Dunelm' and Archidiaconalia Northumbr'.
Locelli.
Miscellaneous Charters.
Obedientaries' Rolls:
Bursars' Rolls, 1406–1437.
Cellarers' Rolls, 1406–1437.
Granator's Roll, 1341.
Obedientaries' Books:
Cartuarium Evidenciarum Communarii.
Registrum Papireum Diversarum Litterarum Cancellarie Dunelmensis.
Receiver-General's Records:
Allerton, no. 189881.
Coroners, no. 188879.
Crayke, no. 189882.
Forester, no. 190030.

Receiver-General's Records—*continued*:
  Howden, no. 190237.
  Instaurer, no. 190307.
  Lead Mines, nos. 190012–15.
  Miscellaneous Ministers, no. 188926.
  Norham, nos. 190004–7.
  Receiver of Durham:
    Rolls, nos. 188714, 188686, 189782, 189809–11, 190184.
    Vouchers, no. 221160.
  Sheriff and Escheator, nos. 189600–5.
  Wards Collectors, no. 188620.
  Works, no. 190043.
Additional Documents, nos. 102–9 (*now* Misc. Charters, nos. 7182–9).

Lambeth Palace Library

Register of Archbishop Courtenay.
Register of Archbishop Arundel.

The Diocesan Registry, Lichfield

Act Books, no. 6 (Registers of Bishops Skirlaw and Scrope).

The Public Record Office

Chancery:
  Early Chancery Proceedings, bundles 1–5.
  Miscellanea:
    Placita in Cancellaria, Tower Series, file 24.
    Diplomatic Documents concerning Scotland, file 12.
  Parliamentary and Council Proceedings, roll 23.
  Charter Rolls, nos. 168–86.
  French Rolls, nos. 100–5.
  Gascon Rolls, nos. 117–18.
  Warrants for the Great Seal, Series I:
    Writs of Privy Seal, files 611–34, 666–82.
    Bills of Privy Seal, files 1091–9.
    Warrants under the Signet, files 1356–67.
    Signed Bills, files 1398–406.
    Regents' Warrants, file 1537.
    Council Warrants, files 1540–5.
  Significations of Excommunication, file 199.
  Miscellaneous Inquisitions, file 274.
  Chancery Files (*Brevia Regia*), Series C, files 124–30.

Exchequer:
  King's Remembrancer: Accounts, Various:
    Hanaper, box 214.
    Nuncii, boxes 321 and 620.
    Unsorted, box 649.
  Lord Treasurer's Remembrancer:
    Foreign Accounts, nos. 47 and 48.
    Originalia Rolls, nos. 183–9.
  Exchequer of Receipt:
    Receipt Rolls, nos. 617–756.
    Issue Rolls, nos. 464–731.
    Warrants for Issues, boxes 15–60.
  Treasury of Receipt: Council and Privy Seal, files 7–58.
King's Bench: *Coram Rege* Rolls, Michaelmas 2 Henry V, and Trinity 14
  Henry VI.
Justices Itinerant: Gaol Delivery Rolls, nos. 191, 199, 208 and 211.
Common Pleas: Feet of Fines, files 88, 89 and 290.
Palatinate of Durham:
  Chancery Records:
    Cursitor's Records:
      Abstracts of Inquisitions *post mortem*, Register II.
      Chancery Enrolments: Rolls of Bishop Langley.
      Warrants and Grants, bundle 1.
      Miscellanea, bundle 206, no. 6.
    Auditor's Records: Sheriffs' Accounts, nos. 2–4.
Duchy of Lancaster:
  Accounts (Various), bundle 32, no. 21.
  Miscellaneous Books, no. 17.
Special Collections:
  Ancient Correspondence, Vols. XLIII and LVII.
  Parliamentary Proxies, files 40–52.
  Rentals and Surveys, portfolio 21, no. 29.
Privy Seal Office: Warrants for the Privy Seal, Series I, files 1–5.

Vatican Library
Thome Trotati Manuale Concilii Pisaniensis.

St Anthony's Hall, York
York Archiepiscopal Registers:
  No. 16 (Scrope).
  No. 17 (Bowet, Part II).
  No. 18 (Bowet, Part I).
  No. 19 (Kemp).

18

2 PRINTED SOURCES

Literary Sources

Archidiaconus (Guido de Bayso). *Rosarium super Decreto.* Venice, 1495.

Brut, The, or the Chronicles of England. Ed. F. W. D. Brie. (Early English Text Society, Original Series, Vols. 131 & 136) 1906, 1908.

Eulogium Historiarum sive Temporis. Ed. F. S. Haydon. (Rolls Series) 1858–63.

Gascoigne, T. *Loci e Libro Veritatum.* Ed. J. E. T. Rogers. Oxford, 1881.

Hardyng, J. *Chronicle.* Ed. H. Ellis. 1812.

Henrici Quinti Gesta. Ed. B. Williams. (English Historical Society) 1850.

Henry the Fifth, Memorials of. Ed. C. A. Cole. (Rolls Series) 1858.

Historical Collection of a Citizen of London in the Fifteenth Century. Ed. J. Gairdner. (Camden Society, Series II, Vol. XVII) 1876.

Incerti Scriptoris Chronicon Angliæ (1399–1455). Ed. J. A. Giles. 1848.

Juvenal des Ursins, J. *Histoire de Charles VI.* Ed. D. Godefroy. Paris, 1653.

Le Fèvre, J. *Chronique.* Ed. F. Morand. (Soc. de l'Histoire de France) 1876, 1881.

London, A Chronicle of. Ed. N. H. Nicolas. 1827.

Melsa, Chronica Monasterii de. Ed. E. A. Bond. (Rolls Series) 1866–8.

Otterbourne, T. *Chronicle.* Ed. T. Hearne. Oxford, 1732.

St. Albans' Chronicle 1406–1420. Ed. V. H. Galbraith. Oxford, 1927.

Saint Denys, Chronique du Religieux de. Ed. L. Bellaguet. (Coll. des Docs. Inédits) 1839–52.

Scotichronicon of J. Fordun with Continuation of W. Bower. Ed. W. Goodall. Edinburgh, 1759.

Scotland, Metrical Chronicle of. Ed. W. B. Turnbull. (Rolls Series) 1858.

Scriptores Tres, Historiæ Dunelmensis. Ed. J. Raine. (Surtees Society, Vol. IX) 1839.

Three Fifteenth Century Chronicles. Ed. J. Gairdner. (Camden Society, Series II, Vol. XXVIII) 1880.

Usk, Adam of. *Chronicle 1377–1421.* Ed. E. Maunde Thompson. 1904.

Walsingham, T. *Historia Anglicana.* Ed. H. T. Riley. (Rolls Series) 1863–4.

——, *Ypodigma Neustriæ.* Ed. H. T. Riley. (Rolls Series) 1876.

Waurin, J. de. *Recueil des Chroniques.* Ed. W. Hardy. (Rolls Series) 1864–91.

Records

Acts of the Parliaments of Scotland. Ed. T. Thompson and C. Innes. (Record Commission) 1814–75.

Ancient Deeds, Descriptive Catalogue of. (Public Record Office) 1890–1915.

Ancient Kalendars and Inventories of the Treasury of H.M. Exchequer. Ed. F. Palgrave. (Record Commission) 1836.

Anglo-Norman Letters and Petitions. Ed. M. D. Legge. (Anglo-Norman Text Society) 1941.

Baye, N. de. *Journal 1400–1417.* Ed. A. Tuety. (Soc. de l'Histoire de France) 1885, 1888.

Bek, Antony, Records of. Ed. C. M. Fraser. (Surtees Society, Vol. CLXII) 1953.

Bekynton, Thomas, Correspondence of. Ed. G. Williams. (Rolls Series) 1872.

Calendar of Charter Rolls. (Public Record Office) 1903–27.

Calendar of Close Rolls. (Public Record Office) 1892– .

Calendar of Documents relating to Scotland 1108–1509. Ed. J. Bain. Edinburgh, 1881–8.

Calendar of Fine Rolls. (Public Record Office) 1911– .

Calendar of Letter-Books of the City of London. Ed. R. R. Sharpe. 1899–1912.

Calendar of Papal Letters. (Public Record Office) 1894– .

Calendar of Patent Rolls. (Public Record Office) 1891– .

Catalogue des Rolles Gascons, Normans et François. Ed. T. Carte. 1753.

Chantries within the County Palatine of Lancaster. Ed. F. R. Raines. (Chetham Society, Vols. LIX & LX) 1862.

Chichele, Henry, Register of. Ed. E. F. Jacob. (Canterbury and York Society) 1937–47.

Coldingham, The Priory of. Ed. J. Raine. (Surtees Society, Vol. XII) 1841.

Collection Générale des Documents Français qui se trouvent en Angleterre. Ed. J. Delpit. Paris, 1847.

Cotton Manuscrit Galba B.1, Le. Ed. Gilliodts van Severen. Brussels, 1896.

Depositions and Ecclesiastical Proceedings. Ed. J. Raine. (Surtees Society, Vol. XXI) 1845.

Deputy Keepers of the Public Records, Reports of the:
    No. 31. Durham Records (Rolls of Bishops de Bury and Hatfield). 1870.
    No. 32. Durham Records (Rolls of Bishop Hatfield, *continued*). 1871.
    No. 33. Durham Records (Rolls of Bishops Skirlaw and Langley). 1872.

No. 34. Durham Records (Rolls of Bishop Neville). 1873.

No. 39. Duchy of Lancaster Records (Inquisitions *post mortem*). 1878.

Durham Account Rolls. Ed. J. T. Fowler. (Surtees Society, Vols. XCIX, C & CII) 1898–1900.

Excerpta Historica. Ed. S. Bentley. 1831.

Foedera, Conventiones, Literæ, etc. Ed. T. Rymer. 1704–35.

Fusoris, Maître Jean, Le Procès de. Ed. L. Mirot. (Mem. de la Soc. de l'Histoire de Paris, Vol. XXVII) 1901.

Hatfield's, Bishop, Survey. Ed. W. Greenwell. (Surtees Society, Vol. XXXII) 1856.

Langley, Thomas, Register of. Ed. R. L. Storey. (Surtees Society, Vols. CLXIV, CLXVI, CLXIX, CLXX, —) 1955– .

Lettres des Rois, Reines et Autres Personnages. Ed. M. Champollion-Figeac. (Coll. des Docs. Inédits) 1839, 1847.

Monasticon Anglicanum. Ed. W. Dugdale. 1817–30.

Northern Convocation, The Records of the. Ed. G. W. Kitchin. (Surtees Society, Vol. CXIII) 1906.

Original Letters illustrative of English History. Ed. H. Ellis. Series I. 1824. Series III. 1846.

Placita de Quo Warranto. Ed. W. Illingworth and J. Caley. (Record Commission) 1818.

Proceedings in Chancery in the Reign of Queen Elizabeth, with Examples of Proceedings from Richard II. Ed. J. Caley and J. Bayley. (Record Commission) 1827–32.

Proceedings and Ordinances of the Privy Council of England. Ed. N. H. Nicolas. (Record Commission) 1834–7.

Registrum Palatinum Dunelmense. Ed. T. D. Hardy. (Rolls Series) 1873–8.

Rotuli Chartarum in Turri Londinensi Asservati 1199–1216. Ed. T. D. Hardy. (Record Commission) 1837.

Rotuli Parliamentorum. 1783.

Rotuli Scotiæ. Ed. D. Macpherson and others. (Record Commission) 1814–19.

Royal Letters, Henry IV. Ed. F. C. Hingeston. (Rolls Series) 1860.

Sacrorum Conciliorum Collectio. Ed. J. D. Mansi. Florence and Venice, 1759–98.

St Giles's Durham, Memorials of. Ed. J. Barmby. (Surtees Society, Vol. XVC) 1895.

Select Cases before the King's Council 1243–1482. Ed. I. S. Leadam and J. F. Baldwin. (Selden Society, Vol. XXXV) 1918.

Statutes of the Realm. Ed. A. Luders and others. (Record Commission) 1810–28.

Testamenta Eboracensia, Vols. I–III. Ed. J. Raine and J. Raine, jnr. (Surtees Society, Vols. IV, XXX & XLV) 1836, 1855 & 1864.

Testamenta Vetusta. Ed. N. H. Nicolas. 1826.

Tunstall, Cuthbert, and James Pilkington, Bishops of Durham, The Registers of. Ed. G. Hinde. (Surtees Society, Vol. CLXI) 1952.

Valor Ecclesiasticus, temp. Henrici VIII. Ed. J. Caley and J. Hunter. (Record Commission) 1810–34.

Wills and Inventories, Vol. I. Ed. J. Raine. (Surtees Society, Vol. II) 1835.

Wills . . . of the Kings and Queens of England, A Collection of all the. Ed. J. Nichols. 1780.

Year Books of Henry VI. 1 Henry VI. Ed. C. H. Williams. (Selden Society, Vol. L) 1933.

York Minster, The Fabric Rolls of. Ed. J. Raine, jnr. (Surtees Society, Vol. XXXV) 1858.

3 MODERN WORKS

Armitage-Smith, J. *John of Gaunt*. Westminster, 1904.

Baines, E. *The History of the County Palatine and Duchy of Lancaster*. 1836.

Baldwin, J. F. *The King's Council in England during the Middle Ages*. Oxford, 1913.

Balfour-Melville, E. W. M. *James I, King of Scots, 1406–1437*. 1936.

Barlow, F. *Durham Jurisdictional Peculiars*. Oxford, 1950.

Bates, C. J. *The Border Holds of Northumberland*. Newcastle-upon-Tyne, 1891.

Bouch, C. M. L. *Prelates and People of the Lake Counties*. Kendal, 1948.

Brand, J. *History of Newcastle-upon-Tyne*. 1789.

Campbell, Lord. *The Lives of the Lord Chancellors*. 1846.

Chrimes, S. B. "Some Letters of John of Lancaster as Warden of the East Marches towards Scotland." (*Speculum*, Vol. XIV) 1939.

Ciaconi. *Vitæ et Res Gestæ Pontificum et S.R.E. Cardinalium*. Rome, 1677.

Clarke, M. V., and V. H. Galbraith. "The Deposition of Richard II." (*Bulletin of John Rylands' Library*, Vol. 14) 1930.

Complete Peerage of England, Scotland, etc. Ed. V. Gibbs. 1910–59.

Creighton, M. *A History of the Papacy from the Great Schism to the Sack of Rome*. 1903–7.

Cristofori, F. *Storia dei Cardinali di Santa Romana Chiesa*. Rome, 1888.

Dictionary of National Biography. 1885–92.

Ehrlich, E. *Proceedings against the Crown (1216–1377)*. (Oxford Studies in Social and Legal History, No. XII) 1921.

Emden, A. B. *A Biographical Register of the University of Oxford to A.D. 1500*. Oxford, 1957–9.

Fabian, The Chronicle of. 1559.

Foss, E. *The Judges of England.* 1848–57.

Fowler, J. T. "On the St. Cuthbert Window in York Minster." (*Yorkshire Archæological Journal*, Vol. IV) 1887.

Fraser, C. M. *A History of Antony Bek.* Oxford, 1957.

Gastrell, F. *Notitia Cestriensis.* Ed. F. R. Raines. (Chetham Society, Vols. VIII, XIX, XXI & XXII) 1845–50.

Godwin, F. *A Catalogue of the Bishops of England.* 1601.

——, *De Præsulibus Angliæ Commentarius.* Ed. W. Richardson. Cambridge, 1743.

Gray, H. L. "Incomes from Land in England in 1436." (*English Historical Review*, Vol. XLIX) 1934.

Hadcock, R. N. "A map of medieval Durham and Northumberland." (*Archæologia Æliana*, Fourth Series, Vol. XVI) 1939.

Harrison, F. *The Painted Glass of York.* 1927.

Hasted, E. *History of Kent.* Canterbury, 1797–1801.

Hennessy, G. *Novum Repertorium Ecclesiasticum Parochiale Londinense.* 1898.

Hodgson, J. F. "The Church of St Andrew Auckland." (*Archaeologia Aeliana*, Vol. XX) 1899.

Hunnisett, R. F. *The Medieval Coroner.* Cambridge, 1961.

Hunter Blair, C. H. "Medieval Seals of the Bishops of Durham." (*Archæologia*, Vol. 72) 1922.

Hutchinson, W. *The History and Antiquities of the County Palatine of Durham.* Newcastle-upon-Tyne, 1785–94.

Jacob, E. F. *Essays in the Conciliar Epoch.* Manchester, 1953.

Kingsford, C. L. "An Historical Collection of the Fifteenth Century." (*English Historical Review*, Vol. XXIX) 1914.

——, *English Historical Literature in the Fifteenth Century.* Oxford, 1913.

——, *Henry V.* 1923.

Knowles, D. *The Religious Orders in England.* Cambridge, 1948–59.

Lapsley, G. T. "The Accounts of a Fifteenth-Century Iron Master." (*English Historical Review*, Vol. XIV) 1899.

——, *The County Palatine of Durham.* 1900.

Leach, A. F. *English Schools at the Reformation.* Westminster, 1896.

Leland, John, *The Itinerary of.* Ed. L. T. Smith. 1906–10.

Le Neve, J. *Fasti Ecclesiæ Anglicanae.* Ed. T. D. Hardy. Oxford, 1854.

Macrae, C. "The English Council and Scotland in 1430." (*English Historical Review*, Vol. LIV) 1939.

Maxwell-Lyte, H. C. *Historical Notes on the Use of the Great Seal of England.* (Public Record Office) 1926.

Northumberland, History of. Newcastle-upon-Tyne and London, 1893–1940.

Oman, C. W. C. *Warwick the Kingmaker*. 1909.

Otway-Ruthven, J. *The King's Secretary and the Signet Office in the XV Century*. Cambridge, 1939.

Pugh, T. B., and C. D. Ross. "The English Baronage and the Income Tax of 1436." *(Bulletin of the Institute of Historical Research,* Vol. XXVI) 1953.

Raine, J. *North Durham*. 1852.

Ramsay, J. H. *Lancaster and York*. Oxford, 1892.

Reid, R. R. "The Office of Warden of the Marches; its Origin and Early History." *(English Historical Review*, Vol. XXXII) 1917.

——, *The King's Council in the North*. 1921.

Rites of Durham, The. Ed. J. T. Fowler. (Surtees Society, Vol. CVII) 1902.

Roskell, J. S. *Knights of the Shire for the County Palatine of Lancaster (1377–1460)*. (Chetham Society, New Series, Vol. 96) 1937.

——, *The Commons in the Parliament of 1422*. Manchester, 1954.

Scammell, G. V. *Hugh du Puiset, Bishop of Durham*. Cambridge, 1956.

Sheriffs, List of. (Public Record Office Lists and Indexes, no. IX) 1898.

Somerville, R. *History of the Duchy of Lancaster*, Vol. I. 1265–1603. 1953.

Steel, A. *The Receipt of the Exchequer 1377–1485*. Cambridge, 1954.

Storey, R. L. "The manor of Burgh-by-Sands." *(Transactions of the Cumberland and Westmorland Antiquarian and Archaeological Society*, New Series, Vol. LIV) 1954.

——, "Marmaduke Lumley, bishop of Carlisle." (Ibid. LV) 1955.

——, "The Wardens of the Marches of England towards Scotland, 1377–1489." *(English Historical Review*, Vol. LXXII) 1957.

——, "English Officers of State, 1399–1485." *(Bulletin of the Institute of Historical Research*, Vol. XXXI) 1958.

——, *Diocesan Administration in the Fifteenth Century*. (St. Anthony's Hall Publications No. 16) York, 1959.

Stubbs, W. *The Constitutional History of England*. Oxford, 1890–6.

——, *Registrum Sacrum Anglicanum*. Oxford, 1897.

Surtees, R. *The History and Antiquities of the County Palatine of Durham*. 1816–40.

Tate, G. *History of Alnwick*. Alnwick, 1866–9.

Thompson, A. Hamilton. *The History of the Hospital and the New College of St Mary in the Newarke, Leicester*. Leicester, 1937.

——, "Thomas Langley, Bishop of Durham, 1406–1437." *(Durham University Journal*, Vol. 38) 1945.

——, *The English Clergy and their Organisation in the Later Middle Ages*. Oxford, 1947.

Tout, T. F. *Chapters in the Administrative History of Medieval England*. Manchester, 1920–33.

Valois, N.   *La France et le Grand Schisme d'Occident*.   Paris, 1896–1902.

Venn, J., and J. A.   *Alumni Cantabrigienses*, Part I.   Cambridge, 1922–7.

Vickers, K. H.   *Humphrey, Duke of Gloucester*.   1907.

Victoria History of the Counties of England:
  Durham, 1905– .
  Lancaster, 1905–14.

Wharton, T.   *Anglia Sacra*.   1691.

Wylie, J. H.   *History of England under Henry the Fourth*.   1884–98.

——, and W. T. Waugh.   *The Reign of Henry the Fifth*.   Cambridge, 1914–29.

INDEX

273